MANAGING INFORMATION SECURITY

SECOND EDITION

T0383270

MANAGING INFORMATION SECURITY

SECOND EDITION

Edited by

JOHN R. VACCA

ELSEVIER

AMSTERDAM • BOSTON • HEIDELBERG • LONDON
NEW YORK • OXFORD • PARIS • SAN DIEGO
SAN FRANCISCO • SYDNEY • TOKYO

Syngress is an imprint of Elsevier

SYNGRESS.

Publisher: Steven Elliot
Senior Developmental Editor: Nathaniel McFadden
Editorial Project Manager: Lindsay Lawrence
Project Manager: Mohanambal Natarajan
Designer: Matthew Limbert

Syngress is an imprint of Elsevier
225 Wyman Street, Waltham, MA 02451, USA

Second edition 2014

Library of Congress Cataloging-in-Publication Data
A catalog record for this book is available from the Library of Congress

British Library Cataloguing in Publication Data
A catalogue record for this book is available from the British Library

For information on all **Syngress** publications,
visit our website at store.elsevier.com/Syngress

ISBN: 978-0-12-416688-2

Printed and bound in USA

14 15 16 17 18   10 9 8 7 6 5 4 3 2 1

This book is dedicated to my wife Bee.

Contents

Acknowledgements

There are many people whose efforts on this book have contributed to its successful completion. I owe each a debt of gratitude and want to take this opportunity to offer my sincere thanks.

A very special thanks to my publisher, Steve Elliot, without whose continued interest and support this book would not have been possible. Senior development editor Nate McFadden provided staunch support and encouragement when it was most needed. Thanks to my production project manager, Mohanambal Natarajan, whose fine work and attention to detail has been invaluable. Thanks also to my marketing manager, Todd Conly, whose efforts on this book have been greatly appreciated. Finally, thanks to all the other people at Morgan Kaufmann Publishers/Elsevier Science & Technology Books, whose many talents and skills are essential to a finished book.

Thanks to my wife, Bee Vacca, for her love, her help, and her understanding of my long work hours. Finally, I wish to thank all the following authors who contributed chapters that were necessary for the completion of this book: Sanjay Bavisi, Rahul Bhaskar, Albert Caballero, Christopher Day, Scott R. Ellis, Errin W. Fulp, Yong Guan, Cem Gurkok, James T. Harmening, Almantas Kakareka, Bhushan Kapoor, Jean-Marc Seigneur.

About the Editor

John Vacca is an information technology consultant, professional writer, editor, reviewer and internationally-known, best-selling author based in Pomeroy, Ohio. Since 1982, John has authored 73 books (some of his most recent books include):

- **Computer and Information Security Handbook, 2E** (*Publisher:* Morgan Kaufmann (an imprint of Elsevier Inc.) (May 31, 2013))
- **Identity Theft (Cybersafety)** (*Publisher:* Chelsea House Pub (April 1, 2012))
- **System Forensics, Investigation, And Response** (*Publisher:* Jones & Bartlett Learning (September 24, 2010)
- **Managing Information Security** (*Publisher:* Syngress (an imprint of Elsevier Inc.) (March 29, 2010))
- **Network and Systems Security** (*Publisher:* Syngress (an imprint of Elsevier Inc.) (March 29, 2010))
- **Computer and Information Security Handbook, 1E** (*Publisher:* Morgan Kaufmann (an imprint of Elsevier Inc.) (June 2, 2009))
- **Biometric Technologies and Verification Systems** (*Publisher:* Elsevier Science & Technology Books (March 16, 2007))

- **Practical Internet Security** (Hardcover): (*Publisher:* Springer (October 18, 2006))
- **Optical Networking Best Practices Handbook** (Hardcover): (*Publisher:* Wiley-Interscience (November 28, 2006))
- **Guide to Wireless Network Security** (*Publisher:* Springer (August 19, 2006)
- **Computer Forensics: Computer Crime Scene Investigation (With CD-ROM), 2nd Edition** (*Publisher:* Charles River Media (May 26, 2005)

and, more than 600 articles in the areas of advanced storage, computer security and aerospace technology (copies of articles and books are available upon request). John was also a configuration management specialist, computer specialist, and the computer security official (CSO) for NASA's space station program (Freedom) and the International Space Station Program, from 1988 until his retirement from NASA in 1995. In addition, John is also an independent online book reviewer. Finally, John was one of the security consultants for the MGM movie titled: "AntiTrust," which was released on January 12, 2001. A detailed copy of my author bio can be viewed at URL: http://www.johnvacca.com. John can be reached at: john2164@windstream.net.

Contributors

Sanjay Bavisi (Chapter 7), President, EC-Council, Selangor, Malaysia

Rahul Bhaskar (Chapter 3), Professor, Department of Information Systems and Decision Sciences, California State University, Fullerton, CA 92834

Albert Caballero, CISSP, GSEC (Chapter 1), Chief Technology Officer_CTO, Digital Era Group, LLC, Surfside, Fl. 33154

Christopher Day, CISSP, NSA: IEM (Chapter 5), Senior Vice President, Secure Information Systems, Terremark Worldwide, Inc., 2 South Biscayne Blvd., Suite 2900, Miami, FL 33131

Scott R. Ellis, EnCE, RCA (Chapter 9), Manager, Infrastructure Engineering Team,kCura, Chicago, IL 60604

Errin W. Fulp (Chapter 6), Professor, Department of Computer Science, Wake Forest University, Winston-Salem, North Carolina 27109

Yong Guan (Chapter 11), Litton Assistant Professor, Department of Electrical and Computer Engineering, Iowa State University, Ames, Iowa 50011

Cem Gurkok (Chapter 10), Threat Intelligence Development Manager, Terremark, Worldwide, Inc., Miami, Florida 33131

James T. Harmening (Chapter 2), President, Computer Bits, Inc., Chicago, Illinois 60602

Almantas Kakareka, CISSP, GSNA, GSEC, CEH (Chapter 8), CTO, Demyo, Inc., Sunny Isles Beach, Florida 33160

Bhushan Kapoor (Chapter 3), Chair, Department of Information Systems and Decision Sciences, California State University, Fullerton, CA 92834

Jean-Marc Seigneur (Chapter 4), Advanced Systems Group, University of Geneva, Switzerland

Introduction

This Managing Information Security derivative book provides a broad overview of information security program elements to assist practitioners and IT professionals in enhancing their skills and knowledge on how to establish and implement an information security program. The material in this book can be referenced for general information on a particular topic or can be used in the decision-making process for managing an information security program. The purpose of this book is to inform information security management practitioners and IT professionals about various aspects of information security that they will be expected to implement and oversee in their respective organizations. In addition, the book provides guidance for facilitating a more consistent approach to information security programs.

Furthermore, this comprehensive book serves as a professional reference to provide the most complete and concise view of how to manage computer security and privacy available. It offers in-depth coverage of computer security theory, technology, and practice as it relates to established technologies; as well as, recent advancements. It explores practical solutions to a wide range of security issues. Individual chapters are authored by leading experts in the field and address the immediate and long term challenges in the contributors' respective areas of expertise.

The book provides information that practitioners and IT professionals can use in building their information security program strategy. In addition, new security vendors are building Ethernet switches that offer full security on every single port at very affordable prices, driving prices down and making competition fiercer for all integrated security products.

The book is therefore useful to any manager who requires a broad overview of information security practices. In addition, in this book, you will also learn how to:

1. Configure tools and utilities to minimize exposure and detect intrusions
2. Create, document and test continuity arrangements for your organization
3. Perform a risk assessment and Business Impact Assessment (BIA) to identify vulnerabilities
4. Select and deploy an alternate site for continuity of mission-critical activities
5. Identify appropriate strategies to recover the infrastructure and processes
6. Organize and manage recovery teams
7. Test and maintain an effective recovery plan in a rapidly changing technology environment
8. Detect and respond to vulnerabilities that put your organization at risk using scanners
9. Employ real-world exploits and evaluate their effect on your systems
10. Configure vulnerability scanners
11. Analyze the results of vulnerability scans
12. Assess vulnerability alerts and advisories

13. Establish a strategy for vulnerability management
14. Build a firewall to protect your network
15. Install and configure proxy-based and stateful-filtering firewalls
16. Provide access to HTTP and FTP services on the Internet
17. Implement publicly accessible servers without compromising security
18. Protect internal IP addresses with NAT and deploy a secure DNS architecture
19. Manage information security risks within your organization
20. Identify security threats to your data and IT infrastructure
21. Recognize appropriate technology to deploy against these threats
22. Adapt your organization's information security policy to operational requirements and assess compliance
23. Effectively communicate information security issues
24. Oversee your organization's ongoing information security

You will also learn to identify vulnerabilities and implement appropriate countermeasures to prevent and mitigate threats to your mission-critical processes. You will learn techniques for creating a business continuity plan (BCP) and the methodology for building an infrastructure that supports its effective implementation.

Knowledge of vulnerability assessment and hacking techniques allows you to detect vulnerabilities before your networks are attacked. In this book, you will learn to configure and use vulnerability scanners to detect weaknesses and prevent network exploitation. You will also acquire the knowledge to assess the risk to your enterprise from an array of vulnerabilities and to minimize your exposure to costly threats.

The firewall has emerged as a primary tool to prevent unauthorized access to valuable data. In this book, you will gain experience installing and configuring a firewall. You will also learn how to allow access to key services while maintaining your organization's security.

Securing information is vital to the success of every organization and is the link to maximizing the benefits of information technology. This book will empower managers with an understanding of the threats and risks to information resources. You will also gain the knowledge of what needs to be done to protect information infrastructures, develop an action plan and monitor threats. You will learn to identify best practices and deploy a security program throughout your organization.

Finally, throughout this book, you will gain practical skills through a series of interactive small-group workshops and evolving case studies. You will also learn how to design and develop a disaster recovery plan, which includes the following:

1. Assessing threats
2. Avoiding disasters
3. Identifying the impact on critical business functions
4. Recognizing alternatives for continuing business functions
5. Planning your continuity project
6. Organizing team structures for use in an emergency
7. Creating a recovery plan from the response to a disaster

In addition, this book is valuable for those involved in selecting, implementing or auditing secure solutions for access into the enterprise. And, it is also valuable for anyone responsible for ensuring the continuity of an organization's critical systems or processes. For example, the reader should have general familiarity with- and have knowledge equivalent to the following:

- Project Management: Skills for Success
- Deploying Internet and Intranet Firewalls
- Implementing Web Security
- Management Skills
- Influence Skills
- Project Risk Management
- Detecting and Analyzing Intrusions
- Vulnerability Assessment
- Disaster Recovery Planning

ORGANIZATION OF THIS BOOK

The book is composed of 11 contributed chapters by leading experts in their fields.

Contributor Albert Caballero (Chapter 1, "Information Security Essentials for IT Managers: Protecting Mission-Critical Systems") begins by discussing how security goes beyond technical controls and encompasses people, technology, policy and operations in a way that few other business objectives do. Information security involves the protection of organizational assets from the disruption of business operations, modification of sensitive data, or disclosure of proprietary information. The protection of this data is usually described as maintaining the confidentiality, integrity, and availability (CIA) of the organization's assets, operations, and information.

As identified throughout this chapter, security goes beyond technical controls and encompasses people, technology, policy, and operations in a way that few other business objectives do. The evolution of a risk-based paradigm, as opposed to a technical solution paradigm for security, has made it clear that a secure organization does not result from securing technical infrastructure alone.

Next, contributor James T. Harmening (Chapter 2, "Security Management Systems") examines documentation requirements and maintaining an effective security system; as well as, assessments. Today, when most companies and government agencies rely on computer networks to store and manage their organizations' data, it is essential that measures are put in place to secure those networks and keep them functioning optimally. Network administrators need to define their security management systems to cover all parts of their computer and network resources.

A security management system starts as a set of policies that dictate the way in which computer resources can be used. The policies are then implemented by the organization's technical departments and enforced. This can be easy for smaller organizations, but can require a team for larger international organizations that have thousands of business processes. Either way, measures need to be put in place to prevent, respond to, and fix security issues that arise in your organization.

Then, contributors Rahul Bhasker and Bhushan Kapoor (Chapter 3, "Information Technology Security Management") discuss the processes that are supported with enabling organizational structure and technology to protect an organization's information technology operations and information technology assets against internal and external threats intentionally or otherwise. Information technology security management can be defined as processes that supported enabling organizational structure and technology to protect an organization's IT operations and assets against internal and external threats, intentional or otherwise. The principle purpose of IT security management is to ensure confidentiality, integrity, and availability (CIA) of IT systems. Fundamentally, security management is a part of the risk management process and business continuity strategy in an organization.

These processes are developed to ensure confidentiality, integrity, and availability of IT systems. There are various aspects to the IT security in an organization that need to be considered. These include security policies and procedures, security organization structure, IT security processes, and rules and regulations.

Contributor Dr. Jean-Marc Seigneur (Chapter 4, "Identity Management") continue by presenting the evolution of identity management requirements. Recent technological advances in user identity management have highlighted the paradigm of federated identity management and user-centric identity management as improved alternatives. The first empowers the management of identity; the second allows users to actively manage their identity information and profiles. It also allows providers to easily deal with privacy aspects regarding user expectations. This problem has been tackled with some trends and emerging solutions, as described in this chapter.

First, Seigneur provides an overview of identity management from Identity 1.0 to 2.0 and higher, with emphasis on user-centric approaches. He surveys how the requirements for user-centric identity management and their associated technologies have evolved, with emphasis on federated approaches and user-centricity. Second, he focuses on related standards XRI and LID, issued from the Yadis project, as well as platforms, mainly ID-WSF, OpenID, InfoCard, Sxip, and Higgins. Finally, he treats identity management in the field of

mobility and focuses on the future of mobile identity management.

Seigneur then surveys how the different most advanced identity management technologies fulfill present day requirements. Then, he discusses how mobility can be achieved in the field of identity management in an ambient intelligent/ubiquitous computing world.

Identity has become a burden in the online world. When it is stolen, it engenders a massive fraud, principally in online services, which generates a lack of confidence in doing business with providers and frustration for users.

Therefore, the whole of society would suffer from the demise of privacy, which is a real human need. Because people have hectic lives and cannot spend their time administering their digital identities, we need consistent identity management platforms and technologies enabling usability and scalability, among other things. In this chapter, Seigneur surveys how the requirements have evolved for mobile user-centric identity management and its associated technologies.

The Internet is increasingly used, but the fact that the Internet has not been developed with an adequate identity layer, is a major security risk. Password fatigue and online fraud are a growing problem and are damaging user confidence.

This chapter has underlined the necessity of mobility and the importance of identity in future ambient intelligent environments. Mobile identity management will have to support a wide range of information technologies and devices with critical requirements such usability on the move, privacy, scalability, and energy-friendliness.

Next, contributor Christopher Day (Chapter 5, "Intrusion Prevention and Detection Systems") discusses the nature of computer system intrusions, those who commit these attacks, and the various technologies that can be utilized to detect and prevent them. With the increasing importance of information systems in today's complex and global economy, it has become mission and business critical to defend those information systems from attack and compromise by any number of adversaries. Intrusion prevention and detection systems are critical components in the defender's arsenal and take on a number of different forms. Formally, intrusion detection systems (IDSs) can be defined as "software or hardware systems that automate the process of monitoring the events occurring in a computer system or network, analyzing them for signs of security problems." Intrusion prevention systems (IPSs) are systems that attempt to actually stop an active attack or security problem. Though there are many IDS and IPS products on the market today, often sold as self-contained, network-attached computer appliances, truly effective intrusion detection and prevention are achieved when viewed as a process coupled with layers of appropriate technologies and products. In this chapter, Day will discuss the nature of computer system intrusions, those who commit these attacks, and the various technologies that can be utilized to detect and prevent them.

It should now be clear that intrusion detection and prevention are not a single tool or product, but a series of layered technologies coupled with the appropriate methodologies and skill sets. Each of the technologies surveyed in this chapter has its own specific strengths and weaknesses, and a truly effective intrusion detection and prevention program must be designed to play to those strengths and minimize the weaknesses. Combining NIDS and NIPS with network session analysis and a comprehensive SIM, for example, helps offset the inherent weakness of each technology; as well as, provide the information security team greater flexibility to bring the right tools to bear for an ever-shifting threat environment.

Next, contributor Errin W. Fulp (Chapter 6, "Firewalls," provides an overview of firewall: policies, designs, features, and configurations. Of course technology is always changing and network firewalls are no exception. However the intent of this chapter is to describe aspects of network firewalls that tend to endure over time.

Providing a secure computing environment continues to be an important and challenging goal of any computer administrator. The difficulty is in part due to the increasing interconnectivity of computers via networks, which includes the Internet. Such interconnectivity brings great economies of scale in terms of resources, services, and knowledge, but it has also introduced new security risks. For example, interconnectivity gives illegitimate users much easier access to vital data and resources from almost anywhere in the world.

Network firewalls are a key component of providing a secure environment. These systems are responsible for controlling access between two networks, which is done by applying a security policy to arriving packets. The policy describes which packets should be accepted and which should be dropped. The firewall inspects the packet header and/or the payload (data portion).

There are several different types of firewalls, each briefly described in this chapter. Firewalls can be categorized based on what they inspect (packet filter, stateful, or application), their implementation (hardware or software), or their location (host or network). Combinations of the categories are possible, and each type has specific advantages and disadvantages.

Improving the performance of the firewall can be achieved by minimizing the rules in the policy (primarily for software firewalls). Moving more popular rules near the beginning of the policy can also reduce the number of rules comparisons that are required. However, the order of certain rules must be maintained (any rules that can match the same packet).

Regardless of the firewall implementation, placement, or design, deployment requires constant vigilance. Developing the appropriate policy (set of rules) requires a detailed understanding of the network topology and the necessary services. If either of these items change (and they certainly will), that will require updating the policy. Finally, it is important to remember that a firewall is not a complete security solution, but is a key part of a security solution.

Then, contributor Sanjay Bavisi (Chapter 7, "Penetration Testing,") shows how penetration testing differs from an actual "hacker attack", some of the ways penetration tests are conducted, how they're controlled, and what organizations might look for when choosing a company to conduct a penetration test for them. Thus, penetration testing is the exploitation of vulnerabilities present in an organization's network. It helps determine which vulnerabilities are exploitable and the degree of information exposure or network control that the organization could expect an attacker to achieve after successfully exploiting a vulnerability. No penetration test is or ever can be "just like a hacker would do it," due to necessary limitations placed on penetration tests conducted by "white hats." Hackers don't have to follow the same rules as the "good guys" and they could care less whether your systems crash during one of their "tests." Bavisi will talk more about this later. Right now, before he can talk any more about penetration testing, he needs to talk about various types of vulnerabilities and how they might be discovered.

Vulnerabilities can be thought of in two broad categories: logical and physical. We normally think of logical vulnerabilities as those associated with the organization's computers, infrastructure devices, software, or applications. Physical vulnerabilities, on the other hand, are normally thought of as those having to do with either the actual physical security of the organization (such as a door that doesn't always lock properly), the sensitive information that "accidentally" ends up in the dumpster, or the vulnerability of the organization's employees to social engineering (a vendor asking to use a computer to send a "quick email" to the boss).

Logical vulnerabilities can be discovered using any number of manual or automated tools and even by browsing the Internet. For those of you who are familiar with Johnny Long's *Google Hacking* books: *"Passwords*, for the *love of God!!!* Google found *passwords!"* The discovery of logical vulnerabilities is usually called *security scanning, vulnerability scanning*, or just *scanning*. Unfortunately, there are a number of "security consultants" who run a scan, put a fancy report cover on the output of the tool, and pass off these scans as a penetration test.

Physical vulnerabilities can be discovered as part of a physical security inspection, a "midnight raid" on the organization's dumpsters, getting information from employees, or via unaccompanied access to a usually nonpublic area. Thus, vulnerabilities might also exist due to a lack of company policies or procedures or an employee's failure to follow the policy or procedure. Regardless of the cause of the vulnerability, it might have the potential to compromise the organization's security. So, of all the vulnerabilities that have been discovered, how do we know which ones pose the greatest danger to the organization's network? We test them! We test them to see which ones we can exploit and exactly what could happen if a "real" attacker exploited that vulnerability.

Because few organizations that have enough money, time, or resources to eliminate every vulnerability discovered, they have to prioritize their efforts; this is one of the best reasons for an organization to conduct a penetration test. At the conclusion of the penetration test, they will know which vulnerabilities can be exploited and what can happen if they are exploited. They can then plan to correct the vulnerabilities based on the amount of critical information exposed or network control gained by exploiting the vulnerability. In other words, a penetration test helps organizations strike a balance between security and business functionality. Sounds like a perfect solution, right? If only it were so!

Next, contributor Almantas Kakareka (Chapter 8, "What Is Vulnerability Assessment?") covers the fundamentals: defining vulnerability, exploit, threat and risk; analyzes vulnerabilities and exploits; configures scanners and shows you how to generates reports; assesses risks in a changing environment; and, show you how to manage vulnerabilities. In computer security, the term *vulnerability* is applied to a weakness in a system that allows an attacker to violate the integrity of that system. Vulnerabilities may result from weak passwords, software bugs, a computer virus or other malware (malicious software), a script code injection, or an SQL injection, just to name a few.

Vulnerabilities always existed, but when the Internet was in its early stage they were not as often used and exploited. The media did not report news of hackers who were getting put in jail for hacking into servers and stealing vital information.

Finally, vulnerability assessment may be performed on many objects, not only computer systems/networks. For example, a physical building can be assessed so it will be clear what parts of the building have what kind of flaw. If the attacker can bypass the security guard at the front door and get into the building via a back door, it is definitely a vulnerability. Actually, going through the back door and using that vulnerability is called an *exploit*. The physical security is one of the most important aspects to be taken into account. If the attackers have physical access to the server, the server is not yours anymore! Just stating, "Your system or network is vulnerable" doesn't provide any useful information. Vulnerability assessment without a comprehensive report is pretty much useless. A vulnerability assessment report should include:

• Identification of vulnerabilities
• Quantity of vulnerabilities

Then, contributor Scott R. Ellis (Chapter 9, "Cyber Forensics") provides an in depth familiarization with computer forensics as a career, a job, and a science. It will help you *avoid mistakes* and find your way through the many aspects of this diverse and rewarding field.

This chapter is intended to provide in-depth information on computer forensics as a career, a job, and a science. It will help you *avoid mistakes* and find your way through the many aspects of this diverse and rewarding field.

Again and again throughout this chapter, a single recurring theme will emerge: Data that has been overwritten cannot, by any conventionally known means, be recovered. If it could be, then Kroll Ontrack and every other giant in the forensics business, would be shouting this service from the rooftops and charging a premium price for it.

Next, contributor **Cem Gurkok** (Chapter 10, **"Cyber Forensics and Incident Response"**), discusses the steps and methods that are needed in order to respond to incidents and conduct cyber forensics investigations. He mainly focuses on Windows systems as target systems and utilizes open- source or freeware tools for discovery and analysis.

Listening to the news on a daily basis suggests that it is a matter of when, rather than if any given computing device will be compromised. Gurkok emphasis that what really matters is how fast one responds to the compromise to mitigate loss and to prevent future incidents. To be able to react with speed, proper plans and procedures need to be implemented beforehand, and tested on a regular basis for preparedness. Part of the response process is to investigate and understand the nature of the compromise.

Finally, in this chapter, Gurkok shows you why cyber forensics is an integral part of incident response that fills the investigative role. He explains that it is a form of forensic science whose aim is to identify, preserve, recover, analyze and present facts and opinions regarding evidence stored on or transferred between digital devices.

Finally, contributor Yong Guan (Chapter 11, "Network Forensics,") continues by helping you determine the path from a victimized network or system through any intermediate systems and communication pathways, back to the point of attack origination or the person who

should be accountable. Today's cyber criminal investigator faces a formidable challenge: tracing network-based cyber criminals. The possibility of becoming a victim of cyber crime is the number-one fear of billions of people. This concern is well founded. The findings in the annual *CSI/FBI Computer Crime and Security Surveys* confirm that cyber crime is real and continues to be a significant threat. Traceback and attribution are performed during or after cyber violations and attacks, to identify where an attack originated, how it propagated, and what computer(s) and person(s) are responsible and should be held accountable.

The goal of network forensics capabilities is to determine the path from a victimized network or system through any intermediate systems and communication pathways, back to the point of attack origination or the person who is accountable. In some cases, the computers launching an attack may themselves be compromised hosts or be controlled remotely. *Attribution* is the process of determining the identity of the source of a cyber attack. Types of attribution can include both digital identity (computer, user account, IP address, or enabling software) and physical identity (the actual person using the computer from which an attack originated).

Finally, in this chapter, Guan discusses the current network forensic techniques in cyber attack traceback. He focuses on the current schemes in IP spoofing traceback and stepping-stone attack attribution. Furthermore, he introduces the traceback issues in Voice over IP, Botmaster, and online fraudsters.

John R. Vacca
Editor-in-Chief

Information Security Essentials for IT Managers
Protecting Mission-Critical Systems

Albert Caballero
Terremark Worldwide, Inc.

1. INFORMATION SECURITY ESSENTIALS FOR IT MANAGERS, OVERVIEW

Information security management as a field is ever increasing in demand and responsibility because most organizations spend increasingly larger percentages of their IT budgets in attempting to manage risk and mitigate intrusions, not to mention the trend in many enterprises of moving all IT operations to an Internet-connected infrastructure, known as enterprise cloud computing.[1] For information security managers, it is crucial to maintain a clear perspective of all the areas of business that require protection. Through collaboration with all business units, security managers must work security into the processes of all aspects of the organization, from employee training to research and development. Security is not an IT problem, it is a business problem.

Information security means protecting information and information systems from unauthorized access, use, disclosure, disruption, modification, or destruction[2]

1. "Cloud computing, the enterprise cloud," Terremark Worldwide Inc. Website, http://www.theenterprisecloud.com/.
2. "Definition of information security," Wikipedia, http://en.wikipedia.org/wiki/Information_security.

Scope of Information Security Management

Information security is a business problem in the sense that the entire organization must frame and solve security problems based on its own strategic drivers, not solely on technical controls aimed to mitigate one type of attack. The evolution of a risk-based paradigm, as opposed to a technical solution paradigm for security, has made it clear that a secure organization does not result from securing technical infrastructure alone. Furthermore, securing the organization's technical infrastructure cannot provide the appropriate protection for these assets, nor will it protect many other information assets that are in no way dependent on technology for their existence or protection. Thus, the organization would be lulled into a false sense of security if it relied on protecting its technical infrastructure alone.[3]

CISSP Ten Domains of Information Security

In the information security industry there have been several initiatives to attempt to define security management and how and when to apply it. The leader in certifying information security professionals is the Internet Security Consortium, with its CISSP (see sidebar, "CISSP Ten Domains: Common Body of Knowledge") certification.[4]

In defining required skills for information security managers, the ISC has arrived at an agreement on ten domains of information security that is known as the *Common Body of Knowledge* (CBK). Every security manager must understand and be well versed in all areas of the CBK.[5]

In addition to individual certification there must be guidelines to turn these skills into actionable items that can be measured and verified according to some international standard or framework. The most widely used standard for maintaining and improving information security is ISO/IEC 17799:2005. ISO 17799 (see Figure 1.1) establishes guidelines and principles for initiating, implementing, maintaining, and improving information security management in an organization.[6]

A new and popular framework to use in conjunction with the CISSP CBK and the ISO 17799 guidelines is ISMM. ISMM is a framework (see Figure 1.2) that describes a five-level evolutionary path of increasingly organized and systematically more mature security layers. It is proposed for the maturity assessment of information security management and the evaluation of the level of security awareness and practice at any organization, whether public or private. Furthermore, it helps us better understand where, and to what extent,

3. Richard A. Caralli, William R. Wilson, "The challenges of security management," Survivable Enterprise Management Team, Networked Systems Survivability Program, Software Engineering Institute, http://www.cert.org/archive/pdf/ESMchallenges.pdf.

4. "CISSP Ten domains" ISC2 Web site https://www.isc2.org/cissp/default.aspx.

5. Micki, Krause, Harold F. Tipton, *Information Security Management Handbook sixth edition*, Auerbach Publications, CRC Press LLC.

6. "ISO 17799 security standards," ISO Web site, http://www.iso.org/iso/support/faqs/faqs_widely_used_standards/widely_used_standards_other/information_security.htm.

CISSP TEN DOMAINS: COMMON BODY OF KNOWLEDGE

- *Access control.* Methods used to enable administrators and managers to define what objects a subject can access through authentication and authorization, providing each subject a list of capabilities it can perform on each object. Important areas include access control security models, identification and authentication technologies, access control administration, and single sign-on technologies.
- *Telecommunications and network security.* Examination of internal, external, public, and private network communication systems, including devices, protocols, and remote access.
- *Information security and risk management.* Including physical, technical, and administrative controls surrounding organizational assets to determine the level of protection and budget warranted by highest to lowest risk. The goal is to reduce potential threats and money loss.
- *Application security.* Application security involves the controls placed within the application programs and operating systems to support the security policy of the organization and measure its effectiveness. Topics include threats, applications development, availability issues, security design and vulnerabilities, and application/data access control.
- *Cryptography.* The use of various methods and techniques such as symmetric and asymmetric encryption to achieve desired levels of confidentiality and integrity. Important areas include encryption protocols and applications and Public Key Infrastructures.

- *Security architecture and design.* This area covers the concepts, principles, and standards used to design and implement secure applications, operating systems, and all platforms based on international evaluation criteria such as Trusted Computer Security Evaluation Criteria (TCSEC) and Common Criteria.
- *Operations security.* Controls over personnel, hardware systems, and auditing and monitoring techniques such as maintenance of AV, training, auditing, and resource protection; preventive, detective, corrective, and recovery controls; and security and fault-tolerance technologies.
- *Business continuity and disaster recovery planning.* The main purpose of this area is to preserve business operations when faced with disruptions or disasters. Important aspects are to identify resource values, perform a business impact analysis, and produce business unit priorities, contingency plans, and crisis management.
- *Legal, regulatory, compliance, and investigations.* Computer crime, government laws and regulations, and geographic locations will determine the types of actions that constitute wrongdoing, what is suitable evidence, and what type of licensing and privacy laws your organization must abide by.
- *Physical (environmental) security.* Concerns itself with threats, risks, and countermeasures to protect facilities, hardware, data, media, and personnel. Main topics include restricted areas, authorization models, intrusion detection, fire detection, and security guards.

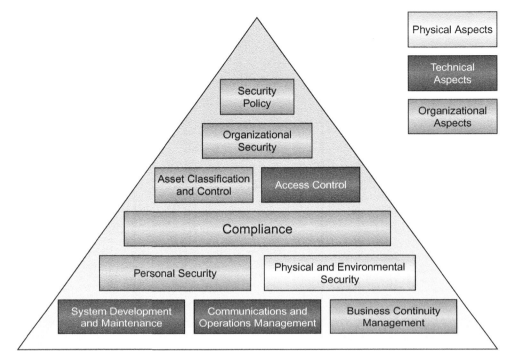

FIGURE 1.1   ISO 17799:2005 security model.[7]

the three main processes of security (prevention, detection, and recovery) are implemented and integrated.

ISMM helps us better understand the application of information security controls outlined in ISO 17799. Figure 1.3 shows a content matrix that defines the scope of applicability between various security controls mentioned in ISO 17799's ten domains and the corresponding scope of applicability on the ISMM Framework.[8]

What is a Threat?

Threats to information systems come in many flavors, some with malicious intent, others with supernatural powers or unexpected surprises. Threats can be deliberate acts of espionage, information extortion, or sabotage, as in many targeted attacks between foreign nations; however, more often than not it happens that the biggest threats can be forces of nature (hurricane, flood) or acts of human error or failure. It is easy to become consumed in attempting to anticipate and mitigate every threat, but this is simply not possible.

7. "ISO 17799 security standards," ISO Web site, http://www.iso.org/iso/support/faqs/faqs_widely_used_standards/widely_used_standards_other/information_security.htm.

8. Saad Saleh AlAboodi, *A New Approach for Assessing the Maturity of Information Security*, CISSP.

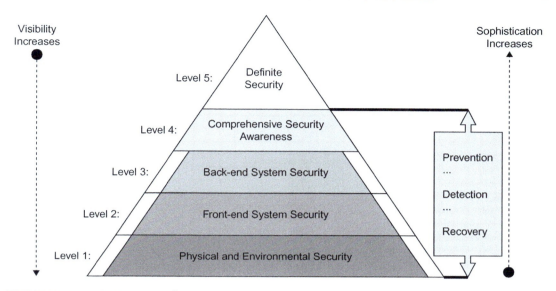

FIGURE 1.2   ISMM framework.[9]

Threat agents are threats only when they are provided the opportunity to take advantage of a vulnerability, and ultimately there is no guarantee that the vulnerability will be exploited. Therefore, determining which threats are important can only be done in the context of your organization. The process by which a threat can actually cause damage to your information assets is as follows: A threat agent *gives rise to* a threat that *exploits* a vulnerability and can *lead to* a security risk that *can damage* your assets and *cause* an exposure. This can be *counter-measured by* a safeguard that *directly affects* the threat agent. Figure 1.4 shows the building blocks of the threat process.

Common Attacks

Threats are exploited with a variety of attacks, some technical, others not so much. Organizations that focus on the technical attacks and neglect items such as policies and procedures or employee training and awareness are setting up information security for failure. The mantra that the IT department or even the security department, by themselves, can secure an organization is as antiquated as black-and-white television. Most threats today are a mixed blend of automated information gathering, social engineering, and combined exploits, giving the perpetrator endless vectors through which to gain access. Examples of attacks vary from a highly technical remote exploit over the Internet, social-engineering an administrative assistant to reset his password, or simply walking right through an unprotected door in the back of your building. All scenarios have the potential

9. Saad Saleh AlAboodi, *A New Approach for Assessing the Maturity of Information Security*, CISSP.

ISO 17799			ISMM (Scope of Applicability)				
Domain Number	Domain Name	Domain Subname	Layer 1	Layer 2	Layer 3	Layer 4	Layer 5
1	Security policy	N/A	✓	✓	✓	✓	
2	Organizational security	Information security infrastructure	✓	✓	✓		
		Security of third-party access	✓	✓	✓	✓	
		Outsourcing	✓	✓	✓	✓	
3	Asset classification and control	Accountability for assets	✓	✓	✓		
		Information classification	✓	✓	✓		
4	Personnel security	Security in job definition and resourcing	✓				
		User training	✓	✓	✓	✓	
		Responding to security incidents/malfunctions	✓	✓	✓	✓	
5	Physical and environmental security	Secure areas	✓				
		Equipment security	✓				
		General controls	✓				
6	Communications and operations management	Operational procedures and responsibilities		✓	✓		
		System planning and acceptance		✓	✓		
		Protection against malicious software		✓			
		Housekeeping		✓	✓		
		Network management			✓		
		Media handling and security	✓				
		Exchange of information and software		✓			
7	Access control	Business requirement for access control	✓	✓	✓		
		User access management		✓			
		User responsibilities		✓			
		Network access control			✓		
		Operating system access control			✓		
		Application access control		✓			
		Monitoring system access and use		✓	✓		
		Mobile computing and teleworking		✓	✓		
8	System development and maintenance	Security requirement of systems		✓	✓		
		Security in application systems		✓			
		Cryptographic controls			✓		
		Security of system files		✓	✓		
		Security in development and support processes		✓	✓		
9	Business continuity management	N/A				✓	✓
10	Compliance	Compliance with legal requirements				✓	
		Review of security policy and compliance				✓	
		System audit considerations				✓	

FIGURE 1.3   A content matrix for ISO 17799 and its scope of applicability.

to be equally devastating to the integrity of the organization. Some of the most common attacks are briefly described in the sidebar, "Common Attacks."[10]

10. Symantec Global Internet, Security Threat Report, Trends for July–December 07, Volume XII, Published April 2008 http://eval.symantec.com/mktginfo/enterprise/white_papers/b-whitepaper_internet_security_threat_report_xiii_04-2008.en-us.pdf.

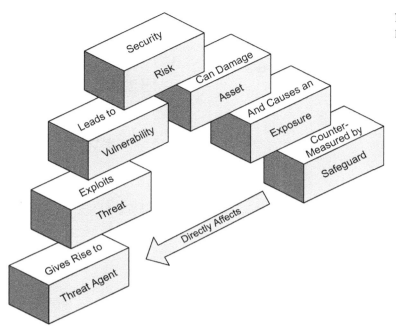

FIGURE 1.4 The threat process.

COMMON ATTACKS

- *Malicious code (malware).* Malware is a broad category; however, it is typically software designed to infiltrate or damage a computer system without the owner's informed consent. As shown in Figure 1.5, the most commonly identifiable types of malware are viruses, worms, backdoors, and Trojans. Particularly difficult to identify are root kits, which alter the kernel of the operating system.

- *Social engineering.* The art of manipulating people into performing actions or divulging confidential information. Similar to a confidence trick or simple fraud, the term typically applies to trickery to gain information or computer system access; in most cases, the attacker never comes face to face with the victim.

- *Industrial espionage.* Industrial espionage describes activities such as theft of trade secrets, bribery, blackmail, and technological surveillance as well as spying on commercial organizations and sometimes governments.

- *Spam, phishing, and hoaxes.* Spamming and phishing (see Figure 1.6), although different, often go hand in hand. Spamming is the abuse of electronic messaging systems to indiscriminately send unsolicited bulk messages, many of which contain hoaxes or other undesirable contents such as links to phishing sites. Phishing is the criminally fraudulent process of attempting to acquire sensitive information such as usernames, passwords, and credit card details by masquerading as a trustworthy entity in an electronic communication.

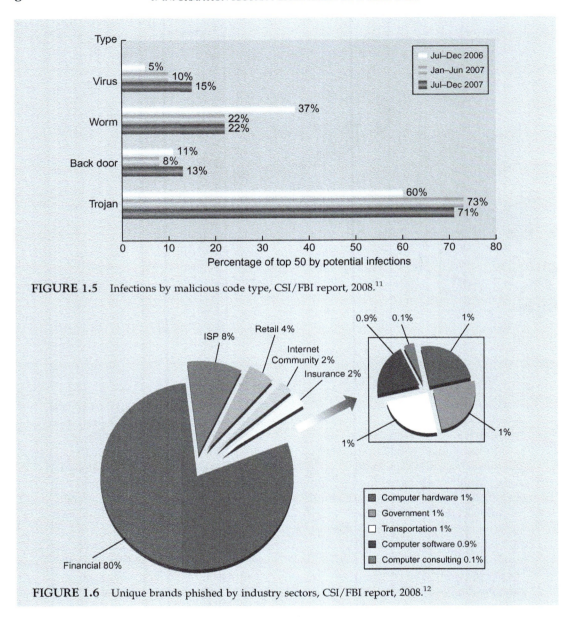

FIGURE 1.5 Infections by malicious code type, CSI/FBI report, 2008.[11]

FIGURE 1.6 Unique brands phished by industry sectors, CSI/FBI report, 2008.[12]

11. Robert Richardson, "2008 CSI Computer Crime & Security Survey," (The latest results from the longest-running project of its kind) http://i.cmpnet.com/v2.gocsi.com/pdf/CSIsurvey2008.pdf.

12. Robert Richardson, "2008 CSI Computer Crime & Security Survey," (The latest results from the longest-running project of its kind) http://i.cmpnet.com/v2.gocsi.com/pdf/CSIsurvey2008.pdf.

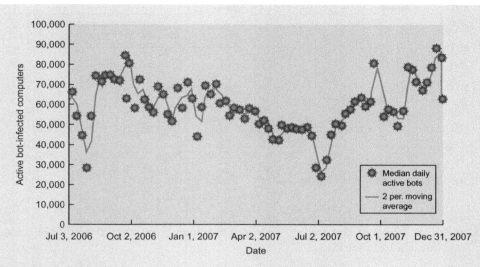

FIGURE 1.7   Botnet activity, CSI/FBI report, 2008.[13]

- *Denial-of-service (DoS) and distributed denial-of-service (DDoS).* These are attempts to make a computer resource unavailable to its intended users. Although the means to carry out, motives for, and targets of a DoS attack may vary, it generally consists of the concerted, malevolent efforts of a person or persons to prevent an Internet site or service from functioning efficiently or at all, temporarily or indefinitely.
- *Botnets.* The term *botnet* (see Figure 1.7) can be used to refer to any group of bots, or software robots, such as IRC bots, but this word is generally used to refer to a collection of compromised computers (called zombies) running software, usually installed via worms, Trojan horses, or backdoors, under a common command-and-control infrastructure. The majority of these computers are running Microsoft Windows operating systems, but other operating systems can be affected.

Impact of Security Breaches

The impact of security breaches on most organizations can be devastating; however, it's not just dollars and cents that are at stake. Aside from the financial burden of having to deal with a security incident, especially if it leads to litigation, other factors could severely damage an organization's ability to operate, or damage the reputation of an organization

13. Robert Richardson, "2008 CSI Computer Crime & Security Survey," (The latest results from the longest-running project of its kind) http://i.cmpnet.com/v2.gocsi.com/pdf/CSIsurvey2008.pdf.

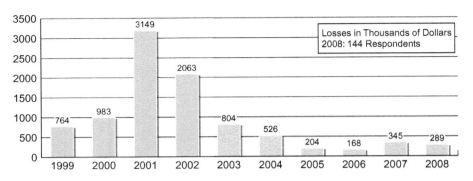

FIGURE 1.8   2008 CSI/FBI Security Survey results.[14]

beyond recovery. Some of the preliminary key findings from the 2008 CSI/FBI Security Report[15] (see Figure 1.8) include:

- Financial fraud cost organizations the most, with an average reported loss of close to $500,000.
- The second most expensive activity was dealing with bots within the network, reported to cost organizations an average of nearly $350,000.
- Virus incidents occurred most frequently, respondents said — at almost half (49%) of respondent organizations.
     Some things to consider:
- How much would it cost your organization if your ecommerce Web server farm went down for 12 hours?
- What if your mainframe database that houses your reservation system was not accessible for an entire afternoon?
- What if your Web site was defaced and rerouted all your customers to a site infected with malicious Java scripts?
- Would any of these scenarios significantly impact your organization's bottom line?

2. PROTECTING MISSION-CRITICAL SYSTEMS

The IT core of any organization is its mission-critical systems. These are systems without which the mission of the organization, whether building aircraft carriers for the U.S. military or packaging Twinkies to deliver to food markets, could not operate. The major components to protecting these systems are detailed throughout this chapter; however, with special emphasis on the big picture an information security manager must keep in

14. Robert Richardson, "2008 CSI Computer Crime & Security Survey," (The latest results from the longest-running project of its kind) http://i.cmpnet.com/v2.gocsi.com/pdf/CSIsurvey2008.pdf.

15. Robert Richardson, "2008 CSI Computer Crime & Security Survey," (The latest results from the longest-running project of its kind) http://i.cmpnet.com/v2.gocsi.com/pdf/CSIsurvey2008.pdf.

mind, there are some key components that are crucial for the success and continuity of any organization. These are information assurance, information risk management, defense in depth, and contingency planning.

Information Assurance

Information assurance is achieved when information and information systems are protected against attacks through the application of security services such as availability, integrity, authentication, confidentiality, and nonrepudiation. The application of these services should be based on the protect, detect, and react paradigm. This means that in addition to incorporating protection mechanisms, organizations need to expect attacks and include attack detection tools and procedures that allow them to react to and recover from these unexpected attacks.[16]

Information Risk Management

Risk is, in essence, the likelihood of something going wrong and damaging your organization or information assets. Due to the ramifications of such risk, an organization should try to reduce the risk to an acceptable level. This process is known as *information risk management*. Risk to an organization and its information assets, similar to threats, comes in many different forms. Some of the most common risks and/or threats are:

- *Physical damage.* Fire, water, vandalism, power loss and natural disasters.
- *Human interaction.* Accidental or intentional action or inaction that can disrupt productivity.
- *Equipment malfunctions.* Failure of systems and peripheral devices.
- *Internal or external attacks.* Hacking, cracking, and attacking.
- *Misuse of data.* Sharing trade secrets; fraud, espionage, and theft.
- *Loss of data.* Intentional or unintentional loss of information through destructive means.
- *Application error.* Computation errors, input errors, and buffer overflows.

The idea of risk management is that threats of any kind must be identified, classified, and evaluated to calculate their damage potential.[17] This is easier said than done.

Administrative, Technical, and Physical Controls

For example, administrative, technical, and physical controls, are as follows:

- Administrative controls consist of organizational policies and guidelines that help minimize the exposure of an organization. They provide a framework by which a business can manage and inform its people how they should conduct themselves while at the workplace and provide clear steps employees can take when they're confronted with a potentially risky situation. Some examples of administrative controls include the

---

16. "Defense in Depth: A practical strategy for achieving Information Assurance in today's highly networked environments," National Security Agency, Information Assurance Solutions Group - STE 6737.

17. Shon Harris, *All in One CISSP Certification Exam Guide 4th Edition*, McGraw Hill Companies.

corporate security policy, password policy, hiring policies, and disciplinary policies that form the basis for the selection and implementation of logical and physical controls. Administrative controls are of paramount importance because technical and physical controls are manifestations of the administrative control policies that are in place.

- Technical controls use software and hardware resources to control access to information and computing systems, to help mitigate the potential for errors and blatant security policy violations. Examples of technical controls include passwords, network- and host-based firewalls, network intrusion detection systems, and access control lists and data encryption. Associated with technical controls is the *Principle of Least Privilege*, which requires that an individual, program, or system process is not granted any more access privileges than are necessary to perform the task.
- Physical controls monitor and protect the physical environment of the workplace and computing facilities. They also monitor and control access to and from such facilities. Separating the network and workplace into functional areas are also physical controls. An important physical control is also separation of duties, which ensures that an individual cannot complete a critical task by herself.

Risk Analysis

During risk analysis there are several units that can help measure risk. Before risk can be measured, though, the organization must identify the vulnerabilities and threats against its mission-critical systems in terms of business continuity. During risk analysis, an organization tries to evaluate the cost for each security control that helps mitigate the risk. If the control is cost effective relative to the exposure of the organization, then the control is put in place. The measure of risk can be determined as a product of threat, vulnerability, and asset values—in other words:

$$Risk = Asset \times Threat \times Vulnerability$$

There are two primary types of risk analysis: quantitative and qualitative. *Quantitative risk analysis* attempts to assign meaningful numbers to all elements of the risk analysis process. It is recommended for large, costly projects that require exact calculations. It is typically performed to examine the viability of a project's cost or time objectives. Quantitative risk analysis provides answers to three questions that cannot be addressed with deterministic risk and project management methodologies such as traditional cost estimating or project scheduling:[18]

- What's the probability of meeting the project objective, given all known risks?
- How much could the overrun or delay be, and therefore how much contingency do we need for the organization's desired level of certainty?
- Where in the project is the most risk, given the model of the project and the totality of all identified and quantified risks?

---

18. Lionel Galway, *Quantitative Risk Analysis for Project Management, A Critical Review*, WR-112-RC, February 2004, Rand.org Web site, http://www.rand.org/pubs/working_papers/2004/RAND_WR112.pdf.

Qualitative risk analysis does not assign numerical values but instead opts for general categorization by severity levels. Where little or no numerical data is available for a risk assessment, the qualitative approach is the most appropriate. The qualitative approach does not require heavy mathematics; instead, it thrives more on the people participating and their backgrounds. Qualitative analysis enables classification of risk that is determined by people's wide experience and knowledge captured within the process. Ultimately it is not an exact science, so the process will count on expert opinions for its base assumptions. The assessment process uses a structured and documented approach and agreed likelihood and consequence evaluation tables. It is also quite common to calculate risk as a single loss expectancy (SLE) or annual loss expectancy (ALE) by project or business function.

Defense in Depth

The principle of *defense in depth* is that layered security mechanisms increase security of a system as a whole. If an attack causes one security mechanism to fail, other mechanisms may still provide the necessary security to protect the system.[19] This is a process that involves people, technology, and operations as key components to its success; however, those are only part of the picture. These organizational layers are difficult to translate into specific technological layers of defenses, and they leave out areas such as security monitoring and metrics. Figure 1.9 shows a mind map that organizes the major categories from both the organizational and technical aspects of defense in depth and takes into account people, policies, monitoring, and security metrics.

Contingency Planning

Contingency planning is necessary in several ways for an organization to be sure it can withstand some sort of security breach or disaster. Among the important steps required to make sure an organization is protected and able to respond to a security breach or disaster are business impact analysis, incident response planning, disaster recovery planning, and business continuity planning. These contingency plans are interrelated in several ways and need to stay that way so that a response team can change from one to the other seamlessly if there is a need. Figure 1.10 shows the relationship between the four types of contingency plans with the major categories defined in each.

Business impact analysis must be performed in every organization to determine exactly which business process is deemed mission-critical and which processes would not seriously hamper business operations should they be unavailable for some time. An important part of a business impact analysis is the recovery strategy that is usually defined at the end of the process. If a thorough business impact analysis is performed, there should be a clear picture of the priority of each organization's highest-impact, therefore risky, business

19. OWASP Definition of Defense in Depth http://www.owasp.org/index.php/Defense_in_depth.

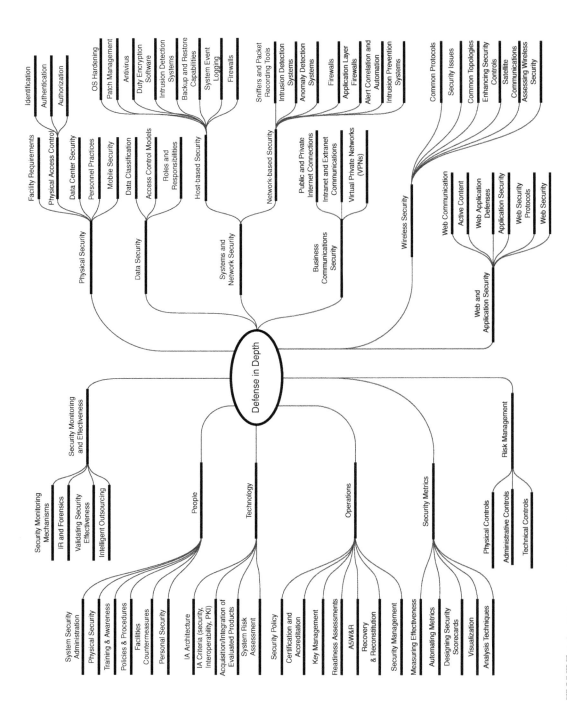

FIGURE 1.9   Defense-in-depth mind map.

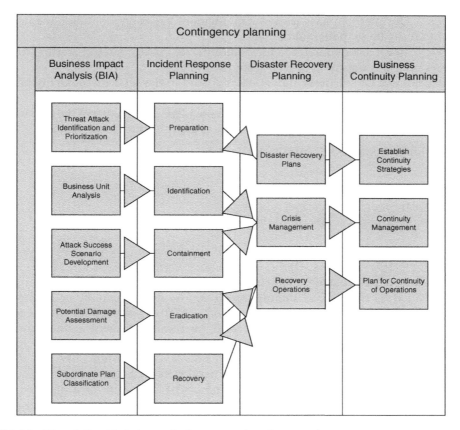

FIGURE 1.10 The relationship between the four types of contingency plans.

processes and assets as well as a clear strategy to recover from an interruption in one of these areas.[20]

An Incident Response (IR) Plan

It is a detailed set of processes and procedures that anticipate, detect, and mitigate the impact of an unexpected event that might compromise information resources and assets. Incident response plans are composed of six major phases:

1. *Preparation.* Planning and readying in the event of a security incident.
2. *Identification.* To identify a set of events that have some negative impact on the business and can be considered a security incident.

20. M. E. Whitman, H. J. Mattord, *Management of Information Security*, Course Technology, 2nd Edition, March 27, 2007.

3. *Containment.* During this phase the security incident has been identified and action is required to mitigate its potential damage.
4. *Eradication.* After it's contained, the incident must be eradicated and studied to make sure it has been thoroughly removed from the system.
5. *Recovery.* Bringing the business and assets involved in the security incident back to normal operations.
6. *Lessons learned.* A thorough review of how the incident occurred and the actions taken to respond to it where the lessons learned get applied to future incidents.

When a threat becomes a valid attack, it is classified as an information security incident if:[21]

- It is directed against information assets.
- It has a realistic chance of success.
- It threatens the confidentiality, integrity, or availability of information assets.

Business Continuity Planning (BCP)

It ensures that critical business functions can continue during a disaster and is most properly managed by the CEO of the organization. The BCP is usually activated and executed concurrently with *disaster recovery planning* (DRP) when needed and reestablishes critical functions at alternate sites (DRP focuses on reestablishment at the primary site). BCP relies on identification of critical business functions and the resources to support them using several continuity strategies, such as exclusive-use options like hot, warm, and cold sites or shared-use options like time-share, service bureaus, or mutual agreements.[22]

Disaster recovery planning is the preparation for and recovery from a disaster. Whether natural or manmade, it is an incident that has become a disaster because the organization is unable to contain or control its impact, or the level of damage or destruction from the incident is so severe that the organization is unable to recover quickly. The key role of DRP is defining how to reestablish operations at the site where the organization is usually located.[23] Key points in a properly designed DRP:

- Clear delegation of roles and responsibilities
- Execution of alert roster and notification of key personnel
- Clear establishment of priorities
- Documentation of the disaster
- Action steps to mitigate the impact
- Alternative implementations for various systems components
- DRP must be tested regularly.

21. M. E. Whitman, H. J. Mattord, *Management of Information Security*, Course Technology, 2nd Edition, March 27, 2007.

22. M. E. Whitman, H. J. Mattord, *Management of Information Security*, Course Technology, 2nd Edition, March 27, 2007.

23. M. E. Whitman, H. J. Mattord, *Management of Information Security*, Course Technology, 2nd Edition, March 27, 2007.

3. INFORMATION SECURITY FROM THE GROUND UP

The core concepts of information security management and protecting mission-critical systems have been explained. Now, how do you actually apply these concepts to your organization from the ground up? You literally start at the ground (physical) level and work yourself up to the top (application) level. This model can be applied to many IT frameworks, ranging from networking models such as OSI or TCP/IP stacks to operating systems or other problems such as organizational information security and protecting mission-critical systems.

There are many areas of security, all of which are interrelated. You can have an extremely hardened system running your ecommerce Web site and database; however, if physical access to the system is obtained by the wrong person, a simple yanking of the right power plug can be game over. In other words, to think that any of the following components is not important to the overall security of your organization is to provide malicious attackers the only thing they need to be successful — that is, the path of least resistance. The next parts of this chapter each contain an overview of the technologies (see Figure 1.11) and processes of which information security managers must be aware to successfully secure the assets of any organization:

- Physical security
- Data security
- Systems and network security
- Business communications security
- Wireless security
- Web and application security
- Security policies and procedures
- Security employee training and awareness.

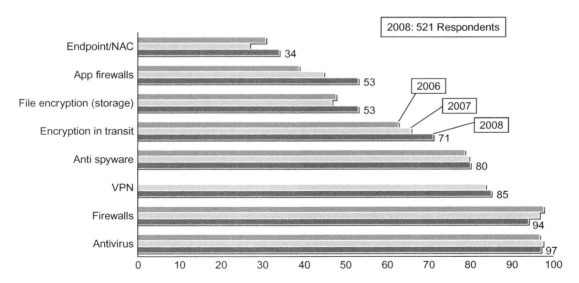

FIGURE 1.11   Security technologies used by organizations, CSI/FBI report, 2008.

Physical Security

Physical security as defined earlier concerns itself with threats, risks, and countermeasures to protect facilities, hardware, data, media and personnel. Main topics include restricted areas, authorization models, intrusion detection, fire detection, and security guards. Therefore physical safeguards must be put in place to protect the organization from damaging consequences. The security rule defines physical safeguards as "physical measures, policies, and procedures to protect a covered entity's electronic information systems and related buildings and equipment, from natural and environmental hazards, and unauthorized intrusion."[24] A brief description of the baseline requirements to implement these safeguards at your facility follow.

Facility Requirements

Entering and accessing information systems to any degree within any organization must be controlled. What's more, it is necessary to understand what is allowed and what's not; if those parameters are clearly defied, the battle is half won. Not every building is a high-security facility, so it's understandable that some of the following items might not apply to your organization; however, there should be a good, clear reason as to why they don't. Sample questions and comments to consider:[25]

- Are policies and procedures developed and implemented that address allowing authorized and limiting unauthorized physical access to electronic information systems and the facility or facilities in which they are housed?
- Do the policies and procedures identify individuals (workforce members, business associates, contractors, etc.) with authorized access by title and/or job function?
- Do the policies and procedures specify the methods used to control physical access, such as door locks, electronic access control systems, security officers, or video monitoring?
  The facility access controls standard has four implementation specifications:[26]
- *Contingency operations.* Establish (and implement as needed) procedures that allow facility access in support of restoration of lost data under the disaster recovery plan and emergency mode operations plan in the event of an emergency.
- *Facility security plan.* Implement policies and procedures to safeguard the facility and the equipment therein from unauthorized physical access, tampering, and theft.
- *Access control and validation procedures.* Implement procedures to control and validate a person's access to facilities based on her role or function, including visitor control and control of access to software programs for testing and revision.
- *Maintenance records.* Implement policies and procedures to document repairs and modifications to the physical components of a facility that are related to security (for example, hardware, walls, doors, and locks).

24. 45 C.F.R. § 164.310 Physical safeguards, http://law.justia.com/us/cfr/title45/45-1.0.1.3.70.3.33.5.html.
25. 45 C.F.R. § 164.310 Physical safeguards, http://law.justia.com/us/cfr/title45/45-1.0.1.3.70.3.33.5.html.
26. 45 C.F.R. § 164.310 Physical safeguards, http://law.justia.com/us/cfr/title45/45-1.0.1.3.70.3.33.5.html.

Administrative, Technical, and Physical Controls

Understanding what it takes to secure a facility is the first step in the process of identifying exactly what type of administrative, technical, and physical controls will be necessary for your particular organization. Translating the needs for security into tangible examples, here are some of the controls that can be put in place to enhance security:

- *Administrative controls.* These include human resources exercises for simulated emergencies such as fire drills or power outages as well as security awareness training and security policies.
- *Technical controls.* These include physical intrusion detection systems and access control equipment such as biometrics.
- *Physical controls.* These include video cameras, guarded gates, man traps, and car traps.

Data Security

Data security is at the core of what needs to be protected in terms of information security and mission-critical systems. Ultimately it is the data that the organization needs to protect in many cases, and usually data is exactly what perpetrators are after, whether trade secrets, customer information, or a database of Social Security numbers — the data is where it's at!

To be able to properly classify and restrict data, the first thing to understand is how data is accessed. Data is accessed by a *subject,* whether that is a person, process, or another application, and what is accessed to retrieve the data is called an *object.* Think of an object as a cookie jar with valuable information in it, and only select subjects have the permissions necessary to dip their hands into the cookie jar and retrieve the data or information that they are looking for. Both subjects and objects can be a number of things acting in a network, depending on what action they are taking at any given moment, as shown in Figure 1.12.

Data Classification

Various *data classification* models are available for different environments. Some security models focus on the confidentiality of the data (such as Bell-La Padula) and use different classifications. For example, the U.S. military uses a model that goes from most confidential (Top Secret) to least confidential (Unclassified) to classify the data on any given system. On the other hand, most corporate entities prefer a model whereby they classify data by business unit (HR, Marketing, R & D . . .) or use terms such as Company Confidential to define items that should not be shared with the public. Other security models focus on the integrity of the data (for example, Bipa); yet others are expressed by mapping security policies to data classification (for example, Clark-Wilson). In every case there are areas that require special attention and clarification.

Access Control Models

Three main *access control models* are in use today: RBAC, DAC, and MAC. In Role-Based Access Control (RBAC), the job function of the individual determines the group he is assigned to and determines the level of access he can attain on certain data and systems.

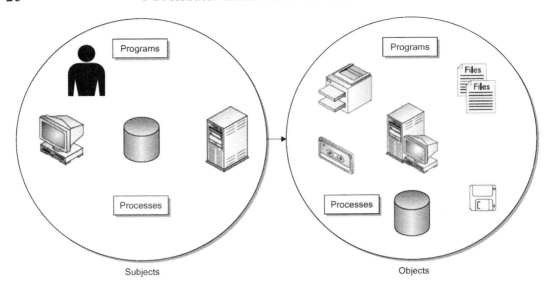

FIGURE 1.12   Subjects access objects.

The level of access is usually defined by IT personnel in accordance with policies and procedures. In Discretionary Access Control (DAC), the end user or creator of the data object is allowed to define who can and who cannot access the data; this has become less popular in recent history. Mandatory Access Control (MAC) is more of a militant style of applying permissions, where permissions are the same across the board to all members of a certain level or class within the organization. The following are data security "need to knows":

- *Authentication versus authorization.* It's crucial to understand that simply because someone becomes authenticated does not mean that they are authorized to view certain data. There needs to be a means by which a person, after gaining access through authentication, is limited in the actions they are authorized to perform on certain data (such as read-only permissions).
- *Protecting data with cryptography* is important for the security of both the organization and its customers. Usually the most important item that an organization needs to protect, aside from trade secrets, is its customers' personal data. If there is a security breach and the data that is stolen or compromised was previously encrypted, the organization can feel more secure in that the collateral damage to their reputation and customer base will be minimized.
- *Data leakage prevention and content management* is an up-and-coming area of data security that has proven extremely useful in preventing sensitive information from leaving an organization. With this relatively new technology, a security administrator can define the types of documents, and further define the content within those documents, that cannot leave the organization and quarantine them for inspection before they hit the public Internet.

- *Securing email systems* is one of the most important and overlooked areas of data security. With access to the mail server, an attacker can snoop through anyone's email, even the company CEO's! Password files, company confidential documents, and contacts for all address books are only some of the things that a compromised mail server can reveal about an organization, not to mention root/administrator access to a system in the internal network.

Systems and Network Security

Systems and network security[27] is at the core of information security. Though physical security is extremely important and a breach could render all your systems and network security safeguards useless, without hardened systems and networks, anyone from the comfort of her own living room can take over your network, access your confidential information, and disrupt your operations at will. Data classification and security are also quite important, if for nothing else to be sure that only those who need to access certain data can and those who do not need access cannot; however, that usually works well for people who play by the rules. In many cases when an attacker gains access to a system, the first order of business is escalation of privileges. This means that the attacker gets in as a regular user and attempts to find ways to gain administrator or root privileges. The following are brief descriptions of each of the components that make for a complete security infrastructure for all host systems and network connected assets.

Host-Based Security

The host system is the core of where data sits and is accessed, so it is therefore also the main target of many intruders. Regardless of the operating system platform that is selected to run certain applications and databases, the principles of hardening systems are the same and apply to host systems as well as network devices, as we will see in the upcoming sections. Steps required to maintain host systems in as secure a state as possible are as follows:

1. *OS hardening.* Guidelines by which a base operating system goes through a series of checks to make sure no unnecessary exposures remain open and that security features are enabled where possible. There is a series of organizations that publish OS hardening Guides for various platforms of operating systems.
2. *Removing unnecessary services.* In any operating system there are usually services that are enabled but have no real business need. It is necessary to go through all the services of your main corporate image, on both the server side and client side, to determine which services are required and which would create a potential vulnerability if left enabled.
3. *Patch management.* All vendors release updates for known vulnerabilities on some kind of schedule. Part of host-based security is making sure that all required vendor patches, at both the operating system and the application level, are applied as quickly as business operations allow on some kind of regular schedule. There should also be an

27. "GSEC, GIAC Security Essentials Outline," SANS Institute, https://www.sans.org/training/description.php?tid=672.

emergency patch procedure in case there is an outbreak and updates need to be pushed out of sequence.

4. *Antivirus.* Possibly more important than patches are antivirus definitions, specifically on desktop and mobile systems. Corporate antivirus software should be installed and updated frequently on all systems in the organization.

5. *Intrusion detection systems (IDSs).* Although many seem to think IDSs are a network security function, there are many good host-based IDS applications, both commercial and open source, that can significantly increase security and act as an early warning system for possibly malicious traffic and/or files for which the AV does not have a definition.

6. *Firewalls.* Host-based firewalls are not as popular as they once were because many big vendors such as Symantec, McAfee, and Checkpoint have moved to a host-based client application that houses all security functions in one. There is also another trend in the industry to move toward application-specific host-based firewalls like those specifically designed to run on a Web or database server, for example.

7. *Data encryption software.* One item often overlooked is encryption of data while it is at rest. Many solutions have recently come onto the market that offer the ability to encrypt sensitive data such as credit card and Social Security numbers that sit on your file server or inside the database server. This is a huge protection in the case of information theft or data leakage.

8. *Backup and restore capabilities.* Without the ability to back up and restore both servers and clients in a timely fashion, an issue that could be resolved in short order can quickly turn into a disaster. Backup procedures should be in place and restored on a regular basis to verify their integrity.

9. *System event logging.* Event logs are significant when you're attempting to investigate the root cause of an issue or incident. In many cases, logging is not turned on by default and needs to be enabled after the core installation of the host operating system. The OS hardening guidelines for your organization should require that logging be enabled.

Network-Based Security

The network is the communication highway for everything that happens between all the host systems. All data at one point or another passes over the wire and is potentially vulnerable to snooping or spying by the wrong person. The controls implemented on the network are similar in nature to those that can be applied to host systems; however, network-based security can be more easily classified into two main categories: detection and prevention. We will discuss security monitoring tools in another section; for now the main functions of network-based security are to either detect a potential incident based on a set of events or prevent a known attack.

Most network-based security devices can perform detect or protect functions in one of two ways: signature-based or anomaly-based. Signature-based detection or prevention is similar to AV signatures that look for known traits of a particular attack or malware. Anomaly-based systems can make decisions based on what is expected to be "normal" on the network or per a certain set of standards (for example, RFC), usually after a period of being installed in what is called "learning" or "monitor" mode.

Intrusion Detection

Intrusion detection is the process of monitoring the events occurring in a computer system or network and analyzing them for signs of possible incidents that are violations or imminent threats of violation of computer security policies, acceptable-use policies, or standard security practices. Incidents have many causes, such as malware (worms, spyware), attackers gaining unauthorized access to systems from the Internet, and authorized system users who misuse their privileges or attempt to gain additional privileges for which they are not authorized.[28] The most common detection technologies and their security functions on the network are as follows:

- *Packet sniffing and recording tools.* These tools are used quite often by networking teams to troubleshoot connectivity issues; however, they can be a security professional's best friend during investigations and root-cause analysis. When properly deployed and maintained, a packet capture device on the network allows security professionals to reconstruct data and reverseengineer malware in a way that is simply not possible without a full packet capture of the communications.
- *Intrusion detection systems.* In these systems, appliances or servers monitor network traffic and run it through a rules engine to determine whether it is malicious according to its signature set. If the traffic is deemed malicious, an alert will fire and notify the monitoring system.
- *Anomaly detection systems.* Aside from the actual packet data traveling on the wire, there are also traffic trends that can be monitored on the switches and routers to determine whether unauthorized or anomalous activity is occurring. With Net-flow and S-flow data that can be sent to an appliance or server, aggregated traffic on the network can be analyzed and can alert a monitoring system if there is a problem. Anomaly detection systems are extremely useful when there is an attack for which the IDS does not have a signature or if there is some activity occurring that is suspicious.

Intrusion Prevention

Intrusion prevention is a system that allows for the active blocking of attacks while they are inline on the network, before they even get to the target host. There are many ways to prevent attacks or unwanted traffic from coming into your network, the most common of which is known as a firewall. Although a firewall is mentioned quite commonly and a lot of people know what a firewall is, there are several different types of controls that can be put in place in addition to a firewall that can seriously help protect the network. Here are the most common prevention technologies:

- *Firewalls.* The purpose of a firewall is to enforce an organization's security policy at the border of two networks. Typically most firewalls are deployed at the edge between the internal network and the Internet (if there is such a thing) and are configured to block

---

28. Karen Scarfone and Peter Mell, NIST Special Publication 800–94: "Guide to Intrusion Detection and Prevention Systems (IDPS)," Recommendations of the National Institute of Standards and Technology, http://csrc.nist.gov/publications/nistpubs/800-94/SP800-94.pdf.

(prevent) any traffic from going in or out that is not allowed by the corporate security policy. There are quite a few different levels of protection a firewall can provide, depending on the type of firewall that is deployed, such as these:

- *Packet filtering.* The most basic type of firewalls perform what is called *stateful packet filtering*, which means that they can remember which side initiated the connection, and rules (called access control lists, or ACLs) can be created based not only on IPs and ports but also depending on the state of the connection (meaning whether the traffic is going into or out of the network).
- *Proxies.* The main difference between proxies and stateful packet-filtering firewalls is that proxies have the ability to terminate and reestablish connections between two end hosts, acting as a proxy for all communications and adding a layer of security and functionality to the regular firewalls.
- *Application layer firewalls.* The app firewalls have become increasingly popular; they are designed to protect certain types of applications (Web or database) and can be configured to perform a level of blocking that is much more intuitive and granular, based not only on network information but also application-specific variables so that administrators can be much more precise in what they are blocking. In addition, app firewalls can typically be loaded with server-side SSL certificates, allowing the appliance to decrypt encrypted traffic, a huge benefit to a typical proxy or stateful firewall.
- *Intrusion prevention systems.* An intrusion prevention system (IPS) is software that has all the capabilities of an intrusion detection system and can also attempt to stop possible incidents using a set of conditions based on signatures or anomalies.

Business Communications Security

Businesses today tend to communicate with many other business entities, not only over the Internet but also through private networks or guest access connections directly to the organization's network, whether wired or wireless. Business partners and contractors conducting business communications obviously tend to need a higher level of access than public users but not as extensive as permanent employees, so how does an organization handle this phenomenon? External parties working on internal projects are also classed as business partners. Some general rules for users to maintain security control of external entities are shown in Figure 1.13.

General Rules for Self-Protection

The general rules for self-protection are as follows:

- Access to a user's own IT system must be protected in such a way that system settings (in the BIOS) can only be changed subject to authentication.
- System start must always be protected by requiring appropriate authentication (requesting the boot password). Exceptions to this rule can apply if:
- Automatic update procedures require this, and the system start can only take place from the built-in hard disk.

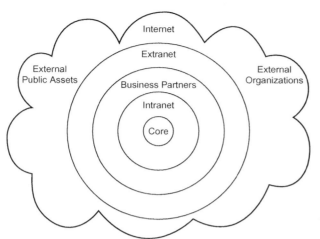

FIGURE 1.13 The business communications cloud.

- The system is equipped for use by a number of persons with their individual user profiles, and system start can only take place from the built-in hard disk.
- Unauthorized access to in-house resources including data areas (shares, folders, mailboxes, calendar, etc.) must be prevented in line with their need for protection. In addition, the necessary authorizations for approved data access must be defined.
- Users are not permitted to operate resources without first defining any authorizations (such as no global sharing). This rule must be observed particularly by those users who are system managers of their own resources.
- Users of an IT system must lock the access links they have opened (for example, by enabling a screensaver or removing the chip card from the card reader), even during short periods of absence from their workstations.
- When work is over, all open access links must be properly closed or protected against system/data access (such as if extensive compilation runs need to take place during the night).
- Deputizing rules for access to the user's own system or data resources must be made in agreement with the manager and the acting employee.

Handling Protection Resources

The handling of protection resources are as follows:

- Employees must ensure that their protection resources cannot be subject to snooping while data required for authentication is being entered (e.g., password entry during login).
- Employees must store all protection resources and records in such a way that they cannot be subjected to snooping or stolen.
- Personal protection resources must never be made available to third parties.
- In the case of chip cards, SecurID tokens, or other protection resources requiring a PIN, the associated PIN (PIN letter) must be stored separately.

- Loss, theft, or disclosure of protection resources is to be reported immediately.
- Protection resources subject to loss, theft, or snooping must be disabled immediately.

Rules for Mobile IT Systems

In addition to the general rules for users, the following rules may also apply for mobile IT systems:

- Extended self-protection.
- A mobile IT system must be safeguarded against theft (that is, secured with a cable lock, locked away in a cupboard).
- The data from a mobile IT system using corporate proprietary information must be safeguarded as appropriate (e.g., encryption). In this connection, CERT rules in particular are to be observed.
- The software provided by the organization for system access control may only be used on the organization's own mobile IT systems.

Operation on Open Networks

Rules for operation on open networks are as follows:

- The mobile IT system must be operated in open network environments using a personal firewall.
- The configuration of the personal firewall must be in accordance with the corporate policy or, in the case of other personal firewall systems, must be subject to restrictive settings.
- A mobile IT system must be operated in an unprotected open network only for the duration of a secure access link to the organization's own network. The connection establishment for the secure access link must be performed as soon as possible, at least within five minutes.
- Simultaneous operation on open networks (protected or unprotected) and the organization's own networks is forbidden at all times.
- Remote access to company internal resources must always be protected by means of strong authentication.
- For the protection of data being transferred via a remote access link, strong encryption must always be used.

Additional Business Communications Guidelines

Additional business communications guidelines should be defined for the following:

- External IT systems may not be connected directly to the intranet. Transmission of corporate proprietary data to external systems should be avoided wherever possible, and copies of confidential or strictly confidential data must never be created on external IT systems.
- Unauthorized access to public data areas (shares, folders, mailboxes, calendars, etc.) is to be prevented. The appropriate authentication checks and authorization requirements must be defined and the operation of resources without such requirements is not permitted (no global sharing).

IEEE Standard or Amendment	Maximum Data Rate	Typical Range	Frequency Band	Comments
802.11	2 Mbps	50–100 meters	2.4 GHz	
802.11a	54 Mbps	50–100 meters	5 GHz	Not compatible with 802.11b
802.11b	11 Mbps	50–100 meters	2.4 GHz	Equipment based on 802.11b has been the dominant WLAN technology
802.11g	54 Mbps	50–100 meters	2.4 GHz	Backward compatible with 802.11b

FIGURE 1.14   IEEE Common Wireless Standards: NIST SP800–97.[29]

- Remote data access operations must be effected using strong authentication and encryption, and managers must obtain permission from the owner of the resources to access.
- For secure remote maintenance by business partners, initialization of the remote maintenance must take place from an internal system, such as via an Internet connection protected by strong encryption. An employee must be present at the system concerned during the entire remote maintenance session to monitor the remote maintenance in accordance with the policy, and the date, nature, and extent of the remote maintenance must be logged at a minimum.

Wireless Security

Wireless networking enables devices with wireless capabilities to use information resources without being physically connected to a network. A wireless local area network (WLAN) is a group of wireless networking nodes within a limited geographic area that is capable of radio communications. WLANs are typically used by devices within a fairly limited range, such as an office building or building campus, and are usually implemented as extensions to existing wired local area networks to provide enhanced user mobility. Since the beginning of wireless networking, many standards and technologies have been developed for WLANs. One of the most active standards organizations that address wireless networking is the Institute of Electrical and Electronics Engineers (IEEE), as outlined in Figure 1.14.[30] Like other wireless technologies, WLANs typically need to support

29. Sheila Frankel, Bernard Eydt, Les Owens, Karen Scarfone, NIST Special Publication 800–97: "Establishing Wireless Robust Security Networks: A Guide to IEEE 802.11i," Recommendations of the National Institute of Standards and Technology, http://csrc.nist.gov/publications/nistpubs/800-97/SP800-97.pdf.

30. Sheila Frankel, Bernard Eydt, Les Owens, Karen Scarfone, NIST Special Publication 800–97: "Establishing Wireless Robust Security Networks: A Guide to IEEE 802.11i," Recommendations of the National Institute of Standards and Technology, http://csrc.nist.gov/publications/nistpubs/800-97/SP800-97.pdf.

several security objectives. This is intended to be accomplished through a combination of security features built into the wireless networking standard. The most common security objectives for WLANs are as follows:

- *Access control.* Restrict the rights of devices or individuals to access a network or resources within a network.
- *Confidentiality.* Ensure that communication cannot be read by unauthorized parties.
- *Integrity.* Detect any intentional or unintentional changes to data that occur in transit.
- *Availability.* Ensure that devices and individuals can access a network and its resources whenever needed.

Access Control

Typically there are two means by which to validate the identities of wireless devices attempting to connect to a WLAN: open-system authentication and shared-key authentication. Neither of these alternatives is secure. The security provided by the default connection means is unacceptable; all it takes for a host to connect to your system is a Service Set Identifier (SSID) for the AP (which is a name that is broadcast in the clear) and, optionally, a MAC Address. The SSID was never intended to be used as an access control feature.

A MAC address is a unique 48-bit value that is permanently assigned to a particular wireless network interface. Many implementations of IEEE 802.11 allow administrators to specify a list of authorized MAC addresses; the AP will permit devices with those MAC addresses only to use the WLAN. This is known as *MAC address filtering.* However, since the MAC address is not encrypted, it is simple to intercept traffic and identify MAC addresses that are allowed past the MAC filter. Unfortunately, almost all WLAN adapters allow applications to set the MAC address, so it is relatively trivial to spoof a MAC address, meaning that attackers can easily gain unauthorized access. Additionally, the AP is not authenticated to the host by open-system authentication. Therefore, the host has to trust that it is communicating to the real AP and not an impostor AP that is using the same SSID. Therefore, open system authentication does not provide reasonable assurance of any identities and can easily be misused to gain unauthorized access to a WLAN or to trick users into connecting to a malicious WLAN.[31]

Confidentiality

The WEP protocol attempts some form of confidentiality by using the RC4 stream cipher algorithm to encrypt wireless communications. The standard for WEP specifies support for a 40-bit WEP key only; however, many vendors offer nonstandard extensions to WEP that support key lengths of up to 128 or even 256 bits. WEP also uses a 24-bit value known as an *initialization vector* (IV) as a seed value for initializing the cryptographic keystream. Ideally, larger key sizes translate to stronger protection, but the cryptographic

31. Sheila Frankel, Bernard Eydt, Les Owens, Karen Scarfone, NIST Special Publication 800–97: "Establishing Wireless Robust Security Networks: A Guide to IEEE 802.11i," Recommendations of the National Institute of Standards and Technology, http://csrc.nist.gov/publications/nistpubs/800-97/SP800-97.pdf.

technique used by WEP has known flaws that are not mitigated by longer keys. WEP is not the secure alternative you're looking for.

A possible threat against confidentiality is network traffic analysis. Eavesdroppers might be able to gain information by monitoring and noting which parties communicate at particular times. Also, analyzing traffic patterns can aid in determining the content of communications; for example, short bursts of activity might be caused by terminal emulation or instant messaging, whereas steady streams of activity might be generated by videoconferencing. More sophisticated analysis might be able to determine the operating systems in use based on the length of certain frames. Other than encrypting communications, IEEE 802.11, like most other network protocols, does not offer any features that might thwart network traffic analysis, such as adding random lengths of padding to messages or sending additional messages with randomly generated data.[32]

Integrity

Data integrity checking for messages transmitted between hosts and APs exists and is designed to reject any messages that have been changed in transit, such as by a manin-the-middle attack. WEP data integrity is based on a simple encrypted checksum — a 32-bit cyclic redundancy check (CRC-32) computed on each payload prior to transmission. The payload and checksum are encrypted using the RC4 keystream, and then transmitted. The receiver decrypts them, recomputes the checksum on the received payload, and compares it with the transmitted checksum. If the checksums are not the same, the transmitted data frame has been altered in transit, and the frame is discarded. Unfortunately, CRC-32 is subject to bit-flipping attacks, which means that an attacker knows which CRC-32 bits will change when message bits are altered. WEP attempts to counter this problem by encrypting the CRC-32 to produce an integrity check value (ICV). WEP's creators believed that an enciphered CRC-32 would be less subject to tampering. However, they did not realize that a property of stream ciphers such as WEP's RC4 is that bit flipping survives the encryption process — the same bits flip whether or not encryption is used. Therefore, the WEP ICV offers no additional protection against bit flipping.[33]

Availability

Individuals who do not have physical access to the WLAN infrastructure can cause a denial of service for the WLAN. One threat is known as jamming, which involves a device that emits electromagnetic energy on the WLAN's frequencies. The energy makes the frequencies unusable by the WLAN, causing a denial of service. Jamming can be performed intentionally by an attacker or unintentionally by a non-WLAN device transmitting on the

32. Sheila Frankel, Bernard Eydt, Les Owens, Karen Scarfone, NIST Special Publication 800–97: "Establishing Wireless Robust Security Networks: A Guide to IEEE 802.11i," Recommendations of the National Institute of Standards and Technology, http://csrc.nist.gov/publications/nistpubs/800-97/SP800-97.pdf.

33. Sheila Frankel, Bernard Eydt, Les Owens Karen, Scarfone, NIST Special Publication 800–97: "Establishing Wireless Robust Security Networks: A Guide to IEEE 802.11i," Recommendations of the National Institute of Standards and Technology, http://csrc.nist.gov/publications/nistpubs/800-97/SP800-97.pdf.

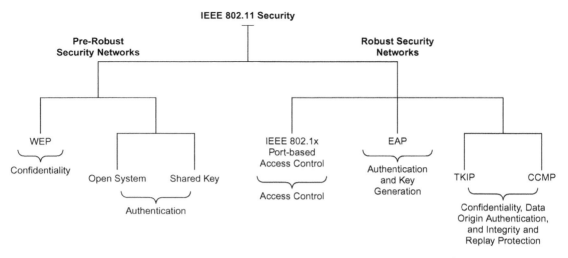

FIGURE 1.15   High-level taxonomy of the major pre-RSN and RSN security mechanisms.[34]

same frequency. Another threat against availability is flooding, which involves an attacker sending large numbers of messages to an AP at such a high rate that the AP cannot process them, or other STAs cannot access the channel, causing a partial or total denial of service. These threats are difficult to counter in any radio-based communications; thus, the IEEE 802.11 standard does not provide any defense against jamming or flooding. Also, as described in Section 3.2.1, attackers can establish rogue APs; if STAs mistakenly attach to a rogue AP instead of a legitimate one, this could make the legitimate WLAN effectively unavailable to users. Although 802.11i protects data frames, it does not offer protection to control or management frames. An attacker can exploit the fact that management frames are not authenticated to deauthenticate a client or to disassociate a client from the network.[35]

Enhancing Security Controls

The IEEE 802.11i amendment allows for enhanced security features beyond WEP and the simple IEEE 802.11 shared-key challenge-response authentication. The amendment introduces the concepts of Robust Security Networks (RSNs) (see Figure 1.15) and Robust Security Network Associations (RSNAs). There are two RSN data confidentiality and integrity protocols defined in IEEE 802.11i—Temporal Key Integrity Protocol (TKIP) and

34. Sheila Frankel, Bernard Eydt, Les Owens Karen, Scarfone, NIST Special Publication 800–97: "Establishing Wireless Robust Security Networks: A Guide to IEEE 802.11i," Recommendations of the National Institute of Standards and Technology, http://csrc.nist.gov/publications/nistpubs/800-97/SP800-97.pdf.

35. Sheila Frankel, Bernard Eydt, Les Owens Karen, Scarfone, NIST Special Publication 800–97: "Establishing Wireless Robust Security Networks: A Guide to IEEE 802.11i," Recommendations of the National Institute of Standards and Technology, http://csrc.nist.gov/publications/nistpubs/800-97/SP800-97.pdf.

Counter Mode with Cipher-Block Chaining Message Authentication Code Protocol (CCMP).

At a high level, RSN includes IEEE 802.1x port-based access control, key management techniques, and the TKIP and CCMP data confidentiality and integrity protocols. These protocols allow for the creation of several diverse types of security networks because of the numerous configuration options. RSN security is at the link level only, providing protection for traffic between a wireless host and its associated AP or between one wireless host and another. It does not provide end-to-end application-level security, such as between a host and an email or Web server, because communication between these entities requires more than just one link. For infrastructure mode, additional measures need to be taken to provide end-to-end security.

The IEEE 802.11i amendment defines an RSN as a wireless network that allows the creation of RSN Associations (RSNAs) only. An RSNA is a security relationship established by the IEEE 802.11i 4-Way Handshake. The 4-Way Handshake validates that the parties to the protocol instance possess a pairwise master key (PMK), synchronize the installation of temporal keys, and confirm the selection of cipher suites. The PMK is the cornerstone of a number of security features absent from WEP. Complete robust security is considered possible only when all devices in the network use RSNAs. In practice, some networks have a mix of RSNAs and non-RSNA connections. A network that allows the creation of both pre-RSN associations (pre-RSNA) and RSNAs is referred to as a Transition Security Network (TSN). A TSN is intended to be an interim means to provide connectivity while an organization migrates to networks based exclusively on RSNAs. RSNAs enable the following security features for IEEE 802.11 WLANs:

- Enhanced user authentication mechanisms
- Cryptographic key management
- Data confidentiality
- Data origin authentication and integrity
- Replay protection

An RSNA relies on IEEE 802.1x to provide an authentication framework. To achieve the robust security of RSNAs, the designers of the IEEE 802.11i amendment used numerous mature cryptographic algorithms and techniques. These algorithms can be categorized as being used for confidentiality, integrity (and data origin authentication), or key generation. All the algorithms specifically referenced in the IEEE 802.11 standard (see Figure 1.16) are symmetric algorithms, which use the same key for two different steps of the algorithm, such as encryption and decryption.

TKIP is a cipher suite for enhancing WEP on pre-RSN hardware without causing significant performance degradation. TKIP works within the processing constraints of first-generation hosts and APs and therefore enables increased security without requiring hardware replacement. TKIP provides the following fundamental security features for IEEE 802.11 WLANs:

- Confidentiality protection using the RC4 algorithm[38]
- Integrity protection against several types of attacks[39] using the Michael message digest algorithm (through generation of a message integrity code [MIC])[40]

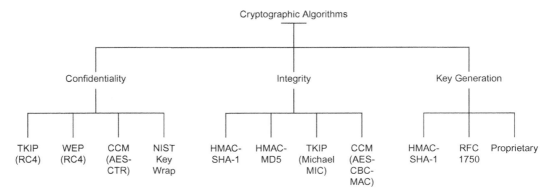

FIGURE 1.16   Taxonomy of the cryptographic algorithms included in the IEEE 802.11 standard.[36]

- Replay prevention through a frame-sequencing technique
- Use of a new encryption key for each frame to prevent attacks, such as the Fluhrer-Mantin-Shamir (FMS) attack, which can compromise WEP-based WLANs[41]
- Implementation of countermeasures whenever the STA or AP encounters a frame with a MIC error, which is a strong indication of an active attack.

Web and Application Security

Web and application security has come to center stage recently because Web sites and other public-facing applications have had so many vulnerabilities reported that it is often trivial to find some part of the application that is vulnerable to one of the many exploits out there. When an attacker compromises a system at the application level, often it is too trivial to take advantage of all the capabilities said application has to offer, including querying the back-end database or accessing proprietary information. In the past it was not necessary to implement security during the development phase of an application, and since most security professionals are not programmers, that worked out just fine; however, due to factors such as rushing software releases and a certain level of complacency where end users expect buggy software and apply patches, the trend of inserting security earlier in the development process is catching steam.

Web Security

Web security is unique to every environment; any application and service that the organization wants to deliver to the customer will have its own way of performing transactions. Static Web sites with little content or searchable areas of course pose the least risk,

36. Sheila Frankel, Bernard Eydt, Les Owens, Karen Scarfone, NIST Special Publication 800–97: "Establishing Wireless Robust Security Networks: A Guide to IEEE 802.11i," Recommendations of the National Institute of Standards and Technology, http://csrc.nist.gov/publications/nistpubs/800-97/SP800-97.pdf.

but they also offer the least functionality. Who wants a Web site they can't sell anything from? Implementing something like a shopping cart or content delivery on your site opens up new, unexpected aspects of Web security. Among the things that need to be considered are whether it is worth developing the application in-house or buying one off the shelf and rely on someone else for the maintenance ad patching. With some of these thoughts in mind, here are some of the biggest threats associated with having a public-facing Web site:

- Vandalism
- Financial fraud
- Privileged access
- Theft of transaction information
- Theft of intellectual property
- Denial-of-service (DoS) attacks
- Input validation errors
- Path or directory traversal
- Unicode encoding
- URL encoding

Some Web application defenses that can be implemented have already been discussed; they include:

- Web application firewalls
- Intrusion prevention systems
- SYN proxies on the firewall

Application Security

An integrated approach to application security (see Figure 1.17) in the organization is required for successful deployment and secure maintenance of all applications. A corporate initiative to define, promote, assure, and measure the security of critical business applications would greatly enhance an organization's overall security. Some of the biggest obstacles, as mentioned in the previous section, are that security professionals are not typically developers, so this means that often application security is left to IT or R & D personnel, which can lead to gaping holes. Components of an application security program consist of:[37]

- *People.* Security architects, managers, technical leads, developers and testers.
- *Policy.* Integrate security steps into your SDLC and ADLC; have security baked in, not bolted on. Find security issues early so that they are easier and cheaper to fix. Measure compliance; are the processes working? Inventory and categorize your applications.
- *Standards.* Which controls are necessary, and when and why? Use standard methods to implement each control. Provide references on how to implement and define requirements.

37. "AppSec2005DC-Anthony Canike-Enterprise AppSec Program PowerPoint Presentation," OWASP, http://www.owasp.org/index.php/Image:AppSec2005DC-Anthony_Canike-Enterprise_AppSec_ Program.ppt.

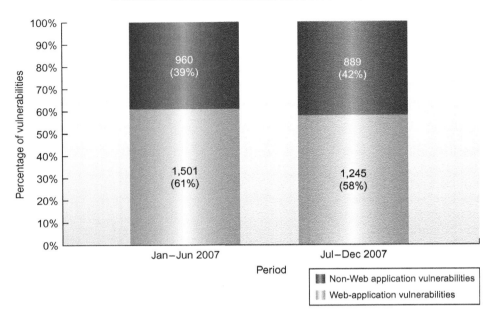

FIGURE 1.17 Symantec Web application vulnerabilities by share.

- *Assessments.* Security architecture/design reviews, security code reviews, application vulnerability tests, risk acceptance review, external penetration test of production applications, white-box philosophy. Look inside the application, and use all the advantages you have such as past reviews, design documents, code, logs, interviews, and so on. Attackers have advantages over you; don't tie your hands.
- *Training.* Take awareness and training seriously. All developers should be performing their own input validation in their code and need to be made aware of the security risks involved in sending unsecure code into production.

Security Policies and Procedures

A quality information security program begins and ends with the correct information security policy (see Figure 1.18). Policies are the least expensive means of control and often the most difficult to implement. An information security policy is a plan that influences and determines the actions taken by employees who are presented with a policy decision regarding information systems. Other components related to a security policy are practices, procedures, and guidelines, which attempt to explain in more detail the actions that are to be taken by employees in any given situation. For policies to be effective, they must be properly disseminated, read, understood, and agreed to by all employees as well as

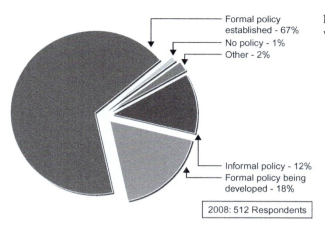

Formal policy established - 67%
No policy - 1%
Other - 2%
Informal policy - 12%
Formal policy being developed - 18%

2008: 512 Respondents

FIGURE 1.18 Information security policy within your organization, CSI/FBI report, 2008.

backed by upper management. Without upper management support, a security policy is bound to fail. Most information security policies should contain at least:

- An overview of the corporate philosophy on security.
- Information about roles and responsibilities for security shared by all members of the organization.
- Statement of purpose.
- Information technology elements needed to define certain controls or decisions.
- The organization's security responsibilities defining the security organization structure.
- References to IT standards and guidelines, such as Government Policies and Guidelines, FISMA, http://iase.disa.mil/policy-guidance/index.html#FISMA and NIST Special Publications (800 Series), and http://csrc.nist.gov/publications/PubsSPs.html.

Some basic rules must be followed when you're shaping a policy:

- Never conflict with the local or federal law.
- Your policy should be able to stand up in court.
- It must be properly supported and administered by management.
- It should contribute to the success of the organization.
- It should involve end users of information systems from the beginning.

Security Employee Training and Awareness

The Security Employee Training and Awareness (SETA) program is a critical component of the information security program. It is the vehicle for disseminating security information that the workforce, including managers, need to do their jobs. In terms of the total security solution, the importance of the workforce in achieving information security goals and the importance of training as a countermeasure cannot be overstated. Establishing and maintaining a robust and relevant information security awareness and training program as part of the overall information security program is the primary conduit for providing employees with the information and tools needed to protect an agency's vital information resources. These programs will ensure that personnel at all levels of the organization understand their information security responsibilities to properly use and protect the information and resources entrusted to them. Agencies that continually train their workforces in organizational security policy and role-based security responsibilities will have a higher rate of success in protecting information.[38]

As cited in audit reports, periodicals, and conference presentations, people are arguably the weakest element in the security formula that is used to secure systems and networks. The people factor, not technology, is a critical one that is often overlooked in the security equation. It is for this reason that the Federal Information Security Management Act (FISMA) and the Office of Personnel Management (OPM) have mandated that more and better attention must be devoted to awareness activities and role-based training, since they are the only security controls that can minimize the inherent risk that results from the people who use, manage, operate, and maintain information systems and networks. Robust and enterprisewide awareness and training programs are needed to address this growing concern.[39]

The Ten Commandments of SETA

The Ten Commandments of SETA consist of the following:

1. Information security is a people, rather than a technical, issue.
2. If you want them to understand, speak their language.
3. If they cannot see it, they will not learn it.
4. Make your point so that you can identify it and so can they.
5. Never lose your sense of humor.
6. Make your point, support it, and conclude it.
7. Always let the recipients know how the behavior that you request will affect them.
8. Ride the tame horses.
9. Formalize your training methodology.
10. Always be timely, even if it means slipping schedules to include urgent information.

Depending on the level of targeted groups within the organization, the goal is first awareness, then training, and eventually the education of all users as to what is acceptable security. Figure 1.19 shows a matrix of teaching methods and measures that can be implemented at each level.

Targeting the right people and providing the right information are crucial when you're developing a security awareness program. Therefore, some of the items that must be kept in mind are focusing on people, not so much on technologies; refraining from using technical jargon; and using every available venue, such as newsletters or memos, online

38. Pauline Bowen, Joan Hash and Mark Wilson, NIST Special Publication 800−100: Information Security Handbook: A Guide for Managers. Recommendations of the National Institute of Standards and Technology, http://csrc.nist.gov/publications/nistpubs/800-100/SP800-100-Mar07-2007.pdf.

39. Pauline Bowen, Joan Hash and Mark Wilson, NIST Special Publication 800−100: Information Security Handbook: A Guide for Managers. Recommendations of the National Institute of Standards and Technology, http://csrc.nist.gov/publications/nistpubs/800-100/SP800-100-Mar07-2007.pdf.

	Awareness	Training	Education
Attribute	"What"	"How"	"Why"
Level	Information	Knowledge	Insight
Objective	Recognition	Skill	Understanding
Teaching Method	<u>Media</u> Videos Newsletters Posters, etc.	<u>Practical Instruction</u> Lecture Case study workshop Hands-on practice	<u>Theoretical Instruction</u> Discussion Seminar Background reading
Test Measure	True/False Multiple Choice (identify learning)	Problem Solving (apply learning)	Essay (interpret learning)
Impact Timeframe	Short-term	Intermediate	Long-term

FIGURE 1.19 Matrix of security teaching methods and measures that can be implemented.

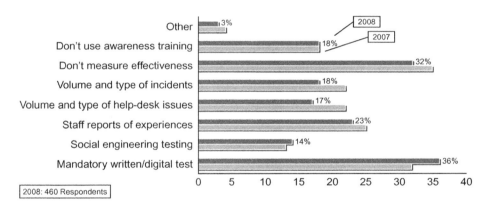

FIGURE 1.20 Awareness training metrics.

demonstrations, and in-person classroom sessions. By not overloading users and helping them understand their roles in information security, you can establish a program that is effective, identifies target audiences, and defines program scope, goals, and objectives. Figure 1.20 presents a snapshot according to the 2008 CSI/FBI Report, showing where the SETA program stands in 460 different U.S. organizations.

4. SECURITY MONITORING AND EFFECTIVENESS

Security monitoring and effectiveness are the next evolutions to a constant presence of security-aware personnel who actively monitor and research events in real time. A substantial number of suspicious events occur within most enterprise networks and computer systems every day and go completely undetected. Only with an effective security monitoring strategy, an incident response plan, and security validation and metrics in place will an optimal level of security be attained. The idea is to automate and correlate as much as possible between both events and vulnerabilities and to build intelligence into security tools so that they alert you if a known bad set of events has occurred or a known vulnerability is actually being attacked.

To come full circle; You need to define a security monitoring and log management strategy, an integrated incident response plan, validation, and penetration exercises against security controls and security metrics to help measure whether there has been improvement in your organization's handling of these issues.

Security Monitoring Mechanisms

Security monitoring involves real-time or near-real-time monitoring of events and activities happening on all your organization's important systems at all times. To properly monitor an organization for technical events that can lead to an incident or an investigation, usually an organization uses a security information and event management (SIEM) and/or log management tool. These tools are used by security analysts and managers to filter through tons of event data and to identify and focus on only the most interesting events.

Understanding the regulatory and forensic impact of event and alert data in any given enterprise takes planning and a thorough understanding of the quantity of data the system will be required to handle (see checklist: "An Agenda For Action When Implementing A Critical Security Mechanism"). The better logs can be stored, understood, and correlated, the better the possibility of detecting an incident in time for mitigation. In this case, what you don't know *will* hurt you. Responding to incidents, identifying anomalous or unauthorized behavior, and securing intellectual property has never been more important.

Incidence Response and Forensic Investigations

Network forensic investigation is the investigation and analysis of all the packets and events generated on any given network in hope of identifying the proverbial needle in a haystack. Tightly related is incident response, which entails acting in a timely manner to an identified anomaly or attack across the system. To be successful, both network investigations and incident response rely heavily on proper event and log management techniques. Before an incident can be responded to there is the challenge of determining whether an event is a routine system event or an actual incident. This requires that there be some framework for incident classification (the process of examining a possible incident and determining whether or not it requires a reaction). Initial reports from end users, intrusion detection systems, host- and network-based malware detection software, and systems administrators are all ways to track and detect incident candidates.[40]

40. M. E. Whitman, H. J. Mattord, *Management of Information Security*, Course Technology, 2nd Edition, March 27, 2007.

AN AGENDA FOR ACTION WHEN IMPLEMENTING A CRITICAL SECURITY MECHANISM

Without a solid log management strategy, it becomes nearly impossible to have the necessary data to perform a forensic investigation; and, without monitoring tools identifying threats and responding to attacks against confidentiality, integrity, or availability, it becomes much more difficult. For a network to be compliant and an incident response or forensics investigation to be successful, it is critical that a mechanism be in place to do the following (check all tasks completed):

_____1. Securely acquire and store raw log data for as long as possible from as many disparate devices as possible while providing search and restore capabilities of these logs for analysis.

_____2. Monitor interesting events coming from all important devices, systems, and applications in as near real time as possible.

_____3. Run regular vulnerability scans on your hosts and devices; and, correlate these vulnerabilities to intrusion detection alerts or other interesting events, identifying high-priority attacks as they happen, and minimizing false positives. SIEM and log management solutions in general can assist in security information monitoring (see Figure 1.21); as well as, regulatory compliance and incident response.

_____4. Aggregate and normalize event data from unrelated network devices, security devices, and application servers into usable information.

_____5. Analyze and correlate information from various sources such as vulnerability scanners, IDS/IPS, firewalls, servers, and so on, to identify attacks as soon as possible and help respond to intrusions more quickly.

_____6. Conduct network forensic analysis on historical or real-time events through visualization and replay of events.

_____7. Create customized reports for better visualization of your organizational security posture.

_____8. Increase the value and performance of existing security devices by providing a consolidated event management and analysis platform.

_____9. Improve the effectiveness and help focus IT risk management personnel on the events that are important.

_____10. Meet regulatory compliance and forensics requirements by securely storing all event data on a network for long-term retention and enabling instant accessibility to archived data.

FIGURE 1.21   Security monitoring.

As mentioned in earlier sections, the phases of an incident usually unfold in the following order: preparation, identification (detection), containment, eradication, recovery and lessons learned. The preparation phase requires detailed understanding of information systems and the threats they face; so to perform proper planning an organization must develop predefined responses that guide users through the steps needed to properly respond to an incident. Predefining incident responses enables rapid reaction without confusion or wasted time and effort, which can be crucial for the success of an incident response. Identification occurs once an actual incident has been confirmed and properly classified as an incident that requires action. At that point the IR team moves from identification to containment. In the containment phase, a number of action steps are taken by the IR team and others. These steps to respond to an incident must occur quickly and may occur concurrently, including notification of key personnel, the assignment of tasks, and documentation of the incident. Containment strategies focus on two tasks: first, stopping the incident from getting any worse, and second, recovering control of the system if it has been hijacked.

Once the incident has been contained and system control regained, eradication can begin, and the IR team must assess the full extent of damage to determine what must be done to restore the system. Immediate determination of the scope of the breach of confidentiality, integrity, and availability of information and information assets is called *incident damage assessment*. Those who document the damage must be trained to collect and preserve evidence in case the incident is part of a crime investigation or results in legal action.

At the moment that the extent of the damage has been determined, the recovery process begins to identify and resolve vulnerabilities that allowed the incident to occur in the first place. The IR team must address the issues found and determine whether they need to install and/or replace/upgrade the safeguards that failed to stop or limit the incident or were missing from system in the first place. Finally, a discussion of lessons learned should always be conducted to prevent future similar incidents from occurring and review what could have been done differently.[41]

Validating Security Effectiveness

The process of validating security effectiveness comprises making sure that the security controls that you have put in place are working as expected and that they are truly mitigating the risks they claim to be mitigating. There is no way to be sure that your network is not vulnerable to something if you haven't validated it yourself. Ensuring that the information security policy addresses your organizational needs and assessing compliance with your security policy across all systems, assets, applications, and people is the only way to have a concrete means of validation.

Here are some areas where actual validation should be performed — in other words, these are areas where assigned IT personnel should go with policy in hand, log in, and verify the settings and reports before the auditors do:

- Verifying operating system settings
- Reviewing security device configuration and management
- Establishing ongoing security tasks
- Maintaining physical security
- Auditing security logs
- Creating an approved product list
- Reviewing encryption strength
- Providing documentation and change control.

Vulnerability Assessments and Penetration Tests

Validating security (see Figure 1.22) with internal as well as external vulnerability assessments and penetration tests is a good way to measure an increase or decrease in overall security, especially if similar assessments are conducted on a regular basis. There are several ways to test security of applications, hosts, and network devices. With a vulnerability assessment, usually limited scanning tools or just one scanning tool is used to determine vulnerabilities that exist in the target system. Then a report is created and the manager reviews a holistic picture of security. With authorized penetration tests it's a little different. In that case the data owner is allowing someone to use just about any means within reason (in other words, many different tools and techniques) to gain access to the system or information. A successful penetration test does not provide the remediation avenues that a vulnerability assessment does; rather, it is a good test of how difficult it would be for someone to truly gain access if he were trying.

41. M. E. Whitman, H. J. Mattord, *Management of Information Security*, Course Technology, 2nd Edition, March 27, 2007.

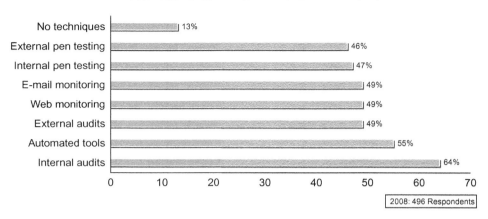

FIGURE 1.22   Security validation techniques, CSI/FBI survey, 2008.

5. SUMMARY

This chapter emphasized how IT managers are expected to develop, document, and implement an organization-wide program to provide information security essentials for protecting mission-critical systems that support the operations and assets of the organization. An effective information security program should include:

- Periodic assessments of risk, including the magnitude of harm that could result from the unauthorized access, use, disclosure, disruption, modification, or destruction of information and information systems that support the operations and assets of the organization.
- Policies and procedures that are based on risk assessments, cost-effectively reduce information security risks to an acceptable level, and ensure that information security is addressed throughout the life cycle of each organizational information system.
- Subordinate plans for providing adequate information security for networks, facilities, information systems, or groups of information systems, as appropriate.
- Security awareness training to inform personnel (including users of information systems that support the operations and assets of the organization) of the information security risks associated with their activities and their responsibilities in complying with organizational policies and procedures designed to reduce these risks.
- Periodic testing and evaluation of the effectiveness of information security policies, procedures, practices, and security controls to be performed with a frequency depending on risk, but no less than annually.
- A process for planning, implementing, evaluating, and documenting remedial actions to address any deficiencies in the information security policies, procedures, and practices of the organization.

- Procedures for detecting, reporting, and responding to security incidents.
- Plans and procedures to ensure continuity of operations for information systems that support the operations and assets of the organization.

In other words, IT managers must be prepared to:

- Plan for security.
- Ensure that appropriate officials are assigned security responsibility.
- Periodically review the security controls in their information systems.
- Authorize system processing prior to operations and, periodically, thereafter.

The preceding management responsibilities presume that responsible IT managers understand the risks and other factors that could adversely affect their missions. Moreover, these managers must understand the current status of their security programs and the security controls planned or in place to protect their information and information systems in order to make informed judgments and investments that appropriately mitigate risk to an acceptable level. The ultimate objective is to conduct the day-to-day operations of the organization and to accomplish the organization's mission critical systems with adequate security, or security commensurate with risk, including the magnitude of harm resulting from the unauthorized access, use, disclosure, disruption, modification, or destruction of information.

Finally, let's move on to the real interactive part of this Chapter: review questions/exercises, hands-on projects, case projects and optional team case project. The answers and/or solutions by chapter can be found in the Online Instructor's Solutions Manual.

CHAPTER REVIEW QUESTIONS/EXERCISES

True/False

1. True or False? Information security management as a field is ever decreasing in demand and responsibility because most organizations spend increasingly larger percentages of their IT budgets in attempting to manage risk and mitigate intrusions, not to mention the trend in many enterprises of moving all IT operations to an Internet-connected infrastructure, known as enterprise cloud computing.
2. True or False? Information security is a business problem in the sense that the entire organization must frame and solve security problems based on its own strategic drivers, not solely on technical controls aimed to mitigate one type of attack.
3. True or False? In defining required skills for information security managers, the ISC has arrived at an agreement on ten domains of information security that is known as the *Common Body of Knowledge* (CBK).
4. True or False? Threats to information systems come in many flavors, some with malicious intent, others with supernatural powers or expected surprises.
5. True or False? Threats are exploited with a variety of attacks, some technical, others not so much.

Multiple Choice

1. The art of manipulating people into performing actions or divulging confidential information, is known as:
   A. Malware
   B. Industrial espionage
   C. Social engineering
   D. Spam
   E. Phishing

2. What describes activities such as theft of trade secrets, bribery, blackmail, and technological surveillance as well as spying on commercial organizations and sometimes governments?
   A. Spam
   B. Phishing
   C. Hoaxes
   D. Industrial espionage
   E. Denial-of-service

3. What is the abuse of electronic messaging systems to indiscriminately send unsolicited bulk messages, many of which contain hoaxes or other undesirable contents such as links to phishing sites?
   A. Spamming
   B. Phishing
   C. Hoaxes
   D. Distributed denial-of-service
   E. All of the Above

4. What is the criminally fraudulent process of attempting to acquire sensitive information such as usernames, passwords, and credit-card details by masquerading as a trustworthy entity in an electronic communication?
   A. Splicing
   B. Phishing
   C. Bending
   D. FSO
   E. Cabling

5. What requires that an individual, program, or system process is not granted any more access privileges than are necessary to perform the task?
   A. Administrative controls
   B. Principle of Least Privilege
   C. Technical controls
   D. Physical controls
   E. Risk analysis

EXERCISE

Problem

What is continuous monitoring?

Hands-On Projects

Project

If your information system is subject to continuous monitoring, does that mean it does not have to undergo security authorization?

Case Projects

Problem

Why is continuous monitoring not replacing the traditional security authorization process?

Optional Team Case Project

Problem

What is front-end security and how does it differ from back-end security?

Security Management Systems

James T. Harmening
Computer Bits, Inc.

1. SECURITY MANAGEMENT SYSTEM STANDARDS

To give organizations a starting point to develop their own security management systems, the International Organization for Standardization (ISO) and the International Electrotechnical Commission (IEC) have developed a family of standards known as the Information Security Management System 27000 Family of Standards. This group of standards, starting with ISO/IEC 27001, gives organizations the ability to certify their security management systems. For more details see WWW.ISO.ORG. As an alternative some organizations are following the SANS 20 Critical Security Controls (http://www.sans.org/critical-security-controls/) set of twenty critical security controls that lead you through a twenty step audit process for your organization.

The ISO/IEC-27001 certification process takes place in several stages. The first stage is an audit of all documentation and policies that currently exist for a system. The documentation is usually based directly on the requirements of the standard, but it does not have to be. Organizations can come up with their own sets of standards, as long as all aspects of the standard are covered. The second stage actually tests the effectiveness of the existing policies. The third stage is a reassessment of the organization to make sure it still meets the requirements. This third stage keeps organizations up to date over time as standards for security management systems change. This certification process is based on a Plan-Do-Check-Act iterative process:

- *Plan* the security management system and create the policies that define it.
- *Do* implement the policies in your organization.
- *Check* to ensure the security management system's policies are protecting the resources they were meant to protect.
- *Act* to respond to incidents that breach the implemented policies.

Managing Information Security
DOI: http://dx.doi.org/10.1016/B978-0-12-416688-2.00002-7

Certifying your security management system helps ensure that you keep the controls and policies constantly up to date to meet certification requirements. Getting certified also demonstrates to your partners and customers that your security management systems will help keep your business running smoothly if network security events were to occur.

Though the ISO/IEC 27000 Family of Standards allows for businesses to optionally get certified, the Federal Information Security Management Act (FISMA) requires all government agencies to develop security management systems. The process of complying with FISMA is very similar to the process of implementing the ISO 27000 family of standards.

The first step of FISMA compliance is determining what constitutes the system you're trying to protect. Next, you need to perform risk assessment to determine what controls you'll need to put in place to protect your system's assets. The last step is actually implementing the planned controls. FISMA then requires mandatory yearly inspections to make sure an organization stays in compliance.

One of the advantages of the Sans 20 Critical Security Controls is the 20 individual touchstones that can be acted upon by the organization. It starts with some basic audit information. In step one you inventory all authorized and unauthorized devices. This may mean accessing each workstation and reviewing the system logs to identify if USB, Music, or phones have been plugged into the computer. The second step is to audit the software in the same way. Many times a user will download software and not know they have violated their organizations I.T. policies. These two basic checks need to be done annually for some organizations and more frequently for others. For more details access the SANS. ORG website.

2. TRAINING REQUIREMENTS

Many security management system training courses for personnel are available over the Internet. These courses provide information for employees setting up security management systems and for those using the computer and network resources of the company that are referenced in the policies of the security management system.

Training should also include creating company security policies and creating user roles that are specific to the organization. Planning policies and roles, ahead of time, will help prevent confusion in the event of a problem, since everyone will know their responsibilities. Documenting these roles is also very important.

3. PRINCIPLES OF INFORMATION SECURITY

The act of securing information has been around for as long as the idea of storing information. Over time, three main objectives of information security have been defined:

- *Confidentiality*. Information is only available to the people or systems that need access to it. This is done by encrypting information that only certain people are able to decrypt or denying access to those who don't need it. This might seem simple at first, but confidentiality must be applied to all aspects of a system. This means preventing access to all backup locations and even log files if those files can contain sensitive information.

- *Integrity*. Information can only be added or updated by those who need to update that data. Unauthorized changes to data cause it to lose its integrity, and access to the information must be cut off to everyone until the information's integrity is restored. Allowing access to compromised data will cause those unauthorized changes to propagate to other areas of the system.
- *Availability*. The information needs to be available in a timely manner when requested. Access to no data is just as bad as access to compromised data. No process can be performed if the data on which the process is based is unavailable.

4. ROLES AND RESPONSIBILITIES OF PERSONNEL

All personnel who come into contact with information systems need to be aware of the risks from improper use of those systems. Network administrators need to know the effects of each change they make to their systems and how that affects the overall security of that system. They also need to be able to efficiently control access to those systems in cases of emergency, when quick action is needed.

Users of those systems need to understand what risks can be caused by their actions and how to comply with company policy. Several roles should be defined within your organization:

- *Chief information officer/director of information technology*. This person is responsible for creating and maintaining the security policies for your organization.
- *Network engineer*. This person is responsible for the physical connection of your network and the connection of your network to the Internet. He or she is also responsible for the routers, firewalls, and switches that connect your organization.
- *Network administrator*. This person handles all other network devices within the organization, such as servers, workstations, printers, copiers, tablets, video conference, smart phones, and wireless access devices. Server and workstation software is also the responsibility of the network administrator.
- *End users*. These people are allowed to operate the computer in accordance with company policies, to perform their daily tasks. They should not have administrator access to their PCs or, especially, servers.

There are also many other specific administrators some companies might require. These are Microsoft Exchange Administrators, Database Administrators, and Active Directory Administrators, to name a few. These administrators should have specific tasks to perform and a specific scope in which to perform them that is stated in the company policy.

5. SECURITY POLICIES

Each organization should develop a company policy detailing the preferred use of company data or company software. An example of a policy is: No person shall transfer any data to any device that was not purchased by the company. This policy can help prevent unauthorized access to company data. Some companies ban all removable media within the organization.

Security policies should govern how the computer is to be used on a day-to-day basis. Very often, computer users are required to have Internet access to do research pertaining to their jobs. This isn't hard to restrict in a specialized setting such as a law firm where only a handful of sites contain pertinent information. In other cases it can be nearly impossible to restrict all Web sites except the ones that contain information that applies to your organization or your research. In those cases it is imperative that you have company policies that dictate what Web sites users are able to visit and for what purposes. When unrestricted Internet access is allowed, it is a good practice to use software that will track the Web sites a user visits, to make sure they are not breaking company policy. For many companies they create a white list of allowable sites, for others they use a black list to prevent certain sites from being accessed. Some of the more advanced firewalls give a list of categories that are allowed or blocked.

6. SECURITY CONTROLS

There are three types of security controls that need to be implemented for a successful security policy to be put into action. They are physical controls, technical controls, and administrative controls.

Physical controls consist of things such as magnetic swipe cards, RFID, or biometric security to prevent access to stored information or network resources. Physical controls also consist of environmental controls such as HVAC units, power generators, and fire suppression systems. One of the most common failures is people leaving their computers on and another person using their computer to gain access to information/data that they should not be allowed to access. Many companies utilize password screen savers or require a computer to be "locked" before they leave their workstation. Another common security measure is to encrypt the drives on a computer. One free whole disk encryption utility commonly deployed is True Crypt. (www.truecrypt.org). This prevents the data from being accessed from a stolen laptop or computer.

Technical controls can also be called software or system controls which are used to limit access to network resources and devices that are used in the organization. They can be individual usernames and passwords used to access individual devices or access control lists that are part of a network operating system. Many organizations are putting in password expiration dates of 30−60 days and even account deletion for accounts not accessed for more than 90 days. In addition, passwords that contain, numbers, upper and lowercase letters, special characters and have a length that exceeds 8 characters are required by some organizations in order to ensure stronger passwords.

Administrative controls consist of policies created by an organization that determine how they will work. These controls guide employees by describing how their jobs are to be done and what resources they are supposed to use to do them. This is probably the weakest section of each companies policies. The lack of written policies makes the implementation of security very difficult. More organizations should spend time setting up their policies and keep their employees up to date on what expectations they have for each employee.

7. NETWORK ACCESS

The first step in developing a security management system is documenting the network resources and which group of users may access those resources. Users should only have access to the resources that they need to complete their jobs efficiently. An example of when this will come in handy is when the president of the company wants access to every network resource and then his computer becomes infected with a virus that starts infecting all network files. Access Control Lists (ACLs) should be planned ahead of time and then implemented on the network to avoid complications with the network ACL hierarchy.

An ACL dictates which users have access to certain network resources. Network administrators usually have access to all files and folders on a server. Department administrators will have access to all files used by their departments. End users will have access to a subset of the department files that they need to perform their jobs. ACLs are developed by the head of IT for an organization and the network administrator and implemented by the network administrator.

Implementing ACLs prevents end users from being able to access sensitive company information and helps them perform their jobs better by not giving them access to information that can act as a distraction.

Access control can also apply to physical access as well as electronic access. Access to certain networking devices could cause an entire organization to stop functioning for a period of time, so access to those devices should be carefully controlled.

Through the use of Remote Authentication Dial In User Service (RADIUS) is an added layer of security to your network. Many of these systems employ a random number generator key fob's that displays a random number and changes it every 30–60 seconds. With this extra step of user authentication a person can combine a private key along with the random number to access the network. For example, an RSA SecureID token generates an 8 digit number, combine that with the users own 4 digit private password, an administrator can help to stop unauthorized access to their system.

8. RISK ASSESSMENT

Before security threats can be blocked, all risks must first be identified and assessed (see checklist: "An Agenda For Action When Identifying And Assessing Risks"). Risk assessment forms the foundation of a good security management system. Network administrators must document all aspects of their network setup. This documentation should provide information on the network firewall, servers, clients, and any other devices physically connected or wirelessly connected to the network.

AN AGENDA FOR ACTION WHEN IDENTIFYING AND ASSESSING RISKS

The most time should be spent documenting how the private computer network will be connected to the Internet for Web browsing and email. Some common security risks that should be identified and assessed are (check all tasks completed):

____1. USB storage devices: Devices that can be used to copy proprietary company data off the internal network. Many organizations use software solutions to disable unused USB ports on a system; others physically block the connections.

____2. Remote control software: Services such as GoToMyPc or Log Me In do not require any special router or firewall configuration to enable remote access.

____3. Email: Filters should be put in place that prevent sensitive company information from simply being emailed outside the organization.

____4. General Internet use: There is always a possibility of downloading a malicious virus from the Internet unless all but trusted and necessary Web sites are restricted to internal users. This can be accomplished by a content-filtering firewall or Web proxy server.

____5. Laptops: Lost laptops pose a very large security risk, depending on the type on data stored on them. Policies need to be put in place to determine what types of information can be stored on these devices and what actions should be taken if a laptop is lost.

____6. Peer-to-peer applications: P2P applications that are used to download illegal music and software cause a risk because the files that are downloaded are not coming from known sources. People who download an illegal version of an application could be downloading a worm that can affect the entire network.

____7. Television/DVR/Blu-Ray Devices: With the expansion of technology, even televisions have internet access and storage.

____8. VOIP telephones: The proliferation of Voice over IP telephones brings another device into our network environment. Some companies prefer to have their phones on a separate physical network, preventing slow response times and bad phone quality, while others have routers and switches that will prioritize the traffic of the phone calls in order to maintain good phone quality.

9. INCIDENT RESPONSE

Knowing what to do in case of a security incident is crucial to being able to track down what happened and how to make sure it never happens again. When a security incident is identified, it is imperative that steps are taken so that forensic evidence is not destroyed in the investigation process. Forensic evidence includes the content of all storage devices attached to the system at the time of the incident and even the contents stored in memory of a running computer.

Using an external hard drive enclosure to browse the content of the hard drive of a compromised system will destroy date and timestamps that a forensic technician can use to tie together various system events.

When a system breach or security issue has been detected, it is recommended to consult someone familiar with forensically sound investigation methods. If forensic methods are not used, it can lead to evidence not being admissible in court if the incident results in a court case.

There are specific steps to take with a computer system, depending on the type of incident that occurred. Unless a system is causing damage to itself by deleting files or folders that can be potential evidence, it is best to leave the system running for the forensic investigator. The forensic investigator will:

- Document what is on the screen by photographing it. He/She will also photograph the actual computer system and all cable connections.
- Capture the contents of the system's memory. This is done using a small utility installed from a removable drive that will create a forensic image of what is in the system's physical memory. This can be used to document Trojan activity. If memory is not imaged and the computer was used to commit a crime, the computer's user can claim that a malicious virus, which was only running in memory, was responsible.
- Turn off the computer. If the system is running a Windows workstation operating system such as Windows Vista Workstation or Windows Azure, the forensic technician will pull the plug on the system. If the system is running a server operating system such as Windows Server 2008, Windows 7 Server, Windows Server 2012, Windows 8 or a Linux- or Unix-based operating system such as Red Hat, Fedora, or Ubuntu, the investigator will properly shut down the system.
- Create a forensic image of the system's hard drive. This is done using imaging software and usually a hardware write-blocker to connect the system's hard drive to the imaging computer. A hardware write-blocker is used to prevent the imaging computer from writing anything at all to the hard drive. Windows, by default, will create a recycle bin on a new volume that it is able to mount, which would cause the evidence to lose forensic value. Investigators are then able to search through the system without making any changes to the original media.

10. SUMMARY

Organizations interested in implementing a comprehensive security management system should start by documenting all business processes that are critical to an organization and then analyzing the risks associated with them, then implement the controls that can protect those processes from external and internal threats. Internet threats are not usually the cause of someone with malicious intent but someone who accidentally downloads a Trojan or accidentally moves or deletes a directory or critical files. The final step is performing recursive checking of the policies your organization has put in place to adjust for new technologies that need to be protected or new ways that external threats can damage your network. The easiest way to implement security management systems is to use the Plan-Do-Act-Check (PDAC) process to step though the necessary procedures. A locked door, a good password, and good supervision of employees is key to good security management.

Finally, let's move on to the real interactive part of this Chapter: review questions/exercises, hands-on projects, case projects and optional team case project. The answers and/or solutions by chapter can be found in the Online Instructor's Solutions Manual.

CHAPTER REVIEW QUESTIONS/EXERCISES

True/False

1. True or False? To give organizations a starting point to develop their own security management systems, the International Organization for Standardization (ISO) and the International Electrotechnical Commission (IEC) have developed a family of standards known as the Information Security Management System 27000 Family of Standards.
2. True or False? Training should also include creating company security policies and creating user roles that are specific to the organization.
3. True or False? The act of securing information has not been around for as long as the idea of storing information.
4. True or False? All personnel who come into contact with information systems need to be aware of the risks from improper use of those systems.
5. True or False? Each organization should not develop a company policy detailing the preferred use of company data or company software.

Multiple Choice

1. _____ what is on the screen by photographing it?
   A. Capture
   B. Turn off
   C. Document
   D. Create
   E. All of the above
2. _____the contents of the system's memory?
   A. Turn off
   B. Document
   C. Create
   D. Capture
   E. All of the above
3. _____the computer?
   A. Capture
   B. Create

C. Document
D. Distribute
E. Turn off

4. _____a forensic image of the system's hard drive?
   A. Create
   B. Turn off
   C. Capture
   D. Document
   E. All of the above

5. Devices that can be used to copy proprietary company data off the internal network are known as:
   A. Remote control software
   B. Email
   C. USB storage
   D. General Internet use
   E. Risk analysis

EXERCISE

Problem

Why should an organization certify their security management system?

Hands-On Projects

Project

How does ISO/IEC 27001 (BS 7799) relate to other security management system standards (ISO 9001 and 14001)?

Case Projects

Problem

Why should an organization invest in implementing an SMS and certifying it using ISO/IEC 27001 (BS 7799-2)?

Optional Team Case Project

Problem

How is risk assessment related to ISO/IEC 27001 (BS 7799)?

Information Technology Security Management

Rahul Bhaskar and Bhushan Kapoor
California State University

1. INFORMATION SECURITY MANAGEMENT STANDARDS

A range of standards are specified by various industry bodies. Although specific to an industry, these standards can be used by any organization and adapted to its goals. Here we discuss the main organizations that set standards related to information security management.

Federal Information Security Management Act

At the U.S. federal level, the National Institute of Standards and Technology (NIST) has specified guidelines for implementing the Federal Information Security Management Act (FISMA). This act aims to provide the following standards shown in Figure 3.1.

The "Federal Information Security Management Framework Recommended by NIST"[1] sidebar describes the risk management framework as specified in FISMA. The activities specified in this framework are paramount in implementing an IT security management plan. Although specified for the federal government, this framework can be used as a guideline by any organization.

---

1. "Federal Information Security Management Act," National Institute of Standards and Technology, http://csrc.nist.gov/groups/SMA/fisma/index.html, 2008 (downloaded 10/20/2008).

Managing Information Security
DOI: http://dx.doi.org/10.1016/B978-0-12-416688-2.00003-9

• Standards for categorizing information and information systems by mission impact
• Standards for minimum security requirements for information and information systems
• Guidance for selecting appropriate security controls for information systems
• Guidance for assessing security controls in information systems and determining security control effectiveness
• Guidance for certifying and accrediting information systems

FIGURE 3.1 Specifications in the Federal Information Security Management Act.[2]

FEDERAL INFORMATION SECURITY MANAGEMENT FRAMEWORK RECOMMENDED BY NIST

Step 1: Categorize

In this step, information systems and internal information should be categorized based on impact.

Step 2: Select

Use the categorization in the first step to select an initial set of security controls for the information system and apply tailoring guidance as appropriate, to obtain a starting point for required controls.

Step 3: Supplement

Assess the risk and local conditions, including the security requirements, specific threat information, and cost/benefit analyses or special circumstances. Supplement the initial set of security controls with the supplement analyses.

Step 4: Document

The original set of security controls and the supplements should be documented.

Step 5: Implement

The security controls you identified and supplemented should be implemented in the organization's information systems.

Step 6: Assess

The security controls should be assessed to determine whether the controls are implemented correctly, are operating as intended, and are producing the desired outcome with respect to meeting the security requirements for the system.

Step 7: Authorize

Upon a determination of the risk to organizational operations, organizational assets, or individuals resulting from their operation, authorize the information systems.

Step 8: Monitor

Monitor and assess selected security controls in the information system on a continuous basis, including documenting changes to the system.

2. "Federal Information Security Management Act," National Institute of Standards and Technology, http://csrc.nist.gov/groups/SMA/fisma/index.html, 2008 (downloaded 10/20/2008).

Security Policy
Organization of Information Security
Asset Management
Human Resources Security
Physical and Environmental Security
Communication and Operations Management
Access Control
Information Systems Acquisition, Development and Maintenance
Information Security Incident Management
Business Continuity Management
Compliance

FIGURE 3.2   International Standards Organization best-practice areas.[3]

International Standards Organization

Another influential international body, the International Standards Organization and the International Electro Technical Commission, published ISO/IEC 17799:2005.[4] These standards establish guidelines and general principles for initiating, implementing, maintaining, and improving information security management in an organization. The objectives outlined provide general guidance on the commonly accepted goals of information security management. The standards consist of best practices of control objectives and controls in the areas of information security management shown in Figure 3.2.

These objectives and controls are intended to be implemented to meet the requirements identified by a risk assessment.

3. "Information technology | Security techniques | Code of practice for information security management, ISO/IEC 17799," The International Standards Organization and The International Electro Technical Commission, www.iso.org/iso (downloaded 10/20/2008).

4. "Information technology | Security techniques | Code of practice for information security management, ISO/IEC 17799," The International Standards Organization and The International Electro Technical Commission, www.iso.org/iso/iso_catalogue/catalogue_tc/catalogue_detail.htm?csnumber=39612, 2005 (downloaded 10/20/2008).

2. OTHER ORGANIZATIONS INVOLVED IN STANDARDS

Other organizations that are involved in information security management include The Internet Society[5] and the Information Security Forum.[6] These are professional societies with members in the thousands. The Internet Society is the organization home for the groups responsible for Internet infrastructure standards, including the Internet Engineering Task Force (IETF) and the Internet Architecture Board (IAB). The Information Security Forum is a global nonprofit organization of several hundred leading organizations in financial services, manufacturing, telecommunications, consumer goods, government, and other areas. It provides research into best practices and advice, summarized in its biannual Standard of Good Practice, which incorporates detailed specifications across many areas.

3. INFORMATION TECHNOLOGY SECURITY ASPECTS

The various aspects to IT security in an organization that must be considered include:

- Security policies and procedures
- Security organization structure
- IT security processes
  - Processes for a business continuity strategy
  - Processes for IT security governance planning
- Rules and regulations

Security Policies and Procedures

Security policies and procedures constitute the main part of any organization's security. These steps are essential for implementing IT security management: authorizing security roles and responsibilities to various security personnel; setting rules for expected behavior from users and security role players; setting rules for business continuity plans; and more. The security policy should be generally agreed to by most personnel in the organization and should have the support of the highest-level management. This helps in prioritization at the overall organization level.

The following list, illustrated in Figure 3.3, is a sample of some of the issues an organization is expected to address in its policies.[7] Note, however, that the universal list is virtually endless, and each organization's list will consist of issues based on several factors,

5. "ISOC's Standards and Technology Activities," Internet Society, www.isoc.org/standards, 2008 (downloaded 10/20/2008).

6. "The Standard of Good Practice," Information Security Forum, https://www.securityforum.org/html/frameset.htm, 2008 (downloaded 10/20/2008).

7. "Information technology | Security techniques | Code of practice for information security management, ISO/IEC 17799," The International Standards Organization and The International Electro Technical Commission, www.iso.org/iso (downloaded 10/20/2008).

Access Control Standards
Accountability
Audit Trails
Backups
Disposal of Media
Disposal of Printed Matter
Information Ownership
Managers Responsibility
Equipment
Communication
Procedures and Processes at Work

FIGURE 3.3   Security aspects an organization is expected to address in its policies.

including its size and the value and sensitivity of the information it owns or deals with. Some important issues included in most security policies are:

- *Access control standards.* These are standards on controlling the access to various systems. These include password change standards.
- *Accountability.* Every user should be responsible for her own accounts. This implies that any activity under a particular user ID should be the responsibility of the user whose ID it is.
- *Audit trails.* There should be an audit trail recorded of all the activities under a user ID. For example, all the login, log-out activities for 30 days should be recorded. Additionally, all unauthorized attempts to access, read, write, and delete data and execute programs should be logged.
- *Backups.* There should be a clearly defined backup policy. Any backups should be kept in a secure area. A clear policy on the frequency of the backups and their recovery should be communicated to the appropriate personnel.
- *Disposal of media.* A clear policy should be defined regarding the disposal of media. This includes a policy on which hardware and storage media, such as disk drives, diskettes, and CD-ROMs, are to be destroyed. The level and method of destruction of business-critical information that is no longer needed should be well defined and documented. Personnel should be trained regularly on the principles to follow.
- *Disposal of printed matter.* Guidelines as to the disposal of printed matter should be specified and implemented throughout the organization. In particular, business-critical materials should be disposed properly and securely.

- *Information ownership.* All the data and information available in the organization should have an assigned owner. The owner should be responsible for deciding on access rights to the information for various personnel.
- *Managers' responsibility.* Managers at all levels should ensure that their staff understands the security policy and adheres to it continuously. They should be held responsible for recording any deviations from the core policy.
- *Equipment.* An organization should have specific guidelines about modems, portable storage, and other devices. These devices should be kept in a secured physical environment.
- *Communication.* Well-defined policy guidelines are needed for communication using corporate information systems. These include communications via emails, instant messaging, and so on.
- *Work procedures and processes.* Employees of an organization should be trained to secure their workstations when not in use. The policy can impose a procedure of logging off before leaving a workstation. It can also include quarantining any device (such as a laptop) brought from outside the organization before plugging it into the network.

Security Organization Structure

Various security-related roles need to be maintained and well defined. These roles and their brief descriptions are described here.[8]

End User

End users have a responsibility to protect information assets on a daily basis through adherence to the security policies that have been set and communicated. End-user compliance with security policies is key to maintaining information security in an organization because this group represents the most consistent users of the organization's information.

Executive Management

Top management plays an important role in protecting the information assets in an organization. Executive management can support the goal of IT security by conveying the extent to which management supports security goals and priorities. Members of the management team should be aware of the risks that they are accepting for the organization through their decisions or failure to make decisions. There are various specific areas on which senior management should focus, but some that are specifically appropriate are user training, inculcating and encouraging a security culture, and identifying the correct policies for IT security governance.

Security Officer

The security officer "directs, coordinates, plans, and organizes information security activities throughout the organization."[9]

8. Tipton and Krause, "Information Security Governance," *Information Security Management Handbook,* Auerbach Publications, 2008.

9. Tipton and Krause, "Information Security Governance," *Information Security Management Handbook,* Auerbach Publications, 2008.

Data/Information Owners

Every organization should have clearly identified data and information owners. These executives or managers should review the classification and access security policies and procedures. They should also be responsible for periodic audit of the information and data and its continuous security. They may appoint a data custodian in case the work required to secure the information and data is extensive and needs more than one person to complete.

Information System Auditor

Information system auditors are responsible for ensuring that the information security policies and procedures have been adhered to. They are also responsible for establishing the baseline, architecture, management direction, and compliance on a continuous basis. They are an essential part of unbiased information about the state of information security in the organization.

Information Technology Personnel

IT personnel are responsible for building IT security controls into the design and implementations of the systems. They are also responsible for testing these controls periodically or whenever there is a change. They work with the executives and other managers to ensure compliance in all the systems under their responsibility.

Systems Administrator

A systems administrator is responsible for configuring the hardware and the operating system to ensure that the information systems and their contents are available for business as and when needed. These adminstrators are placed ideally in an organization to ensure security of these assets. They play a key role because they own access to the most vulnerable information assets of an organization.

IT Security Processes

To achieve effective IT security requires processes related to security management. These processes include business continuity strategy, processes related to IT security governance planning, and IT security management implementation.

Processes for a Business Continuity Strategy

As is the case with any strategy, the business continuity strategy depends on a commitment from senior management. This can include some of the analysis that is obtained by business impact assessment/risk analysis focused on business value drivers (see checklist: "An Agenda For Action For The Contingency Planning Process"). These business value drivers are determined by the main stakeholders from the organizations. Examples of these value drivers are customer service and intellectual property protection.[10]

10. C. R. Jackson, "Developing Realistic Continuity Planning Process Metrics," *Information Security Management Handbook*, Auerbach Publications, 2008.

AN AGENDA FOR ACTION FOR THE CONTINGENCY PLANNING PROCESS

The Disaster Recovery Institute International (DRII) associates eight tasks with the contingency planning process.[11] These are as follows (check all tasks completed):

____1. Business impact analysis, to analyze the impact of outage on critical business function operations.

____2. Risk assessment, to assess the risks to the current infrastructure and the incorporation of safeguards to reduce the likelihood and impact of disasters.

____3. Recovery strategy identification, to develop a variety of disaster scenarios and identify recovery strategies.

____4. Recovery strategy selection, to select the appropriate recovery strategies based on the perceived threats and the time needed to recover.

____5. Contingency plan development, to document the processes, equipment, and facilities required to restore the IT assets.

____6. User training, to develop training programs to enable all affected users to perform their tasks.

____7. Plan verification, for accuracy and adequacy.

____8. Plan maintenance, for continuous upkeep of the plan as needs change.

Processes for IT Security Governance Planning

IT security governance planning includes prioritization as its major function. This helps in utilizing the limited sources of the organization. Determining priorities among the potential conflicting interests is the main focus of these processes. This includes budget setting, resource allocation, and, most important, the political process needed to prioritize in an organization.

Rules and Regulations

An organization is influenced by rules and regulations that influence its business. In a business environment marked by globalization, organizations have to be aware of both national and international rules and regulations. From an information security management perspective, various rules and regulations must be considered. These are listed in Figure 3.4. We give more details on some rules and regulations here:

- The Health Insurance Portability and Accountability Act (HIPAA) requires the adoption of national standards for electronic healthcare transactions and national identifiers for

11. "Contingency Planning Process," DRII — The Institute for Continuity Management, https://www.drii.org/professional_prac/profprac_appen-dix.html#BUSINESS_CONTINUITY_PLANNING_INFORMATION, 2008 (downloaded 10/24/2008).

Health Insurance Portability and Accountability Act (HIPAA)
Gramm-Leach-Bliley Act
Sarbanes-Oxley Act of 2002
Security Breach Notification Laws
Personal Information Protection and Electronic Document Act (PIPEDA)
Computer Fraud and Abuse Act
USA PATRIOT Act

FIGURE 3.4   Rules and regulations related to information security management.

providers, health insurance plans, and employers. Healthcare providers have to protect the personal medical information of the customer to comply with this law. Similarly, the Gramm-Leach-Bliley Act of 1999 (GLBA), also known as the Financial Services Modernization Act of 1999, requires financial companies to protect the information about individuals that it collects during transactions.

- The Sarbanes-Oxley Act of 2002 (SOX). This law requires companies to protect and audit their financial data. The chief information officer and other senior executives are held responsible for reporting and auditing an organization's financial information to regulatory and other agencies.
- State Security Breach Notification Laws (California and many others) require businesses, nonprofits, and state institutions to notify consumers when unencrypted "personal information" might have been compromised, lost, or stolen.
- The Personal Information Protection and Electronics Document Act (PIPEDA) supports and promotes electronic commerce by protecting personal information that is collected, used, or disclosed in certain circumstances, by providing for the use of electronic means to communicate or record information or transactions, and by amending the Canada Evidence Act, the Statutory Instruments Act, and the Statute Revision Act that is in fact the case.
- The Computer Fraud and Abuse Act, or CFAA (also known as Fraud and Related Activity in Connection with Computers), is a U.S. law passed in 1986 and intended to reduce computer crimes. It was amended in 1994, 1996, and 2001 by the U.S.A. PATRIOT Act.[12]

The following sidebar, "Computer Fraud and Abuse Act Criminal Offences," lists criminal offences covered under this law.[13]

12. "Fraud and Related Activities in Relation to the Computers," U.S. Code Collection, Cornell University Law School, www4.law.cornell.edu/uscode/18/1030.html, 2008 (downloaded 10/24/2008).

13. "Fraud and Related Activities in Relation to the Computers," U.S. Code Collection, Cornell University Law School, www4.law.cornell.edu/uscode/18/1030.html, 2008 (downloaded 10/24/2008).

COMPUTER FRAUD AND ABUSE ACT CRIMINAL OFFENCES

(a) Whoever —

(1) having knowingly accessed a computer without authorization or exceeding authorized access, and by means of such conduct having obtained information that has been determined by the United States Government pursuant to an Executive order or statute to require protection against unauthorized disclosure for reasons of national defense or foreign relations, or any restricted data, as defined in paragraph y. of section 11 of the Atomic Energy Act of 1954, with reason to believe that such information so obtained could be used to the injury of the United States, or to the advantage of any foreign nation willfully communicates, delivers, transmits, or causes to be communicated, delivered, or transmitted, or attempts to communicate, deliver, transmit or cause to be communicated, delivered, or transmitted the same to any person not entitled to receive it, or willfully retains the same and fails to deliver it to the officer or employee of the United States entitled to receive it;

(2) intentionally accesses a computer without authorization or exceeds authorized access, and thereby obtains —

(A) information contained in a financial record of a financial institution, or of a card issuer as defined in section 1602 (n) of title 15, or contained in a file of a consumer reporting agency on a consumer, as such terms are defined in the Fair Credit Reporting Act (15 U.S.C. 1681 et seq.);

(B) information from any department or agency of the United States; or

(C) information from any protected computer if the conduct involved an interstate or foreign communication;

(3) intentionally, without authorization to access any nonpublic computer of a department or agency of the United States, accesses such a computer of that department or agency that is exclusively for the use of the Government of the United States or, in the case of a computer not exclusively for such use, is used by or for the Government of the United States and such conduct affects that use by or for the Government of the United States;

(4) knowingly and with intent to defraud, accesses a protected computer without authorization, or exceeds authorized access, and by means of such conduct furthers the intended fraud and obtains anything of value, unless the object of the fraud and the thing obtained consists only of the use of the computer and the value of such use is not more than $5,000 in any 1-year period;

(5)

(A)

(i) knowingly causes the transmission of a program, information, code, or command, and as a result of such conduct, intentionally causes damage without authorization, to a protected computer;

(ii) intentionally accesses a protected computer without authorization, and as a result of such conduct, recklessly causes damage; or

(iii) intentionally accesses a protected computer without authorization, and as a result of such conduct, causes damage; and

(B) by conduct described in clause (i), (ii), or (iii) of subparagraph (A), caused (or, in the case of an attempted offense, would, if completed, have caused) —

(i) loss to 1 or more persons during any 1-year period (and, for purposes of an investigation, prosecution, or other proceeding brought by the United States only, loss resulting from a related course of conduct affecting 1 or more other protected computers) aggregating at least $5,000 in value;

(ii) the modification or impairment, or potential modification or impairment, of the medical examination, diagnosis, treatment, or care of 1 or more individuals;

(iii) physical injury to any person;

(iv) a threat to public health or safety; or

(v) damage affecting a computer system used by or for a government entity in furtherance of the administration of justice, national defense, or national security;

(6) knowingly and with intent to defraud traffics (as defined in section 1029) in any password or similar information through which a computer may be accessed without authorization, if —

(A) such trafficking affects interstate or foreign commerce; or

(B) such computer is used by or for the Government of the United States;

(7) with intent to extort from any person any money or other thing of value, transmits in interstate or foreign commerce any communication containing any threat to cause damage to a protected computer; shall be punished as provided in subsection (c) of this section.

(b) Whoever attempts to commit an offense under subsection (a) of this section shall be punished as provided in subsection (c) of this section.

(c) The punishment for an offense under subsection (a) or (b) of this section is —

(1)

(A) a fine under this title or imprisonment for not more than ten years, or both, in the case of an offense under subsection (a)(1) of this section which does not occur after a conviction for another offense under this section, or an attempt to commit an offense punishable under this subparagraph; and

(B) a fine under this title or imprisonment for not more than twenty years, or both, in the case of an offense under subsection (a)(1) of this section which occurs after a conviction for another offense under this section, or an attempt to commit an offense punishable under this subparagraph;

(2)

(A) except as provided in subparagraph (B), a fine under this title or imprisonment for not more than one year, or both, in the case of an offense under subsection (a)(2), (a)(3), (a)(5)(A)(iii), or (a)(6) of this section which does not occur after a conviction for another offense under this section, or an attempt to commit an offense punishable under this subparagraph;

(B) a fine under this title or imprisonment for not more than 5 years, or both, in the case of an offense under subsection (a)(2), or an attempt to commit an offense punishable under this subparagraph, if —

(i) the offense was committed for purposes of commercial advantage or private financial gain;

(ii) the offense was committed in furtherance of any criminal or tortious act in violation of the Constitution or laws of the United States or of any State; or

(iii) the value of the information obtained exceeds $5,000; and

(C) a fine under this title or imprisonment for not more than ten years, or both, in the case of an offense under subsection (a)(2), (a)(3) or (a)(6) of this section which occurs after a conviction for another offense under this section, or an attempt to commit an offense punishable under this subparagraph;

(3)

(A) a fine under this title or imprisonment for not more than five years, or both, in the case of an offense under subsection (a)(4) or (a)(7) of this section which does not occur after a conviction for another offense under this section, or an attempt to commit an offense punishable under this subparagraph; and

(B) a fine under this title or imprisonment for not more than ten years, or both, in the case of an offense under subsection (a)(4), (a)(5)(A)(iii), or (a)(7) of this section which occurs after a conviction for another offense under this section, or an attempt to commit an offense punishable under this subparagraph;

(4)

(A) except as provided in paragraph (5), a fine under this title, imprisonment for not more than 10 years, or both, in the case of an offense under subsection (a)(5)(A)(i), or an attempt to commit an offense punishable under that subsection;

(B) a fine under this title, imprisonment for not more than 5 years, or both, in the case of an offense under subsection (a)(5)(A)(ii), or an attempt to commit an offense punishable under that subsection;

(C) except as provided in paragraph (5), a fine under this title, imprisonment for not more than 20 years, or both, in the case of an offense under subsection (a)(5)(A)(i) or (a)(5)(A)(ii), or an attempt to commit an offense punishable under either subsection, that occurs after a conviction for another offense under this section; and

(5)

(A) if the offender knowingly or recklessly causes or attempts to cause serious bodily injury from conduct in violation of subsection (a)(5)(A)(i), a fine under this title or imprisonment for not more than 20 years, or both; and

(B) if the offender knowingly or recklessly causes or attempts to cause death from conduct in violation of subsection (a)(5)(A)(i), a fine under this title or imprisonment for any term of years or for life, or both.

(d)

(1) The United States Secret Service shall, in addition to any other agency having such authority, have the authority to investigate offenses under this section.

(2) The Federal Bureau of Investigation shall have primary authority to investigate offenses under subsection (a)(1) for any cases involving espionage, foreign counterintelligence, information protected against unauthorized disclosure for reasons of national defense or foreign relations, or Restricted Data (as that term is defined in section 11y of the Atomic Energy Act of 1954 (42 U.S.C. 2014

(y)), except for offenses affecting the duties of the United States Secret Service pursuant to section 3056 (a) of this title.

(3) Such authority shall be exercised in accordance with an agreement which shall be entered into by the Secretary of the Treasury and the Attorney General.

(e) As used in this section –

(1) the term "computer" means an electronic, magnetic, optical, electrochemical, or other high speed data processing device performing logical, arithmetic, or storage functions, and includes any data storage facility or communications facility directly related to or operating in conjunction with such device, but such term does not include an automated typewriter or typesetter, a portable hand held calculator, or other similar device;

(2) the term "protected computer" means a computer –

(A) exclusively for the use of a financial institution or the United States Government, or, in the case of a computer not exclusively for such use, used by or for a financial institution or the United States Government and the conduct constituting the offense affects that use by or for the financial institution or the Government; or

(B) which is used in interstate or foreign commerce or communication, including a computer located outside the United States that is used in a manner that affects interstate or foreign commerce or communication of the United States;

(3) the term "State" includes the District of Columbia, the Commonwealth of Puerto Rico, and any other commonwealth, possession or territory of the United States;

(4) the term "financial institution" means –

(A) an institution, with deposits insured by the Federal Deposit Insurance Corporation;

(B) the Federal Reserve or a member of the Federal Reserve including any Federal Reserve Bank;

(C) a credit union with accounts insured by the National Credit Union Administration;

(D) a member of the Federal home loan bank system and any home loan bank;

(E) any institution of the Farm Credit System under the Farm Credit Act of 1971;

(F) a broker-dealer registered with the Securities and Exchange Commission pursuant to section 15 of the Securities Exchange Act of 1934;

(G) the Securities Investor Protection Corporation;

(H) a branch or agency of a foreign bank (as such terms are defined in paragraphs (1) and (3) of section 1(b) of the International Banking Act of 1978); and

(I) an organization operating under section 25 or section 25(a) [2] of the Federal Reserve Act;

(5) the term "financial record" means information derived from any record held by a financial institution pertaining to a customer's relationship with the financial institution;

(6) the term "exceeds authorized access" means to access a computer with authorization and to use such access to obtain or alter information in the computer that the accesser is not entitled so to obtain or alter;

(7) the term "department of the United States" means the legislative or judicial branch of the Government or one of the executive departments enumerated in section 101 of title 5;

(8) the term "damage" means any impairment to the integrity or availability of data, a program, a system, or information;

(9) the term "government entity" includes the Government of the United States, any State or political subdivision of the United States, any foreign country, and any state, province, municipality, or other political subdivision of a foreign country;

(10) the term "conviction" shall include a conviction under the law of any State for a crime punishable by imprisonment for more than 1 year, an element of which is unauthorized access, or exceeding authorized access, to a computer;

(11) the term "loss" means any reasonable cost to any victim, including the cost of responding to an offense, conducting a damage assessment, and restoring the data, program, system, or information to its condition prior to the offense, and any revenue lost, cost incurred, or other consequential damages incurred because of interruption of service; and

(12) the term "person" means any individual, firm, corporation, educational institution, financial institution, governmental entity, or legal or other entity.

(f) This section does not prohibit any lawfully authorized investigative,

protective, or intelligence activity of a law enforcement agency of the United States, a State, or a political subdivision of a State, or of an intelligence agency of the United States.

(g) Any person who suffers damage or loss by reason of a violation of this section may maintain a civil action against the violator to obtain compensatory damages and injunctive relief or other equitable relief. A civil action for a violation of this section may be brought only if the conduct involves 1 of the factors set forth in clause (i), (ii), (iii), (iv), or (v) of subsection (a)(5)(B). Damages for a violation involving only conduct described in subsection (a)(5)(B)(i) are limited to economic damages. No action may be brought under this subsection unless such action is begun within 2 years of the date of the act complained of or the date of the discovery of the damage. No action may be brought under this subsection for the negligent design or manufacture of computer hardware, computer software, or firmware.

(h) The Attorney General and the Secretary of the Treasury shall report to the Congress annually, during the first 3 years following the date of the enactment of this subsection, concerning investigations and prosecutions under subsection (a)(5).

Maximum Penalty	
Extent of Damage	
Aggregation of Damage	
Enhancement of Punishment	
Damage to Foreign Computers	
State Law Offenses	
Expanding the Definition of Loss	
Response	

FIGURE 3.5 U.S.A. PATRIOT Act increase in scope and penalties.

The U.S.A. PATRIOT Act of 2001 increased the scope and penalties of this act by:

- Raising the maximum penalty for violations to ten years (from five) for a first offense and 20 years (from ten) for a second offense
- Ensuring that violators only need to intend to cause damage generally, not intend to cause damage or other specified harm over the $5000 statutory damage threshold
- Allowing aggregation of damages to different computers over a year to reach the $5000 threshold
- Enhancing punishment for violations involving any (not just $5000 in) damage to a government computer involved in criminal justice or the military
- Including damage to foreign computers involved in U.S. interstate commerce
- Including state law offenses as priors for sentencing;
- Expanding the definition of loss to expressly include time spent investigating
- Responding (this is why it is important for damage assessment and restoration)

These details are summarized in Figure 3.5.

The PATRIOT Act of 2001 came under criticism for a number of reasons. There are fears that the Act is an invasion of privacy and infringement on freedom of speech. Critics also feel that the Act unfairly expands the powers of the executive branch and strips away many crucial checks and balances.

The original act has a sunset clause that would have caused many of the law's provisions to expire in 2005. The Act was reauthorized in early 2006 with some new safeguards and with expiration dates for its two most controversial powers, which authorize roving wiretaps and secret searches of records.

4. SUMMARY

Information technology security management consists of processes to enable organizational structure and technology to protect an organization's IT operations and assets against internal and external threats, intentional or otherwise. These processes are developed to ensure confidentiality, integrity, and availability of IT systems. There are various aspects to the IT security in an organization that need to be considered. These include security policies and procedures, security organization structure, IT security processes, and rules and regulations.

Security policies and procedures are essential for implementing IT security management: authorizing security roles and responsibilities to various security personnel; setting rules for expected behavior from users and security role players; setting rules for business continuity plans; and more. The security policy should be generally agreed to by most personnel in the organization and have support from high-level management. This helps in prioritization at the overall organization level. The IT security processes are essentially part of an organization's risk management processes and business continuity strategies. In a business environment marked by globalization, organizations have to be aware of both national and international rules and regulations. Their information security and privacy policies must conform to these rules and regulations.

Finally, let's move on to the real interactive part of this Chapter: review questions/exercises, hands-on projects, case projects and optional team case project. The answers and/or solutions by chapter can be found in the Online Instructor's Solutions Manual.

CHAPTER REVIEW QUESTIONS/EXERCISES

True/False

1. True or False? Security policies and procedures do not constitute the main part of any organization's security.
2. True or False? Various security-related roles do not need to be maintained and well defined.
3. True or False? End users have a responsibility to protect information assets on a daily basis through adherence to the security policies that have been set and communicated.
4. True or False? Top management does not play an important role in protecting the information assets in an organization.
5. True or False? The security officer "directs, coordinates, plans, and organizes information security activities throughout the organization.

Multiple Choice

1. Who are responsible for ensuring that the information security policies and procedures have been adhered to?
   A. Information owners
   B. Information system auditors
   C. Security officers

    D. Executive management

    E. All of the above

2. Who is responsible for building IT security controls into the design and implementations of the systems?

    A. Information owners

    B. Information system auditors

    C. IT personnel

    D. Systems Administrator

    E. All of the above

3. Who is responsible for configuring the hardware and the operating system to ensure that the information systems and their contents are available for business as and when needed?

    A. Information System Auditor

    B. Information Owners

    C. Systems Administrator

    D. Security Officer

    E. Executive Management

4. What analyzes the impact of outage on critical business function operations?

    A. Risk assessment

    B. Recovery strategy identification

    C. Recovery strategy selection

    D. Business impact analysis

    E. All of the above

5. What documents the processes, equipment, and facilities required to restore the IT assets?

    A. Contingency plan development

    B. User training

    C. Plan verification

    D. Plan maintenance

    E. Recovery strategy selection

EXERCISE

Problem

Why does an organization need a Business Continuity Plan (BCP)?

Hands-On Projects

Project

How often should the BCP / DR (Disaster Recovery) plans be reviewed?

Case Projects

Problem

What are some guidelines for identifying mission critical functions?

Optional Team Case Project

Problem

Why should an organization certify their IT security management system?

4

Online Identity and User Management Services

Tewfiq El Maliki* and Jean-Marc Seigneur†

*University of Applied Sciences of Geneva, tewfiq.elmaliki@hesge.ch,
†University of Geneva, jean-marc.seigneur@reputaction.com

1. INTRODUCTION

Anytime, anywhere mobile computing is becoming easier, more attractive and even cost-effective: the mobile devices carried by the roaming users offer more and more computing power and functionalities including sensing and providing location-awareness [1]. A lot of computing devices are also deployed in the environments where the users evolve; for example, intelligent home appliances or RFID-enabled fabrics. In this ambient intelligent world, the choices of identity mechanisms will have a large impact on social, cultural, business and political aspects. Moreover, Internet of things will generate more complicated privacy problems [2]. Identity has become a burden on the online world. When it is stolen it engenders a massive fraud, principally in online services which generate a lack of confidence in doing business for providers and frustration for users.

Therefore, the whole of society would suffer from the demise of privacy which is a real human need. As people have hectic live and cannot spend their time administering their digital identities, we need consistent identity management platforms and technologies enabling usability and scalability among others [3]. In this paper, we survey how the requirements have evolved for mobile user-centric identity management and their associated technologies.

The chapter is organized as follows. First, we present the evolution of identity management requirements. Section 4 surveys how the different most advanced identity management technologies fulfill present day requirements. Section 5 covers "social login" that is the major identity management technical solution that has emerged after writing the first version of this book chapter and that has nowadays gained a stronger user adoption than the other solutions surveyed in Section 4 although a few of them are used underneath "social login". Section 6 discusses how mobility can be achieved in the field of identity management in an ambient intelligent/ubiquitous computing world.

2. EVOLUTION OF IDENTITY MANAGEMENT REQUIREMENTS

In this section, we first define what we mean by a digital identity. Later in the chapter, we summarize all the different requirements and detail the most important ones in the following subsections, namely, privacy, usability and mobility.

Digital Identity Definition

A digital identity is a representation of an entity in a specific context [4]. For a long time, a digital identity was considered as the equivalent of our real life identity which indicates some of our attributes:

- Who we are, Name, Citizenship, Birthday;
- What we like, our favorite Reading, Food, Clothes, etc;
- What our reputation is, whether we are honest, without any problems, etc.

A digital identity was seen as an extended identity card or passport containing almost the same information. However, recent work [5] has argued that the link between the real-world identity and a digital identity is not always mandatory. For example, on e-Bay what matters is to know whether the seller's digital identity reputation has been remarkable and that the seller can prove that she controls that digital identity. It is less important to know that her real-world national identity is from the Bermuda Islands, where suing anybody is rather unlikely to succeed. It should be underlined that in a major identity management initiative [6], a digital identity is defined as "the distinguishing character or personality of an individual. An identity consists of traits, attributes, and preferences upon which one may receive personalized services. Such services could exist online, on mobile devices at work, or in many other places", that is, without mentioning a mandatory link to the real-world identity behind the digital identity.

The combination of virtual world with ubiquitous connectivity has changed the physical constraints to entirely new set of requirements as the associated security issues such phishing, spam, and identity theft has emerged. They are aggravated by the mobility of the user, the temporary and anonymity of cyber relationships. We are going toward new truly virtual world with always the implication of human. Therefore, we are facing the problem of determining the identity of our interlocutor and the accuracy of his/her claims. Simply using strong authentication will not resolve all these security issues. Digital identity management is a key issue that will ensure not only the service and functionality expectations but also security and privacy.

Identity Management Overview

A model of identity can been as follows [7]:

- User who wants to access to a service
- Identity Provider (IdP): is the issuer of user identity
- Service Provider (SP): is the relay party imposing identity check
- Identity (Id): is a set user's attributes
- Personal Authentication Device (PDA): Device holding various identifiers and credentials and could be used for mobility

Figure 4.1 lists the main components of identity management. The relationship between entities, identities and identifiers are shown in Figure 4.2, which illustrates that an entity, such as a user, may have multiple identities, and each identity may consist of multiple attributes that can be unique or non-unique identifiers.

Identity management refers to "the process of representing, using, maintaining, deprovisioning and authenticating entities as digital identities in computer networks".

Authentication is the process of verifying claims about holding specific identities. A failure at this stage will threaten the validity in the entire system. The technology is constantly finding stronger authentication using claims based on:

- Something you know: password, PIN
- Something you have: one-time-password
- Something you are: your voice, face, fingerprint (Biometrics)
- Your position
- Some combination of the four.

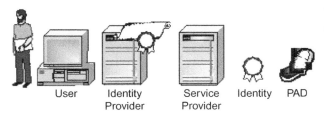

| User | Identity Provider | Service Provider | Identity | PAD |

FIGURE 4.1 Identity management main components.

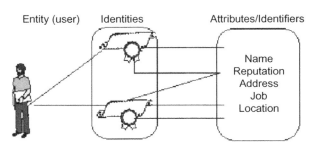

Entity (user)   Identities   Attributes/Identifiers

Name
Reputation
Address
Job
Location

FIGURE 4.2 Relationship between identities, identifiers and entity.

The BT report [3] has highlighted some interesting points to meet the challenges of identity theft and fraud:

- Developing risk calculation and assessment methods
- Monitoring user behavior to calculate risk
- Building trust and value with the user or consumer
- Engaging the cooperation of the user or consumer with transparency and without complexity or shifting the liability to consumer
- Taking a staged approach to authentication deployment and process challenges, using more advanced technologies

Digital identity should mange three connected vertexes: usability, cost and risk as illustrated in Figure 4.3.

The user should be aware of the risk he/she facing if his/her device/software's security is compromised. The usability is the second aspect that should be guaranty to the user unless he/she will find the system difficult which could be a source of security problem. Indeed, a lot of users when they are flooded by passwords write them down and hide them in a secrete place under their keyboard. Furthermore, the difficulty to deploy and manage a large number of identities discourages the use of identity management system. The cost of a system should be well studied and balanced related to risk and usability. Many systems such as one-Time-Password token are not widely used because they are too costly for a widespread deployment for large institutions. Traditionally identity management was seen as service provider centric as it was designed to fulfill the requirements of service provider, such as cost effectiveness and scalability. The users were neglected in many aspects because they were forced to memorize difficult or too many passwords. Identity management systems are elaborated to deal with the following core facets [8]:

- Reducing identity theft: The problem of identity theft is becoming a major one, mainly in the online environment. The providers need more efficient system to tackle this problem.
- Management: The amount of digital identities per person will increase, so the users need convenient support to manage these identities and the corresponding authentication.

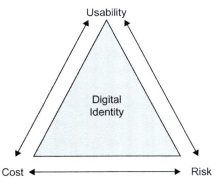

FIGURE 4.3   Digital identity environment to manage.

- Reachability: The management of reachability allows user to handle their contacts to prevent misuse of their address (spam) or unsolicited phone calls.
- Authenticity: Ensuring authenticity with authentication, integrity and non-repudiation mechanisms can prevent from identity theft.
- Anonymity and pseudonymity: providing anonymity prevent from tracking or identifying the users of a service.
- Organization personal data management: A quick method to create, modify a delete work accounts is needed, especially in big organizations.

Without improved usability of identity management [8], for example, weak passwords used by users on many Web sites, the number of successful attacks will remain high. To facilitate interacting with unknown entities, simple recognition rather than authentication of a real-world identity has been proposed, which usually involves manual enrollment steps in the real-world [5]. Usability is indeed enhanced, if there is no manual task needed. There might be a weaker level of security but that level may be sufficient for some actions, such as, logging to a mobile game platform. Single Sign-On (SSO) is the name given to the requirements of eliminating multiple password issues and dangerous password. When we use multiple user Id's and passwords just to use the emails systems and file servers at work, we feel the inconvenience that comes from having multiple identities. The second problem is the scattering of identity data which causes problems for the integration of IT systems. Moreover, it simplifies the end-user experience and enhances security via identity-based access technology.

Microsoft first largest identity management system was Passport Network. It was a very large and widespread Microsoft Internet service to be an identity provider for the MSN and Microsoft properties, and to be an identity provider for the Internet. However, with Passport, Microsoft was suspected by many persons of intending to have an absolute control over the identity information of Internet users and thus exploiting them for its own interests. Passport failed to become the Internet identity management tool. Since then, Microsoft has clearly understood that an identity management solution cannot succeed unless some basic rules are respected [9]. That's why Microsoft's Identity Architect, Kim Cameron, has stated the seven laws of identity. His motivation was purely practical in determining the prerequisites of successful identity management system. He formulated the essential principles to maintain privacy and security.

1. User control and consent over the handling of their data.
2. Minimal disclosure of data, and for specified purpose.
3. Information should only be disclosed to people who have a justifiable need for it.
4. The system must provide identifiers for both bilateral relationships between parties, and for incoming unsolicited communications.
5. It must support diverse operators and technologies.
6. It must be perceived as highly reliable and predictable.
7. There must be a consistent user experience across multiple identity systems and using multiple technologies.

Most systems do not fulfill several of these tests particularly they are deficient in fine-tuning the access control over identity to minimize disclosure of data. The formulated

Cameron's principles are very clear but they are not enough explicit to compare finely identity management systems. That's why we will define explicitly the identity requirements.

Privacy Requirement

Privacy is a central issue, due to the fact that the official authorities of almost all countries have legal strict policies related to identity. It is often treated in the case of identity management because the management deals with personal information and data. Therefore, it is important to give a definition. Alan F. Westin defines privacy as *"the claim of individuals, groups and institutions to determine for themselves, when, how and to what extent information about them is communicated to others"* [2]. However, we will use Cooley's broader definition of privacy [10]: "the right to be let alone", because it also emphasizes the problems related to disturbing the user's attention, for example, by email spam.

User Centricity

The evolution of the identity management system is toward the simplification of user experience and reinforcing authentication. It is well known that a poor usability implies the weakness of authentication. Mainly federated management has responded to some of these requirements by facilitating the use and the managing of identifiers and credentials in the boundary of a federated domain. Nevertheless, it is improbable that only one federated domain will subsist. Moreover, different levels of sensitivity and risks of different services will need different kinds of credentials. It is obvious that we should give users support and atomization of the identity management on the user's side.

A new paradigm must be introduced to solve the problems of usability, scalability and universal SSO. Therefore, a user-oriented paradigm has emerged which is called user-centric identity management. The word user controlled management [11] is the first used to explain user-centric management model. Recent federated identity management systems keep strong end-user controls over how identity information is disseminated amongst members of the federation. This new paradigm gives the user full control over his/her identity by notifying him the information collected and by guarantying his/her consent for any type of manipulation over collected information. A user control and consent is also defined as the first law in Cameron's Laws of Identity [9]. A user-centric identity management system supports the user's control and considers user-centric architecture and usability aspects. There is no uniform definition but "user-centric identity management is understood to mean digital identity infrastructure where an individual end-user has substantially independent control over the dissemination and use of their identifier(s) and personally-identifiable information (PII)."[12] See Figure 4.4. We can also give this definition of user centricity.

> In user-centric identity management the user has the full control over hi/hers identity and consistent user experience during all transaction when accessing his/her services.

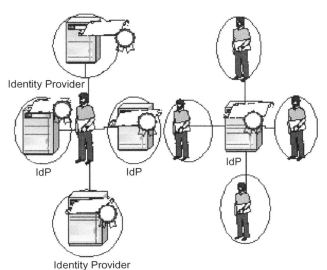

FIGURE 4.4 IdP centric and User-centric models.

In other terms it means that it allows the user to keep at least some or total control over his/her personal data. One of the principles of user-centric identity is the idea that the user of a Web service should have full control over his/her identity information (see checklist: "An Agenda For Action For The User-Centric Identity Paradigm").

AN AGENDA FOR ACTION FOR THE USER-CENTRIC IDENTITY PARADIGM

A lot of technology discussion and solution has been focusing on service provider and rarely on user's perspectives. User-centric identity paradigm is a real evolution because it moves information technology architecture forward for the users with the following advantages. These are as follows (check all tasks completed):

_____1. Empower the total control of users over their privacy.

_____2. Usability, as users are using the same identity for each identity transaction.

_____3. Give a consistent user's experience thanks to uniformity of identity interface.

_____4. Limit identity attacks (Phishing).

_____5. Limit reachability/disturbances, such as spam.

_____6. Review policies on both sides when necessary, identity providers and service providers (Web sites).

_____7. Huge scalability advantages as the Identity Provider does not have to get any prior knowledge about the Service Provider.

_____8. Assure secure conditions when exchanging data.

_____9. Decouple digital identity from applications.

_____10. Pluralism of Operators and Technologies.

User-centricity approach allows the user to gain access anonymously as she detains the full control on his/her identity. Of course, full anonymity [26] and unlinkability may lead to increased misuse by anonymous users. Then, Pseudonymity is alternative which is more suitable to the e-commerce environment. In this regard, anonymity must be guaranty at the application and at network levels. Some frameworks have been proposed to ensure user-centric anonymity using the concepts of One-task Authorization key and Binding Signature [26].

Usability Requirement

The security is also compromised with the proliferation of the user's password and even by it's weakness. Indeed, some users note their passwords on scratch pads, because their memorization poses problem. The recent FFIEC guidance on authentication in online banking reports that "Account fraud and identity theft are frequently the result of single factor (Id/password) authentication exploitation" [14]. From then on, the security must be user oriented as he/her is the effective person concerned with it and a lot of recent attacks take advantage from the lack of awareness of users attacks (i.e. spoofing, pharming and phishing) [15]. Without strong control and improved usability [16] of identity management some attacks will be always possible. To facilitate interacting with unknown entities, simple recognition rather than authentication of a real-world identity, which usually involves manual enrollment steps in the real-world, has been proposed [5]. Usability is indeed enhanced if there is no manual task needed. There might be a weaker level of security reached but that level may be sufficient for some actions, such as, logging to a mobile game platform.

Single Sign-On (SSO) is the name given to the requirements of eliminating multiple password issues and dangerous password. When we use multiple user Id's and passwords just to use the emails systems and file servers at work, we feel the pain that comes from having multiple identities. The second problem is the scattering of identity data which causes problem for the integration of IT systems. Moreover, it simplifies the end-user experience and enhances security via identity-based access technology. Therefore, we offer these features:

- Flexible authentication
- Directory independence
- Session and password management
- Seamless

3. THE REQUIREMENTS FULFILLED BY IDENTITY MANAGEMENT TECHNOLOGIES

This section provides an overview of identity management solutions from identity 1.0 to identity 2.0 and how they address the requirements introduced in Section 2. We will focus on related standards XRI and LID issued from Yadis project and platforms mainly

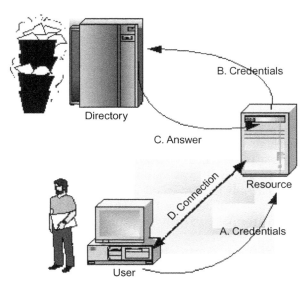

FIGURE 4.5 Identity 1.0 principle.

ID-WSF, OpenID, Higgins, InfoCard and Sxip. At the end, we treat the identity management in the field of mobility.

Evolution of Identity Management

This section provides an overview of almost all identity management 1.0 (See Figure 4.5). First of all, we describe the silo model, then different kind of centralized model and the federated identity management.

4. IDENTITY MANAGEMENT 1.0

In the real world I use my identity card to prove who I am. How about the online world?

The first digital identity appeared when the user was associated with the pair (username, password) or any other shared secret. This method is used for authentication when connecting to an account or a directory. It proves your identity if you follow the guidelines strictly otherwise there is no proof. In fact, it is a single authority using opaque trust decision without any credentials (cryptographic proofs) choice or portability.

In the context of Web access, the user must enroll for every non-related service, generally with different user interfaces and follows diverse policies and protocols. Thus, the user has a non-consistent experience and deals with different identity copies. In addition, some problems related to privacy have also emerged. Indeed, our privacy was potentially invaded by sites. It is clear that sites have a privacy policy, but there is no control from the user on his/her identity. What are the conditions for using these data? How can we improve our privacy? And to what granularity we allow them to use it?

The same problem is revealed when having access to resources. The more resources, the more management we have. It is an asymmetric trust. And, the policy decision maybe opaque.

It allows access with an opaque trust decision and a single centralized authority without a credentials choice. It is a silo model [17] because it is neither portable nor scalable. This is Identity 1.0.

The identity management appeared with these problems in the 1980s. The fist identity management system was the Rec. X.500, developed by ITU [1], covering directory services like Directory Access Protocol (DAP). ISO was also associated to the development of the standard. Like a lot of ITU standards, this one was very heavy and complex. A light version appeared in the 1990s for DAP. It was LDAP which was standardized by the IETF and widespread and adopted by Netscape. Microsoft has invented an equivalent Active Directory, and for users, they introduced Passport. It is also the ITU which standardized X.509 for identities related to certificates. It is the format currently recognized. It is a small file, generated by an authority of certification.

If there is a loss or a usurpation of the certificate, it can always be revoked by the authority of certification. This is for single user and what about business corporations who have automated their procedures and have a proliferation of applications with de-provisioning but still been in a domain-centric model. What about resources shared between domains?

Silo Model

The main identity management system deployed currently in the world of the Internet is known as the silo model, as shown in Figure 4.6. Indeed, the identity provider and service provider are mixed up and they share the same space. The identity management environment is put in place and operated by a single entity for a fixed users' community.

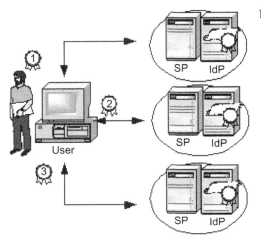

FIGURE 4.6   Identity silo model.

Users of different services must have different accounts and therefore reenter the same information about their identity which increases the difficulty of management. Moreover, the users are overloaded by identity and password to memorize which produces a significant barrier to usage.

A real problem is the forgetfulness of passwords due to the infrequent use of some of these data. This can obviously lead to a higher cost of service provisions. This is for single users, what about Enterprises that have automated their procedures and have a proliferation of applications with de-provisioning but are still in a domain-centric model? What about resources shared between domains?

Silo model is not interoperable and is deficient in many aspects. That's why the federated identity management model is now emerging and it is very appreciated by enterprises. A federated identity management system consists of software components and protocols that handle in a decentralized manner the identity of individuals throughout their identity life cycle [19].

Solution by Aggregation

Aggregating identity information and finding the relationship between identity records is important to aggregate identity. There are some alternatives:

- The first approach consolidates authentication and attributes in only one site and is called a centralized management solution like Microsoft Passport. This solution avoids the redundancies and inconsistencies in the silo model and gives the user a seamless experience [7]. The evolution was as follows [17,19]:
  - Building a single central identity data store which is feasible only for small organizations.
  - Creating a meta-directory that synchronizes data from other identity data stored elsewhere.
  - Creating a virtual directory that provides a single integrated view of the identity data stored.
  - A Single Sign On Identity model which allows users to be authenticated by one service provider.
- The second approach decentralizes the responsibility of IdP to multiple such IdPs which can be selected by the end users. This is a federate system where some attributes of identity are stored in distributed IdPs. A federated directories model, by linking identity data stored together, has emerged. Protocols are defined in several standards such as in Shibboleth [20], Web services federation language 2003.

Centralized vs. Federation Identity Management

Microsoft Passport is a centralized system, entirely controlled by Microsoft and closely tied to other Microsoft products. Individuals and companies have proven to be reluctant adopters of a system so tightly controlled by one dominant company.

Centrally managed repositories in centralized identity infrastructures can't solve the problem of cross-organizational authentication and authorization. This approach has several drawbacks as the IdP does not only become a single point of failure but may also not be trusted. That's why Microsoft Passport was not successful. In contrast, the federation identity will leave the identity resources in their various distributed locations but produce a federation that links them to solve identity duplication, provision and management.

A Simple Centralized Model

A relatively simple centralized identity management model is to build a platform that centralizes identities. A separate entity acts as an exclusive user credentials provider for all service providers. This approach merges both authentication and attributes in only one site. This architecture, which could be called Common user identity management model, is illustrated in Figure 4.7. All identities for each SP are gathered to a unique identity management site (IdP). SPs have to provide each identity to IdP.

In this environment, users can have access to all service providers using the same set of identifiers and credentials. A centralized certificated CAs could be implemented with a PKI or SPKI [21]. This architecture is very efficient in a close domain where users could be identified by a controlled email address. Although such architecture seems to be scalable, the concentration of privacy related information has a lot of difficulties in social acceptance in terms of privacy [22].

Meta-Directories

SPs can share certain identity-related data on a meta-level. This can be implemented by consolidating all service providers' specific identities to a meta-identifier linked to credentials.

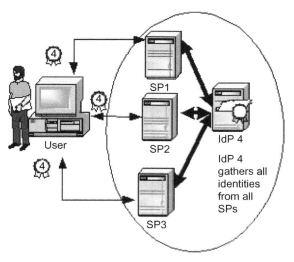

FIGURE 4.7 Simple centralized identity management.

There are collections of directories information from various directory sources. We aggregated them to provide a single view of data. Therefore, we can show these advantages:

- A single point of reference provides an abstraction boundary between application and the actual implementation.
- A single point of administration avoids the multiple directories, too.
- Redundant directory information can be eliminated, reducing the administration tasks.

This approach can be seeing from the user's point of view to his/her password as synchronization across multiple service providers. Thus, the password is automatically changed with all the others.

This architecture can be used in large enterprises where all services are linked to a meta-directory, as shown in Figure 4.8. In this case, the ease-of-use is clear as the administration is done by a single authority.

Virtual Directories

Virtual directories are directories that are not located in the same physical structure as the Web home directory, but look as if they were to Web clients. The actual directories may be at a completely different location in the physical directory structure; for example, on another hard disk or on a remote computer. They are similar in concept to meta-directories in that they provide a single directory view from multiple independent directories. They differ in the means used to accomplish this goal. MD software agents replicate and synchronize data from various directories in what might be batch processes. In contrast, VD provide a single view of multiple directories using real-time queries based on

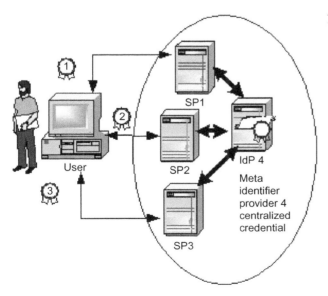

FIGURE 4.8   Meta-directory model.

mapping from fields in the virtual scheme to fields in the physical schemes of the real directories.

Single-Sign-On (SSO)

We use multiple user's Ids and passwords just to use the emails systems and file servers at work and we feel pain from managing multiple identities. The second problem is the scattering of identity data which causes problem for the integration of IT systems.

Single Sign-On (see Figure 4.9) is a solution proposed to eliminate multiple password issues and dangerous password. Moreover, it simplifies the end-user experience and enhances security via identity-based access technology. Therefore, it offers these features:

- Flexible authentication,
- Seamless
- Directory independence and
- Session and password management.

Federated Identity Management

We have seen different approaches to manage user's identity; they are not clearly interoperable and are deficient in unifying standard-based frameworks. On one hand, maintenance of privacy and identity control are fundamental when offering identity to users, on the other hand the same users ask for more easy to use and rapid access. The balance of the two sides leads to federated network identity. That's why these environments are now

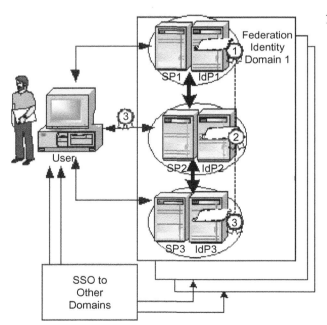

FIGURE 4.9   Single-Sign-On model.

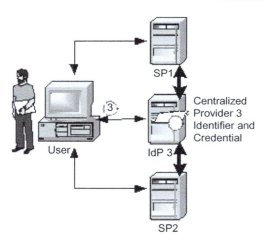

FIGURE 4.10 Federated identity management model.

emerging. A federated identity management system (See Figure 4.10) consists of software components and protocols that handle the identity of individuals throughout their identity life cycle.

This architecture gives the user the illusion that there is a single identifier authority. Even though the user has many identifiers, he doesn't need to know exactly all of them. Only one identifier is enough to have access to all services in the federated domain.

Each SP is responsible for the name space of his users and all SPs are federated by linking the identity domains. Thus, the Federated identity model is based on a set of SPs called a circle of trust by the Liberty Alliance. This set of SPs follows an agreement on mutual security and authentication in order to allow SSO. Indeed, the federated identity management combines SSO and authorization tools using a number of mutual SPs' technologies and standards. This practice makes the recognition and entitlement of user identities by other SPs easy. The Figure 22-10 shows the set of federated domains and the possibility for other SPs to have access to the same user with different identifiers.

The essential difference between federated identity systems and centralized identity management is that there is no single entity that operates the identity management system. Federated systems support multiple identity providers and a distributed and partitioned store for identity information. Therefore, a federated identity network allows a simplified sign-on to users by giving rapid access to resources, but it doesn't require the user's personal information to be stored centrally. With this identity network approach, users authenticate themselves once and can control how their personal information and preferences are used by the service providers.

Federated identity standards, like those produced by the Liberty Alliance [23], provide Single-Sign-On over all offered services and enable users to manage the sharing of their personal information through identity and service providers as well as the use of personalized services in order to give access to convergent services. The interoperability between disparate security systems is assumed by an encapsulation layer through a trust domain which links a set of trusted service providers.

However there are some disadvantages with federated identity management. The first one is the lack of privacy of the user as his/her personal attributes and information can be mapped using correlation between identifiers. Anonymity could be violated. The second one is the scalability of users as they have access to the network from different domains by authentication to their relative IdPs. Therefore, the problem of passwords will continue across multiple federated domains.

A major challenge is to integrate all these components into a distributed network and to deal with these drawbacks. This challenge cannot be taken up without new paradigms and supported standards.

The evolution of identity management system is toward also simplification of user experience and reinforcing authentication. It is very known that a poor usability implies the weakness of authentication. A new paradigm should be introduced to solve those problems while still being compatible at least with federated identity management.

That is why user-centric identity management, has emerged [7,17]. This paradigm is embraced by multiple industry products and initiative such as Microsoft Cardspace [24], Sxip [25] and Higgins Trust Framework [26]. This is Identity 2.0.

Identity 2.0

The user of Internet services is overwhelmed with identities. he/she is seldom able to transfer his/her identity from one site to another. The reputation that he/she gains in one network is useful to transfer to other networks. Nevertheless, he/she cannot profit from his/her constructed reputation and he/she should rebuild his/her identity and reputation another time, and so on. The actual systems don't allow users to decide about the sharing of their attributes related to their identity with other users. This causes a lack of privacy control. Some solutions propose an advanced social system that would model the social interaction like the real world.

The solutions must be easy to use and enable users to share the credentials among many services and must be transparent from the end-user perspective. The principle of modern identity is to separate the acquisition process from the presentation process. It is the same for the identification process and authorization process. Moreover, it provides scalability and privacy. Doing so, we can have more control on my identity.

The scale, security and usability advantages of user-centric identity are what make it the underpinning for Identity 2.0. The main objective of Identity 2.0 protocol is to provide users with full control over their virtual identities. An important aspect of Identity 2.0 is protection against increasingly Web attacks like Phishing attacks as well as the inadvertent disclosure of confidential information while enabling convenient management.

Identity 2.0 would allow users to use one identity respecting transparency and flexibility. It is focused around the user and not around directory or identity provider. It requires identified transactions between users and relaying party using credentials, thus providing more traceable transactions. To maximize the privacy of users, some credentials could be given to the users in advance. Doing so, the IdP could not easily know when the user is utilizing the credentials.

The Identity 2.0 (See Figure 4.11) endorses completely the paradigms of user-centric identity management enabling the full control of user on his/her identity. Service Provider will therefore be required to change their approaches by including request and

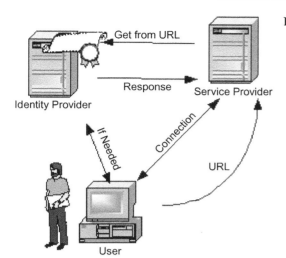

FIGURE 4.11 URL-based Id 2.0.

authentication of users' identity. Identity 2.0 systems are interested in using the concept of a user's identity as credentials about the user, from their attributes like their name, address, to less traditional things like their desires, customer service history, and other attributes that are usually not so much associated with a user identity.

Identity 2.0 Initiatives

When a Website collects data from users he cannot confirm whether or not the collected data is pertinent and reliable as the users often enter nonsense information into online forms. This is due to the lack of Website to control and verify the users' data. Furthermore, due to the law limitation on the requested data, the Website cannot provide true customized services even though users require them. In the other side, users have not direct control on what the Website will do with their data. In addition, the users enter many times the same data when accessing the first time different Websites. Doing so, they have a huge difficulty to manage their large number of identities.

To mitigate these problems, different models of identity management have been considered. One such model, Identity 2.0, proposes an Internet-scalable and user-centric identity architecture that mimics real world interactions.

Many research labs have collaborated to develop the Identity 2.0 Internet based Identity Management services. It is based on the concept of user-centric identity management, supporting enhanced identity verification and privacy, and user consent and control over any access to personal information for Internet-based transactions. There are various Identity 2.0 initiatives:

1. **LID**
2. **XRI**
3. **SAML**
4. **Shibboleth**

5. **ID-WSF**
6. **OpenID**
7. **Microsoft's CardSpace (formerly InfoCard)**
8. **SXIP**
9. **Higgins**

LID

Like LDAP, LID is under the principle of simplicity because many existing identity schemes are too complicated to be largely adoptable. It simplifies more complex protocol; but instead of being less capable due to fewer features, it has run success that their more complex predecessors lacked. This was because their simplification reduced the required complexity to the point where many people could easily support them, and that was one of the goals of LID.

Light-Weight Identity (LID) is a set of protocols capable of representing and using digital identities on the Internet in a simple manner, without relying on any central authority. LID is the original URL-based identity protocol, and part of the OpenID movement.

LID supports digital identities for humans, human organizations and non-humans (software agents, things, Websites, etc.) It implements Yadis, a meta-data discovery service and is pluggable on all levels.

XRI/XDI

We have XRI EXtensible Resource Identifier (see Figure 4.12) and XDI which fractional solution without Web services integrated. They are open standards as they are royalty-free open standards. XRI is about Addressing. XDI is about Data Sharing protocol and uses basically XRI. Both XRI and XDI are being developed under the support of OASIS. I-name and I-number registry services for privacy-protected digital addressing use XRI. It can be used as an identifier for persons, machines and agents.

XRIs offer a human-friendly form of persistent identifier. That's why it is convenient identifier for SSO system. They Supports both persistent and reassignable identifiers in the same syntax and establish a global context symbols. Moreover, they enable identification of the same logical resource across multiple contexts and multiple versions of the same logical resource.

XDI (XRI Data Exchange) is a Secure Distributed Data Sharing Protocol. It is also an architecture and specification for privacy-controlled data exchange where all data is identified using XRIs. The XDI platform includes explicit specification for caching with both push and pull synchronization. XDI universal schema can represent any complex data and have the ability of cross context addressing and linking.

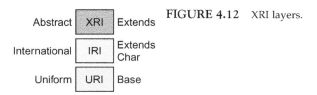

FIGURE 4.12   XRI layers.

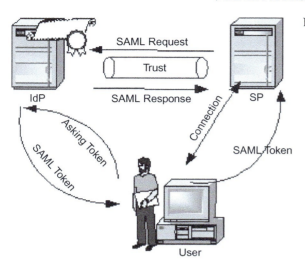

FIGURE 4.13 SAML token exchange.

SAML

The Security Assertion Markup Language (SAML) is an OASIS specification [27] that provides a set of rules for the structure of identity assertions, protocols to move assertions, bindings of protocols for typical message transport mechanisms, and profiles. Indeed, SAML (see Figure 4.13) is a set of XML and SOAP-based services and formats for the exchange of authentication and authorization information between security systems.

The initial versions of SAML v1.0 and v1.1 define protocols for SSO, delegated administration, and policy management. The most recent version is SAML 2.0. It is now a common language to the majority platform to change secure unified assertion. He is very useful and simple as it is based on XML. An assertion is a datum produced by a SAML authority referring to authentication, attribute information, or authorizations applying to the user with respect to a specified resource.

This protocol (see Figure 4.14) enables interoperability between security systems (Browser Single Sign On, Web Services Security, etc.). Other aspects of federated identity management as permission-based attribute sharing are also supported.

An SAML is sometimes criticized for its complexity of the specifications and the relative constraint of its security rules. Recently, the SAML community has shown significant interest in extending SAML to reach less stringent requirements for low-sensitivity use cases. The advantages of SAML are robustness of its security and privacy model, and the guarantee of its interoperability between multiple vendor implementations through the Liberty Alliance's Conformance Program.

Shibboleth

Shibboleth [20] is a project which goal is to allow universities to share the Web resources subject to control access. Thereafter, it allows inter-operation between institutions using it. It develops architectures, policy structure, practical technologies, and an open source implementation. It is building components for both the identity providers and

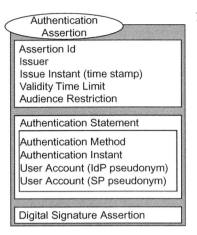

FIGURE 4.14   SAML assertion.

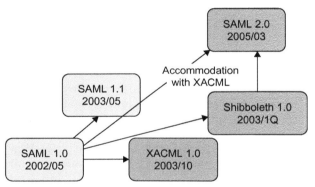

FIGURE 4.15   Convergence between SAML & Shibboleth.

the reliant parties. The key concept includes "federated" management identity whose meaning is almost the same as the Liberty term's [28]. Access control is fundamentally based on user attributes, validated by SAML Assertions. In Figure 4.15, we can see the evolution of SAML, Shibboleth and XACML [29].

ID-WSF

In 2001, a business alliance was formed to serve as open standards organization for federated identity management and it was named Liberty alliance [23,30]. Its goals are to guaranty interoperability, support privacy, and promote adoption of its specifications, guidelines and best practices. The key objectives of the Liberty Alliance (see Figure 4.16) are to:

- Enable users to protect their privacy and identity
- Enable SPs' to manage their clients
- Provide an open federated SSO
- Provide a network identity infrastructure that supports all current emerging network access devices

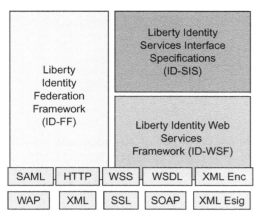

FIGURE 4.16 High-Level Overview of the Liberty Alliance Architecture.

ROADMAP TO INTEROPERABLE FEDERATED IDENTITY SERVICES

The Liberty Alliance's work in the first phase is to enable federated network identity management. It offers among others SSO and linking accounts in the set of SPs' in the boundary of the circle of trust. This work of this phase is referred to as Identity Federation Framework (ID-FF).

In the second phase, the specifications offer enhancing identity federation and interoperable identity-based Web services. This body is referred to as Identity Web Services Framework (ID-WSF). This framework involves support of the new open standard such as WS-Security developed in OASIS. ID-WSF is a platform for the discovery and invocation of identity services – Web services associated with a given identity-. In the typical ID-WSF use case, after a user authenticates to an IdP this fact is asserted to a SP through SAML-based SSO. Embedded within the assertion is information that the SP can optionally use to discover and invoke potentially numerous and distributed identity services for that user. For some scenarios which present an unacceptable privacy risk as it suggests the possibility of a user's identity being exchanged without their consent or even knowledge. ID-WSF has a number of policy mechanisms to guard against this risk but ultimately, it is worth noting that many identity transactions (automated bill payments) already occur without the user's active real-time consent – and users appreciate this efficiency and convenience.

To build additional interoperable identity services such as registration services, contacts, calendar, geo-location services, alert services, it's envisaged to use ID-WSF. This specification is referred to as the Identity Services Interfaces Specifications (ID-SIS).

The Liberty Alliance specifications define the protocol messages, profiles, and processing rules for identity federation and management. They rely heavily on other standards such as SAML and WS-Security which is another OASIS specification that defines mechanisms implemented in SOAP headers.

These mechanisms are designed to enhance SOAP messaging by providing a quality of protection through message integrity, message confidentiality, and single message authentication. Additionally, Liberty has contributed portions of its specification back into the technical committee working on SAML. Other identity management enabling standards include:

- Service Provisioning Markup Language (SPML)
- XML Access Control Markup Language (XACML)
- XML Key Management Specification (XKMS)
- XML Signature
- XML Encryption

The WS-* (the Web Services protocol specifications) are a set of specifications that is currently under development by Microsoft and IBM. It is a part of larger effort to define a security framework for Web services, the resultant of proposals are often referred to as WS-*. It includes specifications as WS-Policy, WS-Security Conversation, WS-Trust, and WS-Federation. This last one has functionality for enabling pseudonyms and attribute-based interactions. Therefore, WS-Trust's has the ability to ensure security tokens as a means of brokering identity and trust across domain boundaries [22].

The Liberty Alliance is developing and delivering specification that enables federate network identity management. Figure 4.16 shows an Overview of the Liberty Alliance architecture as describe in the introduction to the Liberty Alliance identity architecture.

OpenID 2.0

Brad Fitzpatrick is at the origin of the development of the OpenID 1.0. The intent of the OpenID framework is to specify layers that are independent and small enough to be acceptable and adopted by market [12]. OpenID is basically providing simple attribute sharing for low-value transactions. It does not depend on any preconfigured trust model. The version 1.0 has deal with http based URL authentication protocol. OpenID authentication 2.0 is becoming an open platform that supports both URL and XRI user identifiers. In addition, it would like to be modular, lightweight and user oriented. Indeed, OpenID auth. 2.0 allows user to choose/control/manage his/her identity address. Moreover, the user choose his/her Identity Provider and have a large interoperability of his/her identity and can dynamically uses new services that stand out attribute verification and reputation without any loose of features. No software is required on user's side as the user interacts directly with the identity provider's site. This approach jeopardize the user identity because it could be hacked or theft. Moreover the user has no ability to examine tokens before they are sent.

At the beginning of identity management each technology came with its own futures without any interest for others. Later, the OpenID 1.0 community has realized the importance of integrating other technologies as OASIS XRDS which is useful for his simplicity and extensibility.

OpenID Stack

The first layer is for supporting users' identification. Using URL or XRI form, we can identify an user. URL use IP or DNS resolution and is unique and ubiquitously supported. It can be as a personal digital address as used by blogers even though it is not yet largely used.

XRI (EXtensible Resource Identifier) is being developed under the support of OASIS and is about Addressing. I-names are a generic term for XRI authority names that provide abstract identifiers for the entity to which they are assigned. They can be used as the entry point to access data under the control of that authority. Like a domain name, the physical location of the information is transparent to the requester.

OpenID 2.O provides a private digital address to allow a user to be only identified in specific conditions. This is guaranty the user privacy in a public domain.

DISCOVERY Yadis is used for identity service discovery for URLs and XRI resolution protocol for XRIs. The both use OASIS format called XRDS (Extensible Resource Description Sequence). The protocol is simple and describes any type of service.

AUTHENTICATION This service lets a user to prove his/her URL or I-name using credentials (cryptographic proof). This protocol is explained in Figure 4.17. The OpenID doesn't need a centralized authority for enrollment and it is therefore a federated identity management. With the OpenID 2.0 the IdP offers the user the option of selecting a digital address to send to the SP. To ensure anonymity, IdP can randomly generate a digital address used specially for this SP.

DATA TRANSPORT This layer ensures the data exchange between the IdP and SP. It supports push and pulls methods and it is independent from authentication procedures. Therefore, the synchronization of data and secure messaging and other service will be enabled. The data formats are those defined by SAML, SDI (XRI Data interchange) or any other data formats. This approach will enable evolution of the OpenID platform.

The four layers construct the foundation of the OpenID ensuring user centricity (see Figure 4.18). There are three points to guaranty this paradigm:

1. User choose his/her digital identity
2. User choose IdP
3. User choose SP

OpenID is decentralized and well founded and at the same time simple, easy to use and to deploy. It provides open development process and single sign-on for the Web and ease of integration into scripted Web platforms (Drupal, WordPress, etc).

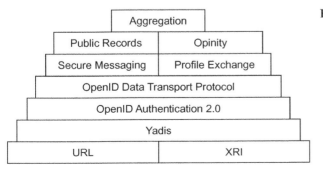

FIGURE 4.17   OpenID protocol stack.

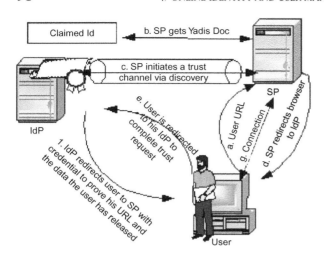

FIGURE 4.18   OpenID 1.1 protocol flow.

So, it is a greater future for him. You can learn about OpenID at openidenabled.com also the community of OpenId can be joined at opened.net.

InfoCard

Rather than invent another technology for creating and representing digital identities, Microsoft has adopted the federated user-centric identity meta-system. This is a serious solution that provides a consistent way to work with multiple digital identities. Using standard protocols that anyone can implement on any platform, the identity meta-system allows the acquisition and use of any kind of security tokens to convey identity.

The "Infocard" is the Microsoft's codename for this new technology that tackles the problem of managing and disclosing identity information. The "InfoCard" implements the core of the Identity Metasystem, using open standard protocols to negotiate, request and broker identity information between trusted IdPs and SPs. "InfoCard" is a technology that helps developers to integrate a consistent identity infrastructure into applications, Web sites and Web services.

By providing a way for users to select identities and more, Windows CardSpace [24] plays an important part in the identity meta-system.

It provides the consistent user experience required by the identity meta-system. It is specifically hardened against tampering and spoofing to protect the end user's digital identities and maintain end-user control. Windows CardSpace enables users to provide their digital identities in a familiar, secure and easy way.

In the terminology of Microsoft, relying party is in our model service provider (SP). To prove an identity over a network, the user emitted credentials which are some proofs about his/her identity. For example in the simplest digital identity the user name is the identity while the password is said to be the authentication credential. In the terminology of Microsoft and others, there are called security token and contain one or more claims. Each claim contains information about the users, like the user name or home address, etc. In addition, security token encloses prove that the claims are correctly emitted by the real user and are belonging to him. This is could be done cryptographically using different forms such as X.509 certificates and Kerberos tickets but unfortunately there are not practical to convoy different kind of claim. The standard SAML as seen before is the indicated one for this purpose as it can be used to define security tokens. Indeed, SAML token could enclose any desired information and thus become as largely useful in the network to show and control digital identity. CardSpace runs on Windows Vista, XP, Server 2003 and Server 2008, based on .NET3, and also uses Web service protocols:

- WS-Trust
- WS-Policy
- WS-SecurityPolicy
- WS-MetaDataExchange

CardSpace runs in a self virtual desktop on the PC. Thereby, it locks out other processes and reduces the possibility of intercepting information by a spyware.

Figure 4.19 shows that the architecture is fitting exactly to the principle of Identity 2.0. The user access one of any of his/her relying parties (SPs) using an application that supports CardSpace.

When the choice is made, the application asks for the requirement of security token of this specific SP that will answer with SP policy. It really contains information about the claims and the accepted token formats. Once this is done, the application passes these requirements to CardSpace which asks the security token from an appropriate identity provider.

Once this security token has been received, CardSpace transmits via application to the relying party. The relying party can then use this token to authenticate the user.

Please note that each identity is emitted by an identity provider and is stored at the user side. It contains the emitter, the kind of security token he/she can issue and the details about the claims' enclose. All difficulties are hidden to the user as he/she has only to choose one of InfoCard when the process of authentication is launched. Indeed, once

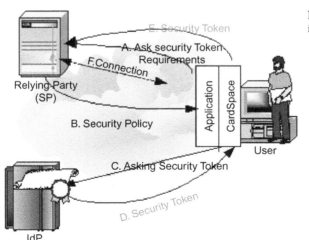

FIGURE 4.19 Interactions among the users, identity providers and relying party.

the requirements information are returned and passed to CardSpace, the system displays the card selection matching the requirements on screen. In this regard, the user has a consistent experience as all applications based on CardSpace will have the same interface, and the user do not have to worry about the protocol used to express identity's security token. The PIN number is entered by user and the choice of his/her card is done in a private Windows desktop to prevent locally-running process.

SXIP 2.0

In 2004, The SXIP 1.0 grows from efforts to build a balanced online identity solution that met the requirements of the entire online community. Indeed, SXIP 2.0 is the new generation of the SXIP 1.0 protocol that was a platform that gives users control over their online identities and enables online communities to have a richer relationship with their membership. SXIP 2.0 defines entities' terminology as:

- Homesite: URL-based identity given by IdP.
- Membersite: SP that uses SXIP 2.0.
- User: equivalent to the user in our model.

The Simple eXtensible Identity Protocol (SXIP) [25] was designed to address the principles defined by the Identity 2.0 model (see Figure 4.20), which proposes an Internet-scalable and user-centric identity architecture that mimics real-world interactions.

If a SP has integrated a SXIP to his Website, which is easy done by using SDKs, he is a Membersite. When a subscriber of SXIP would like to access this Membersite:

1. Types his/her URL address and clicks on [Sxip in]
2. Types his/her URL identity issued by IdP (called Homesite)
3. Browser is redirected to the Homesite

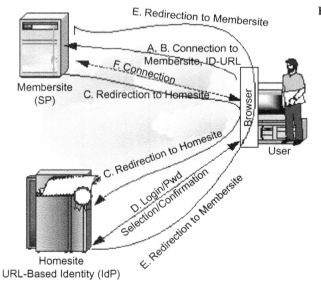

FIGURE 4.20   SXIP entities interactions.

4. Enters his/her username and password, being informed that the Membersite has requested data, selects the related data and verify it and can select to automatically release data for other visit to this Membersite and confirms

5. Browser is redirected to the Membersite

6. Have access to the content of the site.

SXIP 2.0 is a platform based on a fully decentralized architecture providing an open and simple set of process for exchanging identity information. SXIP 2.0 has significantly reduced the problems resulting from moving identity data form one site to another. It is URL-based protocol that allows a seamless user experience and fits exactly to user-centric paradigm. In that sense, the user has full control on his/her identity and has an active role in the exchange of his/her identity data. Therefore, he/she can profit from portable authentication to connect many Websites. Doing so, user has more choice and convenience when exchanging his/her identity data and enables indirectly Websites to offer enhanced services to their subscribers.

SXIP 2.0 provides the following features:

- Decentralized architecture: SXIP 2.0 is completely decentralized and is a federated identity management. The online identity is URL-based and the user identity is separated from the authority that issues the identifiers for this identity. In this regard, we can easily move the location of the identity data without losing the associated identifier.
- Dynamic discovery: A simple and dynamic discovery mechanism ensures that users are always informed online about his/her home site that is exporting identity data.
- Simple implementation: SXIP 2.0 is open source using different high level development languages such as Perl, Python, PHP, and Java. Therefore, the integration of SXIP 2.0 into a Website is effortless. It does not require PKI as it uses a URL-based protocol that do not need it.
- Support for existing technologies: SXIP 2.0 uses simple Web browsers, the primary client and means of data exchange, providing users with choice in the release of their identity data.
- Interoperability: SXIP 2.0 can coexist with other URL-based protocols.
- Richer data at an Internet scale: SXIP 2.0 messages consist of lists of simple name value pairs. It can exchanged simple text, claims using SAML and third-party claims in one exchange and present them in many separate exchange. In addition, the Identity provider is not bothersome every time identity is requested.

Finally by using SXIP 2.0, Websites can also be authoritative about users for data, such as third-party claims. Those are keys to build online reputation, further enriching the online exchange of identity data.

Higgins

Higgins [31] is a project supported principally by IBM and it is a part of IBM's Eclipse open source foundation. It will also offer libraries for Java, C and C++, and plug-ins for popular browsers. It is really an open source trust framework which goals are to support existing and new applications that give users more convenience, privacy and control over their identity information. The aim objective is to develop an extensible, platform-independent, identity protocol-independent, software framework that provides a foundation for user-centric identity management. Indeed, it enables applications to integrate identity, profiles and relationship across heterogeneous systems.

The main goal of Higgins as an identity management systems are interoperability, security and privacy that are a decoupled architecture. This system is a real user-centric based on a federated identity management. The user has the ability to use a pseudonym or simply reply anonymously in case you would not give your name.

We use the term context to cover a range of underlying implementations. A context can be thought of as a distributed container-like object that contains digital identities of multiple people or processes. The platform intends to address four challenges:

- The need to manage multiple contexts,
- The need for interoperability,
- The need to respond to regulatory, public or customer pressure to implement solutions based on trusted infrastructure that offers security and privacy, and
- The lack of common interfaces to identity/networking systems.

Higgins matches exactly the user-centric paradigms because it offers consistent user experience based on card icons for the management and release of identity data. Thereby, there is less vulnerability to Phishing and other attacks. Moreover, user privacy is enabled by sharing only what is needed. Thus, the user has a full control on his/her personal data. Identity Attribute Service enables aggregation and federation of identity systems and even silos. For enterprises, it integrates all data related to identity, profile, reputation, and relationship information across and among complex systems.

Higgins is a trust framework that enables users and enterprises to adopt, share across multiple systems and integrate to new or existing application, digital identity, profiles, and cross-relationship information. In fact, it facilitates as well the integration of different identity management systems as the management of identity, profile, reputation and relationship data across repositories. Using context providers, directories and communications technologies (Microsoft/IBM WS-*, LDAP, email, etc.) can be plugged into the Higgins framework. Higgins has become an Eclipse plug-in, and is a project of the Eclipse Foundation. Any application developed with Higgins will enable users to share identity with other users under a strict control.

Higgins is benefic for developers, users and enterprise. Higgins relieves the developers from knowing all the details of multiple identity systems, thanks to one API that support many protocols and technologies: CardSpace, OpenID, XRI, LDAP, etc. An Application written to the Higgins API can integrate the identity, profile, and relationship information across these heterogeneous systems. The goal of the framework is to be useful in the development of applications accessed through browsers, rich clients, and Web services. Thus, the Higgins Project is supported by IBM and Novell and thwart InfoCard Microsoft's project.

The Higgins framework intents to define in terms of service descriptions, messages and port types consistent with an SOA model and to develop a Java binding and implementation as an initial reference. Applications can use Higgins to create a unified, virtual view of identity, profile and relationship information. A key focus of Higgins is providing a foundation for new "user-centric identity" and personal information management applications.

Finally, Higgins provides virtual integration; user-centric federated management model and trust brokering that are applied to identity, profile and relationship information. Furthermore, Higgins provides common interfaces to identity and thanks to data context it encloses enhanced automation process. Those features are also offered across multiple contexts, disparate systems and implementations. In this regard, Higgins is a full interoperable framework.

The Higgins service acts together with a set of so-called context providers which can represent a department, association, informal network and so on. A context is the environment of Higgins and digital identities, the policies and protocols that govern their interactions. Context providers adjust existing legacy systems to the framework, or implement new ones Context providers may also contain the identities of a machine or human. A context encloses a group of digital identities and their related claims and links. A Context maintains a set of Claims about properties and values (name, address, etc.). It is like security token for Cardspace. The set of profile properties, the set of roles, and the access rights for each role are defined by and controlled by the Context Provider.

Context providers act as adapters to existing systems. Adapter providers can connect for example to LDAP servers, identity management systems like CardSpace, mailing list and social networking systems. A Higgins context provider (see Figure 4.21) has the ability to implement the Context interface and thus empower the applications layered on top of Higgins.

Summarizing Table

The 10 requirements at the top of Table 4.1, are those discussed earlier in the chapter. In this table, white means that the requirement is not covered, grey partially and black fully fulfilled.

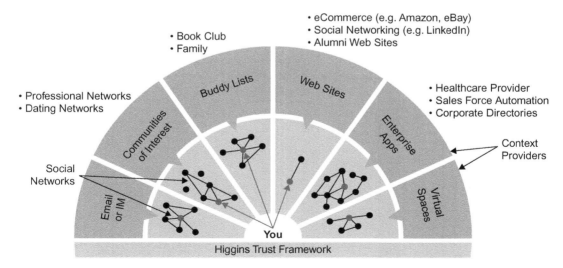

FIGURE 4.21   Higgins Trust Framework and context [26].

TABLE 4.1 Evaluation of Identity 2.0 Technologies

Requirement	Empowering the total control of users over their privacy	Usability, as users are using the same identity for each identity transaction	Giving a consistent user's experience thanks to uniformity of identity interface	Limiting identity attacks i.e. phishing	Limiting reachability/ disturbances, such as spam	Reviewing policies on both sides when necessary, identity providers and service providers	Huge scalability advantages as the identity provider does not have to get any prior knowledge about the service provider	Assuring secure conditions when exchanging data	Decoupling digital identity from applications	Pluralism of operators and technologies
XRI/XDI										
ID/WSF										
Shibboleth										
CardSpace										
OpenID										
SXIP										
Higgins										

At the moment, service providers have to choose between so many authentications and identity management systems and users are left to face the non-convenience of a variety of digital identities. The main initiatives have different priorities and some unique advantages, while overlapping in many areas. The most pressing requirements for users are interoperability, usability and centricity. Thanks to Higgins the majority of identity requirements are guaranty. Therefore, using it, the user is free to visit all Web sites without being worried about the identity management system used by the provider.

5. SOCIAL LOGIN AND USER MANAGEMENT

At the time of the writing of the second version of this book chapter (end of 2012), none of the identity management technologies surveyed earlier in the chapter, have reached major user adoption. A few of them have been discontinued. For example, Sxip went bankrupt [32]. Others have moved very slowly. Higgins has only released a partial implementation of its vision and seems on hold. Liberty Alliance moved to a new initiative called the Kantara initiative [23]. However, a new type of solutions, which was not really expected at time of writing the first version of the book chapter, has emerged and gained quite large users adoption. This type of solutions is provided by major online social networks that have reached mass market very fast and where users have spent time configuring their profile. Then, those major online networks have built on top of previously surveyed standard identity management technological building blocks tools to facilitate logging to other Web sites and online services with the identities managed on their services. The good news is that most of them have based their work on OpenID. Therefore although OpenID is less known by the greater public, it still exists underneath. They are also extensively relying on OAuth [33] that was built when OpenID was investigated for Twitter [34]. It is also possible to authenticate through OAuth but OAuth goes beyond OpenID regarding authorizations (in addition to authentication). The major online social networks providers that have created tools to allow their users to easy log in into other Web sites and services are: Facebook [35], Twitter, LinkedIn [36] and Google [37].

The Web sites and services that use the "social login" tools of one of these providers provide an easier access to their service to users who already have an account on this external provider. With a few confirming clicks, the user has joined the new service without having to spend time filling out her personal information again. Although this solution has gained large adoption because it fulfilled the user-friendliness requirement, there are still a few flaws remaining.

First, there is concern about the privacy protection requirement. For example, based on Facebook privacy bugs and issues due to privacy protection laws in different countries, one cannot claim that a Facebook user is really under control of her personal data disclosed to Facebook. It does not correspond to a user-centric approach. Thus, the Web site or service that reuses Facebook identity management service does not really fulfill the privacy requirement discussed above. The same privacy issues apply to the other "social login" providers.

Second issue concerns allowing users who may not have an account in one of the chosen "social login" provider to still login. Although the "social login" providers have created tools to connect their identity management system to another Web site or service, adding multiple login forms to a Web site or service takes times and may confuse the user as many forms may be possible for registering. In addition, most "social login" providers often change their Application Programming Interface (API) without backward compatibility. Thus, the Web site or service may lose its registration functionality for some time before it can apply the required changes.

It is why a new type of providers has emerged on top of these "social login" providers. Those providers do the hard work to maintain a tool that allows a user to create an account with all the "social login" providers as well as store and manage users information on behalf of the service or Web site that uses this tool. The owners of Web sites and services install this tool on their Web site or service without having to worry when one of the "social login" providers change their API. The price of allowing a user to create an account with any of the main online social networks providers without having to maintain each "social login" module has to be weighed against the subscription price to one of these user management providers such as Janrain [38], OneAll [39], LoginRadius [40] or Gigya [41].

6. IDENTITY 2.0 FOR MOBILE USERS

In this section, we discuss identity management in the realm of mobile computing devices. These devices are used more and more, and have different constraints than fixed desktop computers.

Introduction

The number of devices such as mobile phones, smart cards and RFIDs [42], is increasing daily and becoming huge. Mobile phones have attracted particular interest because of their large penetration and pervasiveness that exceeds that of personal computers. Furthermore, the emergence of both IP-TV and wireless technology has facilitated the proliferation of intelligent devices, mobile phones, RFIDs, and other forms of information technology that are developing at a rapid speed. These devices include a fixed identifier that could be linked to the user's identity. This identifier provides a mobile identity which takes into account information about the location and the mobile user's personal data [43].

Mobile Web 2.0

Mobile Web 2.0 as a content-based service is an up-to-date offering of services within the mobile network. As the number of people having access to mobile devices exceeds those using a desktop computer, *mobile Web* will be a key factor for the next generation network. At the moment, mobile Web suffers from lack of interoperability and usability due to the small screen size and lower computational capability. Fortunately, these limitations are only temporary and within 5 years they will be easily overcome. There will be convergence in the next generation public networks towards the mobile network which will bring mobility to the forefront. Thus, mobile identity management will play a central role in addressing issues such as usability, privacy and security which are key challenges for researcher in the mobile network. Since the initial launch of mobile Web services, customers have increasingly turned to their wireless phones to connect with family and friends and also to obtain the latest news and information or even to produce content with their mobile and then publish them. Mobile Web 2.0 [27] is the enforcement of evolution and will enhance the experience of users by providing connections in an easier and more efficient way. For this reason, it will be welcome by the key actors as a well-established core service identity management for the next generation mobile network. This mobile identity management will be used not only to identify, acquire, access and pay for services but also to offer context-aware services as well as location based services.

Mobility

The mobile identity may not be stored at the same location but could be distributed among many locations, authorities and devices. Indeed, identity is mobile in many respects [1]:

1. There is a device mobility where a person is using the same identity while using different devices;
2. There is a location mobility where a person is using the same devices while changing the location; and
3. There is context mobility where a person is receiving services based on different societal roles: as a parent, as a professional and so on.

The three kind of mobility are not isolated but they interacted more often and became concurrently modified creating much more complex situations that what implied from single mode. Mobile identity management addresses three main challenges: a. usability via context awareness b. trust based on the perception of secure operation and c. the protection of privacy [1].

Evolution of Mobile Identity

Mobile identity management is in its infancy. GSM networks, for example, provide management of SIM identities as a kind of mobile identity management, but they do not meet all the requirements for a complete Mobile identity management. Unlike static identity, already implemented in Web 2.0 identity, dynamic aspects, such as the user's position or the temporal context, gain increasingly importance for new kinds of mobile applications [44].

Mobile identity (MId) infrastructure solutions have evolved over time and can be classified into three solutions. The first proposed solution is just an extension of wired identity management to mobile Internet. This is the widespread solution, which is limited to the users of mobile devices running the same operating system as wired solution. This limitation is expected to evolve over time mainly with the large deployment of Web services. Some specifications, such as Liberty Alliance specifications, have been developed for identity management including mobility. However, several limitations are observed when the MId system is derived from fixed context. These limitations are principally due to the assumptions during their design and they do not match well with extra requirement of mobility [1].

Many improvements such as interoperability, privacy and security are to be operated. Also, older centralized PKI must be replaced by a modern trust management system or at least a decentralized PKI.

The second solution is capable of providing an alternative to the prevalent Internet derived MId infrastructure. This consists of either connected (Cellular phones) or unconnected (Smartcards) mobiles devices.

The third one consists of using implantable radio frequency identity (RFID) devices. This approach is expected to increase rapidly even if the market penetration is smaller than cellular phones.

In addition, the sensitivity risk of data related to different applications and services are seldom at the same level and the number of identifiers used by a person is in constant increasing. Thus, there is a real need of different kind of credentials associated with different kind of applications. Indeed, a tool at the user side capable of managing the credentials and identifies is inevitable. With the increasing capacity of CPU power and the spreading number of mobile phone with a SIM card, mobile phones can be considered as a Personal Authentication Device (PDA). They can hold securely the users' credentials, password and even identities. Thereby, we introduced a new efficient Identity management device at the user side able to facilitate the memorization in one hand, and strengthen the security by limiting the number of passwords and their weakness in other hand. All wired identity management can be deployed using PDA. In addition, many different authentication architectures become possible and easy to implement such as dual channel authentication.

PDA as Solution to Strong Authentication

PDA is a tamper-resistant hardware device which could include smart card and sensors or not. As it is used for authentication it is called a personal authentication device (PDA) [45]. This term has been early used in the context of security by Wong and al. [46]. The approach is the same and the only thing change so far is the performance of the mobile device has radically changed. This is the opportunity to emphasis the user centricity as the PDA could strengthen the user experience and to facilitate the automation and system support of the identity management at the user side. The Figure 4.22 illustrated the combination of PDA and silo model. The user stores his/her identity in the PDA. Whenever he/she would like to connect to a Service provider.

1. He/she authenticates her/himself with a PIN code to use the PDA.
2. The user choose the Password to be used for his/her connection to the specific service provider.
3. The user launch and log to the specific service provider by entering his/her Username and the Password.

The PDA is a good device to tackle the weakness and non-convenience of password authentication. Thereby, we have a user friendly and user centric application and even introducing stronger authentication. The fundamental advantage of PDA comparing with common PC using common operating systems such as windows or linux is that PDA has a robust isolation of processes. Therefore, compromising one application does not compromise all the applications. This advantage is becoming less important for mobile phone as flexibility is introduced by manufacturers a lot of vulnerabilities is also introduced. We have seen many viruses for mobile phones and even nowadays we have viruses for RFID. This vulnerability can compromise authentication and even biometrics authentication. That's why we should be very vigilant in implementing security in PDA devices. An ideal device is the USB stick running a standalone OS, and integrating a biometric reader and mobile network access. A can find some of them with fingerprint reader for a reasonable price.

Two main categories can group many authentication architectures that could be implemented in a PDA. There are single and dual channel authentications. Thereby, the cost, the risk and the non-convenience could be tackled at the same time.

Figure 4.23 illustrates the principle of single channel authentication, which is the first application of the PDA. Figure 4.24 illustrates the second principle of dual-channel authentication, which is more secure.

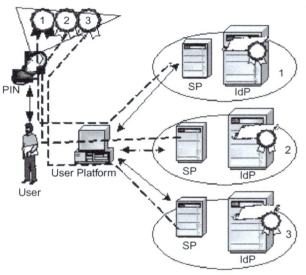

FIGURE 4.22 Integration of PDA in silo model.

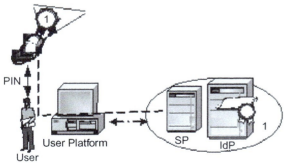

FIGURE 4.23 Single channel authentication.

FIGURE 4.24 Dual channel authentication.

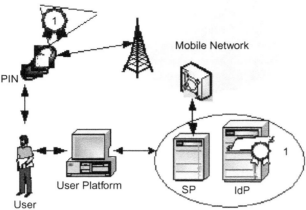

Different Kinds of Strong Authentication Through a Mobile PDA

The mobile network mainly GSM can help to overcome a lot of security vulnerabilities such as phishing or man-in-the-middle. It attracts all business that would like to deploy double channel authentication but are worry about cost and usability. The near-ubiquity of the mobile network has made feasible the utilization of this approach and even being adopted by some banks.

SMS Based One-Time Password (OTP)

The main advantages in mobile network are the facility and usability to send and receive SMSs. Moreover, they could be used to setup and download easily Java program to the mobile device. In addition, mobile devices are using smart card that can securely calculate and store claims.

The cost is minimized by adopting a mobile device using SMS to receive OTP instead of a special hardware that can generate OTP. The scenario implemented by some banks is illustrated in Figure 4.25. First of all, the user switches his/her mobile phone and enters his PIN code then:

1. The user log into his online account by entering his/her Username and Password (U/P)
2. The Web site received the couple U/P
3. The server verifies the couple
4. Send a SMS message with OTP
5. The user reads the message
6. The user enters the OPT into online account
7. The server verify the OPT and give access

The problem of this approach is the fact that the cost is assumed by the service provider. In addition, some drawbacks are very common mainly in some developing countries such as lack of coverage and SMS latency. Of course, the attack of the man-in-the-middle is not overcome by this approach.

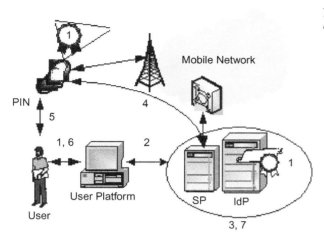

FIGURE 4.25 Scenario of SMS double channel authentication.

Soft Token Application

In this case, the PDA is used as a token emitter. The application is previously downloaded. SMS could be sent to the user in order to set up the application that will play the role of soft token.

The scenario is exactly identical to the SMS but only the user generates his/her OTP using the soft token instead of waiting for a SMS message. The cost is less than the SMS based OTP. This approach is a single channel authentication that is not dependent on mobile network coverage neither on his latency. Furthermore, the attack of the man-in-the-middle is not tackle.

Full Option Mobile Solution

We have seen in the two previously scenarios that the attacks of the man-in-the-middle is not addressed. It exist a counterattack to this security issue consisting of using the second channel to completely control all the transactions over the online connection. Of course, the security of this approach is based on the assumption that it is difficult for an attacker to steal the user's personal mobile phone or to attack the mobile network. Anyway, we have developed an application to crypt the SMS message which minimizes the risk of attacks. The scenario is illustrated in the Figure 4.26 and it is as follows:

1. The user login on online account using token
2. The server receives the token
3. The server verifies the token
4. the access is given to the service
5. the user request a transaction
6. SMS message is send with the requested transaction and a confirmation code
7. The user verifies the transaction
8. He enters the confirmation code
9. The server verifies and execute the transaction
10. The server sends a transaction confirmation

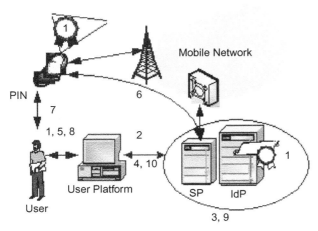

FIGURE 4.26   Secure transaction via SMS.

Future of Mobile User-Centric Identity Management in an Ambient Intelligence (AmI) World

AmI manifests itself through a collection of everyday devices incorporating computing and networking capabilities that enable them to interact with each other, make intelligent decisions and interact with users through user friendly multimodal interfaces. Ambient intelligence is driven by users' needs and the design of its capabilities should be driven by users' requirements.

Ambient Intelligence technologies are expected to combine concepts of ubiquitous computing and intelligent systems putting humans in the center of technological developments. Indeed, the Internet extension to home and mobile networks, the multiplication of modes of connection will make the individual the central point. Therefore, the identity is a challenge in this environment and will guarantee the infatuation with Ambient Intelligence. Moreover, AmI will be the future environment where we shall be surrounded by mobile devices which will be more and more used for mobile interactions with things, places and people.

The low-cost and the shrinking size of sensors as well as the ease of deployment will aid ambient intelligence research efforts for rapid prototyping. Evidently, a sensor combined with unique biometric identifiers is becoming more frequently utilized in access a system, and supposedly provide proof of a person's identity and thus accountability for subsequent actions. To explore these new AmI technologies, it is easier to investigate a scenario related to ubiquitous computing in an ambient intelligence environment.

AmI Scenario

A person having a mobile device, GPS (or equivalent) and an ad-hoc communication network connected to sensors, visits an intelligent environment supermarket and would like to acquire some merchandise. We illustrate below how this person can benefit from mobile identity.

When this person enters the supermarket, he/she is identified by means of his/her mobile device or implemented RFID tag and a special menu is displayed to him/her. His/her profile, related to his/her context identity, announces a discount if there is one.

The members of his/her social network could propose him/her a connection if they are present and even guide him to their location. Merchandise on display could communicate with his/her device to show prices and details. Location-based services could be offered to quickly find his/her specific articles.

His device could help him to find diabetic foods or any restrictions associated with specific articles. A secure Web connection could be initiated to give more information about purchases and the user account.

An adaptive screen could be used by the supermarket to show him/her information that is too extensive for his/her device screen. Payment could be carried out using payment identity stored in his/her device and even a biometric identity to prevent identity theft.

Identity information and profiling should be portable and seamless for interoperability. The identity must be managed to ensure user control. Power and performance management in this environment is a must. The concept of authentication between electronic devices is also highlighted.

In order to use identity management, the user needs an appropriate tool to facilitate the management for the disclosure of personal data. A usable and secure tool should be proposed to help even inexperienced users manage their general security needs when using the network.

We need mobile identity management, which is a concept that allows the user to keep his or her privacy, depending on the situation. By using identity management, the user's device acts in a similar way to the user. In different contexts, the user presents a different appearance. Devices controlled by identity management change their behavior similar to the way in which a user would.

Requirements for Mobile User-centric Identity Management in an AmI world

As the network evolution is toward mobility with the proliferation of ubiquitous and pervasive computing systems, the importance of identity management to build trust relationships in the context of electronic and mobile (e/m) government and business is evident [47,48]. Thereby, all these systems require advanced, automated identity management systems in order to be cost effective and easy to use.

Several mobile devices such as mobile phones, smart cards of RFID are used for mobility. As mobile devices have fixed identifiers, they are essentially providing a mobile identity that can be liked to a user. Mobile identity takes into account location data of mobile users in addition to their personal data. A recent court decision in the UK has established as proof of location of the accused the location trace of his mobile phone which implies a de facto recognition of the identity of a citizen as the identity of her mobile telephones [1].

That is why Mobile identity management (MIdm) is necessary to empower mobile users to manage their mobile identities to enforce their security and privacy interests. Mobile identity management is a special kind of identity management. For this purpose, mobile users must be able to control the disclosure of their mobile identity dependent on the respective service provider and also their location via mobile identity management systems.

Ambient Intelligence emphasizes the principles of secure communication anywhere, anytime, with anything. The evolution of AmI will directly influence identity management with this requirement to ensure mutual interaction between users and things. *Being Anywhere* will imply more and more mobility, interoperability and profiling. *At Anytime* will imply online as well as offline connection as the network does not have a 100% coverage and will imply power as well as performance management in order to optimize use battery. *With anything* will imply sensor use, biometrics and RFID interaction; and *Securely* implies more and more integration of privacy, authentication, anonymity and prevention of identity theft.

From multilateral security [49,50], Jendricke [31] has derived privacy principles for MIdm and we have completed them below with a few other important principles. Management systems are as follows:

1. Context-detection
    a. Sensors
    b. Biometrics
    c. RFID
2. Anonymity
3. Security
    a. Confidentiality
    b. Integrity
    c. Non-repudiation
    d. Availability
4. Privacy
    a. Protection of location information
5. Trustworthiness
    a. Segregation of power, separating knowledge, integrating independent parties
    b. Using Open Source
    c. Trusted seals of approval seal
6. Law Enforcement / Liability
    a. Digital evidence
    b. Digital signatures
    c. Data retention
7. Usability
    a. Comfortable and informative user interfaces
    b. Training and education
    c. Reduction of system' complexity
    d. Raising awareness
8. Affordability
    a. Power of market: Produce MIMS that are competitive and are able to reach a remarkable penetration of market
    b. Using open source building blocks
    c. Subsidies for development, use, operation, etc.
9. Power management: the energy provided by the batteries of mobile devices is limited and that energy must be used with care on energy-friendly applications and services

10. Online and offline identity proof
11. Small screen size and lower computational capability
12. Interoperability
    a. Identity needs to be portable to be understood by any device.

7. SUMMARY

The Internet is being used more and more; but, the fact that the Internet has not been developed with an adequate identity layer is a major security risk. Password fatigue and online fraud are a growing problem and are damaging user confidence. However it is a difficult problem to solve both from a technical point of view and a business model point of view. Users are not prepared to pay themselves for identity management and expect the service provider should provide it to them. It is the reason that a number of major initiatives trying to provide a more adequate identity layer for the Internet surveyed above and already present in the first version of this chapter have been discontinued due to a failing business model, for example, Sxip. If the user experience is too long or require retyping personal information, many users may not take the time to join the new service. "Social login" provided by online social networks has emerged as the main identity management solution adopted by the users to log in to new Web sites and services because they did not have to type their personal information again. It has been to the detriment to the privacy of the users but it is clear that it does not worry the users because they are not able to take into account the effect of this privacy leak in the long term. They prefer accessing the service they want to use, such as Facebook, even if it may impact their privacy in the long term. Thus, although "social login" do not fulfill all identity management requirements that have been presented in this chapter since its first version, "social login" has won over many other identity management initiatives, even if a few of them are still used underneath, e.g., OpenId. User management providers listed in Section 4 and aggregating several "social login" solutions for Web sites and services are promising. Another development concerns mobile identity management and those new user management providers may also play an importation role in this respect.

Finally, let's move on to the real interactive part of this Chapter: review questions/exercises, hands-on projects, case projects and optional team case project. The answers and/or solutions by chapter can be found in the Online Instructor's Solutions Manual.

CHAPTER REVIEW QUESTIONS/EXERCISES

True/False

1. True or False? A digital identity is a representation of an entity in a general context.
2. True or False? Identity management refers to "the process of representing, using, maintaining, deprovisioning and authenticating entities as digital identities in computer networks."

3. True or False? Privacy is a central issue, due to the fact that the official authorities of almost all countries have legal strict policies related to identity.
4. True or False? The evolution of the identity management system is away from the simplification of user experience and reinforcing authentication.
5. True or False? The security is also compromised with the proliferation of the user's password and even by it's strength.

Multiple Choice

1. The main identity management system deployed currently in the world of the Internet is known as the?
   A. Federated identity management model
   B. Identity life cycle
   C. Aggregate identity
   D. Executive management model
   E. Silo model
2. _____ in centralized identity infrastructures, can't solve the problem of cross-organizational authentication and authorization?
   A. Centrally managed repositories
   B. Information system auditors
   C. IT personnel
   D. Systems Administrators
   E. All of the above
3. A relatively simple _____ model is to build a platform that centralizes identities?
   A. Common user identity management
   B. Simple centralized identity management
   C. Unique identity management
   D. Meta directory
   E. Executive Management
4. What provides an abstraction boundary between application and the actual implementation?
   A. Single point of administration
   B. Redundant directory information
   C. Single point of reference
   D. Business impact analysis
   E. All of the above
5. What directories are not located in the same physical structure as the Web home directory, but look as if they were to Web clients?
   A. Single Sign-On
   B. Seamless
   C. Session
   D. Virtual
   E. Flexible

EXERCISE

Problem

What is a digital identity?

Hands-On Projects

Project

Why would a bank issue digital identities?

Case Projects

Problem

Does the digital identity capture the physical signature of the person?

Optional Team Case Project

Problem

What if I am already using digital certificates or credentials?

References

[1] G. Roussos, U. Patel, Mobile Identity Management: An Enacted View, Birkbeck College, University of London, City University, London, 2003.
[2] A. Westin, Privacy and Freedom, Athenaeum, New York, NY, 1967.
[3] J. Madelin, et al., BT report on: comprehensive identity management Balancing cost, risk and convenience in identity management, 2007.
[4] T. Miyata, et al., A survey on identity management protocols and standards, IEICE Trans. Inf. Syst. (2006).
[5] J.-M. Seigneur, Trust, Security and Privacy in Global Computing, PhD Thesis, Trinity College Dublin, 2005.
[6] Introduction to the Liberty Alliance Identity Architecture. Rev. 1.0, March 2003.
[7] A.B. Spantzel, et al., User Centricity: A taxonomy and open issues, IBM Zurich Research Laboratory, 2006.
[8] Independent Center for Privacy Protection (ICPP) and Studio Notarile Genghini(SNG), Identity Management Systems (IMS): Identification and Comparison Study, 2003.
[9] K. Cameron, Laws of Identity, 5/12/2005.
[10] T.M. Cooley, A Treatise on the Law of Torts, Callaghan, Chicago, 1888.
[11] Identity Management Systems (IMS): Identification and Comparison Study, Independent Center for Privacy Protection (ICPP) and Studio Notarile Genghini(SNG), 2003.
[12] David Recordon VeriSign Inc, Drummond Reed, OpenID 2.0: A Platform for User-Centric Identity Management, 2006.
[13] A user centric anonymous authorisation framework in ecommerce environment Richard Au, Harikrishna Vasanta, KimKwang Raymond Choo, Mark Looi Information Security Research Centre Queensland University of Technology, Brisbane, Australia.
[14] Federal financial institutions examination council. Authentication in an internetbanking environment. <http://www.ffiec.gov/press/pr101205.htm>, October 2005.
[15] A. Erzberg, A. Gbara, TrustBar: protecting even Naïve) Web Users from Spoofing and Phishing Attacks. <http://wwwcs.biu.ac.il/~erzbea/papaers/ecommerce/spoofing.htm>, 2004.
[16] Introduction to Usability. <http://www.usabilityfirst.com/intro/index.tx1>, 2005.

[17] A. Jøsang, S. Pope, User Centric Identity Management, AusCERT Conference, 2005.

[18] ITU (International Telecommunication Union), Geneva. <http://www.itu.org/>.

[19] A. Jøsang, et al., Usability and Privacy in identity management architectures, (AISW2007) Ballarat, Australia, 2007.

[20] Internet2, Shibboleth project. <http://shibboleth.Internet2.edu>.

[21] C. Esslison et al., RFC 2693- SPKI Certification Theory. IETF. <http://www.ietf.org/rfc/rfc2693.txt>, Sep. 1999.

[22] T. Miyata, et al., A survey on identity management protocols and standards, IEICE Trans. Inf. Syst. (2006).

[23] Kantara Initiative. <http://kantarainitiative.org/>.

[24] Microsoft, a technical ref. for InfoCard in windows. <http://msdn.microsoft.com/winfx/reference/info-card/,2005>.

[25] J. Merrels, SXIP Identity. DIX: Digital Identity Exchange Protocol. Internet Draft, March 2006.

[26] Higgings trust framework project. <http://www.eclipse.org/higgins/>, 2006.

[27] A. Jaokar, T. Fish. Mobile Web 2.0, a book 2007.

[28] Liberty developer tutorial. <http://www.projectliberty.org/resources/LAP_DIDW_Oct-15_2003_jp.pdf>.

[29] XACML. <http://www.oasis-open.org/committees/tc_home.php?wg_abbrev=xacml>.

[30] Liberty alliance, liberty ID-FF architecture overview. Liberty alliance project, 2005.

[31] U. Jendricke et al., Mobile identity management, UBICOMP, 2002.

[32] Sxip bankruptcy. <http://techcrunch.com/2008/05/22/identity-20-startup-sxips-into-the-deadpool/>.

[33] IETF OAuth. <https://www.ietf.org/mailman/listinfo/oauth>.

[34] Twitter. <http://www.twitter.com>.

[35] Facebook. <http://www.facebook.com>.

[36] LinkedIn. <http://www.linkedin.com>.

[37] Google. <http://www.google.com>.

[38] Janrain. <http://www.janrain.com>.

[39] OneAll. <http://www.oneall.com>.

[40] LoginRadius. <http://www.loginradius.com>.

[41] Gigya. <http://www.gigya.com>.

[42] S. Garfinkel, B. Rosenberg, RFID, Applications, Security and Privacy, Addison Wesley, Boston, 2006.

[43] S.A. Weis, et al., Security and privacy aspects of low-Cost radio frequency identification systems, *Proc. of the First International Conference on Security in Pervasive Computing*, March 2003.

[44] User-centric identity management in open mobile environments Mario Hoffmann Fraunhofer-Institute for secure telecooperation (SIT).

[45] A. Jøsang, et al., Trust Requirements in Identity Management, AISW, 2005.

[46] Wong, et al., Polonius: an identity authentication system, *Proceedings of the 1985 IEEE Symposium on security and Privacy*.

[47] MyGrocer Consortium, Mygrocer whitepaper, 2002.

[48] M. Wieser, The Computer for the twenty-first century, *Scientific American*, 1991.

[49] K. Rannenberg, Multilateral security? a concept and examples for balanced security, *Proc. of the Ninth ACM new security Paradigms Workshop* 2000.

[50] K. Reichenbach, et al., individual management of personal reachability in mobile communications, *Proc. of the IFIP TC11 (Sec'97)*.

Intrusion Prevention and Detection Systems

Christopher Day
Terremark Worldwide, Inc.

1. WHAT IS AN 'INTRUSION' ANYWAY?

Information security concerns itself with the confidentiality, integrity and availability of information systems and the information or data they contain and process. An 'intrusion' then is any action taken by an adversary that has a negative impact on the confidentiality, integrity, or availability of that information. Given such a broad definition of 'intrusion' it is instructive to examine a number of commonly occurring classes of information system (IS) intrusions.

2. PHYSICAL THEFT

Having physical access to a computer system allows an adversary to bypass most security protections put in place to prevent unauthorized access. By stealing a computer system, the adversary has all the physical access he or she could want and unless the sensitive data on the system is strongly encrypted (see sidebar, "Definition of Encryption"), the data is very likely to be compromised. This issue is most prevalent with laptop loss and theft. Given the processing and storage capacity of even low-cost laptops today, a great deal of sensitive information can be put at risk if a laptop containing this data is stolen. In May of 2006, it was revealed that over 26 million military veterans' personal information including names, social security numbers, addresses, and some disability data was on a Veteran Affairs staffer's laptop that was stolen from his home [2a].

The stolen data was of the type that is often used to commit identity theft and due to the large number of impacted veterans, there was a great deal of concern about this theft and the lack of security around such a sensitive collection of data. In another example, in May of 2012 it was revealed that an unencrypted laptop containing medical records for 2,159 patients was stolen Boston Children's Hospital staffer while travelling overseas for a conference [2b].

DEFINITION OF ENCRYPTION

Encryption is the process of protecting the content or meaning of a message or other kinds of data [3]. Modern encryption algorithms are based on complex mathematical functions that scramble the original, clear-text message or data in such a way that makes it difficult or impossible for an adversary to read or access the data without the proper key to reverse the scrambling.

The encryption key is typically a large number of values that when fed into the encryption algorithm scrambles and unscrambles the data being protected and without which it is extremely difficult or impossible to decrypt encrypted data. The science of encryption is called cryptography and is a broad and technical subject.

3. ABUSE OF PRIVILEGES (THE INSIDER THREAT)

An insider is an individual who, due to their role in the organization, has some level of authorized access to the IS environment and systems. The level of access can range from that of a regular user to a system administrator with nearly unlimited privileges. When an insider abuses their privileges the impact can be devastating. Even a relatively limited-privilege user is already starting with an advantage over an outsider due to their knowledge of the IS environment, critical business processes, and potential knowledge of security weaknesses or 'soft spots'. An insider may use their access to steal sensitive data such as customer databases, trade secrets, national security secrets, or personally identifiable information (PII) (see sidebar, "Definition of Personally Identifiable Information"). Because they are a trusted user and given that many intrusion detection systems are designed to monitor for attacks from outsiders, an insider's privileged abuse can go on for a long time unnoticed thus compounding the damage. In 2010, US soldier Bradley Manning allegedly utilized his legitimate access to the Secret Internet Protocol Router Network (SIPRNet) to pass classified information to the whistleblower website WikiLeaks in what has been described as the largest known theft of classified information in US history [4]. An appropriately privileged user may also use their access to make unauthorized modifications to systems that can undermine the security of the environment. These changes can range from creating "backdoor" accounts used to preserve access in the event of termination to installing so-called "logic bombs" which are programs designed to cause damage to systems or data at some predetermined point in time, often as a form of retribution for some real or perceived sleight.

DEFINITION OF PERSONALLY IDENTIFIABLE INFORMATION

Personally Identifiable Information (PII) is a set of information such as name, address, social security number, financial account number, credit card number, and driver's license number. This class of information is considered particularly sensitive due to its value to identify thieves and others who commit financial crimes such as credit card fraud. Most states in the United States have some form of data breach disclosure law which imposes a burden of notification on any organization which suffers unauthorized access, loss, or theft of unencrypted PII. It is worth noting that all of the current laws provide a level of 'Safe Harbor' for organizations that suffer a PII loss if the PII was encrypted. California's SB1386 was the first and arguably most well known of the disclosure laws.

4. UNAUTHORIZED ACCESS BY OUTSIDER

An outsider is considered anyone who does not have authorized access privileges to an information system or environment. To gain access the outsider may try to gain possession of valid system credentials via social engineering or even by guessing username and password pairs in a brute force attack. Alternatively, the outsider may attempt to exploit a vulnerability in the target system to gain access. Often the result of successfully exploiting a system vulnerability leads to some form of high-privileged access to the target, such as an "Administrator" or Administrator-equivalent account on a Microsoft Windows system or "root" or root-equivalent account on a UNIX or Linux-based system. Once an outsider has this level of access on a system he or she effectively "owns" that system and can steal data or use the system as a launching point to attack other systems.

5. MALWARE INFECTION

Malware can be generally defined as "a set of instructions that run on your computer and make your system do something that allow an attacker to make it do what he wants it to do" [5]. Historically, malware (see sidebar, "Classifying Malware") in the form of viruses and worms was more of a disruptive nuisance than a real threat but it has been evolving as the weapon of choice for many attackers due to the increased sophistication, stealthiness, and scalability of intrusion-focused malware. Today, we see malware being used by intruders to gain access to systems, search for valuable data such as PII and passwords, monitor real-time communications, provide remote access/control, and automatically attack other systems just to name a few capabilities. Using malware as an attack method also provides the attacker with a "stand-off" capability that reduces the risk of identification, pursuit, and prosecution. By "stand-off" we mean the ability to launch the malware via a number of anonymous methods such as an insecure, open public wireless access point and once the malware has gained access to the intended target or targets, manage the malware via a distributed command and control system such as Internet Relay Chat (IRC), web site pages, dynamic DNS, as well as completely novel mechanisms. Not only does the command and control network help mask the location and identity of the attacker but it also provides a scalable way to manage many compromised systems at once, maximizing the results for the attacker. In some cases the number of controlled machines can be astronomical, such as with the Storm worm infection which, depending on the estimate, ranged somewhere between one and ten million compromised systems [6]. These large collections of compromised systems are often referred to as "bot-nets".

CLASSIFYING MALWARE

Malware takes many forms but can be roughly classified by function and replication method.

- *Virus*: Self-replicating code that attaches itself to another program. It typically relies on human interaction to start the host program and activate the virus. A virus usually has a limited function set and its creator has no further interaction with it once released. Examples are Melissa, Michelangelo, and Sobig.
- *Worm*: Self-replicating code that propagates over a network, usually without human interaction. Most worms take advantage of a known vulnerability in systems and compromise those that aren't properly patched. Worm creators have begun experimenting with updateable code and payloads, such as seen with the Storm worm [5]. Examples are Code Red, SQL Slammer, and Blaster.
- *Backdoor*: A program that bypasses standard security controls to provide an attacker access, often in a stealthy way. Backdoors rarely have self-replicating capability and are either installed manually by an attacker after compromising a system to facilitate future access or by other self-propagating malware as payload. Examples are Back Orifice, Tini, and netcat (netcat has legitimate uses as well).

- *Trojan Horse*: A program that masquerades as a legitimate, useful program while also performing malicious functions in the background. Trojans are often used to steal data or monitor user actions and can provide a backdoor function as well. Examples of two well-known programs that have had Trojaned versions circulated on the Internet are tcpdump and Kazaa.
- *User-level Rootkit*: Trojan/ backdoor code that modifies operating system software so the attacker can maintain privileged access on a machine but remain hidden. For example, the rootkit will remove malicious processes from user-requested process lists. This form of rootkit is called user-level because it manipulates operating system components utilized by users. This form of rootkit can often be uncovered by the use of trusted tools and software since the core of the operating system is still unaffected. Examples of user-level rootkits are the Linux Rootkit (LRK) family and FakeGINA.
- *Kernel-level Rootkit*: Trojan/ backdoor code that modifies the core or kernel of the operating system to provide the intruder the highest level of access and stealth. A kernel-level rootkit inserts itself into the core of the operating system, the kernel, and intercepts system

calls and thus can remain hidden even from trusted tools brought onto the system from the outside by an investigator. Effectively, nothing the compromised system tells a user can be trusted and detecting and removing kernel-level rootkits is very difficult and often requires advanced technologies and techniques. Examples are Adore and Hacker Defender.

- *Blended Malware*: More recent forms of malware combine features and capabilities discussed above into one program. For example, one might see a Trojan Horse that once activated by the user inserts a backdoor utilizing user-level rootkit capabilities to stay hidden and provide a remote handler with access. Examples of blended malware are Lion and Bugbear.

6. THE ROLE OF THE '0-DAY'

The Holy Grail for vulnerability researchers and exploit writers is to discover a previously unknown and exploitable vulnerability, often referred to as a 0-day exploit (pronounced 'zero day' or 'oh day'). Given that others have not discovered the vulnerability, all systems running the vulnerable code will be unpatched and possible targets for attack and compromise. The danger of a given 0-day is a function of how widespread the vulnerable software is and what level of access it gives the attacker. For example, a reliable 0-day for something as widespread as the ubiquitous Apache Web server that somehow yields root or Administrator-level access to the attacker is far more dangerous and valuable than an exploit that works against an obscure point-of-sale system used by only a few hundred users (unless the attacker's target is that very set of users).

In addition to potentially having a large, vulnerable target set to exploit, the owner of a 0-day also has the advantage that most intrusion detection and prevention systems will not trigger on the exploit for the very fact that it has never been seen before and the various IDS/IPS technologies will not have signature patterns for the exploit yet. We will discuss this issue in more detail later.

It is this combination of many unpatched targets and the ability to potentially evade many forms of intrusion detection and prevention systems that make 0-days such a powerful weapon in the hands of an attacker. Many legitimate security and vulnerability researchers explore software systems to uncover 0-days and report them to the appropriate software vendor in the hopes of preventing malicious individuals from finding and using them first. Those who intend to use 0-days for illicit purposes guard the knowledge of a 0-day very carefully lest it become widely and publically known and effective countermeasures, including vendor software patches, can be deployed.

One of the more disturbing issues regarding 0-days is their lifetimes. The lifetime of a 0-day is the amount of time between the discovery of the vulnerability and public disclosure through vendor or researcher announcement, mailing lists, and so on. By the very nature of 0-day discovery and disclosure it is difficult to get reliable statistics on lifetimes but one vulnerability research organization claims their studies indicate an average 0-day lifetime of 348 days [7]. Hence, if malicious attackers have a high-value 0-day in hand, they may have almost a year to put it to most effective use. If used in a stealthy manner so as not to tip off system defenders, vendors, and researchers this sort of 0-day can yield many high-value compromised systems for the attackers. While there has been no official substantiation, there has been a great deal of speculation that the "Titan Rain" series of attacks against sensitive United States government networks between 2003 and 2005 utilized a set of 0-days against Microsoft software [8,9].

7. THE ROGUE'S GALLERY: ATTACKERS AND MOTIVES

Now that we have examined some of the more common forms computer system intrusions take, it is worthwhile to discuss those who are behind these attacks and attempt to understand their motivations. The appropriate selection of intrusion detection and prevention technologies is dependent on the threat being defended against, the class of adversary and the value of the asset being protected.

While it is always risky to generalize, those who attack computer systems for illicit purposes can be placed into a number of broad categories. At minimum this gives us a "capability spectrum" of attackers to begin to understand motivations and, therefore, threats.

Script Kiddy

The pejorative term "script kiddy" is used to describe those who have little or no skill at writing or understanding how vulnerabilities are discovered and exploits written but download and utilize other's exploits available on the Internet to attack vulnerable systems. Typically, script kiddies are not a threat to a well managed, patched environment as they are usually relegated to using publically known and available exploits for which patches and detection signatures already exist.

Joy Rider

This type of attacker is often represented by those with potentially significant skills in discovering vulnerabilities and writing exploits but who rarely have any real malicious intent when they access systems they are not authorized on. In a sense they are "exploring" for the pleasure of it. However, while their intentions are not directly malicious, their actions can represent a major source of distraction and cost to system administrators who must respond to the intrusion especially if the compromised system contained sensitive data such as PII where a public disclosure may be required.

Mercenary

Since the late nineties there has been a growing market for those who possess the skills to compromise computer systems and are willing to sell them and those willing to purchase these skills [10]. Organized crime is a large consumer of these services and computer crime has seen a significant increase in both frequency and severity over the last decade, primarily

TABLE 5.1 PII Values.

Goods and Services	Percentage	Range of Prices
Financial Accounts	22%	$10–$1,000
Credit Card Information	13%	$.40-$20
Identity Information	9%	$1–$15
eBay Accounts	7%	$1–$8
Scams	7%	$2.5–$50/week for hosting $25 for design
Mailers	6%	$1–$10
Email Addresses	5%	$.83-$10/MB
Email Passwords	5%	$4–$30
Drop (request or offer)	5%	10%–50% of drop amount
Proxies	5%	$1.50–$30

(Complied from Miami Electronic Crimes Task Force and Symantec Global Internet Security Threat Report (2008)).

driven by direct, illicit financial gain and identity theft [11]. In fact, so successful have these groups become that a full-blown market has emerged including support organizations offering technical support for rented bot-nets and online trading environments for the exchange of stolen credit card data and PII. Stolen data has a tangible financial value as can be seen by Table 5.1, which indicates the dollar value ranges for various types of PII.

Nation-State Backed

Nations performing espionage against other nations do not ignore the potential for intelligence gathering via information technology systems. Sometimes this espionage takes the form of malware injection and system compromises such as the previously mentioned Titan Rain attack while other times it may take the form of electronic data interception of unencrypted e-mail and other messaging protocols. A number of nations have developed or are developing an information warfare capability designed to impair or incapacitate an enemy's Internet-connected systems, command-and-control systems, and other information technology capability [12]. These sorts of capabilities were demonstrated in 2007 against Estonia, allegedly by Russian sympathizers, utilizing a sustained series of denial-of-service attacks designed to make certain Websites unreachable as well as interfere with online activities such as e-mail and mission-critical systems such as telephone exchanges [13].

8. A BRIEF INTRODUCTION TO TCP/IP

Throughout the history of computing, there have been numerous networking protocols, the structured rules computers use to communicate with each other, but none have been as successful and become as ubiquitous as the Transmission Control Protocol/Internet Protocol (TCP/IP) suite of protocols. TCP/IP is the protocol suite used on the Internet and the vast majority of enterprise and government networks have now implemented TCP/IP on their networks. Due to this ubiquity almost all attacks against computer systems seen today are designed to be launched over a TCPI/IP network and thus the majority of intrusion detection and prevention systems are designed to operate with and monitor TCP/IP-based networks. Therefore, to better understand the nature of these technologies it is important to have a working knowledge of TCP/IP. While a complete description of TCP/IP is beyond the scope of this chapter, there are numerous excellent references and tutorials for those interested in learning more [14,15]. Three features that have made TCP/IP so popular and widespread are [16]:

1. Open protocol standards that are freely available. This and independence from any particular operating system or computing hardware means TCP/IP can be deployed on nearly any computing device imaginable.
2. Hardware, transmission media and device independence. TCP/IP can operate over numerous physical devices and network types such as Ethernet, Token Ring, optical, radio, and satellite.
3. A consistent and globally scalable addressing scheme. This ensures that any two uniquely addressed network nodes can communicate (notwithstanding any traffic restrictions implemented for security or policy reasons) with each other even if those nodes are on different sides of the planet.

9. THE TCP/IP DATA ARCHITECTURE AND DATA ENCAPSULATION

The best way to describe and visualize the TCP/IP protocol suite is to think of it as a layered stack of functions, as shown in Figure 5.1.

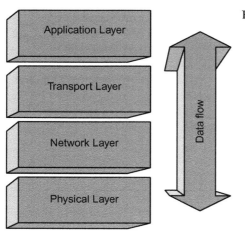

FIGURE 5.1   TCP/IP data architecture stack.

Each layer is responsible for a set of services and capabilities provided to the layers above and below it. This layered model allows developers and engineers to modularize the functionality in a given layer and minimize the impacts of changes on other layers. Each layer performs a series of functions on data as it is prepared for network transport or received from the network. How those functions are performed internal to a given layer is hidden from the other layers and as long as the agreed upon rules and standards are adhered to with regards to how data is passed from layer to layer, the inner workings of a given layer are isolated from any other.

The Application Layer is concerned with applications and processes, including those that users interact with such as browsers, e-mail, instant messaging and other network-aware programs. There may also be numerous applications in the Application Layer running on a computer system that interact with the network but users have little interaction with such as routing protocols.

The Transport Layer is responsible for handling data flow between applications on different hosts on the network. There are two Transport protocols in the TCP/IP suite: the Transport Control Protocol (TCP) and the User Datagram Protocol (UDP). TCP is a connection or session oriented protocol which provides a number of services to the above application such as reliable delivery via Positive Acknowledgement with Retransmission (PAR), packet sequencing to account for out-of-sequence receipt of packets, receive buffer management, and error detection. In contrast, UDP is a low-overhead, connectionless protocol that provides no delivery acknowledgement or other session services. Any necessary application reliability must be built into the application whereas with TCP, the application need not worry about the details of packet delivery. Each protocol serves a specific purpose and allows maximum flexibility to application developers and engineers. There may be numerous network services running on a computer system each built on either TCP or UDP (or, in some cases, both) so both protocols utilize the concept of *ports* to identify a specific network service and direct data appropriately. For example, a computer may be running a Web server and standard Web services are offered on TCP port 80. That same computer could also be running an e-mail system utilizing the Simple Mail Transport Protocol (SMTP) which is by standard offered on TCP port 25. Finally, this server may also be running a Domain Name Server (DNS) server on both TCP and UDP port 53. As can be seen, the concept of ports allows multiple TCP and UDP services to be run on the same computer system without interfering with each other.

The Network Layer is primarily responsible for packet addressing and routing through the network. The Internet Protocol (IP) manages this process within the TCP/IP protocol suite. One very important construct found in IP is the concept of an IP address. Each system running on a TCP/IP network must have at least one unique address for other computer systems to direct traffic to it. An IP address is represented by a 32-bit number which is usually represented as four integers ranging from 0 to 255 separated by decimals such as 192.168.1.254. This representation is often referred to as a *dotted quad*. The IP address actually contains two pieces of information in it: the network address and the node address. To know where the network address ends and the node address begins a *subnet mask* is used to indicate the number of bits in the IP address assigned to the network address and is usually designated as a slash and a number such as '/24'. If the example address of 192.168.1.254

has a subnet mask of /24, then we know that the network address is 24 bits or 192.168.1 and the node address is 254. If we were presented with a subnet mask of /16 then we would know the network address is 192.168 while the node address is 1.254. Subnet masking allows network designers to construct subnets of various sizes ranging from two nodes (a subnet mask of /30) to literally millions of nodes (a subnet of /8) or anything in between. The topic of subnetting and its impact on addressing and routing is a complex one and the interested reader is referred to [14] for more detail.

The Physical Layer is responsible for interaction with the physical network medium. Depending on the specifics of the medium this may include functions such as collision avoidance, the transmission and reception of packets or datagrams, basic error checking, and so on. The Physical Layer handles all of the details of interfacing with the network medium and isolates the upper layers from the physical details.

Another important concept in TCP/IP is that of data encapsulation. Data is passed up and down the stack as it travels from a network-aware program or application in the Application Layer, is packaged for transport across the network by the Transport and Network Layer and eventually placed on the transmission medium (copper or fiber optic cable, radio, satellite, and so on) by the Physical Layer. As data is handed down the stack, each layer adds its own header (a structured collection of fields of data) to the data passed to it by the above layer. Figure 5.2 illustrates three important headers: the IP header, the TCP header, and the UDP header. The reader will note the various headers are where layer-specific constructs such as IP address and TCP or UDP port numbers are placed so the appropriate layer can access this information and act on the accordingly.

The receiving layer is not concerned with the content of the data passed to it, only that the data is given to it in a way compliant with the protocol rules. The Physical Layer places the completed packet (the full collection of headers and application data) onto the transmission medium for handling by the physical network. When a packet is received, the reverse process occurs. As the packet travels up the stack, each layer removes its respective header, inspects the header content for instructions on which upper layer in the protocol stack to hand the remaining data to, and passes the data to the appropriate layer. This process is repeated until all TCP/IP headers have been removed and the appropriate application is handed the data. The encapsulation process is illustrated in Figure 5.3.

To best illustrate these concepts, let us explore a somewhat simplified example. Figure 5.4 illustrates the various steps in this example. Assume a user, Alice, wishes to send an e-mail to her colleague Bob at Cool Company.com:

1. Alice launches her e-mail program and types in Bob's e-mail address, *bob@coolcompany. com*, as well as her message to Bob. Alice's e-mail program constructs a properly formatted SMTP-compliant message, resolves Cool Company's e-mail server address utilizing a DNS query, and passes the message to the TCP component of the Transport Layer for processing.
2. The TCP process adds a TCP header in front of the SMTP message fields including such pertinent information as the source TCP port (randomly chosen as a port number greater than 1024, in this case 1354), the destination port (port 25 for SMTP e-mail), and other TCP-specific information such as sequence numbers and receive buffer sizes.

IP, Version 4 Header

4-bit version	4-bit header length	8-bit type of service	16-bit total packet length (value in bytes)	
16-bit IP/fragment identification			3-bit flags	13-bit fragment offset
8-bit time to live (TTL)		8-bit protcol ID	16-bit header checksum	
32-bit source IP address				
32-bit destination IP address				
options (if present)				
data (inlcuding upper layer headers)				

TCP Header

16-bit source port number		16-bit destination port number	
32-bit sequence number			
32-bit acknowledgement number			
4-bit TCP header length	6-bit reserved	6-bit flags	16-bit window size
16-bit TCP checksum		16-bit urgent pointer	
options (if present)			
data (if any)			

UDP Header

16-bit source port number	16-bit destination port number
16-bit UDP length (header plus data)	16-bit UDP checksum
data (if any)	

(sourced from Request for Comment (RFC) 791, 793, 768)

FIGURE 5.2   IP, TCP, and UDP headers.

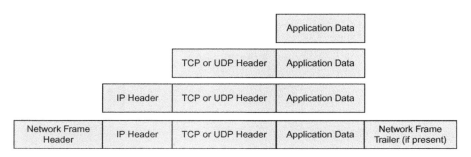

FIGURE 5.3   TCP/IP encapsulation.

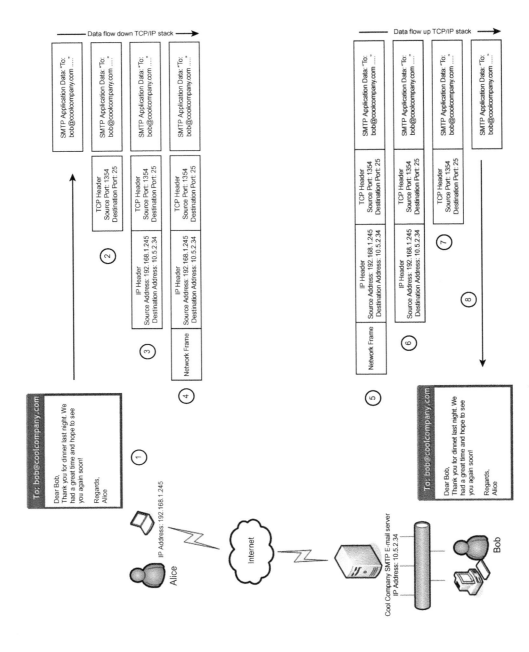

FIGURE 5.4 Application and network interaction example.

3. This new data package (SMTP message plus TCP header) is then handed to the Network Layer and an IP header is added with such important information as the source IP address of Alice's computer, the destination IP address of Cool Company's e-mail server, and other IP specific information such as packet lengths, error-detection checksums, and so on.

4. This complete IP packet is then handed to the Physical Layer for transmission onto the physical network medium, which will add network layer headers as appropriate. Numerous packets may be needed to fully transmit the entire e-mail message depending on the various network media and protocols that must be traversed by the packets as they leave Alice's network and travel the Internet to Cool Company's e-mail server. The details will be handled by the intermediate systems and any required updates or changes to the packet headers will be made by those systems.

5. When Cool Company's e—mail server receives the packets from its local network medium via the Physical Layer, it removes the network frame and hands the remaining data to the Network Layer.

6. The Network Layer strips off the IP header and hands the remaining data to the TCP component of the Transport Layer.

7. The TCP process removes and examines the TCP header to, among other tasks, examine the destination port (again, 25 for e-mail), and finally hand the SMTP message to the SMTP server process.

8. The SMTP application performs further application specific processing as well delivery to Bob's e-mail application by starting the encapsulation process all over again to transit the internal network between Bob's PC and the server.

It is important to understand that network-based computer system attacks can occur at every layer of the TCP/IP stack and thus an effective intrusion detection and prevention program must be able to inspect at each layer and act accordingly. Intruders may manipulate any number of fields within a TCP/IP packet to attempt to bypass security processes or systems including the application-specific data, all in an attempt to gain access and control of the target system.

10. SURVEY OF INTRUSION DETECTION AND PREVENTION TECHNOLOGIES

Now that we have discussed the threats and those who pose them to information systems as well as examined the underlying protocol suite in use on the Internet and enterprise networks today we are prepared to explore the various technologies available to detect and prevent intrusions. It is important to note that while technologies such as firewalls, a robust patching program and disk and file encryption can be part of a powerful intrusion prevention program these are considered static preventative defenses and will not be discussed here. In this section, we will discuss various dynamic systems and technologies that can assist in the detection and prevention of attacks on information systems.

11. ANTI-MALWARE SOFTWARE

We have discussed malware and its various forms previously. Anti-malware software, in the past typically referred to as anti-virus software, is designed to analyze files and programs for known signatures, or patterns, in the data that make up the file or program and indicates malicious code is present. This signature scanning is often accomplished in a multi-tiered approach where the entire hard drive of the computer is scanned sequentially during idle periods and any file accessed is scanned immediately to help prevent dormant code in a file that has not been scanned from becoming active. When an infected file or malicious program is found, it is prevented from running and either quarantined (moved to a location for further inspection by a system administrator) or simply deleted from the system. There are also appliance-based solutions that can be placed on the network to examine certain classes of traffic such as e-mail before being delivered to the end systems.

In any case, the primary weakness of the signature-based scanning method is that if the software does not have a signature for a particular piece of malware then the malware will be effectively invisible to the software and will be able to run without interference. A signature may not exist because a particular instance of the anti-malware software may not have an up to date signature database or the malware may be new or modified so as to avoid detection. To overcome this increasingly common issue, more sophisticated anti-malware software will monitor for known-malicious behavioral patterns instead of, or in addition to, signature based scanning. Behavioral pattern monitoring can take many forms such as observing the system calls all programs make and identifying patterns of calls that are anomalous or known-malicious. Another common method is to create a white list of allowed known-normal activity and prevent all other activity or at least prompt the user when a non-while listed activity is attempted. While these methods overcome some of the limitations of the signature-based model and can help detect previously never seen malware, they come with the price of higher false positive rates and/or additional administrative burdens.

While anti-malware software can be evaded by new or modified malware, it still serves a useful purpose as a component in a defense-in-depth strategy, as illustrated in Figure 5.5. A well maintained anti-malware infrastructure will detect and prevent known forms, thus freeing up resources to focus on other threats, but it can also be used to help speed and simplify containment and eradication of a malware infection once an identifying signature can be developed and deployed.

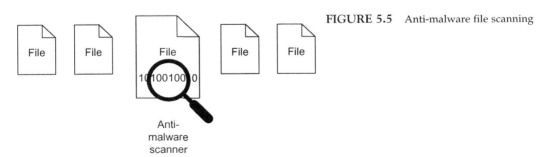

FIGURE 5.5 Anti-malware file scanning

12. NETWORK-BASED INTRUSION DETECTION SYSTEMS

For many years, network-based intrusion detection systems (NIDS) have been the work-horse of information security technology and in many ways have become synonymous with intrusion detection [17]. NIDS function in one of three modes: signature detection, anomaly detection, and hybrid. A signature-based NIDS operates by passively examining all the network traffic flowing past its sensor interface or interfaces and examines the TCP/IP packets for signatures of known attacks as illustrated in Figure 5.6.

TCP/IP packet headers are also often inspected to search for nonsensical header field values sometimes used by attackers in an attempt to circumvent filters and monitors. In much the same way that signature-based anti-malware software can be defeated by never before seen malware or malware sufficiently modified to no longer possess the signature used for detection, signature-based NIDS will be blind to any attack it does not have a signature for. While this can be a very serious limitation, signature-based NIDS are still useful due to most system's ability for the operator to add custom signatures to sensors. This allows security and network engineers to rapidly deploy monitoring and alarming capability on their networks in the event they discover an incident or are suspicious about certain activity. Signature-based NIDS are also useful to monitor for known-attacks and ensure none of those are successful at breaching systems, freeing up resources to investigate or monitor other more serious threats.

NIDS designed to detect anomalies in network traffic build statistical or baseline models for the traffic they monitor and raise an alarm on any traffic that deviates significantly from those models. There are numerous methods for detecting network traffic anomalies

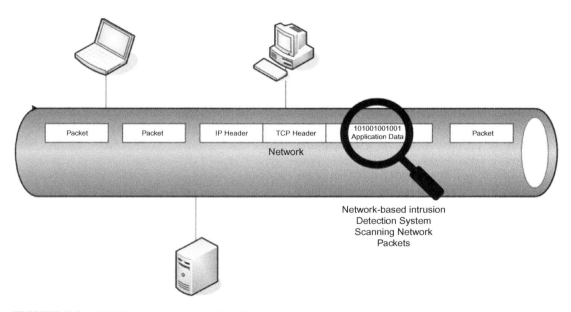

FIGURE 5.6   NIDS device scanning packets flowing past sensor interface.

but one of the most common involves checking traffic for compliance with various protocols standards such as TCP/IP for the underlying traffic and application layer protocols such as HTTP for Web traffic, SMTP for e-mail and so on. Many attacks against applications or the underlying network attempt to cause system malfunctions by violating the protocol standard in ways unanticipated by the system developers and which the targeted protocol handling layer does not deal with properly. Unfortunately, there are entire classes of attacks that do not violate any protocol standard and thus will not be detected by this model of anomaly detection. Another model commonly used is to build a model for user behavior and to generate an alarm when a user deviates from the 'normal' patterns. For example, if Alice never logs into the network after 9 pm and suddenly a logon attempt is seen from Alice's account at 3 am, this would constitute a significant deviation from normal usage patterns and generate an alarm. Some of the main drawbacks of anomaly detection systems are defining the models of what is normal and what is malicious, defining what is a significant enough deviation from the norm to warrant an alarm, and defining a sufficiently comprehensive model or models to cover the immense range of behavioral and traffic patterns that are likely to be seen on any given network. Due to this complexity and the relative immaturity of adaptable, learning anomaly detection technology, there are very few production-quality systems available today. However, due to not relying on static signatures and the potential of a successful implementation of an anomaly detection NIDS for detecting 0-day attacks and new or custom malware is so tantalizing that much research continues in this space.

A hybrid system takes the best qualities of both signature-based and anomaly detection NIDS and integrates them into a single system to attempt to overcome the weaknesses of both models. Many commercial NIDS now implement a hybrid model by utilizing signature matching due to its speed and flexibility while incorporating some level of anomaly detection to, at minimum, flag suspicious traffic for closer examination by those responsible for monitoring the NIDS alerts.

Aside from the primary criticism of signature-based NIDS their depending on static signatures, common additional criticisms of NIDS are they tend to produce a lot of false alerts either due to imprecise signature construction or poor tuning of the sensor to better match the environment, poor event correlation resulting in many alerts for a related incident, the inability to monitor encrypted network traffic, difficulty dealing with very high speed networks such as those operating at 10 gigabits per second, and no ability to intervene during a detected attack. This last criticism is one of the driving reasons behind the development of intrusion prevention systems.

13. NETWORK-BASED INTRUSION PREVENTION SYSTEMS

While NIDS are designed to passively monitor traffic and raise alarms when suspicious traffic is detected, network-based intrusion prevention systems (NIPS) are designed to go one step further and actually try to prevent the attack from succeeding. This is typically achieved by inserting the NIPS device inline with the traffic it is monitoring. Each network packet is inspected and only passed if it does not trigger some sort of alert based on a signature match or anomaly threshold. Suspicious packets are discarded and an alert is generated.

The ability to intervene and stop known attacks, in contrast to the passive monitoring of NIDS, is the greatest benefit of NIPS. However, NIPS suffers from the same drawbacks and limitations as discussed for NIDS such as heavy reliance on static signatures, inability to examine encrypted traffic, and difficulties with very high network speeds. In addition, false alarms are much more significant due to the fact that the NIPS may discard that traffic even though it is not really malicious. If the destination system is business or mission critical, this action could have significant negative impact on the functioning of the system. Thus, great care must be taken to tune the NIPS during a training period where there is no packet discard before allowing it to begin blocking of any detected, malicious traffic.

14. HOST-BASED INTRUSION PREVENTION SYSTEMS

A complementary approach to network-based intrusion prevention is to place the detection and prevention system on the system requiring protection as an installed software package. Host-based intrusion prevention systems (HIPS), while often utilizing some of the same signature-based technology found in NIDS and NIPS, also take advantage of being installed on the protected system to protect by monitoring and analyzing what other processes on the system are doing at a very detailed level. This process monitoring is very similar to that which we discussed in the anti-malware software section and involves observing system calls, interprocess communication, network traffic, and other behavioral patterns for suspicious activity. Another benefit of HIPS is that encrypted network traffic can be analyzed after the decryption process has occurred on the protected system thus providing an opportunity to detect an attack that would have been hidden from a NIPS or NIDS device monitoring network traffic.

Again, as with NIPS and NIDS, HIPS is only as effective as its signature database, anomaly detection model, or behavioral analysis routines. Also, the presence of HIPS on a protected system does incur processing and system resource utilization overhead and on a very busy system, this overhead may be unacceptable. However, given the unique advantages of HIPS, such as being able to inspect encrypted network traffic, it is often used as a complement to NIPS and NIDS in a targeted fashion and this combination can be very effective.

15. SECURITY INFORMATION MANAGEMENT SYSTEMS

Modern network environment generate a tremendous amount of security event and log data via firewalls, network routers and switches, NIDS/NIPS, servers, anti-malware systems and so on. Envisioned as a solution to help manage and analyze all of this information, security information management (SIM) systems have since evolved to provide data reduction, to reduce the sheer quantity of information that must analyzed, and event correlation capabilities that assist a security analyst to make sense of it all [18]. A SIM system not only acts as a centralized repository for such data, it helps organize it and provides an analyst the ability to do complex queries across this entire database. One of the primary benefits of a SIM system is that data from disparate systems is normalized into a uniform database structure thus allowing an analyst to investigate suspicious activity or a known incident across different aspects and elements of the IT environment. Often an intrusion will leave various types of 'footprints' in the logs (see checklist: "An Agenda For Action For Logging Capabilities") of different systems involved in the incident and bringing these all together and providing the complete picture for the analyst or investigator is the job of the SIM.

AN AGENDA FOR ACTION FOR LOGGING CAPABILITIES

Network-based intrusion detection and prevention systems (IDPSs) typically perform extensive logging of data related to detected events. This data can be used to confirm the validity of alerts, to investigate incidents, and to correlate events between the IDPS and other logging sources. Data fields commonly logged by network-based IDPSs include the following (check all tasks completed):

_____1. Timestamp (usually date and time).

_____2. Connection or session ID (typically a consecutive or unique number assigned to each TCP connection or to like groups of packets for connectionless protocols).

_____3. Event or alert type.

_____4. Rating (priority, severity, impact, confidence).

_____5. Network, transport, and application layer protocols.

_____6. Source and destination IP addresses.

_____7. Source and destination TCP or UDP ports, or ICMP types and codes.

_____8. Number of bytes transmitted over the connection.

_____9. Decoded payload data, such as application requests and responses.

_____10. State-related information (authenticated username).

_____11. Prevention action performed (if any).

_____12. Most network-based IDPSs can also perform packet captures. Typically this is done once an alert has occurred, either to record subsequent activity in the connection or to record the entire connection if the IDPS has been temporarily storing the previous packets.

Even with modern and powerful event correlation engines and data reduction routines, however, a SIM system is only as effective as the analyst examining the output. Fundamentally, SIM systems are a reactive technology, like NIDS, and because extracting useful and actionable information from them often requires a strong understanding of the various systems sending data to the SIM, the analysts skill set and experience become very critical to the effectiveness of the SIM as an intrusion detection system [19]. SIM systems also play a significant role during incident response as often times, evidence of an intrusion can be found in the various logs stored on the SIM.

16. NETWORK SESSION ANALYSIS

Network session data represents a high-level summary of 'conversations' occurring between computer systems [20]. No specifics about the content of the conversation such as packet payloads is maintained but various elements about the conversation are kept and can be very useful when investigated an incident or as an indicator of suspicious activity. There are a number of ways to generate and process network session data ranging from vendor specific implementations such as Cisco's NetFlow [21] to session data reconstruction from full traffic analysis using tools such as Argus [22]. However the session data is generated, there are a number of common elements constituting the session such as source IP address, source port, destination IP address, destination port, timestamp information, and an array of metrics about the session such as bytes transferred and packet distribution.

Using the collected session information, an analyst can examine traffic patterns on a network to identify which systems are communicating with each other and identify suspicious sessions that warrant further investigation. For example, a server configured for internal use by users and having no legitimate reason to communicate with addresses on the Internet will cause an alarm to be generated if suddenly a session or sessions appear between the internal server and external addresses. At that point the analyst may suspect a malware infection or other system compromise and investigate further. Numerous other queries can be generated to identify sessions that are abnormal in some way or another such as excessive byte counts, excessive session lifetime, or unexpected ports being utilized. When run over a sufficient timeframe, a baseline for traffic sessions can be established and the analyst can query for sessions that don't fit the baseline. This sort of investigation is a form of anomaly detection based on high-level network data versus the more granular types discussed for NIDS and NIPS.

Another common usage of network session analysis is to combine it with the use of a honeypot or honeynet (see sidebar, "Honeypots and Honeynets"). Any network activity, other than known-good maintenance traffic such as patch downloads, seen on these systems is, by definition, suspicious as there are no production business functions or users assigned to these systems. Their sole purpose is to act as a lure for an intruder. By monitoring network sessions to and from these systems, an early warning can be raised without even necessarily needing to perform any complex analysis.

HONEYPOTS AND HONEYNETS

A honeypot is a computer system designed to act as a lure or trap for intruders. This is most often achieved by configuring the honeypot to look like a production system possibly containing valuable or sensitive information and providing legitimate services but in actuality neither the data or the services are real. A honeypot is carefully monitored and, since there is no legitimate reason for a user to be interacting with it, any activity seen targeting it is immediately considered suspicious. A honeynet is a collection of honeypots designed to mimic a more complex environment than one system can support [23].

17. DIGITAL FORENSICS

Digital forensics is the "application of computer science and investigative procedures for a legal purpose involving the analysis of digital evidence" [24]. Less formally digital forensics is the use of specialized tools and techniques to investigate various forms of computer-oriented crime including fraud, illicit use such as child pornography, and many forms of computer intrusions.

Digital forensics as a field can be divided into two subfields: network forensics and host-based forensics. Network forensics focuses on the use of captured network traffic and session information to investigate computer crime. Host-based forensics focuses on the collection and analysis of digital evidence collected from individual computer systems to investigate computer crime. Digital forensics is a vast topic and a comprehensive discussion is beyond the scope of this chapter and interested readers are referred to [25] for more detail.

In the context of intrusion detection, digital forensic techniques can be utilized to analyze a suspected compromised system in a methodical manner. Forensic investigations are most commonly used when the nature of the intrusion is unclear, such as those perpetrated via a 0-day exploit, but wherein the root cause must be fully understood either to ensure the exploited vulnerability is properly remediated or to support legal proceedings. Due to the increasing use of sophisticated attack tools and stealthy and customized malware designed to evade detection, forensic investigations are becoming increasingly common and sometimes only a detailed and methodical investigation will uncover the nature of an intrusion. The specifics of the intrusion may also require a forensic investigation such as those involving the theft of Personally Identifiable Information (PII) in regions covered by one or more data breach disclosure laws.

18. SYSTEM INTEGRITY VALIDATION

The emergence of powerful and stealthy malware, kernel-level rootkits, and so-called clean-state attack frameworks that leave no trace of an intrusion on a computer's hard drive have given rise to the need for technology that can analyze a running system and its memory and provide a series of metrics regarding the integrity of the system. System integrity validation (SIV) technology is still in its infancy and a very active area of research but primarily focuses on live system memory analysis and the notion of deriving trust from known-good system elements [26]. This is achieved by comparing the system's running state including the processes, threads, data structures, and modules loaded into memory to the static elements on disk that the running state was supposedly loaded from. Through a number of cross-validation processes, discrepancies between what is running in memory and what should be running can be identified. When properly implemented, SIV can be a powerful tool for detecting intrusions, even those utilizing advanced techniques.

19. SUMMARY

It should now be clear that intrusion detection and prevention is not a single tool or product but a series of layered technologies coupled with the appropriate methodologies and skill sets. Each of the technologies surveyed in this chapter have their own specific strengths and weaknesses and a truly effective intrusion detection and prevention program must be designed to play to those strengths and minimize the weaknesses. Combining NIDS and NIPS with network session analysis and a comprehensive SIM, for example, helps to offset the inherent weakness of each technology as well as provides the information security team greater flexibility to bring the right tools to bear for an ever-shifting threat environment.

An essential element in a properly designed intrusion detection and prevention program is an assessment of the threats faced by the organization and a valuation of the assets to be protected. There must be an alignment of the value of the information assets to be protected and the costs of the systems put in place to defend them. The program for an environment processing military secrets and needing to defend against a hostile nation state must be far more exhaustive than that for a single server containing no data of any real value that must simply keep out assorted script kiddies.

For many organizations, however, their information systems are business and mission critical enough to warrant considerable thought and planning with regards to the appropriate choices of technologies, how they will be implemented, and how they will be monitored. Only through flexible, layered, and comprehensive intrusion detection and prevention programs can organizations hope to defend their environment against current and future threats to their information security.

Finally, let's move on to the real interactive part of this Chapter: review questions/exercises, hands-on projects, case projects and optional team case project. The answers and/or solutions by chapter can be found in the Online Instructor's Solutions Manual.

CHAPTER REVIEW QUESTIONS/EXERCISES

True/False

1. True or False? Information security concerns itself with the integrity and availability of information systems and the information or data they contain and process.
2. True or False? Having physical access to a computer system allows an adversary to bypass most security protections put in place to prevent unauthorized access.
3. True or False? An insider is an individual who, due to their role in the organization, has some level of authorized access to the IS environment and systems.
4. True or False? An outsider is considered anyone who does not have authorized access privileges to an information system or environment.
5. True or False? Malware can be generally defined as "a set of instructions that run on your computer and make your system do something that allow an attacker to make it do what he wants it to do."

Multiple Choice

1. What is a self-replicating code that attaches itself to another program?
   A. Worm
   B. Virus
   C. Backdoor
   D. Trojan Horse
   E. User-level Rootkit

2. What is a self-replicating code that propagates over a network, usually without human interaction?
   A. Backdoor
   B. Virus
   C. Worm
   D. Trojan Horse
   E. User-level Rootkit

3. What is a program that bypasses standard security controls to provide an attacker access, often in a stealthy way?
   A. Trojan Horse
   B. Virus
   C. Worm
   D. Backdoor
   E. User-level Rootkit

4. What is a program that masquerades as a legitimate, useful program while also performing malicious functions in the background?
   A. Trojan Horse
   B. Virus
   C. Worm
   D. Backdoor
   E. User-level Rootkit

5. What is the Trojan/ backdoor code that modifies operating system software so the attacker can maintain privileged access on a machine but remain hidden?
   A. Trojan Horse
   B. Virus
   C. Worm
   D. Backdoor
   E. User-level Rootkit

EXERCISE

Problem

How do intrusion detection systems (IDSs) work?

Hands-On Projects

Project

Why should an organization use an IDS, especially when they already have firewalls, anti virus tools, and other security protections on their system?

Case Projects

Problem

What are the different types of IDSs?

Optional Team Case Project

Problem

How do does one go about selecting the best IDS for their organization?

References

[1] NIST Special Publication on Intrusion Detection Systems, NIST, 100 Bureau Drive, Stop 1070, Gaithersburg, MD 20899-1070, [US Department of Commerce, 1401 Constitution Avenue, NW, Washington, DC 20230], 2006.

[2a] M. Bosworth, VA Loses Data on 26 Million Veterans, consumeraffairs.com. <http://www.consumeraffairs.com/news04/2006/05/va_laptop.html>, 2006.

[2b] B. Prince, Stolen Laptop Exposes Boston Hospital Patient Data, darkreading.com. <http://www.darkreading.com/compliance/167901112/security/attacks-breaches/240001031/stolen-laptop-exposes-boston-hospital-patient-data.html>, 2012.

[3] B. Schneier, Applied Cryptograhpy, Wiley, 1996.

[4] S. Fishman, Bradley Manning's Army of One, New York Magazine, July 3, 2011.

[5] E. Skoudis, Malware: *Fighting Malicious Code*, Prentice Hall, 2003.

[6] P. Gutman, World's Most Powerful Supercomputer Goes Online, *Full Disclosure*. <http://seclists.org/fulldisclosure/2007/Aug/0520.html>, 2007.

[7] J. Aitel, The IPO of the 0-day. <http://www.immunityinc.com/downloads/0day_IPO.pdf>, 2007.

[8] M.H. Sachs, Cyber-Threat Analytics. <www.cyber-ta.org/downloads/files/Sachs_Cyber-TA_ThreatOps.ppt>, 2006.

[9] J. Leyden, Chinese Crackers Attack US.Gov, The Register. <http://www.theregister.co.uk/2006/10/09/chinese_crackers_attack_us/>, 2006.

[10] P. Williams, Organized Crime and Cyber-Crime: Implications for Business. <http://www.cert.org/archive/pdf/cybercrime-business.pdf>, 2002.

[11] C. Wilson, Botnets, Cybercrime, and Cyberterrorism: Vulnerabilities and Policy Issues for Congress. <http://fas.org/sgp/crs/terror/RL32114.pdf>, 2008.

[12] M. Graham, Welcome to Cyberwar Country, USA, WIRED. <http://www.wired.com/politics/security/news/2008/02/cyber_command>, 2008.

[13] M. Landler, J. Markoff, <http://www.nytimes.com/2007/05/29/technology/29estonia.html> Digital Fears Emerge After Data Siege in Estonia, New York Times, 2007.

[14] R. Stevens, TCP/IP *Illustrated, Volume 1*: The Protocols, Addison-Wesley Professional, 1994.

[15] D.E. Comer, Internetworking with TCP/IP Vol. 1: Principles, Protocols, and Architecture, fourth ed., Prentice Hall, 2000.

[16] C. Hunt, TCP/IP Network Administration, third ed., O'Reilly Media, Inc., 2002.

[17] S. Northcutt, Network Intrusion Detection, third ed., Sams, 2002.

[18] J.L. Bayuk, Stepping Through the InfoSec Program, ISACA, 2007.

[19] B. Schneier, Security Information Management Systems (SIMS), Schneier on Security. <http://www.schneier.com/blog/archives/2004/10/security_inform.html>, October 20, 2004.

[20] R. Bejtlich, The Tao of Network Security Monitoring: Beyond Intrusion Detection, Addison-Wesley Professional, 2004.

[21] Cisco Website, Cisco IOS NetFlow. <http://www.cisco.com/web/go/netflow>.

[22] Argus Website, Argus — Auditing Network Activity. <http://qosient.com/argus/>, August 13, 2012.

[23] Honeynet Project Website, The Honeynet Project. <www.honeynet.org>, 2012.

[24] K. Zatyko, Commentary: Defining Digital Forensics, Forensics Magazine. <http://www.forensicmag.com/articles.asp?pid=130>, 2007.

[25] K. Jones, Real Digital Forensics: Computer Security and Incident Response, Addison-Wesley Professional, 2005.

[26] Volatile Systems Website, Volatile Systems. <www.volatilesystems.com>, 2012.

6

Firewalls

Dr. Errin W. Fulp
Wake Forest University

1. INTRODUCTION

Providing a secure computing environment continues to be an important and challenging goal of any computer administrator. The difficulty is in part due to the increasing interconnectivity of computers via networks, which includes the Internet. Such interconnectivity brings great economies of scale in terms of resources, services, and knowledge, but it has also introduced new security risks. For example, interconnectivity gives illegitimate users much easier access to vital data and resources from almost anywhere in the world.

In a secure environment it is important to maintain the privacy, integrity, and availability of data and resources. *Privacy* refers to limiting information access and disclosures to authorized users and preventing access by or disclosure to illegitimate users. In the United States, a range of state and federal laws—for example, FERPA, FSMA, and HIPAA—define the legal terms of privacy. *Integrity* is the trustworthiness of information. It includes the idea of *data integrity*, which means data has not been changed inappropriately. It can also include *source integrity*, which means the source of the data is who it claims to be. *Availability* is the accessibility of resources. Of course these security definitions can also form the basis of *reputation*, which is vital to businesses.

2. NETWORK FIREWALLS

Network firewalls (see checklist: "An Agenda For Action For Network Firewalls") are a vital component for maintaining a secure environment and are often the first line of defense against attack. Simply stated, a firewall is responsible for controlling access among devices, such as computers, networks, and servers. Therefore the most common deployment is between a secure and an insecure network (for example, between the computers you control and the Internet), as shown in Figure 6.1.

AN AGENDA FOR ACTION FOR NETWORK FIREWALLS

The following checklist lists the major tasks for network firewalls (check all tasks completed):

_____1. The use of network address translation (NAT) should be considered a form of routing, not a type of firewall.

_____2. Organizations should only permit outbound traffic that uses the source IP addresses in use by the organization.

_____3. Compliance checking is only useful in a firewall when it can block communication that can be harmful to protected systems.

_____4. When choosing the type of firewall to deploy, it is important to decide whether the firewall needs to act as an application proxy.

_____5. Management of personal firewalls should be centralized to help efficiently create, distribute, and enforce policies for all users and groups.

_____6. In general, a firewall should fit into a current network's layout. However, an organization might change its network architecture at the same time as it deploys a firewall as part of an overall security upgrade.

_____7. Different common network architectures lead to very different choices for where to place a firewall, so an organization should assess which architecture works best for its security goals.

_____8. If an edge firewall has a DMZ, consider which outward-facing services should be run from the DMZ and which should remain on the inside network.

_____9. Do not rely on NATs to provide the benefits of firewalls.

_____10. In some environments, putting one firewall behind another may lead to a desired security goal, but in general such multiple layers of firewalls can be troublesome.

_____11. An organization's firewall policy should be based on a comprehensive risk analysis.

_____12. Firewall policies should be based on blocking all inbound and outbound traffic, with exceptions made for desired traffic.

_____13. Policies should take into account the source and destination of the traffic in addition to the content.

_____14. Many types of IPv4 traffic, such as that with invalid or private addresses, should be blocked by default.

_____15. Organizations should have policies for handling incoming and outgoing IPv6 traffic.

_____16. An organization should determine which applications may send traffic into or out of its network and make firewall policies to block traffic for other applications.

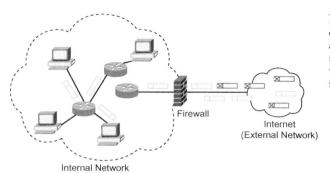

FIGURE 6.1 Example network consisting of an internal network (which is to be secured) and an external network (not trusted). The firewall controls access between these two networks, allowing and denying packets according to a security policy.

Internal Network

However, in response to the richer services provided over modern networks (such as multimedia and encrypted connections), the role of the firewall has grown over time. Advanced firewalls may also perform Network Address Translation (NAT), which allows multiple computers to share a limited number of network addresses (explained later in this chapter). Firewalls may provide service differentiation, giving certain traffic priority to ensure that data is received in a timely fashion. Voice over IP (VoIP) is one type of application that needs differentiation to ensure proper operation. This idea is discussed several times in this chapter, since the use of multimedia services will only continue to increase. Assuming that email and VoIP packets arrive at the firewall at the same time, VoIP packets should be processed first because the application is more susceptible to delays.

Firewalls may also inspect the contents (the data) of packets. This can be done to filter other packets (learn new connections), block packets that contain offensive information, and/or block intrusion attempts. Using the mail analogy again, in this case you open letters and determine what to accept based on what is inside. For example, you unfortunately have to accept bills, but you can deny credit-card solicitations.

3. FIREWALL SECURITY POLICIES

When a packet arrives at a firewall, a security policy is applied to determine the appropriate action. Actions include accepting the packet, which means the packet is allowed to travel to the intended destination. A packet can be denied, which means the packet is not permitted to travel to the intended destination (it is dropped or possibly is bounced back). The firewall may also log information about the packet, which is important to maintain certain services.

It is easy to consider a firewall policy as an ordered list of rules, as shown in Table 6.1. Each firewall rule consists of a set of tuples and an action. Each tuple corresponds to a field in the packet header, and there are five such fields for an Internet packet: Protocol, Source Address, Source Port, Destination Address, and Destination Port.

The firewall rule tuples can be fully specified or contain wildcards (*) in standard prefix format. However, each tuple represents a finite set of values; therefore, the set of all

TABLE 6.1 A Security Policy Consisting of Six Rules, Each of Which Has Five Parts (Tuples)

No.	Protocol	Source		Destination		Action
		IP	Port	IP	Port	
1	UDP	190.1.1.*	*	*	80	deny
2	TCP	180.*	*	180.*	90	accept
3	UDP	210.1.*	*	*	90	accept
4	TCP	210.*	*	220.*	80	accept
5	UDP	190.*	*	*	80	accept
6	*	*	*	*	*	deny

possible packets is also finite. (A more concise mathematical model will be introduced later in the chapter.) It is possible to consider the packet header consisting of tuples, but each tuple must be fully specified.

As packets pass through a firewall, their header information is sequentially compared to the fields of a rule. If a packet's header information is a subset of a rule, it is said to be a match, and the associated action, to accept or reject, is performed. Otherwise, the packet is compared to the next sequential rule. This is considered a *first-match policy* since the action associated with the first rule that is matched is performed. Other matching strategies are discussed at the end of this section.

For example, assume that a packet has the following values in the header: The protocol is TCP, source IP is 210.1.1.1, source port is 3080, destination IP is 220.2.33.8, and destination port is 80. When the packet arrives it is compared to the first rule, which results in no match since the rule is for UDP packets. The firewall then compares the packet second rule, which results in no match since the source IP is different. The packet does not match the third rule, but it does match the fourth rule. The rule action is performed and so the packet is allowed to pass the firewall.

A default rule, or catch-all, is often placed at the end of a policy with action reject. The addition of a default rule makes a policy comprehensive, indicating that every packet will match at least one rule. In the event that a packet matches multiple rules, the action of the first matching rule is taken. Therefore the order of rules is very important.

If a default rule (a rule that matches all possible packets) is placed at the beginning of a first-match policy, no other rule will match. This situation is an anomaly referred to as *shadowing*. We'll talk more about policy anomalies later in this chapter. Policies that employ this form of short-circuit evaluation are called *first-match policies* and account for the majority of firewall implementations.

Rule-Match Policies

Multiple rules of a single firewall policy may match a packet—for example, a packet could match rules 1, 5, and 6 of the policy in Table 6.1. Given multiple possible matches, the rule-match policy describes the rule the firewall will apply to the packet. The previous section described the most popular match policy, first match, which will apply the first rule that is a match.

Other match policies are possible, including best match and last match. For best-match policies, the packet is compared against every rule to determine which rule most closely matches every tuple of the packet. Note that the relative order of the rules in the policy does not impact determining the best-match result; therefore shadowing is not an issue. It is interesting to note that best match is the default criterion for IP routing, which is not surprising since firewalls and routers do perform similar tasks. If a packet matches multiple rules with a last-match criterion, the action of the last rule matched is performed. Note that rule order is important for a last-match policy.

4. A SIMPLE MATHEMATICAL MODEL FOR POLICIES, RULES, AND PACKETS

At this point it is perhaps useful to describe firewall policies, firewall rules, and network packets using set theory.[1] The previous section defined the parts and fields of rules and packets as *tuples*. A tuple can be modeled as a set. For example, assume the tuple for IP source addresses is 198.188.150.*. Then this tuple represents the set of 256 addresses that range from 198.188.150.0 to 198.180.150.255. Each tuple of a packet consists of a single value, which is expected, since a packet only has one source and one destination.

The tuples (which are sets) that form a rule collective define a set of packets that match. For example, consider the following rule:

- Proto = TCP, SIP = 190.150.140.38, SP = 188,
- DIP = 190.180.39.* DP = 80, action = accept

This rule defines a set of 256 unique TCP packet headers with source address 190.150.140.38 and source port 188 destined for any of the 256 computers with destination port 80 and destination IP address 190.180.39.0 through 190.180.39.255, perhaps a Web server farm. Therefore the rule describes a set of 256 packets that will be accepted. If the source port was defined as *, the rule would describe a set of 16,777,216 different packet headers.

$$2^{16} \times 2^8 = 65,536 \times 256 = 16,777,216$$

Using set theory also provides a simple definition of a match. A match occurs when every tuple of a packet is a proper subset of the corresponding rule. In this chapter a proper set can be thought of as one set completely contained within another. For example,

1. Errin W. Fulp, "Optimization of network firewall policies using directed acyclical graphs," In *Proceedings of the IEEE Internet Management Conference*, 2005.

every tuple in the following packet is a proper subset of the preceding rule; therefore it is considered a match:

- Proto = TCP, SIP = 190.150.140.38, SP = 188,
- DIP = 190.180.39.188 DP = 80

A set model can also be used to describe a firewall policy. The list of rules in a firewall policy collectively describes a set of packets. There are three distinct (nonoverlapping) sets of possible packets. The first set, $A(R)$, describes packets that will be accepted by the policy R. The second set, $D(R)$, defines the set of packets that will be dropped by the policy. The last set, $U(R)$, is the set of packets that do not match any rule in the policy. Since the sets do not overlap, the intersection of $A(R)$, $D(R)$, and $U(R)$ should be the empty set.

Using set theory we can also define the set P that describes all possible packet headers, of which there are approximately 7.7×10^{25} possible packet headers. A packet is a single element in this large set.

Using accept, drop, nonmatch, and possible packet sets, we can describe useful attributes of a firewall policy. A firewall policy R is considered comprehensive if any packet from P will match at least one rule. In other words, the union of $A(R)$ and $D(R)$ equals P (therefore $A(R)D(R) = P$), or $U(R)$ is the empty set (therefore $U(R) = \emptyset$). Of course, it is better if a policy is comprehensive, and generally the last rule (catch-all) makes this true.

Finally, these mathematical models also allow the comparison of policies, the most important reason for introducing a somewhat painful section. Assume two firewall policies R and S exist. We can say the two polices are equivalent if the accept, drop, and nonmatch sets are the same. This does not imply that the two policies have the same rules, just that given a packet, both policies will have the same action. This is an important property that will be mentioned again and again in this chapter.

5. FIRST-MATCH FIREWALL POLICY ANOMALIES

As described in the previous sections, for most firewalls the first rule that matches a packet is typically applied. Given this match policy, more specific rules (those that match few packets) typically appear near the beginning of the policy, whereas more general rules are located at the end. Using the set theory model, the number of elements in the rules sets increases as you move toward the last rule.

Unfortunately, it is easy to introduce anomalies when developing and managing a firewall policy. This is especially true as the policy grows in size (number of rules) and complexity. An anomaly is an unintended consequence of adding rules in a certain order.

A simple and very common anomaly is rule shadowing. Shadowing occurs when an earlier rule r_i matches every packet that another lower rule r_j matches, where i and j are rule numbers. Assume rules are numbered sequentially starting at the first rule and $i < j$. Using the mathematical model, shadowing occurs when every tuple in r_j is a proper subset of r_i

For example, shadowing occurs between the following two rules:

- Proto = TCP, SIP = 190.150.140.38, SP = 188,
- DIP = 190.180.39.* DP = 80, action = accept
- Proto = TCP, SIP = 190.150.140.38, SP = 188, DIP = 190.180.39.180 DP = 80, action = drop

What is the problem? Nothing, if the two rules have the same action (there is a performance issue described in the next section). However, if the rules have different actions, there is a potential issue. In the preceding example the second rule is never matched; therefore the packet [Proto = TCP, SIP = 190.150.140.38, SP = 188, DIP = 190.180.39.180 DP = 80] will always be accepted. Was this the intent? If so, the second rule should be removed.

Another policy anomaly is half shadowing, where only a portion of the packets of a later rule matches an earlier rule (although not necessarily half of the packets in the set). For example, consider the following two rules:

- Proto = TCP, SIP = 190.150.140.38, SP = 188,
- DIP = 190.180.39.* DP = 80, action = accept
- Proto = TCP, SIP = 190.150.140.38, SP = *,
- DIP = 190.180.39.180 DP = 80, action = drop

In this example, the second rule is partially shadowed by the first rule. By itself, the second rule will drop any TCP packet arriving from the address 190.150.140.38 and destined for the Web server (because of destination port 80) 190.180.39.180. When the first rule is added, a packet from the address 190.150.140.38 and port 188 will be accepted. Was this the intent? Only the firewall administrator would know. Regardless, it is difficult to detect.

Other firewall policy anomalies are possible. Unfortunately, detecting these problems is not easy, since the anomaly may be introduced on purpose (then technically it is not an anomaly). This has created a new area of research, and some software packages are available to help find problems. However, only the administrator can ultimately determine whether the rule ordering is correct. Note that best-match policies do not have these issues, and this reason is often used to promote their use. However, best-match policies are typically considered difficult for the administrator to manage.

6. POLICY OPTIMIZATION

Given that a network firewall will inspect all packets transmitted between multiple networks, these devices need to determine the appropriate match with minimal delay. Often the number of firewall rules in a policy will impact the firewall performance. Given that every rule requires some processing time, more rules will require more time, on average. There are a few ways to improve firewall performance with regard to the security policy. Note that this section is more applicable to software-based than hardware-based firewalls.

Policy Reordering

Given a security policy, it may be possible to reorder the rules such that more popular rules appear earlier.[2] *More popular* refers to how often the rule is a match. For example,

2. Errin W. Fulp, "Optimization of network firewall policies using directed acyclical graphs," In *Proceedings of the IEEE Internet Management Conference*, 2005.

over time it is possible to determine how many times a rule is matched. Dividing this number by the total number of packets matched for the entire policy yields the probability that this rule is considered the first match.

If the match policy is first match, then placing more popular rules earlier in the policy will reduce the average number of rule comparisons. The average number of rule comparisons performed, $E[n]$, is given by the following equation:

$$E[n] = \sum_{i=1}^{n} i \times p_i$$

where n is the number of rules in the policy and p_i is the probability that rule i is the first match. Although reordering is advantageous, it must be done so that the policy's integrity is maintained.

Policy integrity refers to the policy intent, so the policy will accept and deny the same packets before and after the reorganization of rules. For example, rule six in Table 29.1 may be the most popular rule (the default deny), but placing it at the beginning of the policy does not maintain integrity. However, if rule two is more popular than rule one, it could be placed at the beginning of the policy and integrity will be maintained. Therefore the order between certain rules must be maintained.

This can be described mathematically using the models introduced in the earlier section. Assume a firewall policy R exists. After reordering the rules, let's call the firewall policy S. If $A(R) = A(S)$ and $D(R) = D(S)$, then the policies R and S are equivalent and integrity is maintained. As a result S can be used in place of R in the firewall, which should improve performance.

Although a simple concept, reordering rules to maintain integrity is provably difficult for large policies.[3,4] Fortunately, commercial software packages are now available to optimize rules to improve performance.

Combining Rules

Another method for improving firewall performance is removing unnecessary rules. This can be accomplished by first removing redundant rules (rules that are shadowed with the same action). For example, the second rule here is unnecessary:

- Proto = TCP, SIP = 190.150.140.38, SP = 188,
- DIP = 190.180.39.* DP = 80, action = drop
- Proto = TCP, SIP = 190.150.140.38, SP = 188,
- DIP = 190.180.39.180 DP = 80, action = drop

3. Errin W. Fulp, "Optimization of network firewall policies using directed acyclical graphs," In *Proceedings of the IEEE Internet Management Conference*, 2005.

4. M. Yoon and Z. S. Zhang, "Reducing the size of rule set in a firewall," In *Proceedings of the IEEE International Conference on Communications*, 2007.

This is because the first rule matches any packet the second rule does, and the first rule has the same action (different actions would be an anomaly, as described in the earlier sections).

Another example occurs when two nonshadowing rules can be combined into a single rule. Consider the following two rules:

- Proto = TCP, SIP = 190.150.140.38, SP = 188,
- DIP = 190.180.39.* DP = 80, action = accept
- Proto = UDP, SIP = 190.150.140.38, SP = 188,
- DIP = 190.180.39.* DP = 80, action = accept

These two rules can be combined into the following rule, which substitutes the wildcard for the protocol field:

- Proto = *, SIP = 190.150.140.38, SP = 188,
- DIP = 190.180.39.* DP = 80, action = accept

Combining rules to form a smaller policy is better in terms of performance as well as management in most cases, since fewer rules should be easier for the administrator to understand. Finding such combinations takes practice; fortunately, there are some software packages available to help.

Default Accept or Deny?

It may be worth a few lines to discuss whether a default accept policy provides better performance than a default deny. This debate occurs from time to time; generally speaking, the question is better answered with regard to management of the policy and security. Is it easier to define the appropriate policy in terms of what is denied or what should be accepted?

Assuming that the administrator defines one (accepted or denied), the default behavior becomes the other. A "define what is accepted and default deny" is the most common. It can be considered pessimistic, since it assumes that if you are not certain about a packet, then drop it.

7. FIREWALL TYPES

Firewalls can be categorized into three general classes: packet filters, stateful firewalls, and application layer firewalls.[5] Each type provides a certain type of security and is best described within the context of a network layer model—for example, the Open Systems Interconnect (OSI) or TCP/IP model, as shown in Figure 6.2.

Recall that the TCP/IP model consists of four basic layers: data link, networking (IP), transport (TCP and UDP), and application. Each layer is responsible for providing a certain service to the layer above it. The first layer (data link) is responsible for transmitting information across the local area network (LAN); examples include Ethernet and 802.11

5. J.R. Vacca and S. R. Ellis, *Firewalls Jumpstart for Network and Systems Administrators*, Elsevier, 2005.

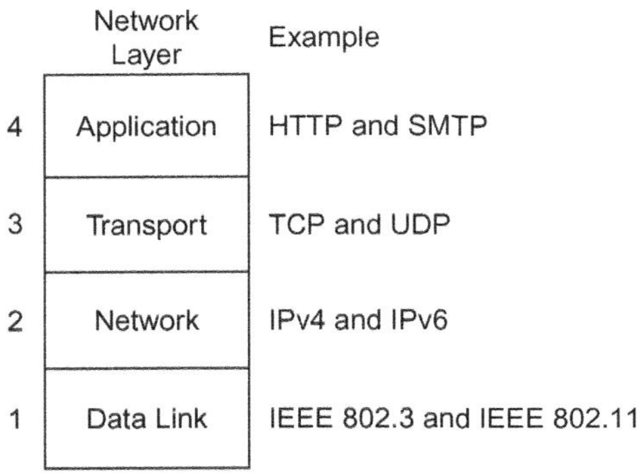

	Network Layer	Example
4	Application	HTTP and SMTP
3	Transport	TCP and UDP
2	Network	IPv4 and IPv6
1	Data Link	IEEE 802.3 and IEEE 802.11

FIGURE 6.2 Layered model for computer networks and example implementations for each layer.

networks. The network layer (routing, implemented IP) concerns routing information across interconnected LANs. The third layer (transport, implemented as TCP and UDP) concerns the end-to-end connection between communicating devices. The highest layer (application) is the application using the network.

Packet Filter

A packet filter is the most basic type of a firewall since it only filters at the network and transport layers (layers two and three). Therefore a packet filter's operations are similar to a network router's. The packet filter receives a packet, determines the appropriate action based on the policy, then performs the action on the packet. This will be based on the information from the network and transport layers. Therefore, a packet filter only considers the IP addresses (layer two information), the port numbers (layer one information), and the transport protocol type (layer three information). Furthermore, since all this information resides in the packet header, there is no need to inspect the packet data (payload). It is possible to filter based on the data link layer, but this chapter only considers the network layer and above. Another important note is that the packet filter has no memory (or state) regarding the packets that have arrived and departed.

Stateful Packet Firewalls

Stateful firewalls perform the same operations as packet filters but also maintain state about the packets that have arrived. Given this additional functionality, it is now possible to create firewall rules that allow network sessions (sender and receiver are allowed to communicate), which is critical given the client/server nature of most communications (that is, if you send packets, you probably expect something back). Also note the change in terminology from packet filter to firewall. Many people say that when state is added to a packet filter, it becomes a firewall. This is really a matter of opinion.

For example, assume a user located in the internal (protected) network wants to contact a Web server located in the Internet. The request would be sent from the user to the Web server, and the Web server would respond with the requested information. A packet filter would require two rules, one allowing departing packets (user to Web server) and another allowing arriving packets (Web server to user). There are several problems with this approach, since it is difficult to determine in advance what Web servers a user will connect to. Consider having to add a new rule for every Web server that is or would ever be contacted.

A stateful firewall allows connection tracking, which can allow the arriving packets associated with an accepted departing connection. Recall that a connection or session can be considered all the packets belonging to the conversation between computers, both sender to receiver, and vice versa. Using the Web server example, a single stateful rule can be created that accepts any Web requests from the secure network and the associated return packets. A simple way to add this capability is to have the firewall add to the policy a new rule allowing return packets. Of course, this new rule would be eliminated once the connection is finished. Knowing when a connection is finished is not an easy task, and ultimately timers are involved. Regardless, stateful rules were a significant advancement for network firewalls.

Application Layer Firewalls

Application layer firewalls can filter traffic at the network, transport, and application layer. Filtering at the application layer also introduces new services, such as proxies. Application proxies are simply intermediaries for network connections. Assume that a user in the internal network wants to connect to a server in the external network. The connection of the user would terminate at the firewall; the firewall would then create a connection to the Web server. It is important to note that this occurs seamlessly to the user and server.

As a result of the proxy the firewall can potentially inspect the contents of the packets, which is similar to an intrusion detection system (IDS). This is increasingly important since a growing number of applications, as well as illegitimate users, are using nonstandard port numbers to transmit data. Application layer firewalls are also necessary if an existing connection may require the establishment of another connection—for example, the Common Object Resource Broker Architecture (CORBA).

Increasingly, firewalls and other security devices are being merged into a single device that can simplify management. For example, an intrusion prevention system (IPS) is a combination firewall and IDS. An IPS can filter packets based on the header, but it can also scan the packet contents (payload) for viruses, spam, and certain types of attacks.

8. HOST AND NETWORK FIREWALLS

Firewalls can also be categorized based on where they are implemented or what they are intended to protect—host or network.[6] Host firewalls typically protect only one computer. Host firewalls reside on the computer they are intended to protect and are implemented in software (this is described in the next section).

6. J.R. Vacca and S. R. Ellis, *Firewalls Jumpstart for Network and Systems Administrators*, Elsevier, 2005.

In contrast, network firewalls are typically standalone devices. Located at the gateway (s) of a network (for example, the point at which a network is connected to the Internet), a network firewall is designed to protect all the computers in the internal network. As a result, a network firewall must be able to handle high bandwidth, as fast as the incoming connection, and process packets quickly. A network firewall gives administrators a single point at which to implement and manage security, but it is also a single point of failure.

There are many different network configurations that involve firewalls. Each provides different levels of security and management complexity. These configurations are described in detail in a later section.

9. SOFTWARE AND HARDWARE FIREWALL IMPLEMENTATIONS

As described in the previous sections, a firewall applies a policy to an arriving packet to determine the appropriate match. The policy is an ordered list of rules, and typically the first rule that matches the packet is performed. This operation can be performed primarily in either software or hardware. Performance is the principal reason to choose one implementation.

Software firewalls are application software that can execute on commercial hardware. Most operating systems provide a firewall to protect the host computer (often called a *host firewall*). For example, iptables is the firewall application provided as a part of the Linux operating system. Several major firewall companies offer a software version of their network firewall. It is possible to buy off-the-shelf hardware (for example, a server) and run the firewall software. The advantage of software firewalls is their ability to upgrade without replacing the hardware. In addition, it is easier to add new features—for example, iptables can easily perform stateful filtering, NATing, and quality-of-service (QoS) operations. It is as simple as updating and configuring the firewall software.

Hardware firewalls rely on hardware to perform packet filtering. The policy and matching operation is performed in dedicated hardware—for example, using a field-programmable gate array (FPGA). The major advantages of a hardware firewall are increased bandwidth and reduced latency. Note that bandwidth is the number of packets a firewall can process per unit of time, and latency is the amount of time require to process a packet. They are not the same thing, and IETF RFC 3511 provides a detailed description of the process of testing firewall performance.[7]

Hardware firewalls can operate at faster bandwidths, which translates to more packets per second (10 Gbps is easily achieved). In addition, hardware firewalls can operate faster since processing is performed in dedicated hardware. The firewall operates almost at wireline speeds; therefore, very little delay is added to accepted packets. This is important since more applications, such as multimedia, need QoS for their operation. The disadvantage is that upgrading the firewall may require replacement of hardware, which can be more expensive.

7. B. Hickman, D. Newman, S. Tadjudin, and T. Martin, *Benchmarking Methodology for Firewall Performance*, IETF RFC 3511, 2003.

10. CHOOSING THE CORRECT FIREWALL

The previous sections have described several categories of firewalls. Firewalls can be packet filters or stateful firewalls and/or provide application layer processing; implemented at the host or network or implemented in software or hardware. Given the possible combinations, it can be difficult to choose the appropriate technology.

When determining the appropriate technology, it is important to first understand the current and future security needs of the computer system being protected. Given a large number of hosts, a network firewall is probably the easiest to manage. Requiring and relying on every computer in an internal network to operate a host firewall may not be realistic.

Furthermore, updating the policy in a multiple host-based firewall system would be difficult. However, a single network firewall may imply that a single policy is suitable for all computers in the internal network. This generally is not the case when there are servers and computers in the internal network. More expensive network firewalls will allow the implementation of multiple policies or objects (described in more detail in the next section). Of course, if speed is an issue, a hardware firewall may justify the generally higher cost.

If scanning for viruses and spam and/or discovering network attacks are also requirements, a more advanced firewall is needed. Sometimes called an intrusion prevention system (IPS), these advanced devices filter based on packet headers and inspect the data transmitted for certain signatures. In addition, these devices can monitor traffic (usage and connection patterns) for attacks. For example, a computer that attempts to connect to a range of ports on another computer is probably *port scanning*. This can be done to determine what network-oriented programs are running and in some cases even the operating system can be determined. It is a good idea to block this type of network reconnaissance, which an advanced firewall can do.

Although already introduced in this chapter, it is worth mentioning IETF RFC 3511 again. This document describes how firewalls should be tested to measure performance. This information helps the buyer understand the performance numbers cited by manufacturers. It is also important to ask whether the device was tested under RFC 3511 conditions.

11. FIREWALL PLACEMENT AND NETWORK TOPOLOGY

A simple firewall typically separates two networks: one trusted (internal—for example, the corporate network) and one untrusted (external—for example, the Internet). In this simple arrangement, one security policy is applied to secure all the devices connected to the internal network. This may be sufficient if all the computers perform the same duties, such as desktop computers; however, if the internal network consists of different types of computers (in terms of the services provided), a single policy or level of protection is not sufficient or is difficult to create and maintain.

For example, the security policy for a Web server will be different from the security policy for a desktop computer. This is primarily due to the type of external network access each type of computer needs. Web servers would probably accept almost any unsolicited HTTP (port 80) requests arriving from the Internet. However, desktop computers probably do not serve Web pages and should not be subject to such requests.

Therefore it is reasonable to expect that different classes of computers will need different security policies. Assume an internal network consists of one Web server and several desktop computers. It is possible to locate the Web server on the outside, on the firewall (on the side of the external network), but that would leave the Web server without any firewall protection. Furthermore, given that the Web server is on the outside, should the administrator trust it?

Of course, the Web server could be located in the internal network (see Figure 6.3) and a rule can be added to the policy to allow Web traffic to the Web server (often called *poking a hole*). However, if the Web server is compromised, the remaining computers in the internal network are vulnerable. Most attacks are multistage, which means the first target of attack is rarely the objective. Most attackers use one computer to compromise another until the objective is achieved. Therefore it is a good practice to separate machines and services, even in the internal network.

Demilitarized Zones

Another strategy often employed to provide different types of protection is a *demilitarized zone* (DMZ), as shown in Figure 6.3. Assume the firewall has three connections (sometimes called a *multihomed* device)—one for the external network (Internet), one for the Web server, and another for the internal network. For each connection to the firewall (referred to as an *interface*), a different firewall policy can be enforced, providing different forms of protection. The connection for the Web server is called the DMZ, and it prevents users from the external network getting direct access to the other computers in the internal

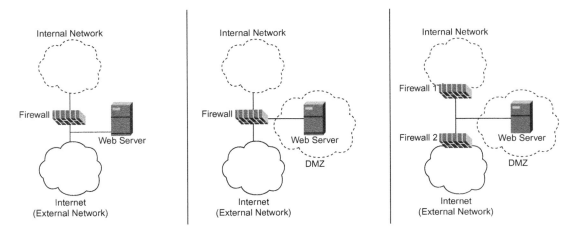

FIGURE 6.3   Example firewall configurations. Left configuration has a Web server outside the internal network. The middle configuration has the Web server in a demilitarized zone. The right configuration is another example of a demilitarized zone.

network. Furthermore, if the Web server is compromised, the internal network still has some protection, since the intruder would have to cross the firewall again to access the internal network.

If the firewall only supports two interfaces (or just one policy), multiple firewalls can be used to achieve the same DMZ effect. The first firewall would be placed between the external network and the Web server. The second firewall would connect the Web server to the internal network. Given this design, the first firewall policy would be less restrictive than the second. Again, different levels of security are now possible.

Grouping machines together based on similar firewall security needs is increasingly common and is seen as a good practice. Large networks may have server farms or a group of servers that perform similar services. As such, each farm is connected to a firewall and given a unique security policy. For example, users from the internal network may have access to administrative servers, but Web servers may have no access to the administrative servers. Such groupings are also referred to as *enclaves*.

Perimeter Networks

A perimeter network is a subnetwork of computers located outside the internal network.[8] Given this definition, a DMZ can be considered a type of perimeter network. The primary difference between a DMZ and a perimeter network is the way packets arriving and departing the subnetwork are managed.

In a perimeter network, the device that connects the external network to the perimeter network is a *router*, whereas a DMZ uses a firewall to connect to the Internet. For a DMZ, a firewall policy will be applied to all packets arriving from the external network (Internet). The firewall can also perform advanced services such as NATing and packet payload inspection. Therefore it is easy to see that a DMZ offers a higher level of protection to the computers that are part of the perimeter and internal networks.

Two-Router Configuration

Another interconnection of subnetworks is the two-router configuration.[9] This system consists of an external router, a bastion host, an internal router, and an internal network. The *bastion host* is a computer that serves as a filter and/or proxy for computers located in the internal network.

Before describing the specifics of the two-router configuration, let's define the duties of a bastion host. A bastion host is the first device any external computer will contact before accessing a computer in the internal network. Therefore the bastion host is fully exposed to the Internet and should be made as secure as possible. There are several types of bastion hosts, including victim machines that provide insecure but necessary services. For our discussion the bastion host will provide proxy services, shielding (to a limited degree) internal computers from external threats.

8. J.R. Vacca and S. R. Ellis, *Firewalls Jumpstart for Network and Systems Administrators*, Elsevier, 2005.

9. J.R. Vacca and S. R. Ellis, *Firewalls Jumpstart for Network and Systems Administrators*, Elsevier, 2005.

For the two-router configuration, the external network connects to the external router, which connects to the bastion host. The bastion host then connects to the internal router, which also connects to the internal network. The routers can provide limited filtering, whereas the bastion host provides a variety of proxy services—for example, HTTP, SSH, IRC, and FTP. This provides some level of security, since attackers are unaware of some internal network details. The bastion host can be viewed as a part of a very small perimeter network.

Compared to the DMZ, a two-router system provides less security. If the bastion host is compromised, the computers in the internal network are not immediately vulnerable, but it would only be a matter of time before they were. Therefore the two-router design should be limited to separating internal subnetworks. If the internal router is a firewall, the design is considerably more secure.

Dual-Homed Host

A *dual-homed host* system consists of a single computer separating the external network from internal computers.[10] Therefore the dual-homed computer needs at least two network interface cards (NICs). One NIC connects to the external network; the other connects to the internal network—hence the term *dual-homed*. The internal connection is generally a switch that connects the other internal computers.

The dual-homed computer is the location where all traffic arriving and departing the internal network can be processed. The dual-homed computer can perform various tasks such as packet filtering, payload inspection, NAT, and proxy services. Given the simple design and low cost, this setup is popular for home networks. Unfortunately, the dual-homed approach introduces a single point of failure. If the computer fails, then the internal network is isolated from the external network. Therefore this approach is not appropriate for businesses that rely on the Internet.

Network Configuration Summary

This section described various network configurations that can be used to provide varying levels of security. There are certainly variations, but this part of the chapter attempted to describe the most prevalent:

- *Demilitarized zones (DMZs)*. When correctly configured, DMZs provide a reasonable level of security. Servers that need to be available to the external network are placed outside the internal network but have a firewall between them and the external network.
- *Perimeter networks*. A perimeter network consists of a subnetwork of systems (again, those that need to be available to the external network) located outside the internal network. The perimeter subnetwork is separated from the external network by a router that can provide some basic packet filtering.

10. J.R. Vacca and S. R. Ellis, *Firewalls Jumpstart for Network and Systems Administrators*, Elsevier, 2005.

- *Two-router configuration.* The two-router configuration places a bastion host between the internal and external networks. One router is placed between the internal network and bastion host, and the other router is placed between the bastion host and the external network. The bastion host provides proxy services, which affords some security (but not much).
- *Dual-homed configuration.* A dual-homed configuration has one computer that has at least two network connections—one connected to the external network and another to the internal network. All traffic must transmit through the dual-homed system; thus is can act as a firewall, NAT, and/or IDS. Unfortunately, this system has a single point of failure.

12. FIREWALL INSTALLATION AND CONFIGURATION

Before a firewall is actually deployed, it is important to determine the required services and realize the vulnerabilities that may exist in the computer system that is to be secured. Determining the services requires a detailed understanding of how the computers in the network are interconnected, both physically and from a service-oriented perspective. This is commonly referred to as *object discovery*.

For example, given a database server, which services should the server provide? Which computers should be allowed to connect? Restated, which ports should be open and to whom? Often object discovery is difficult since it is common that a server will be asked to do various tasks over time. Generally a multiservice server is cheaper (one server providing Web, email, and database), but it is rarely more secure. For example, if a multiservice server is compromised via one service, the other services are vulnerable to attack. In other words, the rules in the firewall policy are usually established by the list of available services and secure computers.

Scanning for vulnerabilities is also helpful when you're installing a firewall. Several open-source tools are available to detect system vulnerabilities, including netstat, which shows open services. Why not simply patch the vulnerability? Perhaps the patch is not available yet, or perhaps the application is deemed necessary but it is simply insecure (FTP is an example). Network mappers such as Nessus are also valuable in showing what information about the internal network is available from the outside. Knowing the internal network layout is invaluable in attacking a system, since must modern attacks are multistaged. This means that one type of system vulnerability is typically leveraged to gain access elsewhere within the network.

A simple and unfortunately common security risk is a Web server that is connected to another internal server for data. Assume that Network File System (NFS) is used to gain access to remote data. If the Web server is compromised, which will probably occur at some time, then all the data inside the data server may be at risk (depending on how permissions have been set) and access to the data could be the true objective of the attacker. Therefore, understanding the interconnection of internal machines can help identify possible multistage attacks.

Of course the process of determining services, access rights, and vulnerabilities is not a one-time occurrence. This process should repeat over time as new computers, operating systems, users, and so on are introduced. Furthermore, firewall changes can cause disruption to legitimate users; these cases require tracing routes, defining objects, and reading policies. Managing a firewall and its policy requires constant vigilance.

13. SUPPORTING OUTGOING SERVICES THROUGH FIREWALL CONFIGURATION

As described in the first section, a firewall and the policy govern access to and from an internal network (the network being administered). A firewall applies a policy to arriving packets, then determines the type of access. The policy can be represented as an ordered set of rules; again, assume that the first-match criterion is used. When a packet arrives, it is compared to the first rule to determine whether it is a match. If it is, then the associated action is performed; otherwise the next rule is tested. Actions include accepting, denying, and logging the packet.

For a simple packet filter, each rule in the policy will describe a certain range of packet headers that it will match. This range of packets is then defined by describing certain parts of the packet header in the rule. For the Internet (TCP/IP networks) there are five such parts that can be described: source IP, source port, destination IP, destination port, and protocol.

Recall that the source IP is the address of the computer that originated the packet. The source port is the number associated with the application that originated the packet. Given the IP address and port number, it is possible to determine the machine and application, within reason. The destination IP and port number describe the computer and the program that will receive the packet. Therefore, given these four pieces of information, it is possible to control the access to and from a certain computer and program. The fifth piece of information is the communication protocol, UDP or TCP.

At this point it is important to also consider the direction of traffic. When referring to a packet, did it come from the external network and is it destined for an internal computer, or vice versa? If the packet is considered inbound, the source and destination addresses are in one order; outbound would reverse the order. Unfortunately, many firewalls will consider any arriving packet as inbound, regardless of where it originated (external or internal network), so the administrator must consider the direction when designing the policy. For example, iptables considers packets as locally or nonlocally generated. Locally generated packets are created at the computer running the firewall; all others are nonlocal, regardless of the source network.

Many firewalls can go beyond the five tuples (TCP/IP packet header parts) described. It is not uncommon to have a rule check the Medium Access Control (MAC) address or hardware address. This can be applied to filter-spoofed addresses. Filtering on the Type of Service (ToS) field is also possible to treat packets differently—for better service, for example.

As previously described, maintaining the state of a connection is important for filtering traffic. For example, maintaining state allows the returning traffic to be accepted if the request was initiated from the internal network. Note that in these simple cases we are only considering two computers communicating—for example, an internal workstation connecting to an external Web server.

Forms of State

The state of a connection can be divided into three main categories: new, established, and related. The new state indicates that this is the first packet in a connection. The established state has observed traffic from both directions, so the minimum requirement is that the source computer sends a packet and receives a packet in reply. The new state will change to *established* once the reply packet is processed by the firewall.

The third type of state is *related*, which is somewhat complicated. A connection is considered related if it is associated with an established connection. Therefore an established connection may create a new connection, separate from the original, which is considered related. The common example of this process is the File Transfer Protocol (FTP), which is used to transmit data from a source computer to a destination computer. The process begins with one connection from source to destination on port 21, the command connection. If there is data to be transferred, a second connection is created on port 20 for the data. Hence the data connection is related to the initial control connection. To simplify the firewall policy, it is possible to add a single rule to permit related connections.

In the previous example, the two computers communicating remained the same, but new connections were created, which can be managed in a table. However, understanding related connections is problematic for many new services. One example is the Common Object Resource Broker Architecture (CORBA), which allows software components to be executed on different computers. This communication model may initiate new connections from different computers, similar to peer-to-peer networking. Therefore it is difficult to associate related connections.

Payload Inspection

Although firewalls originally only inspected the packet header, content filtering is increasingly commonplace. In this case the packet payload (also called *contents* or *data)* is examined for certain patterns (analogous to searching for certain words on a page). These patterns, or signatures, could be for inappropriate or illegal content, spam email messages, or intrusion attempts. For example, it is possible to search for certain URLs in the packet payload.

The patterned searched for is often called a *signature*. If the pattern is found, the packet can be simply dropped, or the administrator may want to log the connection. In terms of intrusion signatures, this includes known patterns that may cause a buffer overflow in a network service.

Content filtering can be used to provide differentiated services as well. For example if the firewall can detect that a connection is used for multimedia, it may be possible to provide more bandwidth or disconnect it, depending on the policy. Of course, content filtering assumes that the content is available (readable), which is not the case when encryption is used. For example, many worms encrypt their communications to prevent content filtering at the firewall.

Examining the packet payload normally requires significantly more processing time than normal header inspection. A signature may actually contain several patterns to match, specifying where they should occur relative to the packet beginning and the distance between patterns in the signature. This is only a short list of potential signature characteristics.

A signature can also span multiple packets—for example, a 20-byte signature could occur over two 10-byte IP fragments. Recall that IP may fragment packets based on the maximum transfer unit (MTU) of a link. Therefore the system may have to reassemble fragments before the scanning can begin. This necessary reassembly will further delay the transmission of data, which is problematic for certain types of applications (for example, multimedia). However, at this point, the discussion is more about intrusion detection systems (IDSs) than firewalls.

Over the years several techniques have been developed to decrease the amount of time required for payload inspection. Faster searching algorithms, dedicated hardware, and parallel searching techniques have all shown promise in this regard. However, payload inspection at high bandwidths with low latency often requires expensive equipment.

14. SECURE EXTERNAL SERVICES PROVISIONING

Often we need a server that will provide services that are widely available to the external network. A Web server is a simple example of providing a service (Web pages) to a potentially large set of users (both honest and dishonest). As a result the server will be subjected to malicious intrusion attempts during its deployment.

Therefore systems that provide external services are often deployed on the edge or perimeter of the internal network. Given the location, it is it important to maintain secure communications between it and other servers. For example, assume that the Web server needs to access a database server for content (PHP and MySQL); the connection between these machines must be secure to ensure proper operation.

A common solution to secure communications is the use of a virtual private network (VPN), which uses encryption to tunnel through an insecure network and provide secrecy. Advanced firewalls can create VPNs to different destinations, including mobile users. The first and most popular protocol for VPN is Internet Security Protocol (IPsec), which consists of standards from IPv6 ported to IPv4.

15. NETWORK FIREWALLS FOR VOICE AND VIDEO APPLICATIONS

The next generation of network applications is expected to better leverage different forms of media. This is evident with the increased use of Voice over IP (VoIP) instead of traditional line-line telephones. Teleconferencing is another application that is seeing a steady increase in use because it provides an easy method for collaborating with others.

Teleoperations is another example that is seeing recent growth. These applications allow operators to control equipment that is at another location over the network (for example, telemedicine). Of course these examples assume that the network can provide QoS guarantees, but that is a separate discussion.

Generally speaking, these applications require special handling by network firewalls. In addition, they normally use more than one connection. For example, the audio, video, and control information of a multimedia application often uses multiple network connections.

Multimedia applications also use multiple transport protocols. Control messages can be sent using TCP, which provides a reliable service between the sender and receiver. The media (voice and/or video) is typically sent using UDP. Often Realtime Transport Protocol (RTP) is used, but this protocol is built on UDP. UDP is unreliable but faster than TCP, which is more important for multimedia applications.

As a result, these connections must be carefully managed by the firewall to ensure the proper operation of the application. This includes maintaining state across multiple connections and ensuring that packets are filtered with minimal delay.

Packet Filtering H.323

There are a few multimedia standards for transmitting voice and video over the Internet. Session Initiation Protocol (SIP) and H.323 are two examples commonly found in the Internet. The section briefly describes H.323 to illustrate the support required by network firewalls.

H.323 is the International Telecommunications Union (ITU) standard for videoconferencing. It is a high-level standard that uses other lower-level standards for the actual setup, transmission, control, and tear-down of a videoconference. For example, G.711 is used for encoding and decoding speech, and H.245 is used to negotiate the connections.

During H.323's operation, one port will be used for call setup using the static port 1720 (easy for firewalls). Each datastream will require one dynamically allocated TCP port for control and one dynamically allocated UDP port for data. As previously described, audio and video are transmitted separately.

Therefore an H.323 session will generate at least eight dynamic connections, which makes packet processing at the firewall very difficult. How does a firewall know which ports to open for an H.323 session? This is referred as a *lack of symmetry* between the computer located in the internal network and the computer located in the external network.

A stateful firewall can inspect the packet payloads and determine the dynamic connection port numbers. This information (negotiated port numbers) is placed in higher-level protocols, which are difficult to quickly parse and can be vendor specific.

In 2005 the ITU ratified the H.460.17/.18/.19 standards, which describe how to allow H.323 to traverse a firewall (or a NAT router/firewall, which essentially has the same problem). H.460.17 and H.460.18 deal with signaling, whereas H.460.19 concerns media. The H.460 standards require the deployment of stateful firewalls and updated H.323 equipment. This is a solution, but it remains a complex problem.

16. FIREWALLS AND IMPORTANT ADMINISTRATIVE SERVICE PROTOCOLS

There are a large number of administrative network protocols that are used to manage computer systems. These protocols are typically not complex to control at the firewall since dynamic connections are not used and little state information is necessary. The administrator should be aware of these services when designing the security policy, since many can be leveraged for attacks. This section reviews some of these important protocols.

Routing Protocols

Routing protocols are used to distribute routing information between routing devices. This information will change over time based on network conditions; therefore this information is critical to ensure that packets will get to their destinations. Of course, attackers can also use routing protocols for attacks. For example, maliciously setting routes such that a certain network is not reachable can be considered a denial-of-service (DoS) attack. Securing routers and routing protocols is a continuing area of research. The firewall can help prevent these attacks (typically by not forwarding such information).

In considering routing protocols, it is important to first determine which devices in the internal network will need to receive and submit routing information. More than likely only devices that are directly connected to the external network will need to receive and respond to external routing changes—for example, the gateway router(s) for the internal network. This is primarily due to the hierarchical nature of routing tables, which does not require an external host to know the routing specifics of a distant subnetwork. As a result, there is typically no need to forward routing information from the external network into the internal network, and vice versa.

Routing Information Protocol (RIP) is the oldest routing protocol for the Internet. The two versions of RIP differ primarily by the inclusion of security measures. RIPv1 is the original protocol, and RIPv2 is the same but supports classless addresses and includes some security. Devices that use RIP will periodically (approximately every 30 seconds) broadcast routing information to neighboring hosts. The information sent by a host describes the devices they are directly connected to and the cost. RIP is not very scalable so is primarily used for small networks. RIP uses UDP to broadcast messages; port 520 is used by servers, whereas clients use a port above 1023.

Another routing protocol is Open Short Path First (OSPF), which was developed after RIP. As such OSPF is considered an improvement because it converges faster and it incorporates authentication. Interestingly, OSPF is not built on the transport layer but instead talks directly to IP. It is considered protocol 89 by the IP layer. OSPF messages are broadcast using two special multicast IP addresses: 224.0.0.5 (all SPF/link state routers) and 224.0.0.6 (all designated routers). The use of multicast addresses and setting the packet Time to Live (TTL) to one (which is done by OSPF) typically means a firewall will not pass this routing information.

Internet Control Message Protocol

Internet Control Message Protocol (ICMP) is used to send control messages to network devices and hosts. Routers and other network devices monitor the operation of the network. When an error occurs, these devices can send a message using ICMP. Messages that can be sent include destination unreachable, time exceeded, and echo request.

Although ICMP was intended to help manage the network, unfortunately attackers can use it as well. Several attacks are based on ICMP messages since they were originally allowed through the firewall. For example, simply forging a "destination unreachable" ICMP message can cause problems.

The program ping is one program that uses ICMP to determine whether a system is connected to the Internet (it uses the ICMP messages Echo Request and Echo Reply). However, this program can also be used for a smurf attack, which causes a large number of unsolicited ping replies to be sent toward one computer. As a result most firewall administrators do not allow ping requests or replies across the firewall.

Another program that uses ICMP is traceroute, which determines the path (list of routers) between a source and destination. Finding the path is done by sending multiple packets, each with an increasing TTL number (starting at one). When a router encounters a packet that it cannot forward due to the TTL, an ICMP message is sent back to the source. This reveals the router on the path (assuming that the path remains the same during the process). Most administrators do not want to provide this information, since it can show addresses assigned to hosts, which is useful to attackers. As a result firewalls are often configured to only allow traceroute requests originating from the internal network or limiting replies to traceroute originating from known external computers.

ICMP is built on the IP layer, like TCP and UDP. A firewall can filter these messages based on the message code field, which is a number that corresponds to each type of error message. Although this section described the problems with allowing ICMP messages through the firewall, an administrator may not want to block all ICMP packets. For example, Maximum Transfer Unit (MTU) messages are important for the transmission of packets and probably should be allowed.

Network Time Protocol

Network Time Protocol (NTP) is a protocol that allows the synchronization of system clocks (from desktops to servers). Having synchronized clocks is not only convenient but required for many distributed applications. Therefore the firewall policy must allow the NTP service if the time comes from an external server.

NTP is a built-on UDP, where port 123 is used for NTP server communication and NTP clients use port 1023 (for example, a desktop). Unfortunately, like many legacy protocols, NTP suffers from security issues. It is possible to spoof NTP packets, causing clocks to set to various times (an issue for certain services that run periodically). There are several cases of NTP misuse and abuse where servers are the victim of DoS attacks.

As a result, if clock synchronization is needed, it may be better to provide an internal NTP server (master clock) that synchronizes the remaining clocks in the internal network. If synchronization is needed by an NTP server in the Internet, consider using a bastion host.

Central Log File Management

Almost every operating system maintains a system log where important information about a system's state is reported. This log is a valuable resource for managing system resources and investigating security issues.

Given that almost every system (especially a server) generates log messages, having this information at a central location is beneficial. The protocol syslog provides this functionality, whereby messages can be forwarded to a syslog server, where they are stored. An attacker will commonly attempt to flood the syslog server with fake messages in an effort to cover their steps or to cause the server disk to fill, causing syslog to stop.

Syslog runs on UDP, where syslog servers listen to UDP port 514 and clients (sending log messages) use a port above 1023. Note that a syslog server will not send a message back to the client, but the syslog log server can communicate, normally using port 514.

Generally allowing syslog communication between the external and internal network is not needed or advised. Syslog communications should be limited to internal computers and servers; otherwise a VPN should be used to prevent abuse from others and to keep the information in the messages private.

Dynamic Host Configuration Protocol

The Dynamic Host Configuration Protocol (DHCP) provides computers essential information when connecting to an IP network. This is necessary because a computer (for example, a mobile laptop) does not have an IP address to use.

The computer needing an IP address will first send a broadcast request for an IP address. A DHCP server will reply with the IP address, netmask, and gateway router information the computer should use. The address provided comes from a pool of available IP addresses, which is managed by the DHCP server. Therefore the DHCP provides a method of sharing IP addresses among a group of hosts that will change over time.

The actual exchange of information is more elaborate than described here, but this is enough information for our discussion. In general the DHCP server providing addresses will be located in the internal network. As a result, this information should not be transmitted across the firewall that separates the internal and external networks. Why would you want to provide IP addresses to computers in the external network?

17. INTERNAL IP SERVICES PROTECTION

Domain Name Server (DNS) provides the translation between the hostname and the IP address, which is necessary to send packets in the Internet. Given the number of hostnames in the Internet, DNS is built on a hierarchical structure. The local DNS server cannot store all the possible hostnames and IP addresses, so this server will need to occasionally request a translation from another DNS server located in the external network. As a result it is important to configure the firewall to permit this type of lookup.

In many cases the service provider provides the address of a DNS server that can be used to translate external hostnames. There is no need to manage a local DNS server in this case. However, it is possible to manage a local DNS, which allows the internal network to use local hostnames (these can be published to the external network). Some advanced firewalls can provide DNS, which can help hide internal computer hostnames

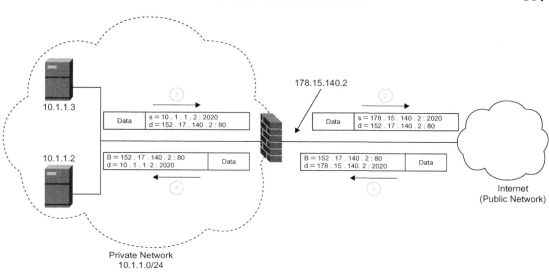

FIGURE 6.4 Example source Network Address Translation (NAT). The connection originates from a computer in the internal network and is sent to a computer in the external network. Note the address and port number exchange performed at the firewall.

and IP addresses. As a result, external computers have a limited view of the internal network.

Another important service that can be provided by the firewall is Network Address Translation (NAT). NAT is a popular method for sharing a smaller set of IP addresses across a larger number of computers. Recall that every packet has a source IP, source port, destination IP, and destination port. Assume that a small network only has one external IP address but has multiple computers that need to access the Internet. Note the external address is a routable address, whereas the internal computers would use a private address (addresses have no meaning outside the internal network). NAT will allow the internal machines to share the single external IP address.[11]

When a packet arrives from a computer in the internal network, its source address is replaced with the external address, as shown in Figure 6.4. The packet is sent to the destination computer, which returns a packet. The return packet has the external address (which is routable), so it is forwarded to the firewall. The firewall can then replace the external destination address with the correct internal destination address. What if multiple internal machines send a packet to a server in the external network? The firewall will replace the source address with the external address, but how will the firewall differentiate the return packets? NAT will also change the source port number, so each connection can be separated.

11. B. Hickman, D. Newman, S. Tadjudin, and T. Martin, *Benchmarking Methodology for Firewall Performance*, IETF RFC 3511, 2003.

The NAT process described in the preceding paragraph is *source NAT*,[12] which works for packets initiated in the internal network. There is also *destination NAT*, which works in a similar fashion for packets initiated in the external network. In this case the firewall needs to know which machine to forward packets to in the internal network.

18. FIREWALL REMOTE ACCESS CONFIGURATION

As described in the first section, firewalls are deployed to help maintain the privacy of data and authenticate the source. Privacy can be provided using encryption, for which there are several possible algorithms to use. These algorithms can be categorized as either secret key or public key. Secret key techniques use the same key to encrypt and decrypt information. Examples include IDEA, RC4, Twofish, and AES. Though secret key algorithms are fast, they require the key to be distributed between the two parties in advance, which is not trivial.

Public key encryption uses two keys—one to encrypt (the public key) and another to decrypt (the private key). The public key can be freely available for others to use to encrypt messages for the owner of the private key, since only the private key can decrypt a message. Key management sounds easy, but secure key distribution is difficult. How do you know the public key obtained is the correct one? Perhaps it is a man-in-middle attack. The Public Key Infrastructure (PKI), one method of distributing public keys, depends on a system of trusted key servers.

Authentication is another important component of security; it attempts to confirm a person is who he or she claims to be. This can be done based on what the user has (ID card or security token) or by something a person knows (for example, a password). A very familiar method of authentication is requesting a username and password, which is common for VPNs.

Secrecy and authentication are also important when an entity manages multiple separate networks. In this case the administrator would like to interconnect the networks but must do so using an insecure network (for example, the Internet).

Tunneling from one firewall to another firewall can create a secure interconnection. This can be done using application proxies or VPN. Application firewalls implement a proxy for each application supported. A user first contacts the firewall and authenticates before connecting to the server. The firewall then connects to the destination firewall, which then connects to the destination server. Three connections are thus involved.

An alternative is to construct a VPN from one firewall to another. Now a secure connection exists between the two networks. However, note that the VPN could also be used as an easy connection for an attacker who has successfully broken into one of the networks.

It is also important to note that tunneling can be used to transport packets over a network with a different transport protocol—for example, carrying TCP/IP traffic over Frame Relay.

12. K. Egevang and P. Francis, *The IP Network Address Translator (NAT)*, IETF RFC 1631, 1994.

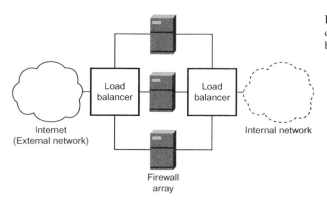

FIGURE 6.5 Load-balancing firewall array consisting of a three-firewall array and a load balancer.

19. LOAD BALANCING AND FIREWALL ARRAYS

As network speeds continue to increase, firewalls must continue to process packets with minimal delay (latency). Unfortunately, firewalls that can operate at these extreme data rates are also typically very expensive and cannot easily be upgraded to meet future demands. Load-balancing firewalls can provide an answer to this important problem.[13]

Load balancing (or *parallelization)* provides a scalable firewall solution for high-bandwidth networks and/or low-latency applications. This approach consists of an array of firewalls that process arriving packets in parallel. A simple system would consist of two load balancers connected to an array of firewalls, where each firewall is identically configured (same firewall policy), as depicted in Figure 6.5. One balancer connects to the Internet, then to the array (arriving traffic); the other balancer connects to the internal network, then to the array (departing traffic). Of course, one load balancer can be used instead of two separate load balancers.

When a packet arrives, it is sent to a firewall that currently has the lightest load (fewest number of packets awaiting processing), hence the term *load balancing*. As a result, the amount of traffic each firewall must process is roughly $1/n$ of the total traffic, where n is the number of firewalls in the array.

As with any new firewall implementation, the integrity of the policy must be maintained. This means that given a policy, a traditional single firewall and a load-balancing firewall will accept the same packets and deny the same packets. For static rules, integrity is provided, since the policy is duplicated at every firewall; therefore the set of accepted and denied packets at each firewall is also the same. As will be discussed in the next sections, maintaining integrity for stateful rules is not easy.

---

13. Errin W. Fulp and Ryan J. Farley, "A function-parallel architecture for high-speed firewalls," In *Proceedings of the IEEE International Conference on Communications*, 2006.

Load Balancing in Real Life

A simple supermarket analogy can help describe the system and the potential performance increase. Consider a market consisting of an array of n cashiers. As with the firewall system, each cashier in the market is identical and performs the same duties. When a customer wants to pay for her items, she is directed to the cashier with the shortest line. The load balancer is the entity that would direct the customer, but in reality such a person rarely exists. A customer must guess which line is actually the best to join, which as we all know is not simple to determine.

Obviously, as more cashiers are added, the market can check out more customers. This is akin to increasing the bandwidth of the firewall system. Another important advantage of a load-balancing system is robustness. Even if a cashier takes a break (or a firewall in the array fails), the system will still function properly, albeit more slowly.

How to Balance the Load

An important problem with load-balancing firewalls is how to quickly balance the lines (queues) of packets. We are all aware that customers require different amounts of time to check out of a market. This is dependent on the number of items (which is observable) and their ability to pay (not easily observable). Similarly, it is difficult to determine how much time a packet will require at a firewall (for software-based systems). It will depend on the number of rules, organization of the rules, and which rule the packet will match.

A more important problem with load balancing is how to maintain state. As described in the preceding sections, some firewall rules will maintain the state of a connection. For example, a firewall rule may allow traffic arriving from the Internet only if an internal computer requested it. If this is the case, a new temporary rule will be generated to handle traffic arriving from the Internet. In a parallel system, where should this rule reside? Which firewall? The objective is to ensure that the integrity of the policy is maintained in the load-balancing system.

To use the market analogy again (and this will be a stretch), assume that a mother leaves her credit card with one cashier, then sends her children into the market to buy certain items. When the children are ready to pay for their items they must go to the cashier that has the credit card. If the children don't know which cashier has the credit card the load balancer must not only balance lines but also check a list to make certain the children join the correct line.

Maintaining state increases the amount of time the load balancer will spend per packet, which increases the latency of the system. An alternative solution is it to replicate the stateful rules across every firewall (or the credit card across every cashier). This requires an interconnection and state-aware program per firewall. Maintaining network connections is also difficult for applications that dynamically create new connections. Examples include FTP (one connection for control, the other for data), multimedia, and CORBA. Again, a new rule must be added to handle the new traffic.

Advantages and Disadvantages of Load Balancing

Given these issues, firewall load balancing is still done. There are several advantages and disadvantages to this approach. Disadvantages of load balancing include:

- *Load balancing is not trivial.* The load balancer seeks to ensure that the lines of packets across the array of firewalls remains equal. However, this assumes that the balancer can predict how much time a packet will require.
- *Maintaining state is difficult.* All packets that belong to a session will need to traverse the same firewall, or state information must be shared across the firewalls. Either solution is difficult to manage.

There are several advantages to load balancing:

- *Scalable solution for higher throughput.* If higher throughput is needed, adding more firewalls is simple and cost effective.
- *Robustness.* If a firewall fails in the array, the integrity of the system remains. The only loss is throughput.
- *Easy policy management.* If the rules change, simply update the policy at each firewall.

The load balancer can be implemented in software or hardware. Hardware load balancers provide better performance, but they will also have a much higher price.

20. HIGHLY AVAILABLE FIREWALLS

As previously discussed, a network firewall is generally considered easier to manage than multiple host-based firewalls. The administrator only manages one firewall and one policy, but this design also introduces a single point of failure. If the network firewall fails in the system, the entire internal network is isolated from the Internet. As a result, there is a real need to provide a highly available, or robust, firewall system.

The load-balancing system described in the previous section provides a greater degree of robustness. If a firewall in the array fails, the system is still functional; however, the capacity of the system is reduced, which is considered acceptable under the circumstances. Unfortunately, the design still has a single point of failure—the load distributor. If the load distributor fails, the entire system fails.

A simple solution to this problem simply replicates the load distributor. The incoming connection is duplicated to both load distributors, and the distributors are then connected to the firewalls in the array. The distributors are interconnected via a lifeline to detect failure and possibly share information.

Load Balancer Operation

The two load balancers described in the previous section can operate in one of two modes: active-backup or active-active. In active-backup mode, one balancer operates as normal distributing packets to minimize delays and maintain state information. The second distributor is in backup mode and monitors the status of the active load balancer and duplicates any necessary state information. Upon load-balance failure, the backup device can quickly take over operation.

In contrast, active-active operation operates both load balancers in parallel. When a packet arrives at the system, it is processed by one of the load balancers, which forwards the packet to a firewall in the array. Of course, this seems as though there will be a load balancer for the load balancers, but this is not necessary. Under active-active mode, the load balancers use the lifeline to synchronize and determine which packets to process. Although the active-active mode can increase performance by using both load balancers simultaneously, it is more difficult to implement and complex to manage.

Interconnection of Load Balancers and Firewalls

In our simple example, the additional load balancer requires double the number of ports per firewall (one per load balancer). This design provides greater robustness but may also be cost prohibitive.

An alternative solution uses active-active mode and divides the array into two equal groups. One group is then connected to one load-balancer and the other group is connected to the other. For example, consider an array of six firewalls. Three firewalls would be connected to one load balancer and the other six firewalls connected to the second load balancer. Although this design only requires one port per firewall (on one side), if a load balancer fails, half the firewalls are nonoperational.

21. FIREWALL MANAGEMENT

Once a firewall has been deployed and policy created, it is important to determine whether it is providing the desired security. Auditing is the process of verifying the firewall and policy and consists of two steps. First, the administrator should determine whether the firewall is secure. If an attacker can exploit the firewall, the attacker has a significant advantage. Consider the information that can be gained just from knowing the firewall policy.

The firewall should be in a secure location and have the latest security patches (recall that many firewalls are implemented in software). Also ensure that the firewall only provides the necessary services, such as SSH, if remote access to the firewall is needed. Exploiting a firewall operating system or provided services is the most common method for breaking into a firewall. Therefore the services and access should be tightly controlled. User authentication with good passwords and secure connections should always be used.

Once the firewall has been secured, the administrator should review the policy and verify that it provides the security desired. Does it block the illegitimate traffic and permit legitimate traffic? This is not a trivial task, given the first-match criterion and the number of rules in the policy. It is easy to create firewall policies with anomalies, such as shadowing (a subsequent rule that is never matched because of an earlier rule). Some software packages are available to assist this process, but in general it is a difficult problem.

An administrator should periodically audit the firewall rules and test the policy to verify that the system performs as expected. In addition, the system should undergo penetration testing to verify correct implementation. This includes seeded and blind penetration testing. *Seeded testing* includes detailed information about the network and configuration, so target systems and services can be tested. *Blind testing* is done without any knowledge of the system, so it is more complete but also more time consuming.

Keeping backups of configurations and policies should be done in case of hardware failure or an intrusion. Logging at the firewall should also be performed, which can help measure performance. In addition, logs can show connections over time, which is useful for forensics and verifying whether the security policy is sufficient.

22. SUMMARY

Network firewalls are a key component of providing a secure environment. These systems are responsible for controlling access between two networks, which is done by applying a security policy to arriving packets. The policy describes which packets should be accepted and which should be dropped. The firewall inspects the packet header and/or the payload (data portion).

There are several different types of firewalls, each briefly described in this chapter. Firewalls can be categorized based on what they inspect (packet filter, stateful, or application), their implementation (hardware or software), or their location (host or network). Combinations of the categories are possible, and each type has specific advantages and disadvantages.

Placement of the firewall with respect to servers and internal computers is key to the way these systems will be protected. Often servers that are externally available, such as Web servers, will be located away from other internal computers. This is often accomplished by placing these servers in a demilitarized zone (DMZ). A different security policy is applied to these computers so the access between computers in the DMZ and the internal network is limited.

Improving the performance of the firewall can be achieved by minimizing the rules in the policy (primarily for software firewalls). Moving more popular rules near the beginning of the policy can also reduce the number of rules comparisons that are required. However, the order of certain rules must be maintained (any rules that can match the same packet).

Parallel firewalls can provide greater performance improvements. These systems consist of a load balancer and an array of firewalls, where all the firewalls in the array are identical. When a packet arrives at the system, it is sent to one of the firewalls in the array. The load balancer maintains short packet queues, which can provide greater system bandwidth and possibly a lower latency.

Regardless of the firewall implementation, placement, or design, deployment requires constant vigilance. Developing the appropriate policy (set of rules) requires a detailed understanding of the network topology and the necessary services. If either of these items change (and they certainly will), that will require updating the policy. Finally, it is important to remember that a firewall is not a complete security solution but is a key part of a security solution.

Finally, let's move on to the real interactive part of this Chapter: review questions/exercises, hands-on projects, case projects and optional team case project. The answers and/or solutions by chapter can be found in the Online Instructor's Solutions Manual.

CHAPTER REVIEW QUESTIONS/EXERCISES

True/False

1. True or False? Network firewalls are a vital component for maintaining a secure environment and are often the first line of defense against attack.
2. True or False? When a packet arrives at a firewall, a hacker policy is applied to determine the appropriate action.
3. True or False? Multiple rules of a single firewall policy may match a packet—for example, a packet could match rules 2, 6, and 7 of the policy.
4. True or False? For most firewalls, the first rule that matches a packet is not typically applied.
5. True or False? Given that a network firewall will not inspect all packets transmitted between multiple networks, these devices need to determine the appropriate match with minimal delay.

Multiple Choice

1. What refers to how often the rule is a match?
   A. Worm
   B. Virus
   C. Backdoor
   D. More popular
   E. User-level Rootkit
2. What is the most basic type of a firewall since it only filters at the network and transport layers (layers two and three)?
   A. Backdoor
   B. Virus
   C. Worm
   D. Packet filter
   E. User-level Rootkit
3. What perform the same operations as packet filters, but also maintain state about the packets that have arrived?
   A. Stateful firewalls
   B. Virus
   C. Worm
   D. Backdoor
   E. User-level Rootkit

4. What can filter traffic at the network, transport, and application layer?
   A. Application layer firewalls
   B. Virus
   C. Worm
   D. Backdoor
   E. User-level Rootkit
5. What can also be categorized based on where they are implemented or what they are intended to protect—host or network?
   A. Trojan Horse
   B. Firewalls
   C. Worm
   D. Backdoor
   E. User-level Rootkit

EXERCISE

Problem

Create a firewall policy that specifies how firewalls should handle inbound and outbound network traffic.

Hands-On Projects

Project

Identify all requirements that should be considered when determining which firewall to implement.

Case Projects

Problem

Create rulesets that implement the organization's firewall policy while supporting firewall performance.

Optional Team Case Project

Problem

Manage firewall architectures, policies, software, and other components throughout the life of the firewall solutions.

Penetration Testing

Sanjay Bavisi
EC-Council

1. INTRODUCTION

Last year I walked into a restaurant in Rochester, New York, with a business partner; I was wearing an EC-Council official polo shirt. The back of the shirt was embroidered with the words "Licensed Penetration Tester." On reading those words on my shirt, a group of young executives seated behind me started an intense dialogue among themselves.

They were obviously not amused at my "behavior," since that was a restaurant for decent people! On my way out, I walked up to them and asked if they were amazed at what that statement meant. They replied "Absolutely!" When I explained to them the meaning of a Licensed Penetration Tester, they gave a loud laugh and apologized to me. They admitted that they had thought I was a pervert.

Each time I am at an airport, I get some stares when I put on that shirt. So the question is, what is penetration testing?

2. WHAT IS PENETRATION TESTING?

Penetration testing is the exploitation of vulnerabilities present in an organization's network. It helps determine which vulnerabilities are exploitable and the degree of information exposure or network control that the organization could expect an attacker to achieve after successfully exploiting a vulnerability. No penetration test is or ever can be "just like a hacker would do it," due to necessary limitations placed on penetration tests conducted by "white hats." Hackers don't have to follow the same rules as the "good guys" and they could care less whether your systems crash during one of their "tests." We'll talk more about this later. Right now, before we can talk any more about penetration testing, we need to talk about various types of vulnerabilities and how they might be discovered.

Before we can exploit a vulnerability in a penetration test, we have to discover what vulnerabilities exist within (and outside of) the organization. A vulnerability is a potential weakness in an organization's security. I use the term "potential" because not all vulnerabilities are exploitable or worth exploiting. A flaw may exist and may even be documented, but perhaps no one has figured out (yet) how to exploit it. Some vulnerabilities, although exploitable, might not yield enough information in return for the time or resources necessary to exploit them. Why break into a bank and steal only a dollar? That doesn't make much sense, does it?

Vulnerabilities can be thought of in two broad categories: logical and physical. We normally think of logical vulnerabilities as those associated with the organization's computers, infrastructure devices, software, or applications. Physical vulnerabilities, on the other hand, are normally thought of as those having to do with either the actual physical security of the organization (such as a door that doesn't always lock properly), the sensitive information that "accidentally" ends up in the dumpster, or the vulnerability of the organization's employees to social engineering (a vendor asking to use a computer to send a "quick email" to the boss).

Logical vulnerabilities can be discovered using any number of manual or automated tools and even by browsing the Internet. For those of you who are familiar with Johnny Long's *Google Hacking* books: *"Passwords,* for the *love of God!!!* Google found *passwords!"* The discovery of logical vulnerabilities is usually called *security scanning, vulnerability scanning,* or just *scanning.* Unfortunately, there are a number of "security consultants" who run a scan, put a fancy report cover on the output of the tool, and pass off these scans as a penetration test.

Physical vulnerabilities can be discovered as part of a physical security inspection, a "midnight raid" on the organization's dumpsters, getting information from employees, or via unaccompanied access to a usually nonpublic area (I really need to use the bathroom!).

Vulnerabilities might also exist due to a lack of company policies or procedures or an employee's failure to follow the policy or procedure. Regardless of the cause of the vulnerability, it might have the potential to compromise the organization's security. So, of all the vulnerabilities that have been discovered, how do we know which ones pose the greatest danger to the organization's network? We test them! We test them to see which ones we can exploit and exactly what could happen if a "real" attacker exploited that vulnerability.

Because few organizations that I know of have enough money, time, or resources to eliminate every vulnerability discovered, they have to prioritize their efforts; this is one of the best reasons for an organization to conduct a penetration test. At the conclusion of the penetration test, they will know which vulnerabilities can be exploited and what can happen if they are exploited. They can then plan to correct the vulnerabilities based on the amount of critical information exposed or network control gained by exploiting the vulnerability. In other words, a penetration test helps organizations strike a balance between security and business functionality. Sounds like a perfect solution, right? If only it were so!

There are organizations that do not care about the "true risks" that their organizations face. Instead, they are more interested in being able to tell their shareholders or their regulating agencies that they've conducted a penetration test and "passed" it. If the penetration test is structured so that only certain systems are tested, or if the test is conducted during a known timeframe, the test results will be favorable to the organization, but the test isn't a true reflection of its network security posture. This kind of "boutique testing" can lead to a false sense of security for the organization, its employees, and its stakeholders.

3. HOW DOES PENETRATION TESTING DIFFER FROM AN ACTUAL "HACK?"

Earlier, I mentioned that penetration testing isn't and never can be "just like a hacker would do it." How come? Except in the case of "directed" sabotage or espionage, it's not personal between your organization and attackers. They don't care who you are, where you are, or what your organization does to earn its living. They just want to hack something. The easier it is to attack your network, the more likely it is that you'll be a target. Ask your network administrator to look at the network intrusion detection logs (or look at them yourself if you're a network admin). See how many times in a 24-hour period your organization's network gets scanned for potential vulnerabilities.

Once an attacker has decided that you're his or her (yes, there *are* female hackers—good ones, too!) next target, they may take weeks or months to perform the first step of an attack: reconnaissance. As a penetration tester or company providing penetration testing services, I doubt that you're going to get hired to spend six months doing reconnaissance and another couple of months conducting an attack. So, the first difference between a penetration test and a real attack is the length of time taken to conduct all the activities needed to produce a successful outcome. As "good guys," we don't have the luxury of time that the "bad guys" do. So we're handicapped to begin with. The two things I tell clients are:

1. I cannot spend the months planning to attack you like a real hacker can
2. I cannot break the law, I am limited by a code of ethics, and have to maintain "ethical" boundaries.

In some (not all) cases, once attackers find a suitable vulnerability to attack, they will. They don't care that the vulnerability resides on a mission-critical system, if the vulnerability will crash the system, or that the system might become unusable in the middle of the busiest time of day. If that vulnerability doesn't "pan out," they find another and try again. They keep it up until they run out of vulnerabilities that they can exploit, or they're discovered, or they manage to successfully breach the network or crash the system. Penetration test teams normally don't have this luxury, either. Usually the test team has X amount of time to find a vulnerability and get in or the test is over and the network is declared "safe and secure." If the test team didn't have enough time to test all the vulnerabilities—oh, well. The test is still over, they still didn't get in, and so our network *must* be safe! Few seem to think about the fact that a "real" attacker may, just by blind luck, choose one of the unable-to-be-tested-because-of-time-limitations vulnerabilities and be able to waltz right into the network without being detected. One of the most important things for a tester and/or clients to grasp is the fact that no test will find everything, there are always things that can be missed, be it due to time constraints, or the team did not have the right conditions to find the weakness. It is best to proceed with the understanding that there will always be things we might miss, our job as a tester is to find what we can within the scope of the assessment and time constraints. At the end of the day, the goal of the test is to provide the client a report that will assist them in improving their security posture, there is no such thing as perfect security and there will never be.

Some systems are declared "off limits" to testing because they're "too important to have crash" during a test. An organization may specify that testing can only occur during certain hours or on certain days because of a real or perceived impact on business operations. This is the second difference between a penetration test and a real attack: Hackers don't play by any rules. They attack what they want when they want and how they want. Just to be clear: I'm not advocating denial-of-service testing during the busiest time of an organization's day, or unrestricted testing at any time. I'm just trying to make a point that *no* system is too critical to test. From a hacker's perspective, there are no "off-limits" systems, just opportunities for attack. We'll talk more about differences between real attacks and penetration tests when we talk about the various types of testing in the next section. For example, in a bank or financial company you never get to test their financial databases, there is just too much risk, and when that is the revenue that the company uses to survive they are not going to let you test it, and real hackers would not have this limitation.

4. TYPES OF PENETRATION TESTING

Some sources classify penetration testing into two types—internal and external—and then talk about the "variations" of these types of tests based on the amount of information the test team has been given about the organization prior to starting the test. Other sources use a reverse-classification system, typing the penetration test based on the amount of information available to the test team and then the location from which the test is conducted. I much prefer the latter method, since it removes any chance of misunderstanding about what testing is going to be conducted where. *Warning:* If you're planning to take the CISSP or some of the other network security certification examinations, stick with the "old skool" "classification by location, then type" definitions for penetration testing types and variations.

When a penetration test is conducted against Internet-facing hosts, it is known as *external testing*. When conducted against hosts inside the organization's internal network, it is known as *internal testing*. Obviously, a complete penetration test will encompass testing of both external and internal hosts. The "variations" of penetration tests are normally classified based on how much information the test team has been given about the organization. The three most commonly used terms for penetration types are *white-box, gray-box,* and *black-box testing.* Before we talk about these penetration testing variations, you need to understand that we can conduct any of them (white, gray, or black) either externally or internally. If we want a complete test, we need to test both externally *and* internally. Got it? Good! Now we can talk about what is involved with each type of testing.

We'll start with white-box testing. The "official" definition of white-box testing usually includes verbiage about providing information so as to be able to assess the security of a specific target or assess security against a specific attack. There are several problems with this definition in real life. The first is that it sounds as though you would only conduct a white-box test if you were looking to verify the security of one specific host or looking to verify the security of your network against one specific attack. But it would be foolhardy to test for only one vulnerability. Since the "variations" we're talking about are supposed to be centered on the amount of information available to the test team, let's look at a white-box test from an information availability perspective.

Who in your organization knows the most about your network? Probably the network administrator. Any organization that has recently terminated employment of a network administrator or member of the IT Department under less than favorable circumstances has a big problem. There is the potential that the organization's network could be attacked by this former employee who has extreme knowledge about the network. In a white-box test, therefore, the test team should be given about the same amount of information that a network administrator would have. Probably the team won't be given passwords, but they'll be given network ranges, topologies, and so on.

Gray-box testing, by "official" definition, provides "some" knowledge to the test team, about the sort of thing a normal, unprivileged user might have: hostnames, maybe a few IP addresses, the fact that the organization allows senior management to "remote" into the network, and so on. Common, though not necessarily public, knowledge about the "inner workings" of the organization's network is the level of information provided to the test team. Some sources claim that this testing type (as well as the information disclosed in a white-box test) "puts the tester at an advantage" over an attacker because the test team possesses information that an attacker wouldn't have. But that's not necessarily the case. Any organization that has terminated a "normal user" has the potential for an attack based on that user's inside knowledge of the network.

Now let's talk about everyone's favorite: black-box penetration testing. Again, we'll start with the common definition, which usually says something like "provides the test team with little or no information except for possibly the company name." The test team is required to obtain all their attack information from public sources such as the Internet. There's usually some sentence somewhere in the description that says how a black-box test is always much better than any other type of test because it most closely mimics the way an attacker would conduct an attack. The definition might be right (and I might even be inclined to agree with it) if the organization has never terminated a network admin or any other employee with network access. I might also be more in agreement with this train of thought if the majority of attacks were conducted by unknown persons from the far reaches of the globe instead of former employees or currently employed "insiders"!

Depending on what article or book you happen to be reading at the time, you might also see references to application penetration testing, Web penetration testing, shrink-wrap penetration testing, wireless penetration testing, telephony penetration testing, Bluetooth penetration testing ... and the list goes on. I've seen every possible device in a network listed as a separate penetration test. The bottom line is that if it's present in the network, an organization needs to discover what vulnerabilities exist on it and then test those vulnerabilities to discover what could happen if they're successfully exploited.

I guess since Morgan Kaufmann asked me to write this chapter, I can give you my opinion: I don't like black-box penetration testing. I don't want any network of mine tested "just like a hacker would do it." I want my network tested *better* than any hacker ever could, because I don't want to end up on the front page of *The New York Times* as the subject of a "latest breach" article. My client's data are much too important to take that chance.

The success of every penetration test rests on the experience of the test team. If some hacker has more experience than the test team I hire, I'm in trouble! So how do I even the odds? Instead of hiring a team to do a black box, in which they're going to spend hours searching for information and poking around, I give them the necessary information to test the network thoroughly, right up front. By doing so, their time is actually spent testing the network, not carrying out a high-tech scavenger hunt. Any good penetration test team is still going to do reconnaissance and tell me what information is available about my organization from public sources anyway. No, I'm not going to give up the administrative password to my network. But I am going to tell them what my IP ranges are, whether or not I have wireless, and whether I allow remote access into the network, among other things.

In addition to the types and variations of penetration testing, we also need to talk about announced and unannounced testing. Which of these two methods will be used depends on whether your intent is to test the network itself or the network's security staff. In an announced test, the penetration testing team works in "full cooperation" with the IT staff and the IT staff has "full knowledge" about the test, such as what will be tested and when. In an unannounced test, only specific members of the tested organization (usually the higher levels of management) are aware that the testing will take place. Even they may only know a "window" of time for testing, not the exact times or dates.

If you follow the published guidelines, an unannounced test is used when testing an organization's incident response capability is called for. Announced tests are used when the organization simply wants to test network devices. Is this really how it happens in the real world? Sometimes it isn't.

Most organizations that conduct annual testing do so at about the same time every year, especially if it's a government organization. So there's really no such thing as an "unannounced" test. Everyone knows that sometime between X and Y dates, they're going to be tested. In some organizations this means that during that timeframe there suddenly appears to be an increased awareness of network security. Machines get patched quicker. Logs are reviewed daily. Abnormal activities are reported immediately. After the testing window is over, however, it's back to the same old routine until the next testing window, next year.

What about announced testing, you ask? Think about it: If you're a network administrator and you know a test is coming, you're going to make sure that everything is as good as you can make it. Once again, there's that increased emphasis on security—until the testing window is over, that is.

Let's take a minute to recap what we've talked about so far. We've learned that a penetration test is used to exploit discovered vulnerabilities and to help determine what an attacker could do if they successfully exploited a vulnerability. We learned that not all vulnerabilities are actually a concern, because there might not be a way to exploit them or what we'd get by exploiting them wouldn't justify the time or effort we spent in doing so. We learned that there are different types and variations of penetration tests, that they can be announced or unannounced, and that none of them are actually "just like a hacker would do it." Probably the most important thing we've learned so far is that if we really and truly want to protect our network from a real-life attack, we have to offset the biggest advantage that a hacker has: time. We discovered that we can do this by giving the testing team sufficient information to thoroughly test the network instead of surfing the Internet on our dime. In today's penetration testing world , when we get hired to do a general penetration test, we inform the client that the level of skill we are going to emulate, shall be the skill set of an average hacker within the parameters set by the client. This means we will use a combination of tools and manual techniques and proven methodologies. Given the general scope of the assignment, this will not enable us to reverse engineer all of the applications and run debugging tools to find vulnerabilities, and write our own exploits, as it is too time consuming and obviously outside of the scope of the engagement.

5. PHASES OF PENETRATION TESTING

There are three phases in a penetration test, and they mimic the phases that an attacker would use to conduct a real attack. These phases are the pre-attack phase, the attack phase, and the post-attack phase, as shown in Figure 7.1.

The activities that take place in each phase (as far as the penetration testing team is concerned) depend on how the rules of engagement have specified that the penetration test be conducted. To give you a more complete picture, we talk about these phases from the perspective of a hacker and from that of a penetration team conducting the test under "black-box" conditions.

The Pre-Attack Phase

The pre-attack phase (see Figure 7.2) consists of the penetration team's or hacker's attempts to investigate or explore the potential target. This reconnaissance effort is normally categorized into two types: active reconnaissance and passive reconnaissance.

Beginning with passive reconnaissance, which does not "touch" the network and is therefore undetectable by the target organization, the hacker or penetration tester will gather as much information as possible about the target company. Once all available sources for passive reconnaissance have been exhausted, the test team or attacker may move into active reconnaissance.

During active reconnaissance, the attacker may actually "touch" the network, thereby increasing the chance that they will be detected or alert the target that someone is "rattling

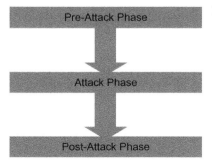

FIGURE 7.1   The three phases in a penetration test.

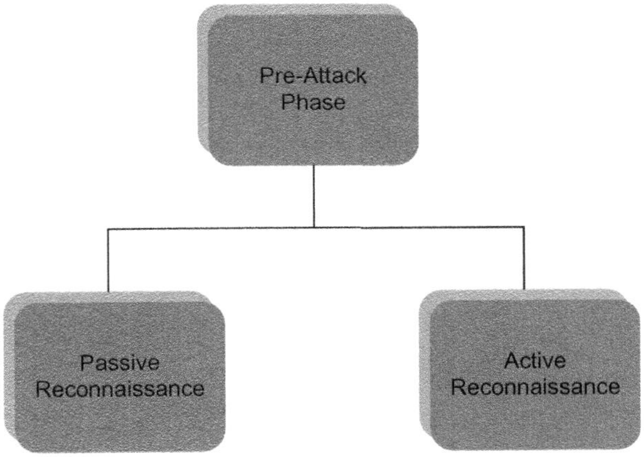

FIGURE 7.2   The pre-attack phase.

the doorknobs." Some of the information gathered during reconnaissance can be used to produce a provisional map of the network infrastructure for planning a more coordinated attack strategy later. Ultimately it boils down to information gathering in all its many forms. Hackers will often spend more time on pre-attack or reconnaissance activities than on the actual attack itself.

The Attack Phase

This stage involves the actual compromise of the target. The hacker or test team may exploit a logical or physical vulnerability discovered during the pre-attack phase or use other methods such as a weak security policy to gain access to a system. The important point here is to understand that although there could be several possible vulnerabilities, the hacker needs only one to be successful to compromise the network.

By comparison, a penetration test team will be interested in finding and exploiting as many vulnerabilities as possible because neither the organization nor the test team will know which vulnerability a hacker will choose to exploit first (see Figure 7.3). Once inside, the attacker may attempt to escalate his or her privileges, install one or more applications to sustain their access, further exploit the compromised system, and/or attempt to extend their control to other systems within the network. When they've finished having their way with the system or network, they will attempt to eliminate all evidence of their presence in a process some call "covering their tracks."

The Post-Attack Phase

The post-attack phase is unique to the penetration test team. It revolves around returning any modified system(s) to the pretest state. With the exception of covering their tracks, a real attacker couldn't care less about returning a compromised system to its original state. The longer the system remains compromised, the longer they can legitimately claim credit for "pwning" (owning) the system.

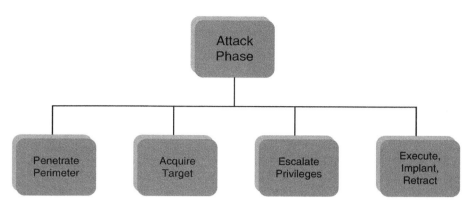

FIGURE 7.3   The attack phase.

Obviously, in a real penetration test, the following list would include reversal of each and every change made to the network to restore it to its pre-attack state. Some of the activities that the test team may have to accomplish are shown here:

- Removal of any files, tools, exploits, or other test-created objects uploaded to the system during testing
- Removal or reversal of any changes to the registry made during system testing
- Reversal of any access control list (ACL) changes to file(s) or folder(s) or other system or user object(s)
- Restoration of the system, network devices, and network infrastructure to the state the network was in prior to the beginning of the test

The key element for the penetration test team to be able to restore the network or system to its pre-attack state is documentation. The penetration testing team documents every step of every action taken during the test, for two reasons. The obvious one is so that they can reverse their steps to "cleanse" the system or network. The second reason is to ensure repeatability of the test. Why is repeatability an issue?

An important part of the penetration test team's job is not only to find and exploit vulnerabilities but also to recommend appropriate mitigation strategies for discovered vulnerabilities. This is especially true for those vulnerabilities that were successfully exploited. After the tested organization implements the recommended corrections, it should repeat the penetration test team's actions to ensure that the vulnerability has indeed been eliminated and that the applied mitigation has not had "unintended consequences" by creating a new vulnerability. The only way to do that is to recreate the original test that found the vulnerability in the first place, make sure it's gone, and then make sure there are no new vulnerabilities as a result of fixing the original problem.

As you might imagine, there are lots of possible ways for Murphy to stick his nose into the process we just talked about. How do penetration test teams and tested organizations try to keep Murphy at bay? Rules!

6. DEFINING WHAT'S EXPECTED

Someone once said: "You can't win the game if you don't know the rules!" That statement makes good sense for a penetration test team as well. Every penetration test must have a clearly defined set of rules by which the penetration test "game" is played. These rules are put into place to help protect both the tested organization and the penetration test team from errors of omission and commission (under normal circumstances). According to the National Institute of Standards and Technology (NIST), the "rule book" for penetration tests is often called the "Rules of Engagement." Rules of Engagement define things like which IP addresses or hosts are and are not allowed to be tested, which techniques are and are not allowed to be used, when testing is permitted or prohibited, points of contact for both the test team and the tested organization, IP addresses of machines from which testing is conducted, and measures to prevent escalation of an incident response to law enforcement, just to name a few.

There isn't a standard format for the Rules of Engagement, so it is not the only document that can be used to control a penetration test. Based on the complexity of the tested organization and the scope of the penetration test, the penetration test team may also use detailed test plan(s) for either or both logical and physical testing. In addition to these documents, both the client and the penetration test company conducting the operation will require some type of formal contact that spells out either explicitly, or incorporates by reference, such items as how discovered sensitive material will be handled, an indemnification statement, nondisclosure statement, fees, project schedule, reporting, and responsibilities. These are but a few of the many items that penetration testing control documents cover, but they should be sufficient for you to understand that all aspects of the penetration test need to be described somewhere in a document.

We now know what's expected during the penetration test. Armed with this information, how does the penetration test team plan to deliver the goods? It starts with a methodology.

7. THE NEED FOR A METHODOLOGY

When you leave for vacation and you've never been to your destination before, you're likely make a list of things you need or want to do before, during, or after the trip. You might also take a map along so you know how to get there and not get lost or sidetracked along the way. Penetration test teams also use a map of sorts. It's called their *methodology*.

A methodology is simply a way to ensure that a particular activity is conducted in a standard manner, with documented and repeatable results. It's a planning tool to help ensure that all mandatory aspects of an activity are performed.

Just as a map will show you various ways to get to your destination, a good penetration testing methodology does not restrict the test team to a single way of compromising the network. While on the road to your dream vacation, you might find your planned route closed or under construction and you might have to make a detour. You might want to do some sightseeing, or maybe visit long-lost relatives along the way.

Similarly, in a penetration test, your primary attack strategy might not work, forcing you to find a way around a particular network device, firewall, or intrusion prevention system. While exploiting one vulnerability, you may discover another one that leads you to a different host or a different subnet. A well-written methodology allows the test team the leeway necessary to explore these "targets of opportunity" while still ultimately guiding them to the stated goals of the test.

Most penetration test companies will have developed a standard methodology that covers all aspects of a penetration test. This baseline methodology document is the starting point for planning a particular test. Once the control documentation has been finalized, the penetration test team will know exactly what they can and cannot test. They will then modify that baseline methodology based on the scope statement in the Rules of Engagement for the penetration test that they are going to conduct.

Different clients are subject to different regulatory requirements such as HIPAA, Sarbanes-Oxley, Gramm-Leach-Bliley, or others, so the penetration test team's methodology must also be flexible enough to cover these and other government or private industry regulations.

In a minute, we'll talk about the sources of penetration testing methodologies, but for now, just understand that a methodology is not a "nice to have," it's a "must have." Without a methodology to be used as the basis to plan and execute a penetration test, there is no reliability. The team will be lost in the network, never knowing if they've fulfilled the requirements of the test or not until they're writing the report. By then, it's too late—for them and for the organization.

8. PENETRATION TESTING METHODOLOGIES

Back to our map example for a minute. Unless you're a cartographer, you're probably not going to make your own map to get to your dream vacation destination. You'll rely on a map that someone else has drawn, tested, and published. The same holds true for penetration testing methodologies. Before we talk about how a methodology, any methodology, is used in a penetration test, let's discuss penetration testing methodologies in general. There are probably as many different methodologies as there are companies conducting penetration tests, but all of them fit into one of two broad categories: open source or proprietary.

Open-source methodologies are just that: available for use by anyone. Probably the best-known open-source methodology, and de facto standard, is the Open Source Security Testing Methodology Manual (OSSTMM), the brainchild of Pete Herzog. You can get the latest copy of this document at www.isecom.org. Another valuable open-source methodology is the Open Web Application Security Project (OWASP), geared to securing Web applications, available at www.owasp.org.

Proprietary methodologies have been developed by particular entities offering network security services or certifications. The specific details of the processes that produce the output of the methodology are usually kept private. Companies wanting to use these proprietary methodologies must usually undergo specific training in their use and abide by quality standards set by the methodology proponent. Some examples of proprietary methodologies include IBM, ISS, Foundstone, and our own EC Council Licensed Penetrator Tester methodology.

9. METHODOLOGY IN ACTION

A comprehensive penetration test is a systematic analysis of all security controls in place at the tested organization. The penetration test team will look at not only the logical and physical vulnerabilities that are present but also at the tested organization's policies and procedures to assess whether or not the controls in place adequately protect the organization's information infrastructure.

Let's examine the use of a penetration testing methodology in more detail to demonstrate how it's used to conduct a penetration test. Of course, as the President of the EC-Council, I'm going to take the liberty of using our LPT methodology as the example.

EC-Council LPT Methodology

Figure 7.4 is a block representation of some of the major areas of the LPT methodology as taught in the EC-Council's Licensed Penetration Tester certification course. The first two rows of the diagram (except for the Wireless Network Penetration Testing block) represent a fairly normal sequence of events in the conduct of a penetration test. The test team will normally start by gathering information, then proceed with vulnerability

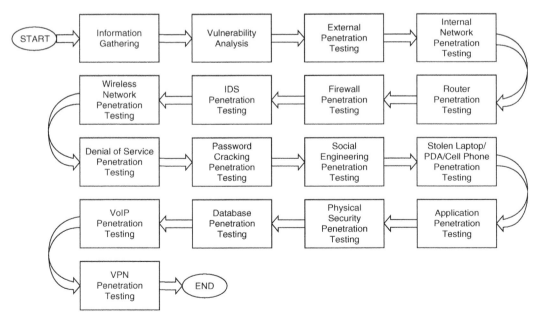

FIGURE 7.4   Block representation of some of the major areas of the LPT methodology.

discovery and analysis, followed by penetration testing from the network perimeter, and graduating to the internal network.

After that, beginning with wireless testing, what the test team actually does will depend on what applications or services are present in the network and what is allowed to be tested under the Rules of Engagement. I've chosen not to show every specific step in the process as part of the diagram. After all, if I told you everything, there wouldn't be any reason for you to get certified as a Licensed Penetration Tester, would there?

The methodology (and course) assumes that the penetration test team has been given authorization to conduct a complete test of the target network, including using denial-of-service tactics so that we can acquaint our LPT candidates with the breadth of testing they may be called on to perform. In real life, a test team may seldom actually perform DoS testing, but members of the penetration test team must still be proficient in conducting this type of test, to make recommendations in their reports as to the possible consequences of an attacker conducting a DoS attack on the company's network infrastructure. Here I give you a quick overview of each of the components.

Information Gathering

The main purpose of information gathering is to understand more about the target company. As we've already talked about, there are a number of ways to gather information about the company from public domain sources such as the Internet, newspapers, and third-party information sources.

Vulnerability Analysis

Before you can attack, you have to find the weak points. A vulnerability analysis is the process of identifying logical weaknesses in computers and networks as well as physical weaknesses and weaknesses in policies, procedures, and practices relating to the network and the organization.

External Penetration Testing

External testing is normally conducted before internal testing. It exploits discovered vulnerabilities that are accessible from the Internet to help determine the degree of information exposure or network control that could be achieved by the successful exploitation of a particular vulnerability from outside the network.

Internal Network Penetration Testing

Internal testing is normally conducted after external testing. It exploits discovered vulnerabilities that are accessible from inside the organization to help determine the degree of information exposure or network control that could be achieved by the successful exploitation of a particular vulnerability from inside the network.

Router Penetration Testing

Depending on where they are located in the network infrastructure, routers may forward data to points inside or outside the target organization's network. Take down a router; take down all hosts connected to that router. Because of their importance, routers that connect the target organization to the Internet may be tested twice: once from the Internet and again from inside the network.

Firewall Penetration Testing

Firewall(s) are another critical network infrastructure component that may be tested multiple times, depending on where they reside in the infrastructure. Firewalls that are exposed to the Internet are a primary line of defense for the tested organization and so will usually be tested from the Internet and from within the DMZ for both ingress and egress vulnerabilities and proper rule sets. Internal firewalls are often used to segregate portions of the internal network from each other. Those firewalls are also tested from both sides and for ingress and egress filtering to ensure that only applicable traffic can be passed.

IDS Penetration Testing

As networks have grown more complex and the methods to attack them have multiplied, more and more organizations have come to rely on intrusion detection (and prevention) systems (IDS/IPS) to give them warning or prevent an intrusion from occurring. The test team will be extremely interested in testing these devices for any vulnerabilities that will allow an attacker to circumvent setting of the IPS/IDS alarms.

Wireless Network Penetration Testing

If the target company uses wireless (and who doesn't these days), the test team will focus on the availability of "outside" wireless networks that can be accessed by employees of the target company (effectively circumventing the company's firewalls), the "reach" of the company's own wireless signal outside the physical confines of the company's buildings, and the type and strength of encryption employed by the wireless network. With the explosion of smart phones this has expanded significantly, and requires much time and consideration in the testing methodology if an organization is syncing their smart phones, or more importantly using a Blackberry Enterprise Server (BES), one of our Master Trainers while doing a penetration test for a large financial organization was able to compromise the BES and this machine holds all of the files from the Blackberry device, over the years the Blackberry has made improvements in their security, but when an organization deploys a BES then they have accepted the risk that if that gets a vulnerability and is compromised then all of the data that is stored on ALL of the organizations Blackberry devices is compromised, think about that, what do you have on your Blackberry today? It is not only Blackberry, but all of the smart phones carry with them similar risks, not to mention each and every application on the device is susceptible to the same vulnerabilities as our systems have been for years. There is a saying " Hack the iPhone, there is an app for that."

Denial-of-Service Penetration Testing

If the test team is lucky enough to land a penetration test that includes DoS testing, they will focus on crashing the company's Web sites and flooding the sites or the internal network with enough traffic to bring normal business processes to a standstill or a crawl.

They may also attempt to cause a DoS by locking out user accounts instead of trying to crack the passwords.

Password-Cracking Penetration Testing

Need we say more?

Social Engineering Penetration Testing

The test team may use both computer- and human-based techniques to try to obtain not only sensitive and/or nonpublic information directly from employees but also to gain unescorted access to areas of the company that are normally off-limits to the public. Once alone in an off-limits area, the social engineer may then try to obtain additional sensitive or nonpublic information about the company, its data, or its customers. This has taken on a whole new level, whereas before the most common method was by phone, we now have all the email attacks, and the variants that have proven largely successful, and now with the advent of social networking by the vast majority of the online population the attack surface for this has no boundaries, and it is not just Facebook and Twitter, it is the combination of these different profiles that can be used to social engineer information from perspective victims.

Stolen Laptop, PDA, and Cell Phone Penetration Testing

Some organizations take great pains to secure the equipment that is located within the physical confines of their buildings but fail to have adequate policies and procedures in place to maintain that security when mobile equipment leaves the premises. The test team attempts to temporarily "liberate" mobile equipment and then conducts testing to gain access to the data stored on those devices. They will most often attempt to target either or both members of the IT Department and the senior members of an organization in the hopes that their mobile devices will contain the most useful data.

Application Penetration Testing

The test team will perform meticulous testing of an application to check for code-related or "back-end" vulnerabilities that might allow access to the application itself, the underlying operating system, or the data that the application can access.

Physical Security Penetration Testing

The test team may attempt to gain access to the organizational facilities before, during, or after business hours using techniques meant to defeat physical access control systems or alarms. They may also conduct an overt "walk-thorough" accompanied by a member of the tested organization to provide the tested company with an "objective perspective" of the physical security controls in place. Either as a part of physical security testing or as a part of social engineering, the team may rifle through the organization's refuse to discover what discarded information could be used by an attacker to compromise the organization and to observe employee reaction to an unknown individual going through the trash.

Database Penetration Testing

The test team may attempt to directly access data contained in the database using account password-cracking techniques or indirectly access data by manipulating triggers and stored procedures that are executed by the database engine.

Voice-Over-IP Penetration Testing

The test team may attempt to gain access to the VoIP network for the purpose of recording conversations or to perform a DoS to the company's voice communications network. In some cases, if the organization has not followed the established "best practices" for VoIP, the team may attempt to use the VoIP network as a jumping-off point to conduct further compromise of the organization's network backbone.

VPN Penetration Testing

A number of companies allow at least some of their employees to work remotely, either from home or while they are "on the road." In either case, a VPN represents a trusted connection to the internal network. The test team will attempt to gain access to the VPN by either compromising the remote endpoint or gaining access to the VPN tunnel so that they have a "blessed" connection to the internal company network.

In addition to testing the applicable items in the blocks on the previous diagram, the penetration test team must also be familiar with and able to test for compliance with the regulatory requirements to which the tested organization is subject. Each standard has specific areas that must be tested, the process and procedures of which may not be part of a standard penetration test.

I'm sure that as you read the previous paragraphs, there was a nagging thought in the back of your mind: What are the risks involved? Let's talk about the risks.

10. PENETRATION TESTING RISKS

The difference between a real attack and a penetration test is the penetration tester's intent, authority to conduct the test, and lack of malice. Because penetration testers may use the same tools and procedures as a real attacker, it should be obvious that penetration testing can have serious repercussions if it's not performed correctly.

Even if your target company ceased all operations for the time the penetration test was being conducted, there is still a danger of data loss, corruption, or system crashes that might require a reinstall from "bare metal." Few, if any, companies can afford to stop functioning while a penetration test is being performed. Therefore it is incumbent on both the target organization and the penetration test team to do everything in their power to prevent an interruption of normal business processes during penetration testing operations.

Target companies should be urged to back up all their critical data before testing begins. They should always have IT personnel present to immediately begin restoration in the unfortunate event that a system crashes or otherwise becomes unavailable. The test team must be prepared to lend all possible assistance to the target company in helping to restore any system that is affected by penetration testing activities.

11. LIABILITY ISSUES

Although we just discussed some of the risks involved with conducting a penetration test, the issue of liability deserves its own special section. A botched penetration test can mean serious liability for the penetration test company that conducted the testing. The penetration test company should ensure that the documentation for the penetration test includes a liability waiver.

The waiver must be signed by an authorized representative of the target company and state that the penetration testing firm cannot be held responsible for the consequences of items such as:

- Damage to systems
- Unintentional denial-of-service conditions
- Data corruption
- System crashes or unavailability
- Loss of business income

12. LEGAL CONSEQUENCES

The legal consequences of a penetration test gone wrong can be devastating to both the target company and the penetration testers performing the test. The company may become the target of lawsuits by customers. The penetration testers may become the target of lawsuits by the target company. The only winners in this situation are the lawyers. It is imperative that proper written permission is obtained from the target company before *any* testing is conducted.

Legal remedies are normally contained in a penetration testing contract that is drawn up in addition to the testing control documentation. Both the penetration test company and the target company should seek legal counsel to review the agreement and to protect their interests. The authorization to perform testing must come from a senior member of the test company, and that senior member must be someone who has the authority to authorize such testing, not just the network administrator or LAN manager.

Authorized representatives of both the penetration test company and the target company must sign the penetration testing contract to indicate that they agree with its contents and the contents of all documentation that may be included or included by reference, such as the Rules of Engagement, the test plan, and other test control documentation.

13. "GET OUT OF JAIL FREE" CARD

We just talked about how the target company and the penetration test company protect themselves. What about that individual team member crawling around in the dumpster at 2:00 A.M., or the unfortunate team member who's managed to get into the company president's office and log onto his or her computer? What protection do those individuals have when that 600-pound gorilla of a security guard clamps his hand on their shoulder and asks what they're doing?

A "Get Out of Jail Free" card might just work wonders in these and other cases. Though not really a card, it's usually requested by the penetration test team as "extra insurance" during testing. It is presented if they're detained or apprehended while in the performance of their duties, as proof that their actions are sanctioned by the officers of the company. The card may actually be a letter on the tested company's letterhead and signed by the senior officer authorizing the test. It states the specific tasks that can be performed under the protection of the letter and specifically names the bearer.

It contains language that the bearer is conducting activities and testing under the auspices of a contract and that no violation of policy or crime is or has been committed. It includes a 24-hour contact number to verify the validity of the letter. As you can imagine, these "Get Out of Jail Free" cards are *very* sensitive and are usually distributed to team members immediately before testing begins, collected, and returned to the target company immediately after the end of any testing requiring their use.

There is a tremendous amount of work involved in conducting a thorough and comprehensive penetration test. What we've just discussed is but a 40,000-foot flyover of what actually happens during the process. But we're not done yet! The one area that we haven't discussed is the personnel performing these tests.

14. PENETRATION TESTING CONSULTANTS

The quality of the penetration test performed for a client is directly dependent on the quality of the consultants performing the work, singularly and in the aggregate. There are hundreds if not thousands of self-proclaimed "security services providers" out there, both companies and individuals. If I'm in need of a penetration test, how can I possibly know whether the firm or individual I'm going to select is really and truly qualified to test my network comprehensively, accurately, and safely? What if I end up hiring a consultancy that employs hackers? What if the consultant(s) aren't hackers, but they just don't know what they're doing?

In these, the last pages of this chapter, I want to talk about the people who perform penetration testing services. First, you get another dose of my personal opinion. Then we'll talk about security services providers, those who provide penetration testing services. We'll talk about some of the questions that you might want to ask about their operations and their employees. Here's a hint for you: If the company is evasive in answering the questions or outright refuses to answer them—run!

What determines whether or not a penetration tester is "experienced"? There are few benchmarks to test the knowledge of a penetration tester. You can't ask her for a score: "Yes, I've performed 27 penetration tests, been successful in compromising 23 of those networks, and the overall degree of difficulty of each one of those tests was 7 on a scale of 1 to 10."

There really isn't a Better Business Bureau for penetration testers. You can't go to a Web site and see that XSecurity has had three complaints filed against them for crashing networks they've been testing or that "John Smith" has tested nine networks that were hacked within the following 24 hours. (Whoa! What an idea ... ! Nah, wouldn't work.) Few companies would want to admit that they chose the wrong person or company to test their networks, and that kind of information would surely be used by attackers in the "intelligence-gathering phase" as a source of information for future attacks on any company that chose to report. Well, if we can't do that, what can we do?

We pretty much have to rely on "word of mouth" that such-and-such a company does a good job. We have to pretty much rely on the fact that the tester has been certified to a basic standard of knowledge by a reputable certification body. We pretty much have to rely on the skill set of the individual penetration tester and that "the whole is more than the sum of its parts" thing called synergy, which is created when a group of penetration testers works together as a team.

I'm not going to insult you by telling you how to go ask for recommendations. I will tell you that there are security certification providers who are better than others and who hold their candidates to a higher standard of knowledge and professionalism than others. Since it's hard to measure the "synergy" angle, let's take a closer look at what skill sets should be present on the penetration team that you hire.

15. REQUIRED SKILL SETS

Your penetration test "dream team" should be well versed in areas such as these:

- Networking concepts
- Hardware devices such as routers, firewalls, and IDS/IPS
- Hacking techniques (ethical hacking, of course!)
- Databases
- Open-source technologies
- Operating systems
- Wireless protocols
- Applications
- Protocols
- Many others

That's a rather long list to demonstrate a simple concept: Your penetration team should be able to show proof that they have knowledge about all the hardware, software, services, and protocols in use within your network.

Okay. They have technical skills. Is that enough?

16. ACCOMPLISHMENTS

Are the members of the test team "bookworms" or have they had practical experience in their areas of expertise? Have they contributed to the security community (see checklist: "An Agenda For Action For The Experiences Of The Test Team")?

AN AGENDA FOR ACTION FOR THE EXPERIENCES OF THE TEST TEAM

The checklist that follows should give you some indication of questions you can ask to determine the "experiences" of your test team (check all tasks completed):

_____1. Have they conducted research and development in the security arena?

_____2. Have they published research papers or articles in technical journals?

_____3. Have they presented at seminars, either locally or internationally?

_____4. What certifications do they hold?

_____5. Where are those certifications from?

_____6. Do they maintain membership/ affiliation/ accreditation in organizations such as the EC-Council, ISC2, ISACA, and others?

_____7. Have they written or contributed to security-related books and articles?

_____8. How about some simple questions to ask of the company that will perform your test?

---

17. HIRING A PENETRATION TESTER

Here are some of the questions you might consider asking prospective security service providers or things to think about when hiring a test team:

- Is providing security services the primary mission of the security service provider, or is this just an "additional revenue source" for another company?
- Does the company offer a comprehensive suite of services tailored to your specific requirements, or do they just offer service packages?
- Does the supplier have a methodology? Does their methodology follow a recognized authority in security such as OSSTMM, OWASP, or LPT?
- Does the supplier hire former hackers? Do they perform background checks on their employees?
- Can they distinguish (and articulate) between infrastructure and application testing?
- How many consultants does the supplier have who perform penetration testing? How long have those consultants been practicing?
- What will the final report look like? Does it meet your needs? Is the supplier willing to modify the format to suit your needs (within reason)?
- Is the report just a list of what's wrong, or does it contain mitigation strategies that will be tailored to your particular situation?
- Is the supplier a recognized contributor to the security community?
- Do they have references available to attest to the quality of work already performed?
- That ought to get a company started down the road to hiring a good penetration test team. Now let's talk about why a company should hire you, either as an individual or as a member of a penetration testing team.

18. WHY SHOULD A COMPANY HIRE YOU?

When a prospective client needs a penetration test, they may publish a request for proposal (RFP) or just make an announcement that they are accepting solicitations for security services. When all the bids come in, they will only consider the most qualified candidates. How to you make sure that your or your company's bid doesn't end up in the "circular file?"

Qualifications

Highlight your or your company's qualifications to perform the desired services. Don't rely on "alphabet soup" after your name or your team's names to highlight qualifications. Take the time to explain the meaning of CISSP, LPT, or MCSE.

Work Experience

The company will provide some information about itself. Align your response by highlighting work (without naming specific clients!) in the same or related fields and of related size.

Cutting-Edge Technical Skills

It doesn't bode well when you list one of your primary skills as "MCSE in Windows NT 3.51 and NT 4.0 or higher." Maintain your technical proficiency and showcase your most recent and most highly regarded certification accomplishments, such as CCNA, CEH, CHFI, CCNP, MCSE, LPT, CISA, and CISM.

Communication Skills

Whether your communicate with the prospective client through written or verbal methods, made sure you are well written or well spoken. Spell-check your written documents, and then look them over again. There are some errors that spell checkers just won't find. "Dude, I'm gonna hack yer network!" isn't going to cut it in a second-round presentation.

Attitude

Let's face it: Most of us in the security arena have a bit of an ego and sometimes come off as a bit arrogant. Though that may hold some sway with your peers, it won't help your case with a prospective client. Polite and professional at all times is the rule.

Team Skills

There is no synergy if there is no team. You must be a good team player who can deal with subordinates, superiors, and clients professionally, even in the most critical moments of an engagement.

Okay. You've done all this. What else do you need to know to get hired? What about the concerns of the company that will hire you?

Company Concerns

You can have a sterling record and the best qualifications around and still not get hired. Here are some of the "influencing factors" companies may consider when looking to hire a penetration testing team:

- Companies usually want to work in collaboration with reputable and well-established firms such as Foundstone, ISS, EC-Council, and others.
- Companies may want to verify the tools that will be run during a test and the equipment on which the tools run.
- Companies will want references for the individuals on the team as well as recommendations about the company itself.
- Companies demand security-related certifications such as CISSP, CEH, and TICSA to confirm the authenticity of the testing company.
- Companies usually have an aversion to hiring those who are known or suspected hackers.
- Companies may require security clearances.
- Companies may inquire about how and where their data will be stored while in the testing company's possession.

Okay, you get the idea, right?

19. SUMMARY

Anybody got an aspirin? I'm sure you probably need one after reading all the information I've tried to throw at you in this chapter. I've only barely scratched the surface of what a penetration test is, what it's meant to accomplish, how it's done, and how you report the findings to the client, but I'm out of space to tell you more.

Let me take these last couple of inches on the page to summarize. If you've got a network, the question is not "if you'll be attacked," but "when." If you're going to make your network as safe as possible, you need to find the weaknesses and then test them to see which ones are really, truly the things that need to be fixed "yesterday." If you only conduct a penetration test once a year, a real hacker has 364 "unbirthdays" in which to attack and compromise your network. Don't give them the opportunity. Get someone on your staff certified as an ethical hacker and a Licensed Penetration Tester so that they can perform ethical hacks and penetrations on a regular basis to help protect your network.

Finally, let's move on to the real interactive part of this Chapter: review questions/exercises, hands-on projects, case projects and optional team case project. The answers and/or solutions by chapter can be found in the Online Instructor's Solutions Manual.

CHAPTER REVIEW QUESTIONS/EXERCISES

True/False

1. True or False? Penetration testing is the exploitation of vulnerabilities absent in an organization's network.
2. True or False? Some sources classify penetration testing into two types—internal and external—and then talk about the "variations" of these types of tests based on the amount of information the test team has been given about the organization prior to starting the test.
3. True or False? When a penetration test is conducted against Internet-facing hosts, it is known as *external testing*.
4. True or False? There are three phases in a penetration test, and they mimic the phases that an attacker would use to conduct a real attack.
5. True or False? The pre-attack phase consists of the penetration team's or hacker's attempts to investigate or explore the potential target.

Multiple Choice

1. What stage involves the actual compromise of the target?
   A. Worm Phase
   B. Virus Phase
   C. Backdoor Phase
   D. More popular Phase
   E. Attack Phase
2. What is unique to the penetration test team?
   A. Backdoor Phase
   B. Virus Phase
   C. Post-Attack Phase
   D. Packet filter Phase
   E. User-level Rootkit Phase
3. What is simply a way to ensure that a particular activity is conducted in a standard manner, with documented and repeatable results?
   A. Stateful firewalls
   B. Virus
   C. Methodology
   D. Backdoor
   E. User-level Rootkit
4. What have been developed by particular entities offering network security services or certifications?
   A. Application layer firewalls
   B. Proprietary methodologies
   C. Worms
   D. Backdoors
   E. User-level Rootkit

5. What test is a systematic analysis of all security controls in place at the tested organization?
   A. Trojan Horse
   B. Firewalls
   C. Worm
   D. Comprehensive penetration
   E. User-level Rootkit

EXERCISE

Problem

Penetration testing can also be useful for determining?

Hands-On Projects

Project

The discovery phase of penetration testing includes two parts. The first part is the start of actual testing, and covers information gathering and scanning. Network port and service identification is conducted to identify potential targets. In addition to port and service identification, what other techniques are used to gather information on the targeted network?

Case Projects

Problem

While vulnerability scanners check only for the possible existence of a vulnerability, the attack phase of a penetration test exploits the vulnerability to confirm its existence. Most vulnerabilities exploited by penetration testing fall into which of the following categories?

Optional Team Case Project

Problem

Identify some penetration testing logistics.

What is Vulnerability Assessment?

Almantas Kakareka

Demyo, Inc.

1. INTRODUCTION

In computer security, the term *vulnerability* is applied to a weakness in a system that allows an attacker to violate the integrity of that system. Vulnerabilities may result from weak passwords, software bugs, a computer virus or other malware (malicious software), a script code injection, or from unchecked user input, just to name a few.

A security risk is classified as vulnerability if it is recognized as a possible means of attack. A security risk with one or more known instances of a working or fully implemented attack is classified as an *exploit*. Constructs in programming languages that are difficult to use properly can be large sources of vulnerabilities.

Vulnerabilities always existed, but when the Internet was in its early stage they were not as often used and exploited. The media did not report news of hackers who were getting put in jail for hacking into servers and stealing vital information.

Vulnerability assessment may be performed on many objects, not only computer systems/networks. For example, a physical building can be assessed so it will be clear what parts of the building have what kind of flaw. If the attacker can bypass the security guard at the front door and get into the building via a back door, it is definitely vulnerability. Actually, going through the back door and using that vulnerability is called an *exploit*. The physical security is one of the most important aspects to be taken into account. If the attackers have physical access to the server, the server is not yours anymore! Just stating, "Your system or network is vulnerable" doesn't provide any useful information. Vulnerability assessment without a comprehensive report is pretty much useless. A vulnerability assessment report should include:

- Identification of vulnerabilities
- Risk rating of each vulnerability (Critical, High, Medium, Low)
- Quantity of vulnerabilities

It is enough to find one critical vulnerability, which means the whole network is at risk, as shown in Figure 8.1.

FIGURE 8.1 One critical vulnerability affects the entire network.

Vulnerabilities should be sorted by severity and then by servers/services. Critical vulnerabilities should be at the top of the report and should be listed in descending order, that is, critical, then high, medium, and low.

2. REPORTING

Reporting capability is of growing importance to administrators in a documentation-oriented business climate where you must not only be able to do your job, you must also provide written proof of how you've done it. In fact, respondents to Sunbelt's survey[1] indicate that flexible and prioritizing reporting is their number-one favorite feature.

A scan might return hundreds or thousands of results, but the data is useless unless it is organized in a way that can be understood. That means that ideally you will be able to sort and cross-reference the data, export it to other programs and formats (such as CSV, HTML, XML, MHT, MDB, Excel, Word, and/or various databases), view it in different ways, and easily compare it to the results of earlier scans.

Comprehensive, flexible, and customizable reporting is used within your department to provide a guideline of technical steps you need to take, but that's not all. Good reports also give you the ammunition you need to justify to management the costs of implementing security measures.

3. THE "IT WON'T HAPPEN TO US" FACTOR

Practical matters aside, CEOs, CIOs, and administrators are all human beings and thus subject to normal human tendencies—including the tendency to assume that bad things happen to "other people," not to us. Organizational decision makers assume that their companies aren't likely targets for hackers ("Why would an attacker want to break into the network of Widgets, Inc., when they could go after the Department of Defense or Microsoft or someone else who's much more interesting?").[1]

4. WHY VULNERABILITY ASSESSMENT?

Organizations have a tremendous opportunity to use information technologies to increase their productivity. Securing information and communications systems will be a

1. "Vulnerability Assessment Scanning:Why Sunbelt Network Security Inspector (SNSI)?" Sunbelt Software, [http://img2.insight.com/graphics/uk/content/microsite/sunbelt/sunbelt_network_security_inspector_whitepaper.pdf], February 2004.

necessary factor in taking advantage of all this increased connectivity, speed, and information. However, no security measure will guarantee a risk-free environment in which to operate. In fact, many organizations need to provide easier user access to portions of their information systems, thereby increasing potential exposure. Administrative error, for example, is a primary cause of vulnerabilities that can be exploited by a novice hacker, whether an outsider or insider in the organization. Routine use of vulnerability assessment tools along with immediate response to identified problems will alleviate this risk. It follows, therefore, that routine vulnerability assessment should be a standard element of every organization's security policy. Vulnerability assessment is used to find unknown problems in the systems. The main purpose of vulnerability assessment is to find out what systems have flaws and take action to mitigate the risk. Some industry standards such as DSS PCI require organizations to perform vulnerability assessments on their networks. The sidebar "DSS PCI Compliance" gives a brief look.

DSS PCI Compliance

PCI DSS stands for Payment Card Industry Data Security Standard. This standard was developed by leading credit-card companies to help merchants be secure and follow common security criteria to protect sensitive customers' credit-card data. Before that every credit card company had a similar standard to protect customer data on the merchant side. Any company that does transactions via credit cards needs to be PCI compliant. One of the requirements to be PCI compliant is to regularly test security systems and processes. This can be achieved via vulnerability assessment. Small companies that don't process a lot of transactions are allowed to do self-assessment via questionnaire. Big companies that process a lot of transactions are required to be audited by third parties.[2]

5. PENETRATION TESTING VERSUS VULNERABILITY ASSESSMENT

There seems to be a certain amount of confusion within the security industry about the difference between penetration testing and vulnerability assessment. They are often classified as the same thing but in fact they are not. Penetration testing sounds a lot more exciting, but most people actually want a vulnerability assessment and not a penetration test, so many projects are labeled as penetration tests when in fact they are 100% vulnerability assessments.

A penetration test mainly consists of a vulnerability assessment, but it goes one step further. A penetration test is a method for evaluating the security of a computer system or network by simulating an attack by a malicious hacker. The process involves an active analysis of the system for any weaknesses, technical flaws, or vulnerabilities. This analysis is carried out from the position of a potential attacker and will involve active exploitation

---

2. PCI Security Standards Council, Copyright© 2006–2013 PCI Security Standards Council, LLC. All rights reserved. [www.pcisecuritystandards.org], 2013.

of security vulnerabilities. Any security issues that are found will be presented to the system owner, together with an assessment of their impact and often with a proposal for mitigation or a technical solution.

A vulnerability assessment is what most companies generally do, since the systems they are testing are live production systems and can't afford to be disrupted by active exploits that might crash the system. Vulnerability assessment is the process of identifying and quantifying vulnerabilities in a system. The system being studied could be a physical facility such as a nuclear power plant, a computer system, or a larger system (for example, the communications infrastructure or water infrastructure of a region). Vulnerability assessment has many things in common with risk assessment. Assessments are typically performed according to the following steps:

1. Cataloging assets and capabilities (resources) in a system
2. Assigning quantifiable value and importance to the resources
3. Identifying the vulnerabilities or potential threats to each resource
4. Mitigating or eliminating the most serious vulnerabilities for the most valuable resources

This is generally what a security company is contracted to do, from a technical perspective—not to actually penetrate the systems but to assess and document the possible vulnerabilities and to recommend mitigation measures and improvements. Vulnerability detection, mitigation, notification, and remediation are linked, as shown in Figure 8.2.[3]

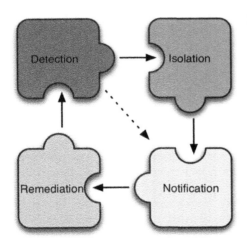

FIGURE 8.2   Vulnerability mitigation cycle.

3. Darknet, © Darknet—The Darkside 2000—2013. [www.darknet.org.uk/2006/04/penetration-testing-vs-vulnerability-assessment/], 2013.

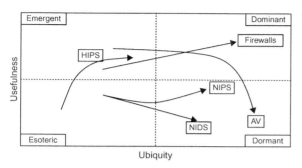

FIGURE 8.3 Usefulness/ubiquity relationship.

6. VULNERABILITY ASSESSMENT GOAL

The theoretical goal of network scanning is elevated security on all systems or establishing a network-wide minimal operation standard. Figure 8.3 shows how usefulness is related to ubiquity:

- HIPS: Host-Based Intrusion Prevention System
- NIDS: Network-Based Intrusion Detection System
- AV: Antivirus
- NIPS: Network-Based Intrusion Prevention System

7. MAPPING THE NETWORK

Before we start scanning the network we have to find out what machines are alive on it. Most of the scanners have a built-in network mapping tool, usually the Nmap network mapping tool running behind the scenes. The Nmap Security Scanner is a free and open-source utility used by millions of people for network discovery, administration, inventory, and security auditing. Nmap uses raw IP packets in novel ways to determine what hosts are available on a network, what services (application name and version) those hosts are offering, what operating systems they are running, what type of packet filters or firewalls are in use, and more. Nmap was named "Information Security Product of the Year" by *Linux Journal* and *Info World*. It was also used by hackers in the movies *Matrix Reloaded, Die Hard* 4, and *Bourne Ultimatum*. Nmap runs on all major computer operating systems, plus the Amiga. Nmap has a traditional command-line interface, as shown in Figure 8.4; and, zenmap is the official nmap security scanner GUI (see Figure 8.5).

It is a multiplatform (Linux, Windows, Mac OS X, BSD, etc.), free and open-source application that aims to make Nmap easy for beginners to use while providing advanced features for experienced Nmap users. Frequently used scans can be saved as profiles to make them easy to run repeatedly. A command creator allows interactive creation of Nmap command lines. Scan results can be saved and viewed later. Saved scan results can be compared with one another to see how they differ. The results of recent scans are stored in a searchable database.

```
sh-3.2# nmap -sV scanme.nmap.org

Starting Nmap 5.61TEST4 ( http://nmap.org ) at 2012-02-25 15:08 EST
Nmap scan report for scanme.nmap.org (74.207.244.221)
Host is up (0.17s latency).
Not shown: 994 closed ports
PORT      STATE     SERVICE      VERSION
22/tcp    open      ssh          OpenSSH 5.3p1 Debian 3ubuntu7 (protocol 2.0)
25/tcp    filtered  smtp
80/tcp    open      http         Apache httpd 2.2.14 ((Ubuntu))
646/tcp   filtered  ldp
1720/tcp  filtered  H.323/Q.931
9929/tcp  open      nping-echo   Nping echo
Service Info: OS: Linux; CPE: cpe:/o:linux:kernel

Service detection performed. Please report any incorrect results at http://
Nmap done: 1 IP address (1 host up) scanned in 11.31 seconds
sh-3.2#
```

FIGURE 8.4   Nmap command-line interface.

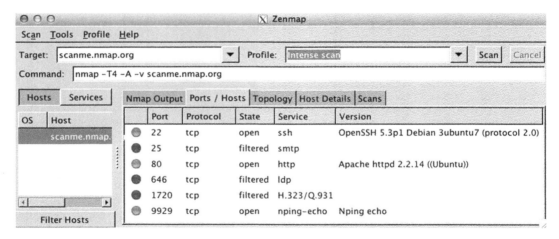

FIGURE 8.5   Zenmap graphical user interface.

Gordon Lyon (better known by his nickname, Fyodor) released Nmap in 1997 and continues to coordinate its development. He also maintains the Insecure.Org, Nmap.Org, SecLists.Org, and SecTools.Org security resource sites and has written seminal papers on OS detection and stealth port scanning. He is a founding member of the Honeynet project and coauthored the books *Know Your Enemy: Honeynets* and *Stealing the Network: How to*

Own a Continent. Gordon is President of Computer Professionals for Social Responsibility (CPSR), which has promoted free speech, security, and privacy since 1981.[4]

Some systems might be disconnected from the network. Obviously, if the system is not connected to any network at all it will have a lower priority for scanning. However, it shouldn't be left in the dark and not be scanned at all, because there might be other non-network related flaws, for example, a Firewire exploit that can be used to unlock the Windows XP SP2 system. Exploits work like this: An attacker approaches a locked Windows XP SP2 station, plugs a Firewire cable into it, and uses special commands to unlock the locked machine. This technique is possible because Firewire has direct access to RAM. The system will accept any password and unlock the computer.[5]

8. SELECTING THE RIGHT SCANNERS

Scanners alone don't solve the problem; using scanners well helps solve *part* of the problem. Start with one scanner but consider more than one. It is a good practice to use more than one scanner. This way you can compare results from a couple of them. Some scanners are more focused on particular services. Typical scanner architecture is shown in Figure 8.6.

For example, Nessus is an outstanding general-purpose scanner, but Web application-oriented scanners such as HP Web Inspect or Hailstorm will do a much better job of scanning a web application. In an ideal situation, scanners would not be needed because everyone would maintain patches and tested hosts, routers, gateways, workstations, and servers. However, the real world is different; we are humans and we tend to forget to install updates, patch systems, and/or configure systems properly. Malicious code will always find a way into your network! If a system is connected to the network, that means there is a possibility that this system will be infected at some time in the future. The chances might be higher or lower depending on the system's maintenance level. The system will never be secure 100%. There is no such thing as 100% security; if well maintained, it might be 99.9999999999% secure, but never 100%. There is a joke that says, if you want to make a computer secure, you have to disconnect it from the network and power outlet and then put it into a safe and lock it. This system will be *almost* 100% secure (although not useful), because social engineering cons may call your employees and ask them to remove that system from the safe and plug it back into the network.[6,7]

4. insecure.org, http://insecure.org/fyodor/

5. Nilay Patel, "Windows passwords easily bypassed over Firewire," © 2013 AOL Inc. All rights reserved. [http://www.engadget.com/2008/03/04/windows-passwords-easily-bypassed-over-firewire/], Mar 4th, 2008.

6. Hewlett-Packard Development Company, L.P. © 2013 Hewlett-Packard Development Company, L.P. [http://www.hpenterprisesecurity.com/], 2013.

7. "Cenzic Desktop: Application Security for Cloud and Web," © 2012 Cenzic, Inc. All rights reserved. Cenzic, Inc., 655 Campbell Technology Parkway, Suite #100Campbell, CA 95008 [http://www.cenzic.com/products/desktop/index.html], 2013.

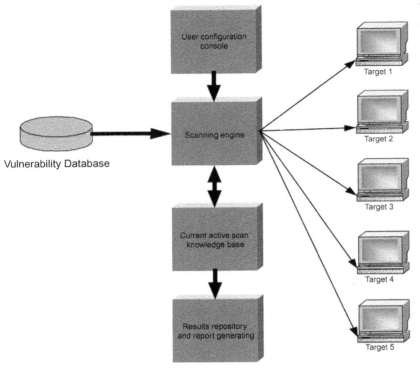

FIGURE   8.6   Typical
scanner architecture.

TABLE 8.1   Pros and Cons of Central Scans and Local Scans.

	Centrally Controlled and Accessed Scanning	**Decentralized Scanning**
Pros	Easy to maintain	Scan managers can scan at will
Cons	Slow; most scans must be queued	Patching of the scanner is often overlooked

9. CENTRAL SCANS VERSUS LOCAL SCANS

The question arises: Should we scan locally or centrally? Should we scan the whole network at once, or should we scan the network based on subdomains and virtual LANs? Table 8.1 shows pros and cons of each method.

With localized scanning and central scanning verification, central scanning becomes a verification audit. The question again arises, should we scan locally or centrally? The answer is both. Central scans give overall visibility into the network. Local scans may have higher visibility into the local network. Centrally driven scans serve as the baseline. Locally driven scans are key to vulnerability reduction. Scanning tools should support both methodologies. Scan managers should be empowered to police their own area and enforce policy. So what will hackers target? Script kiddies will target any easily exploitable system; dedicated hackers will target some particular network/organization (see sidebar, "Who Is the Target?").

Who is the Target?

"We are not a target." How many times have you heard this statement? Many people think that they don't have anything to hide, they don't have secrets, and thus nobody will hack them. Hackers are not only after secrets but after resources as well. They may want to use your machine for hosting files, use it as a source to attack other systems, or just try some new exploits against it.

If you don't have any juicy information, you might not be a target for a skilled hacker, but you will always be a target for script kiddies. In hacker culture terms, *script kiddie* describes an inexperienced hacker who is using available tools, usually with a GUI, to do any malicious activity. Script kiddies lack technical expertise to write or create any tools by themselves. They try to infect or deface as many systems as they can with the least possible effort. If they can't hack your system/site in a couple of minutes, usually they move to an easier target. It's rather different with skilled hackers, who seek financial or other benefits from hacking the system. They spend a lot of time just exploring the system and collecting as much information as possible before trying to hack it. The proper way of hacking is data mining and writing scripts that will automate the whole process, thus making it fast and hard to respond to.

10. DEFENSE IN DEPTH STRATEGY

Defense in depth is an information assurance (IA) strategy in which multiple layers of defense are placed throughout an IT system. Defense in depth addresses security vulnerabilities in personnel, technology, and operations for the duration of the system's life cycle. The idea behind this approach is to defend a system against any particular attack using several varying methods. It is a layering tactic, conceived by the National Security Agency (NSA) as a comprehensive approach to information and electronic security. Defense in depth was originally a military strategy that seeks to delay, rather than prevent, the advance of an attacker by yielding space in order to buy time. The placement of protection mechanisms, procedures, and policies is intended to increase the dependability of an IT system where multiple layers of defense prevent espionage and direct attacks against critical systems. In terms of computer network defense, defense-in-depth measures should not only prevent security breaches, they should give an organization time to detect and respond to an attack, thereby reducing and mitigating the impact of a breach. Using more than one of the following layers constitutes defense in depth:

- Physical security (deadbolt locks)
- Authentication and password security
- Antivirus software (host based and network based)

- Firewalls (hardware or software)
- Demilitarized zones (DMZs)
- Intrusion detection systems (IDSs)
- Intrusion prevention systems (IPSs)
- Packet filters (deep packet inspection appliances and stateful firewalls)
- Routers and switches
- Proxy servers
- Virtual private networks (VPNs)
- Logging and auditing
- Biometrics
- Timed access control
- Proprietary software/hardware not available to the public

11. VULNERABILITY ASSESSMENT TOOLS

There are many vulnerability assessment tools. Popular scanning tools according to www.sectools.org are listed here.

Nessus

Nessus is one of the most popular and capable vulnerability scanners, particularly for UNIX systems. It was initially free and open source, but they closed the source code in 2005 and removed the free "Registered Feed" version in 2008. It now costs $1,200 per year, which still beats many of its competitors. A free "Home Feed" is also available, though it is limited and only licensed for home network use. Nessus is constantly updated, with more than 46,000 plugins. Key features include remote and local (authenticated) security checks, a client/server architecture with a web-based interface, and an embedded scripting language for writing your own plugins or understanding the existing ones. The open-source version of Nessus was forked by a group of users who still develop it under the OpenVAS name.

GFI LANguard

This is a network security and vulnerability scanner designed to help with patch management, network and software audits, and vulnerability assessments. The price is based on the number of IP addresses you wish to scan. A free trial version of up to 5 IP addresses is available.

Retina

Commercial vulnerability assessment scanner by eEye. Like Nessus, Retina's function is to scan all the hosts on a network and report on any vulnerabilities found. It was written by eEye, well known for security research.

Core Impact

Core Impact isn't cheap (be prepared to spend at least $30,000), but it is widely considered to be the most powerful exploitation tool available. It sports a large, regularly updated database of professional exploits, and can do neat tricks like exploiting one machine and then establishing an encrypted tunnel through that machine to reach and exploit other boxes. Other good options include Metasploit and Canvas.

ISS Internet Scanner

Application-level vulnerability assessment Internet Scanner started off in 1992 as a tiny open-source scanner by Christopher Klaus. Now he has grown ISS into a billion-dollar company with myriad security products.

X-Scan

A general scanner for scanning network vulnerabilities, X-Scan is a multithreaded, plug-in-supported vulnerability scanner. X-Scan includes many features, including full NASL support, detecting service types, remote OS type/version detection, weak user/ password pairs, and more. You may be able to find newer versions available at the X-Scan site if you can deal with most of the page being written in Chinese.

12. SARA

Security Auditor's Research Assistant SARA is a vulnerability assessment tool that was derived from the infamous SATAN scanner. Updates are released twice a month and the company tries to leverage other software created by the open-source community (such as Nmap and Samba).

QualysGuard

A Web-based vulnerability scanner delivered as a service over the Web, QualysGuard eliminates the burden of deploying, maintaining, and updating vulnerability management software or implementing ad hoc security applications. Clients securely access QualysGuard through an easy-to-use Web interface. QualysGuard features 5000+ unique vulnerability checks, an inference-based scanning engine, and automated daily updates to the QualysGuard vulnerability knowledge base.

13. SAINT

Security Administrator's Integrated Network Tool (SAINT) is another commercial vulnerability assessment tool (like Nessus, ISS Internet Scanner, or Retina). It runs on Unix and used to be free and open source but is now a commercial product.

14. MBSA

Microsoft Baseline Security Analyzer (MBSA) is an easy-to-use tool designed for the IT professional that helps small and medium-sized businesses determine their security state in accordance with Microsoft security recommendations, and offers specific remediation guidance. Built on the Windows Update Agent and Microsoft Update infrastructure, MBSA ensures consistency with other Microsoft management products, including Microsoft Update (MU), Windows Server Update Services (WSUS), Systems Management Server (SMS), and Microsoft Operations Manager (MOM). Apparently MBSA, on average, scans over three million computers each week.[8]

15. SCANNER PERFORMANCE

A vulnerability scanner can use a lot of network bandwidth, so you want the scanning process to complete as quickly as possible. Of course, the more vulnerabilities in the database and the more comprehensive the scan, the longer it will take, so this can be a tradeoff. One way to increase performance is through the use of multiple scanners on the enterprise network, which can report back to one system that aggregates the results.

16. SCAN VERIFICATION

The best practice is to use few scanners during your vulnerability assessment, then use more than one scanning tool to find more vulnerabilities. Scan your networks with different scanners from different vendors and compare the results. Also consider penetration testing, that is, hire white/gray-hat hackers to hack your own systems.

17. SCANNING CORNERSTONES

All orphaned systems should be treated as hostile. Something in your organization that is not maintained or touched poses the largest threat. For example, say that you have a Web server and you inspect every byte of DHTML and make sure it has no flaws, but you totally forget to maintain the SMTP service with open relay that it is also running. Attackers might not be able to deface or harm your Web page, but they will be using the SMTP server to send out spam emails via your server. As a result, your company's IP ranges will be put into spammer lists such as spamhaus and spamcop.[9,10]

8. "SecTools.Org: Top 125 Network Security Tools," SecTools.Org [www.sectools.org], 2013.

9. The Spamhaus Project Ltd., © 1998–2013 The Spamhaus Project Ltd. All rights reserved. [www.spamhaus.org], 2013.

10. Cisco Systems, Inc., ©1992–2010 Cisco Systems, Inc. All rights reserved. [www.spamcop.net], 2010.

18. NETWORK SCANNING COUNTERMEASURES

A company wants to scan its own networks, but at the same time the company should take countermeasures to protect itself from being scanned by hackers. Here is a checklist of countermeasures (see checklist: "An Agenda For Action For The Use Of Network Scanning Countermeasures") to use when you're considering technical modifications to networks and filtering devices to reduce the effectiveness of network scanning and probing undertaken by attackers.

AN AGENDA FOR ACTION FOR THE USE OF NETWORK SCANNING COUNTERMEASURES

Here is a checklist of network scanning countermeasures; and, if a commercial firewall is in use (check all tasks completed):

_____1. Filter inbound Internet Control Message Protocol (ICMP) message types at border routers and firewalls. This forces attackers to use full-blown TCP port scans against all your IP addresses to map your network correctly.

_____2. Filter all outbound ICMP type 3 unreachable messages at border routers and firewalls to prevent UDP port scanning and firewalking from being effective.

_____3. Consider configuring Internet firewalls so that they can identify port scans and throttle the connections accordingly. You can configure commercial firewall appliances (such as those from Check Point, NetScreen, and WatchGuard) to prevent fast port scans and SYN floods being launched against your networks. On the open-source side, many tools such as port sentry can identify port scans and drop all packets from the source IP address for a given period of time.

_____4. Assess the way that your network firewall and IDS devices handle fragmented IP packets by using fragtest and fragroute when performing scanning and probing exercises. Some devices crash or fail under conditions in which high volumes of fragmented packets are being processed.

_____5. Ensure that your routing and filtering mechanisms (both firewalls and routers) can't be bypassed using specific source ports or source-routing techniques.

_____6. If you house publicly accessible FTP services, ensure that your firewalls aren't vulnerable to stateful circumvention attacks relating to malformed PORT and PASV commands.

If a commercial firewall is in use, ensure the following:

_____7. The latest firmware and latest service pack is installed.

_____8. Antispoofing rules have been correctly defined so that the device doesn't accept packets with private spoofed source addresses on its external interfaces.

_____9. Investigate using inbound proxy servers in your environment if you require a high level of security. A proxy server will not forward fragmented or malformed packets, so it isn't possible to launch FIN scanning or other stealth methods.

_____10. Be aware of your own network configuration and its publicly accessible ports by launching TCP and UDP port scans along with ICMP probes against your own IP address space. It is surprising how many large companies still don't properly undertake even simple port-scanning exercises.[11]

19. VULNERABILITY DISCLOSURE DATE

The time of disclosure of vulnerability is defined differently in the security community and industry. It is most commonly referred to as "a kind of public disclosure of security information by a certain party." Usually vulnerability information is discussed on a mailing list or published on a security Web site and results in a security advisory afterward. Mailing list named "Full Disclosure Mailing List" is a perfect example how vulnerabilities are disclosed to public. It is a must read for any person interested in IT security. This mailing list is free of charge and is available at http://seclists.org/fulldisclosure/.

The *time of disclosure* is the first date that security vulnerability is described on a channel where the disclosed information on the vulnerability has to fulfill the following requirements:

- The information is freely available to the public.
- The vulnerability information is published by a trusted and independent channel/ source.
- The vulnerability has undergone analysis by experts such that risk rating information is included upon disclosure.

The method of disclosing vulnerabilities is a topic of debate in the computer security community. Some advocate immediate full disclosure of information about vulnerabilities once they are discovered. Others argue for limiting disclosure to the users placed at greatest risk and only releasing full details after a delay, if ever. Such delays may allow those notified to fix the problem by developing and applying patches, but they can also increase the risk to those not privy to full details. This debate has a long history in security; see full disclosure and security through obscurity. More recently a new form of commercial vulnerability disclosure has taken shape, as some commercial security companies offer money for exclusive disclosures of zero-day vulnerabilities. Those offers

11. Chris McNab, Network Security Assessment, O'Rielly, Chapter 4: IP Network Scanning [www. trustmatta.com/downloads/pdf/Matta_IP_Network_Scanning.pdf], pp. 36–72, 2013.

provide a legitimate market for the purchase and sale of vulnerability information from the security community.

From the security perspective, a free and public disclosure is successful only if the affected parties get the relevant information prior to potential hackers; if they did not, the hackers could take immediate advantage of the revealed exploit. With security through obscurity, the same rule applies but this time rests on the hackers finding the vulnerability themselves, as opposed to being given the information from another source. The disadvantage here is that fewer people have full knowledge of the vulnerability and can aid in finding similar or related scenarios.

It should be unbiased to enable a fair dissemination of security-critical information. Most often a channel is considered trusted when it is a widely accepted source of security information in the industry (such as CERT, SecurityFocus, Secunia, www.exploit-db.com). Analysis and risk rating ensure the quality of the disclosed information. The analysis must include enough details to allow a concerned user of the software to assess his individual risk or take immediate action to protect his assets.

Find Security Holes before they Become Problems

Vulnerabilities can be classified into two major categories:

- Those related to errors made by programmers in writing the code for the software
- Those related to misconfigurations of the software's settings that leave systems less secure than they could be (improperly secured accounts, running of unneeded services, etc.)

Vulnerability scanners can identify both types. Vulnerability assessment tools have been around for many years. They've been used by network administrators and misused by hackers to discover exploitable vulnerabilities in systems and networks of all kinds. One of the early well-known Unix scanners, System Administrator Tool for Analyzing Networks (SATAN), later morphed into SAINT (Security Administrator's Integrated Network Tool). These names illustrate the disparate dual nature of the purposes to which such tools can be put.

In the hands of a would-be intruder, vulnerability scanners become a means of finding victims and determining those victims' weak points, like an undercover intelligence operative who infiltrates the opposition's supposedly secure location and gathers information that can be used to launch a full-scale attack. However, in the hands of those who are charged with protecting their networks, these scanners are a vital proactive defense mechanism that allows you to see your systems through the eyes of the enemy and take steps to lock the doors, board up the windows, and plug up seldom used passageways through which the "bad guys" could enter, before they get a chance.

In fact, the first scanners were designed as hacking tools, but this is a case in which the bad guys' weapons have been appropriated and used to defend against them. By "fighting fire with fire," administrators gain a much-needed advantage. For the first time, they are able to battle intruders proactively.[8] Once the vulnerabilities are found, we have to remove them (see sidebar, "Identifying and Removing Vulnerabilities").

IDENTIFYING AND REMOVING VULNERABILITIES

Many software tools can aid in the discovery (and sometimes removal) of vulnerabilities in a computer system. Though these tools can provide an auditor with a good overview of possible vulnerabilities present, they cannot replace human judgment. Relying solely on scanners will yield false positives and a limited-scope view of the problems present in the system.

Vulnerabilities have been found in every major operating system including Windows, Mac OS, various forms of Unix and Linux, OpenVMS, and others. The only way to reduce the chance of a vulnerability being used against a system is through constant vigilance, including careful system maintenance (e.g., applying software patches), best practices in deployment (e.g., the use of firewalls and access controls), and auditing during development and throughout the deployment life cycle.

20. PROACTIVE SECURITY VERSUS REACTIVE SECURITY

There are two basic methods of dealing with security breaches:

- The *reactive method* is passive; when a breach occurs, you respond to it, doing damage control at the same time you track down how the intruder or attacker got in and cut off that means of access so it won't happen again.
- The *proactive method* is active; instead of waiting for the hackers to show you where you're vulnerable, you put on your own hacker hat in relation to your own network and set out to find the vulnerabilities yourself, before anyone else discovers and exploits them.

The best security strategy employs both reactive and proactive mechanisms. Intrusion detection systems (IDS), for example, are reactive in that they detect suspicious network activity so that you can respond to it appropriately.

Vulnerability assessment scanning is a proactive tool that gives you the power to anticipate vulnerabilities and keep out attackers instead of spending much more time and money responding to attack after attack. The goal of proactive security is to prevent attacks before they happen, thus decreasing the load on reactive mechanisms. Being proactive is more cost effective and usually easier; the difference can be illustrated by contrasting the time and cost required to clean up after vandals break into your home or office with the effort and money required to simply install better locks that will keep them out.

Despite the initial outlay for vulnerability assessment scanners and the time spent administering them, potential return on investment is very high in the form of time and money saved when attacks are prevented. *Threat Intelligence* is another example of proactive security methods. The goal of threat intelligence is to monitor dark corners of Internet for hacks, exploits, malicious code being sent to your networks. For example company XYZ, Inc. receives threat intelligence information that one of their web servers administrator level access is for sale in Russian underground forums. For this company it will be so much cheaper to shut down the server as soon as possible, so there will be the least amount of damage done.[12]

21. VULNERABILITY CAUSES

The following are examples of vulnerability causes:

- Password management flaws
- Fundamental operating system design flaws
- Software bugs
- Unchecked user input

Password Management Flaws

The computer user uses weak passwords that could be discovered by brute force. The computer user stores the password on the computer where a program can access it. User has so many accounts on different web sites, that it is impossible to have a different password and still remember it. The result: user uses the same password on many web sites (déjà vu anyone?).

Fundamental Operating System Design Flaws

The operating system designer chooses to enforce suboptimal policies on user/program management. For example, operating systems with policies such as *default permit* grant every program and every user full access to the entire computer. This operating system flaw allows viruses and malware to execute commands on behalf of the administrator.

Software Bugs

The programmer leaves an exploitable bug in a software program. The software bug may allow an attacker to misuse an application through (for example) bypassing access control checks or executing commands on the system hosting the application. Also the programmer's failure to check the size of data buffers, which can then be overflowed, can cause corruption of the stack or heap areas of memory (including causing the computer to execute code provided by the attacker).

Unchecked User Input

The program assumes that all user input is safe. Programs that do not check user input can allow unintended direct execution of commands or SQL statements (known as Buffer

12. "Threat Intelligence," © 2013 Demyo, Inc., Demyo, Inc. [http://demyo.com/services/threat-intelligence/], 2013.

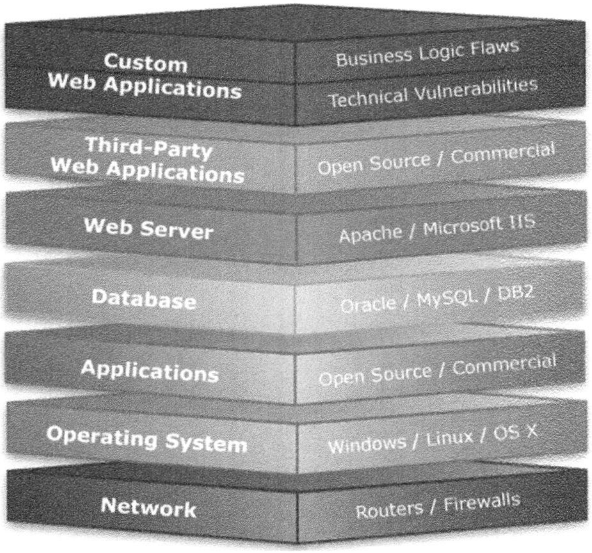

FIGURE 8.7   Vulnerabilities with the biggest impact.

overflows, SQL injection, or other non-validated inputs). For example a form on the web page is asking how old are you? A regular user would enter 32, a hacker would try -3.2, which is somewhat legit input. The goal for entering bogus data is to find out how application reacts and monitor for input validation flaws. The biggest impact on the organization would be if vulnerabilities were found in core devices on the network (routers, firewalls, etc.), as shown in Figure 8.7.

22. DIY VULNERABILITY ASSESSMENT

If you perform credit-card transactions online, you're most likely PCI DSS compliant or working on getting there. In either case, it is much better to resolve compliancy issues on an ongoing basis rather than stare at a truck-load of problems as the auditor walks into your office. Though writing and reviewing policies and procedures is a big part of reaching your goal, being aware of the vulnerabilities in your environment and understanding how to remediate them are just as important. For most small businesses, vulnerability assessments sound like a lot of work and time that you just don't have. What if you could have a complete understanding of all vulnerabilities in your network and a fairly basic resolution for each, outlined in a single report within a couple of hours? Sound good? What if I also told you the tool that can make this happen is currently free and doesn't require an IT genius to run it? Sounding better?

It isn't very pretty and it's not always right, but it can give you some valuable insight into your environment. Tenable's Nessus vulnerability scanner is one of the most widely used tools in professional vulnerability assessments today. In its default configuration, all you need to do is provide the tool with a range of IP addresses and click Go. It will then compare its database of known vulnerabilities against the responses it receives from your network devices, gathering as much information as possible without killing your network or servers, usually. It does have some very dangerous plug-ins that are disabled by default, and you can throttle down the amount of bandwidth it uses to keep the network noise levels to a minimum. The best part about Nessus is that it's, very well documented, and used by over 75,000 organizations worldwide, so you know you're dealing with trustworthy product. I urge you to take a look Tenable's enterprise offerings as well. You might just be surprised at how easy it is to perform a basic do-it-yourself vulnerability assessment! Related links:

- Tenable's Nessus: www.nessus.org
- Tenable Network Security: www.tenablesecurity.com

23. SUMMARY

Network and host-based vulnerability assessment tools are extremely useful in determining what vulnerabilities might exist on a particular network. However, these tools are not useful if the vulnerability knowledge base is not kept current. Also, these tools can only take a snapshot of the systems at a particular point in time. Systems administrators will continually update code on the target systems and will continuously add/delete services and configure the system. All found vulnerabilities should be promptly patched (especially critical ones).

Finally, let's move on to the real interactive part of this Chapter: review questions/exercises, hands-on projects, case projects and optional team case project. The answers and/or solutions by chapter can be found in the Online Instructor's Solutions Manual.

CHAPTER REVIEW QUESTIONS/EXERCISES

True/False

1. True or False? Reporting capability is of growing importance to administrators in a documentation-oriented business climate where you must not only be able to do your job, you must also provide written proof of how you've done it.
2. True or False? Organizations have a tremendous opportunity to use information technologies to increase their productivity.
3. True or False? PCI DSS stands for Payment Card Information Data Security Standard.
4. True or False? There seems to be a certain amount of confusion within the security industry about the similarities between penetration testing and vulnerability assessment.
5. True or False? The theoretical goal of network scanning is elevated security on all systems or establishing a network-wide minimal operation standard.

Multiple Choice

1. What runs on all major computer operating systems, plus the Amiga.?
   A. Nmap
   B. Zenmap
   C. Security scanner GUI
   D. More popular Phase
   E. Attack Phase

2. What is an outstanding general-purpose scanner, but Web application-oriented scanners such as HP Web Inspect or Hailstorm will do a much better job of scanning a web application?
   A. Nessus
   B. SATAN
   C. Central
   D. Local
   E. User-level Rootkit scan

3. With localized scanning and central scanning verification, central scanning becomes a:
   A. Stateful firewall
   B. Virus
   C. Methodology
   D. Verification audit
   E. User-level Rootkit

4. What is an information assurance (IA) strategy in which multiple layers of defense are placed throughout an IT system?
   A. Physical security
   B. Authentication and password security
   C. Defense in depth
   D. Antivirus software
   E. Firewalls Rootkit

5. What is one of the most popular and capable vulnerability scanners, particularly for UNIX systems?
   A. Nessus
   B. GFI LANguard
   C. Retina
   D. Core Impact
   E. ISS Internet Scanner

EXERCISE

Problem

What will happen if a Vulnerability is exploited and who exploits vulnerabilities?

Hands-On Projects

Project

Will scanning interrupt or affect the servers?

Case Projects

Problem

What is Open Vulnerability and Assessment Language (OVAL®)?

Optional Team Case Project

Problem

How is OVAL different from commercial vulnerability scanners?

9

Cyber Forensics

Scott R. Ellis
kCura Corporation

---

1. WHAT IS CYBER FORENSICS?

Definition: Cyber forensics is the acquisition, preservation, and analysis of electronically stored information (ESI) in such a way that ensures its admissibility for use as either evidence, exhibits, or demonstratives in a court of law.

Rather than discussing at great length what cyber forensics is (the rest of the chapter will take care of that), let's, for the sake of clarity, define what cyber forensics is *not*. It is not an arcane ability to tap into a vast, secret repository of information about every single thing that ever happened on, or to, a computer. Often, it involves handling hardware in unique circumstances and doing things with both hardware and software that are not, typically, things that the makers or manufacturers ever intended (see sidebar: "Angular Momentum").

Not every single thing a user ever did on a computer is 100% knowable beyond a shadow of a doubt or even beyond reasonable doubt. Some things are certainly *knowable* with varying degrees of certainty. and there is nothing that can happen on a computer through the use of a keyboard and a mouse that cannot be replicated with a software program or macro of some sort. It is fitting, then, that many of the arguments of cyber forensics become philosophical, and that *degrees of certainty* exist and beg definition. Such as: How heavy is the burden of proof? Right away, lest arrogant thoughtlessness prevail, anyone undertaking a study of cyber forensics must understand the core principles of what it means to be in a position of authority and to what varying degrees of certainty an examiner may attest to without finding he has overstepped his mandate (see sidebar, "Angular Momentum"). The sections "Testifying in Court" and "Beginning to End in Court" in this chapter, and the article "Cyber forensics and Ethics, Green Home Plate Gallery View," address these concerns as they relate to ethics and testimonial work.

ANGULAR MOMENTUM

Hard drive platters spin very fast. The 5¼-inch floppy disk of the 1980s has evolved into heavy, metallic platters that spin at ridiculous speeds. If your car wheels turned at 10,000 RPM, you would zip along at 1000 mph. Some hard drives spin at 15,000 RPM. That's really fast. But though HD platters will not disintegrate (as CD-ROMs have been known to do), anecdotal evidence suggests that in larger, heavier drives, the bearings can become so hot that they liquefy, effectively stopping the drive in its tracks. Basic knowledge of surface coating magnetic properties tells us that if the surface of a hard drive becomes overly hot, the basic magnetic properties, the "zeroes and ones" stored by the particulate magnetic domains, will become unstable. The stability of these zeroes and ones maintains the consistency of the logical data stored by the medium. The high speeds of large, heavy hard drives generate heat and ultimately result in drive failure.

Forensic technicians are often required to handle hard drives, sometimes while they have power attached to them. For example, a computer may need to be moved while it still has power attached to it. Here is where a note about angular momentum becomes necessary: A spinning object translates pressure applied to its axis of rotation 90 degrees from the direction of the force applied to it. Most hard drives are designed to park the heads at even the slightest amount of detected g-shock. They claim to be able to withstand thousands of "g's," but this simply means that if the hard drive was parked on a neutron star it would still be able to park its heads. This is a relatively meaningless, static attribute. Most people should understand that if you drop your computer, you may damage the internal mechanics of a hard drive and, if the

platters are spinning, the drive may be scored. Older drives, those that are more than three years old, are especially susceptible to damage. Precautions should be taken to keep older drives vibration free and cool.

With very slight, gentle pressures, a spinning hard drive can be handled much as you would handle a gyro and with little potential for damage. It can be handled in a way that won't cause the heads to park.

Note: Older drives are the exception, and any slight motion at all can cause them to stop functioning.

Most hard drives have piezoelectric shock detectors that will cause the heads to park the instant a certain g-shock value is reached. Piezoelectrics work under the principle that when a force is exerted along a particular axis, certain types of crystals will emit an electrical charge. Just like their pocket-lighter counterparts, they don't always work and eventually become either desensitized or oversensitized; if the internal mechanism of the hard drive is out of tolerance, the shock detector may either work or it won't park the heads correctly and the heads will shred the surface of the platters. Or, if it does work, it may thrash the surface anyway as the heads park and unpark during multiple, repeated shocks. A large, heavy drive (such as a 1 TB drive) will behave exactly as would any heavy disk spinning about an axis—just like a gyro (see Figure 9.1). So, when a vector of force is applied to a drive and it is forced to turn in the same direction as the vector, instead of its natural 90 degree offset, the potential for damage to the drive increases dramatically.

Such is the case of a computer mounted in brackets inside a PC in transit. The internal, spinning platters of the drive try to shift in opposition to the direction the external

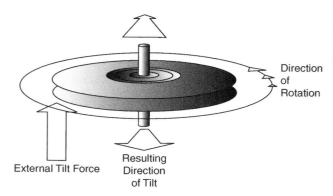

FIGURE 9.1 A spinning object distributes applied force differently than a stationary object. Handle operating hard drives with extreme care.

drive turned; it is an internal tug of war. As the platters attempt to lean forward, the drive leans to the left instead. If there is any play in the bearings at all, the cushion of air that floats the drive heads can be disrupted and the surface of the platters can scratch. If you must move a spinning drive (and sometimes you must), be very careful, go very slowly, and let the drive do all the work. If you must transport a running hard drive, ensure that the internal drive is rotating about the x axis, that it is horizontally mounted inside the computer, and that there is an external shock pad. Some PCs have vertically mounted drives.

Foam padding beneath the computer is essential. If you are in the business of transporting running computers that have been seized, a floating platform of some sort wouldn't be a bad idea. A lot of vibrations, bumps, and jars can shred less durably manufactured HDs. This author once shredded his own laptop hard drive by leaving it turned on, carrying it 15 city blocks, and then for an hour-long ride on the train. You can transport and move computers your entire life and not have an issue. But the one time you do, it could be an unacceptable and unrecoverable loss.

Never move an older computer. If the computer cannot be shut down, then the acquisition of the computer must be completed on site. Any time a computer is to be moved while it's running, everyone involved in the decision-making process should sign off on the procedure and be aware of the risk.

Lesson learned: Always make sure that a laptop put into standby mode has actually gone into standby mode before closing the lid. Windows can be tricky like that sometimes.

2. ANALYSIS OF DATA

Never underestimate the power of a maze. There are two types of mazes that maze experts generally agree on: unicursive and multicursive. In the unicursive maze, the maze has only one answer; you wind along a path and with a little patience you end up at the end. Multicursory mazes, according to the experts, are full of wrong turns and dead ends.

The fact of the matter is, however, when one sets foot into a multicursive maze, one need only recognize that it is, in fact, two unicursory mazes put together, with the path through the maze being the seam. If you take the unicursory tack and simply *always stay to the right (or the left*, as long as you are consistent), you will traverse the entire maze and have no choice but to traverse and complete it successfully.

This is not a section about mazes, but they are analogous in that there are two approaches to cyber forensics: one that churns through every last bit of data and one that takes shortcuts. This is called *analysis*. Quite often as a forensic analyst, the sheer amount of data that needs to be sifted will seem enormous and unrelenting. But there is a path that, if you know it, you can follow it through to success. Here are a few guidelines on how to go about conducting an investigation. For starters, we talk about a feature that is built into most forensic toolsets. It allows the examiner to "reveal all" in a fashion that can place hundreds of thousands of files at the fingertips for examination. It can also create a bad situation, legally and ethically.

Cyber Forensics and Ethics, Green Home Plate Gallery View[1]

A simplified version of this article was published on the Chicago Bar Association blog in late 2007. This is the original version, unaltered.

EnCase is a commonly used forensic software program that allows a cyber forensic technologist to conduct an investigation of a forensic hard disk copy. One of the functions of the software is something known as "green-home-plate-gallery-view." This function allows the forensic technologist to create, in *plain view*, a gallery of every single image on the computer.

In EnCase, the entire folder view structure of a computer is laid out just as in Windows Explorer with the exception that to the left of every folder entry are two boxes. One is shaped like a square, and the other like a little "home plate" that turns green when you click on it; hence the "green-home-plate." The technical name for the home plate box is "Set Included Folders." With a single click, every single file *entry* in that folder and its sub-folders becomes visible in a table view. An additional option allows the examiner to switch from a table view of entries to a gallery view of *thumbnails*. Both operations together create the "green-home-plate-gallery-view" action.

With two clicks of the mouse, the licensed EnCase user can gather up every single image that exists on the computer and place it into a single, scrollable, thumbnail gallery. In a court-ordered investigation where the search may be for text-based documents such as correspondence, green-home-plate-gallery-view has the potential of being *misused* to visually search the computer for imaged/scanned documents. I emphasize *misused* because, ultimately, this action puts every single image on the computer in *plain view*. It is akin to policemen showing up for a domestic abuse response with an x-ray machine in tow and x-raying the contents of the whole house.

Because this action enables one to view every single image on a computer, including those that may not have anything to do with the forensic search at hand, it raises a question of ethics, and possibly even legality. Can a forensic examiner green-home-plate-gallery-view without reasonable cause?

1. "Cyber forensics and ethics," Green Home Plate Gallery View, Chicago Bar Association Blog, September 2007.

In terms of a search where the search or motion specifically authorized searching for text-based "documents," green-home-plate-gallery-view is not the correct approach, nor is it the most efficient. The action exceeds the scope of the search and it may raise questions regarding the violation of rights and/or privacy. To some inexperienced examiners, it may seem to be the quickest and easiest route to locating all the documents on a computer. More experienced examiners may use it as a quick litmus test to "peek under the hood" to see if there are documents on the computer.

Many documents that are responsive to the search may be in the form of image scans or PDFs. Green-home-plate-gallery-view renders them visible and available, just for the scrolling. Therein lies the problem: If anything incriminating turns up, it also has the ring of truth in a court of law when the examiner suggests that he was innocently searching for financial documents when he inadvertently discovered, in *plain view*, offensive materials that were outside the scope of his original mandate. But just because something has the ring of truth does not mean that the bell's been rung.

For inexperienced investigators, green-home-plate-gallery-view (see Figure 9.2) may truly seem to be the only recourse and it may also be the one that has yielded the most convictions. However, because there is a more efficient method to capture and detect text, one that can protect privacy and follows the constraints of the search mandate, it should be used.

Current forensic technology allows us, through electronic file signature analysis, sizing, and typing of images, to capture and export every image from the subject file system. Next, through optical character recognition (OCR), the experienced professional can detect every image that has text and discard those that do not. In this manner, images are protected from being viewed, the subject's privacy is protected, and all images with text are located efficiently. The resultant set can then be hashed and reintroduced into EnCase as single files, hashed, and indexed so that the notable files can be bookmarked and a report generated.

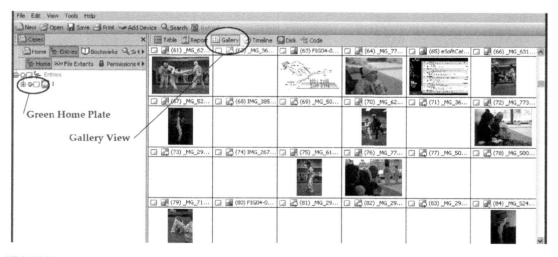

FIGURE 9.2   Green-home-plate-gallery-view.

Technically, this is a more difficult process because it requires extensive knowledge of imaging, electronic file signature analysis, automated OCR discovery techniques, and hash libraries. But to a trained technician, this is actually faster than green-home-plate-gallery-view, which may yield thousands of images and may take hundreds of hours to accurately review.

In practice, the easiest way is seldom the most ethical way to solve a problem; neither is it always the most efficient method of getting a job done. Currently, there are many such similar scenarios that exist within the discipline of cyber forensics. As the forensic technology industry grows and evolves, professional organizations may eventually emerge that will provide codes of ethics and some syncretism in regard to these issues. For now, however, it falls on attorneys to retain experienced cyber forensic technologists who place importance on developing appropriate ethical protocols. Only when these protocols are in place can we successfully understand the breadth and scope of searches and prevent possible violations of privacy.

Database Reconstruction

A disk that hosts an active database is a very busy place. Again and again throughout this chapter, a single recurring theme will emerge: Data that has been overwritten cannot, by any conventionally known means, be recovered. If it could be, then Kroll Ontrack and every other giant in the forensics business would be shouting this service from the roof-tops and charging a premium price for it. Experimentally, accurate statistics on the amount of data that will be overwritten by the seemingly random action of a write head may be available, but most likely it functions by rules that are different for every system based on the amount of usage, the size of the files, and the size of the unallocated clusters. Anecdotally, the formula goes something like this; the rules change under any given circumstances, but this story goes a long way toward telling how much data will be available:

On a server purposed with storing surveillance video, there are three physical hard drives. Drive C serves as the operating system (OS) disk and program files disk; Drives E and F, 350 gigabytes (GB) each, serve as storage disks. When the remote DVR units synchronize each evening, every other file writes to every other disk of the two storage drives. Thirty-day-old files automatically get deleted by the synchronization tool.

After eight months of use, the entire unallocated clusters of each drive, 115 GB on one drive and 123 GB on the other, are completely filled with MPG data. An additional 45 GB of archived deleted files are available to be recovered from each drive.

In this case, the database data were MPG movie files. In many databases, the data, the records (as the database indexes and grows and shrinks and is compacted and opti-mized), will grow to populate the unallocated clusters. Database records found in the unallocated clusters are not an indicator of deleted records. Database records that exist in the unallocated clusters that don't exist in the live database *are* a sign of deleted records.

Lesson learned: Don't believe everything you see. Check it out and be sure. Get second, third, and fourth opinions when you're uncertain.

3. CYBER FORENSICS IN THE COURT SYSTEM

Cyber forensics is one of the few cyber-related fields in which the practitioner will be found in the courtroom on a given number of days of the year. With that in mind, the following sections are derived from the author's experiences in the courtroom, the lessons learned there, and the preparation leading up to giving testimony. To most lawyers and judges, cyber forensics is a mysterious black art. It is as much a discipline of the art to demystify and explain results in plain English as it is to conduct an examination. It was with special consideration of the growing prevalence of the use of electronically stored information (ESI) in the courtroom, and the general unfamiliarity with how it must be handled as evidence, that spawned the idea for the sidebar "Preserving Digital Evidence in the Age of eDiscovery."

PRESERVING DIGITAL EVIDENCE IN THE AGE OF EDISCOVERY[2]

Society has awoken in these past few years to the realities of being immersed in the digital world. With that, the harsh realities of how we conduct ourselves in this age of binary processing are beginning to take form in terms of both new laws and new ways of doing business. In many actions, both civil and criminal, digital documents are the new "smoking gun." And with the new Federal laws that open the floodgates of accessibility to your digital media, the sanctions for mishandling such evidence become a fact of law and a major concern.

At some point, most of us (any of us) could become involved in litigation. Divorce, damage suits, patent infringement, intellectual property theft, and employee misconduct are just some examples of cases we see. When it comes to digital evidence, most people simply aren't sure of their responsibilities. They don't know how to handle the requests for and subsequent handling of the massive amounts of data that can be crucial to every case. Like the proverbial smoking gun, "digital evidence" must be handled properly.

Recently, a friend forwarded us an article about a case ruling in which a routine email exhibit was found inadmissible due to authenticity and hearsay issues. What we should take away from that ruling is that electronically stored information (ESI), just like any other evidence, must clear standard evidentiary hurdles. Whenever ESI is offered as evidence, the following evidence rules must be considered.

In most courts, there are four types of evidence. Cyber files that are extracted from a subject machine and presented in court typically fall into one or more of these types:

- *Documentary evidence* is paper or digital evidence that contains human language. It must meet the authenticity requirements outlined below. It is also unique in that it may be disallowed if it contains hearsay. Emails fall into the category of documentary evidence.
- *Real evidence* must be competent (authenticated), relevant, and material. For example, a computer that was

2. Scott R. Ellis, "Preserving digital evidence in the age of ediscovery," *Daily Southtown*, 2007.

involved in a court matter would be considered real evidence provided that it hasn't been changed, altered, or accessed in a way that destroyed the evidence. The ability to use these items as evidence may be contingent on this fact, and that's is why preservation of a cyber or digital media must be done.

- *Witness testimony*. With ESI, the technician should be able to verify how he retrieved the evidence and that the evidence is what it purports to be, and he should be able to speak to all aspects of computer use. The witness must both remember what he saw and be able to communicate it.

- *Demonstrative evidence* uses things like PowerPoint, photographs, or cyber-aided design (CAD) drawings of crime scenes to demonstrate or reconstruct an event. For example, a flowchart that details how a person goes to a Web site, enters her credit-card number, and makes a purchase would be considered demonstrative.

For any of these items to be submitted in court, they each must, to varying degrees, pass the admissibility requirements of relevance, materiality, and competence. For evidence to be *relevant*, it must make the event it is trying to prove either more or less probable. A forensic analyst may discover a certain Web page on the subject hard drive that shows the subject visited a Web site where flowers are sold and that he made a purchase. In addition to perhaps a credit-card statement, this shows that it is more probable that the subject of an investigation visited the site on his computer at a certain time and location.

Materiality means that something not only proves the fact (it is relevant to the fact that it is trying to prove) but is also *material* to the issues in the case. The fact that the subject of the investigation purchased flowers on a Web site may not be material to the matter at hand.

Finally, *competency* is the area where the forensic side of things becomes most important. Assuming that the purchase of flowers from a Web site is material (perhaps it is a stalking case), how the evidence was obtained and what happened to it after that will be put under a microscope by both the judge and the party objecting to the evidence. The best evidence collection experts are trained professionals with extensive experience in their field. The best attorneys will understand this and will use experts when and where needed. Spoliation results from mishandled ESI, and spoiled data is generally inadmissible. It rests upon everyone involved in a case—IT directors, business owners, and attorneys—to get it right. Cyber forensics experts cannot undo damage that has been done, but if involved in the *beginning*, they can prevent it from happening.

4. UNDERSTANDING INTERNET HISTORY

Of the many aspects of user activity, the Internet history is usually of the greatest interest. In most investigations, people such as HR, employers, and law enforcement seek to understand the subject's use of the Internet. What Web sites did he visit? When did he visit them? Did he visit them more than once? The article "What Have You Been Clicking On" (see sidebar) seeks to demystify the concept of temporary Internet files (TIF).

WHAT HAVE YOU BEEN CLICKING ON?

You've probably heard the rumor that whenever you click on something on a Web page, you leave a deeply rooted trail behind you for anyone (with the right technology) to see. In cyber forensics, just like in archeology, these pieces that a user leaves behind are called *artifacts*. An artifact is a thing made by a human. It tells the story of a behavior that happened in the past.

On your computer, that story is told by metadata stored in databases as well as by files stored on your local machine. They reside in numerous places, but this article will address just three: Internet history, Web cache, and temporary Internet files (TIF). Because Internet Explorer (IE) was developed in a time when bandwidth was precious, storing data locally prevents a browser from having to retrieve the same data every time the same Web page is visited. Also, at the time, no established technology existed that, through a Web browser, could show data on a local machine without first putting the file on the local machine. A Web browser, essentially, was a piece of software that combined FTP and document-viewing technology into one application platform, complete with its own protocol, HTTP.

In IE, press **Ctrl + H** to view your history. This will show a list of links to all the sites that were viewed over a period of four weeks. The history database only stores the name and date the site was visited. It holds no information about files that may be cached locally. That's the job of the Web cache.

To go back further in history, an Internet history viewer is needed. A Google search for "history.dat viewer" will turn up a few free tools.

The Web cache database, index.dat, is located in the TIF folder; it tracks the date, the time the Web page downloaded, the original Web page filename, and its local name and location in the TIF. Information stays in the index.dat for a long time, much longer than four weeks. You will notice that if you set your computer date back a few weeks and then press **Ctrl + H**, you can always pull the last four weeks of data for as long as you have had your computer (and not cleared your cache). Using a third-party viewer to view the Web cache shows you with certainty the date and origination of a Web page. The Web cache is a detailed inventory of everything in the TIF. Some history viewers will show Web cache information, too.

The TIF is a set of local folders where IE stores Web pages your computer has downloaded. Typically, the size varies depending on user settings. But Web sites are usually small, so 500 MB can hold thousands of Web pages and images! Viewing these files may be necessary. Web mail, financial, and browsing interests are all stored in the TIF. However, malicious software activity, such as pop-ups, exploits, viruses, and Trojans, can cause many strange files to appear in the TIF. For this reason, files that are in the TIF should be compared to their entry in the Web cache. Time stamps on files in the TIF may or may not accurately show when a file was written to disk. System scans periodically alter Last Accessed and Date Modified time stamps! Because of hard-disk caching and delayed writing, the Date Created time stamp may not be the actual time the file arrived. Cyber forensics uses special tools to analyze the TIF, but much is still left to individual interpretations.

Inspection of all the user's Internet artifacts, when intact, can reveal what a user was doing and whether or not a click trail exists. Looking just at time stamps or IE history isn't enough. Users can easily delete IE history, and time stamps aren't always accurate. Missing history can disrupt the trail. Missing Web cache entries or time stamp–altering system scans can destroy the trail. Any conclusions are best not preceded by a suspended leap through the air (you may land badly and trip and hurt yourself). Rather, check for viruses and bad patching, and get the artifacts straight. If there is a click trail, it will be revealed by the Web cache, the files in the TIF, and the history. Bear in mind that when pieces are missing, the reliability of the click trail erodes, and professional examination may be warranted.

5. TEMPORARY RESTRAINING ORDERS AND LABOR DISPUTES

A temporary restraining order (TRO) will often be issued in intellectual property or employment contract disputes. The role of the forensic examiner in a TRO may be multifold, or it may be limited to a simple, one-time acquisition of a hard drive. Often when an employee leaves an organization under less than amicable terms, accusations will be fired in both directions and the resulting lawsuit will be a many-headed beast. Attorneys on both sides may file motions that result in forensic analysis of emails, user activity, and possible contract violations as well as extraction of information from financial and customer relationship management (CRM) databases.

Divorce

Typically the forensic work done in a divorce case will involve collecting information about one of the parties to be used to show that trust has been violated. Dating sites, pornography, financial sites, expatriate sites, and email should be collected and reviewed.

Patent Infringement

When one company begins selling a part that is patented by another company, a lawsuit will likely be filed in federal court. Subsequently, the offending company will be required to produce all the invoices relating to sales of that product. This is where a forensic examiner may be required. The infringed-on party may find through their own research that a company has purchased the part from the infringer and that the sale has not been reported. A thorough examination of the financial system will reveal all the sales. It is wise when doing this sort of work to contact the financial system vendor to get a data dictionary that defines all the fields and the purpose of the tables.

Invoice data is easy to collect. It will typically reside in just two tables: a header and a detail table. These tables will contain customer codes that will need to be joined to the customer table, so knowing some SQL will be a great help. Using the database server for the specific database technology of the software is the gold standard for this sort of work. Getting the collection to launch into VMware is the platinum standard, but sometimes an image won't want to boot. Software utilities such as Live View do a great job of preparing the image for deployment in a virtualized environment.

When to Acquire, When to Capture Acquisition

When a forensics practitioner needs to capture the data on a hard disk, he/she does so in a way that is forensically sound. This means that, through any actions on the part of the examiner, no data on the hard drive is altered and a complete and total copy of the surface of the hard drive platters is captured. Here are some common terms used to describe this process:

- Collection
- Mirror
- Ghost
- Copy
- Acquisition

Any of these terms is sufficient to describe the process. The one that attorneys typically use is *mirror* because they seem to understand it best. A "forensic" acquisition simply means that the drive was write-protected by either a software or hardware write blocker while the acquisition was performed.

Acquisition of an entire hard drive is the standard approach in any case that will require a deep analysis of the behaviors and activities of the user. It is not always the standard procedure. However, most people will agree that a forensic procedure must be used whenever information is copied from a PC. Forensic, enterprise, and ediscovery cases all vary in their requirements for the amount of data that must be captured. In discovery, much of what is located on a computer may be deemed "inaccessible," which is really just fancy lawyer talk for "it costs too much to get it." Undeleting data from hundreds of computers in a single discovery action in a civil case would be a very rare thing to happen and would only take place if massive malfeasance was suspected. In these cases, forensic creation of logical evidence files allows the examiner to capture and copy relevant information without altering the data.

Creating Forensic Images Using Software and Hardware Write Blockers

Both software and hardware write blockers are available. Software write blockers are versatile and come in two flavors. One is a module that "plugs" into the forensic software and can generally be used to write block any port on the computer. The other method of software write blocking is to use a forensic boot disk. This will boot the computer from the hard drive. Developing checklists that can be repeatable procedures is an ideal way to ensure solid results in any investigation.

Software write blockers are limited by the port speed of the port they are blocking, plus some overhead for the write-blocking process. But then, all write blockers are limited in this manner.

Hardware write blockers are normally optimized for speed. Forensic copying tools such as Logicube and Tableau are two examples of hardware write blockers, though there are many companies now that make them. LogiCube will both hash and image a drive at a rate of about 3 GB a minute. They are small and portable and can replace the need for bulky PCs on a job site. There are also appliances and large enterprise software packages that are designed to automate and alleviate the labor requirements of large discovery/disclosure acquisitions that may span thousands of computers.

Live Capture of Relevant Files

Before conducting any sort of a capture, all steps should be documented and reviewed with counsel before proceeding. Preferably, attorneys from both sides on a matter and the judge agree to the procedure before it is enacted. Whenever a new procedure or technique is introduced late on the job site, if there are auditors or observers present, the attorneys will argue, which can delay the work by several hours. Most forensic software can be loaded to a USB drive and launched on a live system with negligible forensic impact to the operating environment. Random Access Memory (RAM) captures are becoming more popular; currently this is the only way to capture an image of physical RAM. Certain companies are rumored to be creating physical RAM write blockers. Launching a forensic application on a running system will destroy a substantial amount of physical RAM as well as the paging file. If either RAM or the paging file is needed, the capture must be done with a write blocker.

Once the forensic tool is launched, either with a write blocker or on a live system, the local drive may be previewed. The examiner may only be interested in Word documents, for example. Signature analysis is a lengthy process in preview mode, as are most searches. A better method, if subterfuge is not expected: Filtering the table pane by extension produces a list of all the docs. "Exporting" them will damage the forensic information, so instead you need to create a logical evidence file (LEF). Using EnCase, a user can create a condition to view all the .DOC files and then dump the files into a logical evidence file in about 30 seconds. Once the logical evidence file is created, it can later be used to create a CD-ROM. There are special modules available that will allow an exact extraction of native files to CD to allow further processing for a review tool.

Redundant Array of Independent (or Inexpensive) Disks (RAID)

Acquiring an entire RAID set disk by disk and then reassembling them in EnCase is probably the easiest way of dealing with a RAID and may be the only way to capture a software RAID. Hardware RAIDs can be most efficiently captured using a boot disk. This allows the capture of a single volume that contains all the unique data in an array. It can be trickier to configure and as with everything, practice makes perfect. Be sure you understand how it works. The worst thing that can happen is that the wrong disk or an unreadable disk gets imaged and the job has to be redone at your expense.

File System Analyses

FAT12, FAT16, and FAT32 are all types of file systems. Special circumstances aside, most forensic examiners will find themselves regularly dealing with either FAT or NTFS file systems. FAT differs from NTFS primarily in the way that it stores information about how it stores information. Largely, from the average forensic examiner's standpoint, very little about the internal workings of these file systems is relevant. Most modern forensic software will do the work of reconstructing and extracting information from these systems, at the system level, for you. Nonetheless, an understanding of these systems is critical because, at any given time, an examiner *just might* need to know it. The following are some examples showing where you might need to know about the file system:

- Rebuilding RAID arrays
- Locating lost or moved partitions
- Discussions of more advanced information that can be gleaned from entries in the MFT or FAT

The difference between FAT12, 16, and 32 is in the size of each item in the File Allocation Table (FAT). Each has a correspondingly sized entry in the FAT. For example, FAT12 has a 12-bit entry in the FAT. Each 12-bit sequence represents a cluster. This places a limitation on the file system regarding the number of file extents available to a file. The FAT stores the following information:

- Fragmentation
- Used or unused clusters
- A list of entries that correspond to each cluster on the partition
- Marks a cluster as used, reserved, unused, or bad
- The cluster number of the next cluster in the chain

Sector information is stored in the directory. In the FAT file system, directories are actually files that contain as many 32-byte slots as there are entries in the folder. This is also where deleted entries from a folder can be discovered. Figure 9.3 shows how the sector view is represented by a common forensic analysis tool.

NTFS

NTFS is a significant advancement in terms of data storage. It allows for long filenames, almost unlimited storage, and a more efficient method of accessing information. It also

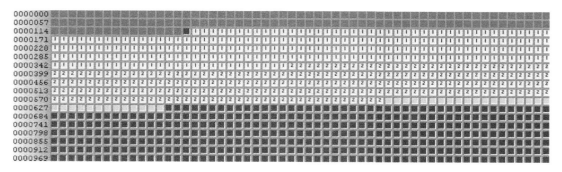

FIGURE 9.3   The sector view.

provides for much greater latency in deleted files, that is, deleted files stick around a lot longer in NTFS than they do in FAT. The following items are unique to NTFS. Instead of keeping the filenames in folder files, the entire file structure of NTFS is retained in a flat file database called the Master File Table (MFT):

- Improved support for metadata
- Advanced data structuring improves performance and reliability
- Improved disk space utilization with a maximum disk size of 7.8 TB, or 2^{64} sectors; sector sizes can vary in NTFS and are most easily controlled using a third-party partitioning tool such as Partition Magic.
- Greater security

The Role of the Forensic Examiner in Investigations and File Recovery

The forensic examiner is at his best when he is searching for deleted files and attempting to reconstruct a pattern of user behavior. The sidebar "Oops! Did I Delete That?" first appeared in the Chicago *Daily Southtown* column "Bits You Can Use." In addition, this section also includes a discussion of data recovery and an insurance investigation article (see sidebar, "Don't Touch That Computer! Data Recovery Following Fire, Flood, or Storm").

OOPS! DID I DELETE THAT?

The file is gone. It's not in the recycle bin. You've done a complete search of your files for it, and now the panic sets in. It's vanished. You may have even asked people to look through their email because maybe you sent it to them (you didn't). Oops. Now what?

Hours, days, maybe even years of hard work seem to be lost. Wait! Don't touch that PC! Every action you take on your PC at this point may be destroying what is left of your file. It's not too late yet. You've possibly heard that things that are deleted are never really deleted, but you may also think that it will cost you thousands of dollars to recover deleted files once you've emptied the recycle bin. Suffice it to say, unless you are embroiled in complicated ediscovery or forensic legal proceedings where preservation is a requirement, recovering some deleted files for you may cost no more than a tune-up for your car.

Now the part where I told you: "Don't touch that PC!" I meant it. Seriously: Don't touch that PC. The second you realize you've lost a file, stop doing anything. Don't visit any Web sites. Don't install software. Don't reformat your hard drive, do a Windows repair, or install undelete software. In fact, if it's not a server or running a shared database application, pull the plug from the back of the PC. Every time you "write" to your hard drive, you run the risk that you are destroying your lost file. In the case of one author we helped, ten years of a book were "deleted." With immediate professional help, her files were recovered.

Whether you accidentally pulled your USB drive from the slot without stopping it first (corrupting your MFT), intentionally deleted it, or have discovered an "OS not found" message when you booted your PC, you need your files back and you need them now. However, if you made the mistake of actually overwriting a file with a file that has the same name and thereby replaced it, "Abandon hope all ye who enter here." Your file is trashed, and all that may be left are some scraps of the old file, parts that didn't get overwritten but can be extracted from file slack. If your hard drive is physically damaged, you may also be looking at an expensive recovery.

Here's the quick version of how deleted files become "obliterated" and unrecoverable:

Step 1: The MFT that contains a reference to your file marks the deleted file space as available.

Step 2: The actual sectors where the deleted file resides *might* be either completely or partially overwritten.

Step 3: The MFT record for the deleted file is overwritten and destroyed. Any ability to *easily* recover your deleted file at this point is lost.

Step 4: The sectors on the PC that contain your deleted file *are* overwritten and eventually only slight traces of your lost file remain. Sometimes the MFT record may be destroyed before the actual sectors are overwritten. This happens a lot, and these files are recoverable with a little extra work.

It's tremendously amazing how fast this process can occur. It's equally amazing how slowly this process can occur. Recently I retrieved hundreds of files from a system that had periodically been deleting files, and new files were written to the disk on a daily basis. Yet recovery software successfully recovered hundreds of complete files from nearly six months ago! A lot of free space on the disk contributed to this success. A disk that is in use and is nearly full will be proportionally less likely to contain old, deleted files.

The equipment and training investment to perform these operations is high, so expect that labor costs will be higher, but you can also expect some degree of success when attempting to recover files that have been accidentally deleted. Let me leave you with two dire warnings: Disks that have experienced surface damage (scored platters) are unrecoverable with current technology. And never, ever, ever disrupt power to your PC when it's performing a defrag. The results are disastrous.

DON'T TOUCH THAT COMPUTER! DATA RECOVERY FOLLOWING FIRE, FLOOD, OR STORM

Fire, flood, earthquakes, landslides, and other catastrophes often result in damaged cyber equipment—and loss of electronic data. For claims managers and adjusters, this data loss can manifest itself in an overwhelming number of insurance claims, costing insurers millions of dollars each year.

The improper handling of computers immediately following a catastrophic event is possibly one of the leading causes of data loss—and once a drive has been improperly handled, the chances of data retrieval plummet. Adjusters often assume a complete loss when, in fact, there are methods that can save or salvage data on even the most damaged computers.

Methods to Save or Salvage Data

One of the first steps toward salvaging cyber data is to focus on the preservation of the hard drive. Hard drives are highly precise instruments, and warping of drive components by even fractions of a millimeter will cause damage to occur in the very first moments of booting up. During these moments the drive head can shred the surface of the platters, rendering the data unrecoverable.

Hard drives are preserved in different ways, depending on the damaging event. If the drive is submerged in a flood, the drive should be removed and resubmerged in clean, distilled water and shipped to an expert. It is important that this is done immediately. Hard drive platters that are allowed to corrode after being exposed to water, especially if the drive experienced seepage, will oxidize and data will be destroyed. A professional can completely disassemble the drive to ensure that all of its parts are dry, determine what level of damage has already occurred, and then decide how to proceed with the recovery. Care must always be taken during removal from the site to prevent the drive from breaking open and being exposed to dust.

Fire or Smoke Damage

After a fire or a flood, the hard drive should not be moved and in no circumstances should it be powered up. A certified cyber forensic expert with experience in handling damaged drives should be immediately contacted. Typically, these experts will be able to dismantle the drive and move it without causing further damage. They are able to assess the external damage and arrive at a decision that will safely triage the drive for further recovery steps. Fire-damaged drives should never be moved or handled by laymen.

Shock Damage

Shock damage can occur when someone drops a computer or it is damaged via an automobile accident; in more catastrophic scenarios, shock damage can result when servers fall through floors during a fire or are even damaged by bulldozers that are removing debris. This type of crushing damage often results in bending of the platters and can be extensive. As in fire and flood circumstances, the drive should be isolated and power should not be applied.

A drive that has been damaged by shock presents a unique challenge: from the outside, the computer may look fine. This is typical of many claims involving laptop computers damaged during an automobile collision. If the computer consultant can verify that the drive was powered down at the time the accident occurred, most will be comfortable attempting to power up a drive that has been in a collision, to begin the data capture process. At the first sign of a change in the dynamics of the drive, a head clicking or a drive spinning down, power will be cut from the drive and the restoration will continue in a clean room where the drive will be opened up and protected from harmful dust.

The Importance of Off-Site Cyber Backup

One of the best ways to maximize cyber data recovery efforts is to have off-site cyber backup. For adjusters arriving at the scene, this should be one of the first questions asked. An offsite backup can take many forms. Some involve the use of special data centers that synchronize data constantly. There are companies that provide this service. Other backups, for smaller companies, may be as mundane (but effective) as removing a tape backup of critical data from the site on a daily basis. With proper rotation and several tapes, a complete backup of data is always offsite. Prices for these services vary widely depending on how much data needs to be backed up and how often.

Case Studies

Scenario 1

John ran a home-based IT business. After his home burned down, John posted an insurance claim for a $500,000 loss for lost income, damaged cyber equipment, and lost wages. He also charged the insurance company $60,000 for the three months he spent recovering data from the drives. Because he was only able to recover 25% of the data, he posted an additional claim for the cost of reconstructing the Web sites that he hosted from his home.

For the cyber forensic consultant, this case raised several questions. As an IT professional, John should have known better than to touch the hard drive and attempt to recover any of the data himself. Also, when a claimant intentionally or unintentionally inflicts damage on his or her own property after an event, who is responsible? Through a thorough evaluation of the circumstances and intense questioning of the claimant, the claim was eventually reduced to a substantially smaller amount.

Scenario 2

Sammie's Flowers has 113 retail outlets and one central headquarters where they keep photography, custom software, catalog masters, and the like. There is no offsite backup. Everything is on CD-ROMs or on the hard drive of the company's server.

One night lightning struck the headquarters building and it burned down. An IT appraiser lacking the appropriate cyber forensic skills evaluated the cyber equipment after the fire. No attempts were made to recover data from the hard drives or to start the computers; because of their damaged physical condition, they were simply thrown into a dumpster.

One year later, the insured filed a claim for $37 million. Under the terms of the insured's policy, coverage for valuable papers and business personal property was most pertinent to the case. The policy limit for valuable papers is small and easily reached. The coverage limit for business personal property, on the other hand, *will* cover the $37 million claim—if the court decides that the cyber data that was lost qualifies as "business valuable papers." Though this case is still pending, the cost of resolving this claim could be astronomic, and had a cyber data recovery expert been consulted, the claim amount could have been reduced by millions.

Scenario 3

Alisa, a professional photographer, was in a car accident that damaged her laptop computer. She had been using the PC at a rest stop prior to the accident and later reported to the adjuster that when she booted it up after the accident she heard "a strange clicking and clacking sound." Unfortunately for Alisa, that was the sound of data being destroyed. She posted a $500,000 claim to her insurance company under her business policy—including the cost of 2000 lost images and the cost of equipment, site, model, and agency fees for a one-day photography shoot. Had the PC, which had a noticeable crack in it caused by the accident, been professionally handled, the chances are good the data could have been recovered and the claim would have been significantly reduced.

Cyber equipment is always at risk of being damaged—whether by flood, fire, lightning, or other catastrophic means. However, damage does not always equal data loss. Indeed, companies and their adjusters can be quick to write off damaged storage media when, in fact, recovery may be possible. By taking the immediate measures of protecting the computers from touch and power and by calling in professional cyber forensic experts to assess the damage, insurers can reap the benefits in reduced claim amounts.

Password Recovery

The following is a short list of the ways and types of passwords that can be recovered. Many useful tools that can be downloaded from the Internet for free will crack open system files that store passwords. Software programs, such as Peachtree (a financial database), Windows 8, certain FTP programs, and the like all store passwords in a way that allows their easy retrieval.

Recovering license keys for software is often an important step in reconstructing or virtualizing a disk image. Like passwords, without a valid license key the software won't work. There are a number of useful programs that can recover software license keys from the registry of a computer that can be found with a quick Google search. Understanding the mind of the user can also be helpful in locating things such as password storage tools or simply thinking to search a computer for the word *password*. Many, many Web sites will pass the password down to a client machine through the Password field in HTML documents. Some developers have wised up to this "feature" and they strip it out before it comes down, but most of them do it on the client side. This means that with the proper intercepting tool, the password can be captured midstream on its way down to the client, before it gets stripped out.

Password cracking can be achieved with a minimal amount of skill and a great deal of patience. Having some idea of what the password is before cracking it will be helpful. You can also purchase both online services as well as software tools that will strip the password right out of a file, removing it completely. Word documents are particularly vulnerable, and zip files are particularly invulnerable. However, there is a method (and a free download) that can figure out the password of a zip file if a sample of a file that is known to be in the zip can be provided.

File Carving

In most investigations, the very first place a file system examination begins is with live files. Live files are those files that still have MFT entries. Link file, trash bin, Outlook Temporary (OLK) folders, recent items, ISO lists, Internet history, TIF, and thumb databases all constitute a discernible, unique pattern of user activity. As such, they hold particular interest. By exploring these files an examiner can make determinations about file origins, the usage of files, the distribution of files, and of course the current location of the files. But sometimes the subject has been very clever and removed all traces of activity. Or the suspect item may be a server, used merely as a repository for the files. Or maybe someone just wants to recover a file that they deleted a long, long time ago (see sidebar, "Oops, Did I Delete That?").

When such need arises, the vast graveyard called the *unallocated clusters* could hold the last hope that the file can be recovered. By searching the unallocated clusters using a search tool designed for such things, and by using a known keyword in the file, one may locate the portion within the unallocated clusters where a file used to reside. Typically, search hits will be stored under a tab or in a particular area of the forensic toolset, and they may be browsed, one by one, along with a small excerpt from the surrounding bits. By clicking on the search hit, another pane of the software window may show a more expanded view of the hit location. If it is a document, with text, then that is great and you may see other words that were also known to have been in the target file. Now, in TV shows like *CSI*, of course the document is always there, and by running some reverse 128-bit decrytion sequencer to an inverted 12-bit decryption sequencer that reloops the hashing algorithm through a 256-bit decompiler by rethreading it into a multiplexing file marker, they can just right click and say "export this" and the file will print out, even if it's not even on the computer that is being examined and never was. (Yes, I made all that up.)

In the real world, more often than not we find that our examinations are spurred and motivated and wholly created by someone's abject paranoia. In these cases, no amount of digging will ever create the evidence that they want to see. That leaves only creative use of time stamps on documents to attempt to create an aroma of guilt about the subject piece. Sometimes we find that even after rooting through 300 GB of unallocated clusters, leaving no stone unturned, the *file just isn't there*. But sometimes, all pessimism aside, we find little bits and pieces of interesting things all salted around throughout the unallocated clusters.

The first place to turn is the automated carvers. By familiarizing ourselves with the hexadecimal patterns of file signatures (and I've provided a nice table for you here), we may view the hex of the unallocated clusters in a hex editor or in the hex pane of the examination tool. Or possibly we already know the type of file. Let's say that we know the type of file because our client told us that they only use Word as their document editor. We scroll to the beginning of the section of text, which might look like this:

Figure sample file signature
From the text pane view of EnCase:
Ð Ï · à¡ ± á · · · · · · · · · · · · · · · > · · · þÿ · · · · · · · · ·
From the Hex view:
00 00 00 00 00 00 00 00 00 00 00 00 00 00 00 4F 6F 70 73
21 20 20 44 69 64
20 49 20 64 65 6C 65 74 65 20 74 68 61 74 3F 0D 42 79
20 53 63 6F 74 74 20
52 2E 20 45 6C 6C 69 73 0D 73 65 6C 6C 69 73 40 75 73
2E 72 67 6C 2E 63 6F
6D 0D 0D 54 68 65 20 66 69 6C 65 20 69 73 20 67 6F 6E

65 2E 20 20 49 74 92
73 20 6E 6F 74 20 69 6E 20 74 68 65 20 72 65 63 79 63
6C 65 20 62 69 6E 2E
20 59 6F 75 92 76 65 20 64 6F 6E 65 20 61 20 63 6F 6D
70 6C 65 74 65 20 73

Scrolling down in the text pane, we then find the following:

············· Oops! Did I delete that? By Scott R. Ellis The file is gone. It's not in the recycle bin. You've ....

By simply visually scanning the unallocated clusters, we can pick up where the file begins and, if the file signature isn't in the provided list of signatures or if for some reason the carving scripts in the forensic software are incorrectly pulling files, they may need to be manually set up. Truly, for Word files, that is all you need to know. You need to be able to determine the end and the beginning of a file. Some software will ignore data in the file before and after the beginning and end of file signatures. This is true for many, many file types; I can't tell you which ones because I haven't tried them all. There are some file types that need a valid end-of-file (EOF) marker, but most don't. However, if you *don't* capture the true EOF (sensible marker or no), the file may look like garbage or all the original formatting will be scrambled or it won't open. Some JPEG viewers (such as Adobe Photoshop) will throw an error if the EOF is not found. Others, such as Internet Explorer, won't even notice. Here's the trick—and it is a trick, and don't let anyone tell you differently; they might not teach this in your average university cyber forensics class: Starting with the file signature, highlight as many of the unallocated clusters *after* the file signature that you think would possibly be big enough to hold the entire file size. Now double that, and export it as raw data. Give it a .DOC extension and open it in Word. *Voilá!* The file has been reconstructed. Word will know where the document ends and it will show you that document. If you happen to catch a few extra documents at the end, or a JPG or whatever, Word will ignore them and show only the first document.

Unless some sort of drastic "wiping action" has taken place, as in the use of a third-party utility to delete data, I have almost always found that a great deal of deleted data is *immediately* available in EnCase (forensic software) within 20–25 minutes after a hard disk image is mounted, simply by running "recover folders" and sitting back and waiting while it runs. This is especially true when the drive has not been used at all since the time the data was deleted. Preferably, counsel will have taken steps to ensure that this is the case when a computer is the prime subject of an investigation. Often this is not the case, however. Many attorneys, IT, and HR directors "poke around" for information all on their own.

It is conceivable that up to 80% of deleted data on a computer may be readily available, without the necessity of carving, for up to two or three years, as long as the computer hasn't seen extreme use (large amounts of files, or large amounts of copying and moving of very large files) that could conceivably overwrite the data.

Even so, searching unallocated clusters for file types typically does not require the creation of an index. Depending on the size of the drive, it may take four or five hours for the carving process to complete, and it may or may not be entirely successful, depending on the type of files that are being carved. For example, MPEG videos do not carve well at all, but there are ways around that. DOC and XLS files usually carve out quite nicely.

Indexing is something that is done strictly for the purpose of searching massive amounts of files for large numbers of keywords. We rarely use EnCase to search for keywords; we have found it better to use Relativity, our review environment, to allow the people who are interested in the keywords to do the keyword searching themselves as they perform their review. Relativity is built on an SQL platform on which indexing is a known and stable technology.

In other words (as in the bottom line), spending 15 to 25 minutes with a drive, an experienced examiner can provide a very succinct answer as to how long it would take to provide the files that they want. And, very likely, the answer could be, "Another 30 minutes and it will be yours." Including time to set up, extract, and copy to disk, if everything is in perfect order, two hours is the upper limit. This is based on the foundation that the deleted data they are looking for was deleted in the last couple of weeks of the use of the computer. If they need to go back more than a couple of months, an examiner may end up carving into the unallocated clusters to find "lost" files—these are files for which part of or all of the master file table entry has been obliterated and portions of the files themselves may be overwritten.

Carving is considered one of the consummate forensic skills. Regardless of the few shortcuts that exist, carving requires a deep, disk-level knowledge of how files are stored, and it requires a certain intuition that cannot be "book taught." Examiners gain this talent from years of looking at raw disk data. Regardless, even the most efficient and skilled of carvers will turn to their automated carving tools. Two things that the carving tools excel at is carving out images and print spool files (EMFs). What are they really bad at? The tools I use don't even begin to work properly to carve out email files. General regular program (GREP) searching doesn't provide for branching logic, so you can't locate a qualified email header, every single time, and capture the end of it. The best you can do is create your own script to carve out the emails. GREP does not allow for any sort of true logic that would be useful or even efficient at capturing something as complex as the many variations of email headers that exist, but it does allow for many alterations of a single search term to be formulated with a single expression. For example, the words *house, housing, houses*, and *housed* could all be searched for with a single statement such as "hous[(e)|(es)|(ing)|(ed)]". GREP can be useful, but it is not really a shortcut. Each option added to a GREP statement doubles the length of time the search will take to run. Searching for *house (s)* has the same run time as two separate keywords for *house* and *houses*. It also allows for efficient pattern matching. For example, if you wanted to find all the phone numbers on a computer for three particular area codes, you could formulate a GREP expression like this. Using a test file and running the search each time, an expression can be built that finds phone numbers in any of three area codes:

(708)|(312)|(847) Checks for the three area codes [\(]?(708)|(312)|(847)[\-\)\.]? Checks for parentheses and other formatting
[\(]?(708)|(312)|(847)[\-\)\.]?###[\-\.]?#### Checks for the rest of the number

This statement will find any 10-digit string that is formatted like a phone number, as well as any 10-digit string that contains one of the three area codes. This last option, to check for any 10-digit number string, if run against an entire OS, will likely return numerous results that aren't phone numbers. The question marks render the search for phone number formatting optional.

The following are the characters that are used to formulate a GREP expression. Typically, the best use of GREP is its ability to formulate pattern-matching searches. In GREP, the following symbols are used to formulate an expression:

.   The period is a wildcard and means a space must be occupied by any character.
*   The asterisk is a wildcard that means any character or no character. It will match multiple repetitions of the character as well.
?   The character preceding the question mark must repeat 0 or 1 times. It provides instructions as to how to search for the character or grouping that precedes it.
+   This is like the question mark, only it *must* exist at least one or more times.
#   Matches a number.
[•]   Matches a list of characters. *[hH]i* matches *hi* and *Hi* (but not *hHi!*).
∧   This is a "not" and will exclude a part from a string.
[-]   A range of characters such as (a-z) will find any single letter, a through z.
\   This will escape the standard GREP search symbols so that it may be included as part of the search. For example, a search string that has the (symbol in it (such as a phone number) needs to have the parentheses escaped so that the string can be included as part of the search.
| This is an "or." See previous sample search for area codes.
\x   Searches for the indicated hex string.

By preceding a hex character with \x marks the next two characters as hexadecimal characters. Using this to locate a known hex string is more efficient than relying on it to be interpreted from Unicode or UTF.

Most forensic applications have stock scripts included that can carve for you. Many of the popular cyber forensics applications can carve for you. They have scripted modules that will run, and all you have to do is select the signature you want and *voilá*, it carves it right out of the unallocated clusters for you. Sounds pretty slick, and it is slick—when it works. The problem is that some files, such as MPEG video, don't have a set signature at the beginning and end of each file. So how can we carve them? Running an MPEG carver will make a mess. It's a far better thing to do a "carve" by locating MPEG data, highlighting it, exporting it to a file, and giving it an MPEG extension.

Things to Know: How Time Stamps Work

Let's take an example: Bob in accounting has been discovered to be pilfering from the cash box. A forensics examiner is called in to examine his cyber system to see if he has been engaging in any activities that would be against company policy and to see if he has been accessing areas of the network that he shouldn't be. They want to know what he has been working on. A quick examination of his PC turns up a very large cache of pornography. A casual glance at the Entry Modified time stamp shows that the images were created nearly one year before Bob's employment, so automatically the investigator disregards the images and moves onto his search for evidence of copying and deleting sensitive files to his local machine. The investigator begins to look at the deleted files. His view is filtered, so he is not looking at anything but deleted files. He leaves the view in "gallery" view so that he can see telltale images that may give clues as to any Web sites used during the timeframe of the suspected breaches. To his surprise, the investigator begins seeing images from that porn cache. He notices now that when a deleted file is overwritten, in the gallery view of the software the image that overwrote the deleted file is displayed. He makes the logical conclusion that the Entry Modified time stamp is somehow wrong.

On a Windows XP machine, an archive file is extracted. Entry Modified time stamps are xx:xx:xx, even though the archive was extracted to the file system on yy:yy:yy. Normally when a file is created on a system, it takes on the system date as its Date Created time stamp. Such is not the case with zip files.

Entry Modified, in the world of cyber forensics, is that illustrious time stamp that has cinched many a case. It is a hidden time stamp that users never see, and few of them actually know about it. As such, they cannot change it. A very little-known fact about the Entry Modified time stamp is that it is constrained. It can be no later than the Date Created time stamp. (This is not true in Vista.) When a zip file is created, the Date Created and Date Modified time stamps become the same.

Experimental Evidence

Examining and understanding how time stamps behave on individual PCs and operating systems provide some of the greatest challenges facing forensic examiners. This is not due to any great difficulty, but rather because of the difficulty in clearly explaining it to others. This examiner once read a quote from a prosecutor in a local newspaper that said, "We will clearly show that he viewed the image on three separate occasions." In court the defense's expert disabused her of the notion she held that Last Written, Last Accessed, Entry Modified, and Date Created time stamps were convenient little recordings of user activity. Rather, they are references mostly used by the operating system for its own arcane purposes. Table 9.1 compares the three known Windows time stamps with the four time stamps in EnCase.

TABLE 9.1 Comparison of Three Known Windows Time stamps with the Four EnCase Time Stamps

Windows	EnCase	Purpose
Date Created	Date Created	Typically this is the first time a file appeared on a system. It is not always accurate.
Date Modified	Last Written	Usually this is the time when a system last finished writing or changing information in a file.
Last Accessed	Last Accessed	This time stamp can be altered by any number of user and system actions. It should not be interpreted as the file having been opened and viewed.
N/A	Entry Modified	This is a system pointer that is inaccessible to users through the Explorer interface. It changes when the file changes size.

TABLE 9.2 Date Created Time Stamp

ID	Name	Last Accessed	File Created	Entry Modified
1	*IMG_3521.CR2*	*04/28/08 01:56:07PM*	*12/23/07 10:40:53AM*	*03/15/08 09:11:15AM*
2	IMG_3521.CR2	04/28/08 01:56:07PM	12/23/07 10:40:53AM	04/28/08 01:57:12PM

TABLE 9.3 Altering the Entry Modified Time Stamp

ID	Name	Last Accessed	File Created	Entry Modified
1	*IMG_3521.CR2*	*04/28/08 01:56:07PM*	*12/23/07 10:40:53AM*	*03/15/08 09:11:15AM*
2	IMG_3521.CR2	05/21/08 03:32:01PM	12/23/07 10:40:53AM	05/21/08 03:32:01PM

XP

A zip file was created using a file with a Date Created time stamp of 12/23/07 10:40:53AM (see ID 1 in Table 19.2). It was then extracted and the time stamps were examined.

Using Windows XP compressed folders, the file was then extracted to a separate file on a different system (ID 2 in Table 9.2). Date Created and Entry Modified time stamps, upon extraction, inherited the original Date Created time stamp of 12/23/12 10:40:53AM and Last Accessed of 04/28/13 01:56:07PM.

The system Entry Modified (not to be confused with Date Modified) became 04/28/13 01:57:12PM.

Various operating systems can perform various operations that will, *en masse*, alter the Entry Modified time stamp (see Table 9.3). For example, a tape restoration of a series of directories will create a time stamp adjustment in Entry Modified that corresponds to the date of the restoration. The original file is on another system somewhere and is inaccessible to the investigator (because he doesn't know about it).

In Table 9.3, Entry Modified becomes a part of a larger pattern of time stamps after an OS event. On a computer on which most of the time stamps have an Entry Modified time stamp that is sequential to a specific timeframe, it is now more difficult to determine when the file actually arrived on the system. As long as the date stamps are not inherited from the overwriting file by the overwritten file, examining the files that were overwritten by ID2 (Table 19.3), can reveal a No Later Than time. In other words, the file could not have appeared on the system prior to the file that it overwrote.

Vista

A zip file was created using a file with a Date Created time stamp of dd:mm:yyyy(a) and a date modified of dd:mm:yy(a). Using Windows Vista compressed folders, the file was then extracted to a separate file on the same system. Date Modified time stamps, on extraction, inherited the original time stamp of dd:mm:yyyy(a), but the Date Created time stamp reflected the true date. This is a significant change from XP. There are also tools available that will allow a user to mass-edit time stamps. Forensic examiners must always bear in mind that there are some very savvy users who research and understand antiforensics.

Email Headers and Time Stamps, Email Receipts, and Bounced Messages

There is much confusion in the ediscovery industry and in cyber forensics in general about how best to interpret email time stamps. Though it might not offer the perfect "every case" solution, this section reveals the intricacies of dealing with time stamps and how to interpret them correctly.

Regarding sources of email, SMTP has to relay email to its own domain. HELO/EHLO allows a user to connect to the SMTP port and send email.

As most of us are aware, in 2007 the U.S. Congress enacted the Energy Policy Act of 2005 (http://www.epa.gov/oust/fedlaws/publ_109-058.pdf, Section 110. Daylight Savings). This act was passed into law by President George W. Bush on August 8, 2005. Among other provisions, such as subsidies for wind energy, reducing air pollution, and providing tax breaks to homeowners for making energy-conserving changes to their homes, it amended the Uniform Time Act of 1966 by changing the start and end dates for Daylight Savings Time (DST) beginning in 2007. Previously, clocks would be set ahead by an hour on the first Sunday of April and set back on the last Sunday of October. The new law changed this as follows: Starting in 2007 clocks were set ahead one hour on the first Sunday of March and then set back on the first Sunday in November. Aside from the additional confusion now facing everyone when we review email and attempt to translate Greenwich Mean Time (GMT) to a sensible local time, probably the only true noteworthy aspect of this new law is the extra daylight time afforded to children trick-or-treating on Halloween. Many observers have questioned whether or not the act actually resulted in a net energy savings.

In a world of remote Web-based email servers, it has been observed that some email sent through a Web mail interface will bear the time stamp of the time zone wherein the server resides. Either your server is in the Central Time zone or the clock on the server is set to the wrong time/time zone. Servers that send email mark the header of the email with the GMT stamp numerical value (noted in bold in the example that follows) as opposed to the actual time zone stamp. For example, instead of saying 08:00 CST, the header will say 08:00 (-0600). The GMT differential is used so that every email client interprets that stamp based on the time zone and time setting of itself and is able to account for things like Daylight Savings Time offsets. This is a dynamic interpretation; if I change the time zone of my computer, it will change the way Outlook *shows* me the time of each email, but it doesn't actually physically change the email itself. For example, if an email server is located in Colorado, every email I send appears to have been sent from the Mountain Time zone. My email client interprets the Time Received of an email based on when my server received the mail, *not* when my email client downloads the email from my server.

If a server is in the Central Time zone and the client is in Mountain Time, the normal Web mail interface will not be cognizant of the client's time zone. Hence those are the times you'll see. I checked a Webmail account on a server in California that I use and it does the same thing. Here I've broken up the header to show step by step how it moved.

Here is, first, the entire header in its original context, followed by a breakdown of how I interpret each transaction in the header:

```
***********************************************

       Received: from p01c11m096.mxlogic.net (208.65.144.247) by mail.us.rgl.com
       (192.168.0.12) with Microsoft SMTP Server id 8.0.751.0; Fri, 30 Nov 200721:03:15-0700
       Received: from unknown [65.54.246.112] (EHLO bay0-omc1-s40.bay0.hotmail.com)
       by p01c11m096.mxlogic.net (mxl_mta-5.2.0-1) with ESMTP id 23cd0574.3307895728.120458.00-105.
       p01c11m096. mxlogic.net (envelope-from <timezone32@hotmail.com>); Fri, 30 Nov 2007 20:59:46-0700
       (MST)
       Received: from BAY108-W37 ([65.54.162.137]) by bay0-omc1-s40.bay0.hotmail.com
       with Microsoft SMTPSVC(6.0.3790.3959); Fri, 30 Nov 2007 19:59:46-0800
       Message-ID: <BAY108-W374BF59F8292A9D2C95F08BA720@phx.gbl>
       Return-Path: timezone32@hotmail.com
       Content-Type: multipart/alternative; boundary = " = _reb-r538638D0-t4750DC32"
       X-Originating-IP: [71.212.198.249]
       From: Test Account <timezone3@hotmail.com>
       To: Bill Nelson <attorney@attorney12345.com>, Scott
       Ellis <sellis@us.rgl.com>
       Subject: FW: Norton Anti Virus
       Date: Fri, 30 Nov 2007 21:59:46 -0600
       Importance: Normal
       In-Reply-To: <BAY108-W26EE80CDDA1C4C632124ABA720@phx.gbl>
       References: <BAY108-W26EE80CDDA1C4C632124ABA720@phx.gbl>
       MIME-Version: 1.0
       X-OriginalArrivalTime: 01 Dec 2007 03:59:46.0488
       (UTC) FILETIME = [9CAC5B80:01C833CE]
       X-Processed-By: Rebuild v2.0-0
       X-Spam: [F = 0.0038471784; B = 0.500(0);
       spf = 0.500; CM = 0.500; S = 0.010(2007110801);
       MH = 0.500(2007113048); R = 0.276(1071030201529);
       SC = none; SS = 0.500]
       X-MAIL-FROM: <timezone3@hotmail.com>
       X-SOURCE-IP: [65.54.246.112]
       X-AnalysisOut: [v = 1.0 c = 0 a = Db0T9Pbbji75CibVO CAA:9
       a = rYVTvsE0vOPdh0IEP8MA:]
       X-AnalysisOut: [7 a = TaS_S6-EMopkTzdPlCr4MVJL5D QA:4
       a = NCG-xuS670wA:10 a = T-0]
       X-AnalysisOut:[QtiWyBeMA:10a = r9zUxlSq4yJzxRie7pAA:7
       a = EWQMng83CrhB0XWP0h]
       X-AnalysisOut: [vbCEdheDsA:4 a = EfJqPEOeqlMA:10
       a = 37WNUvjkh6kA:10]


***********************************

```

Looks like a bunch of garbage, right? Here it is, step by step, transaction by transaction, in reverse chronological order:

1. My server in Colorado receives the email (GMT differential is in bold):

```
       Received: from p01c11m096.mxlogic.net (208.65.144.247) by mail.us.rgl.com
       (192.168.0.12) with Microsoft SMTP Server id 8.0.751.0; Fri, 30 Nov 2007 21:03:15 -0700
```

2. Prior to that, my mail-filtering service in Colorado receives the email:

> Received: from unknown [65.54.246.112] (EHLO bay0-omc1-s40.bay0.hotmail.com)
> by p01c11m096.mxlogic.net (mxl_mta-5.2.0-1) with ESMTP id
> 23cd0574.3307895728.120458.00-105.p01c11m096.
> mxlogic.net (envelope-from
> <timezone3@hotmail.com>); Fri, 30 Nov 2007 20:59:46 -0700 (MST)

— The email server receives the sender's email in this next section. On most networks, the mail server is rarely the same machine on which a user created the email. This next item in the header of the email shows that the email server is located in the Pacific Time zone. 65.54.246.112, the x-origin stamp, is the actual IP address of the computer that sent the email:

> Received: from BAY108-W37 ([65.54.162.137]) by bay0-omc1-s40.bay0.hotmail.com
> with Microsoft SMTPSVC(6.0.3790.3959); Fri, 30 Nov 2007 19:59:46 **-0800**
> Message-ID: <BAY108-W374BF59F8292A9D2C95F08BA720@phx.gbl>
> Return-Path: timezone310@hotmail.com

— This content was produced on the server where the Webmail application resides. Technically, the email was created on the Web client application with only one degree of separation between the originating IP and the sender IP. By examining the order and type of IP addresses logged in the header, a trail can be created that shows the path of mail servers that the email traversed before arriving at its destination. This machine is the one that is likely in the Central Time zone, since it can be verified by the -0600 in the following. The X-originating IP address is the IP address of the sender's external Internet connection IP address in her house and the X-Source IP address is the IP address of the Webmail server she logged into on this day. This IP address is also subject to change because they have many Webmail servers as well. In fact, comparisons to older emails sent on different dates show that it is different. Originating IP address is also subject to change since a DSL or cable Internet is very likely a dynamic account, but it (likely) won't change as frequently as the X-source:

> Content-Type: multipart/alternative; boundary = " = _ reb-r538638D0-t4750DC32"
> X-Originating-IP: [71.212.198.249]
> From: Test Account <@hotmail.com>
> To: Bill Nelson <attorney@attorney12345.com>, Scott
> Ellis <sellis@us.rgl.com>
> Subject: FW: Norton Anti Virus
> Date: Fri, 30 Nov 2007 21:59:46 **-0600**
> Importance: Normal
> In-Reply-To: <BAY108-W26EE80CDDA1C4C632124 ABA 720@phx.gbl>
> References: <BAY108-W26EE80CDDA1C4C632124 ABA7 20@phx.gbl>
> MIME-Version: 1.0
> X-OriginalArrivalTime: 01 Dec 2007 03:59:46.0488

(UTC) FILETIME = [9CAC5B80:01C833CE]
X-Processed-By: Rebuild v2.0-0
X-Spam: [F = 0.0038471784; B = 0.500(0); spf = 0.500;
CM = 0.500; 5 = 0.010(2007110801); MH = 0.500(2007113 048); R = 0.276(1071030201529); SC = none;
SS = 0.500]
X-MAIL-FROM: <timezone310@hotmail.com>
X-SOURCE-IP: [65.54.246.112]
X-AnalysisOut: [v = 10c = 0a = Db0T9Pbbji75CibVOCAA:9
a = rYVTvsE0vOPdh0IEP8MA:]
X-AnalysisOut:[7a = TaS_S6-EMopkTzdPlCr4MVJL5DQA:4
a = NCG-xuS670wA:10a = T-0]
X-AnalysisOut: [QtiWyBeMA:10 a = r9zUxlSq4yJzxRie 7p AA:7 a = EWQMng83CrhB0XWP0h]
X-AnalysisOut: [vbCEdheDsA:4 a = EfJqPEOeqlMA:10 a = 37WNUvjkh6kA:10]
From: Test Account [mailto:timezone310@hotmail.com
Sent: Friday, November 30, 2007 10:00 PM
To: Bill Nelson; Scott Ellis
Subject: FW: Norton Anti Virus
Bill and Scott,
By the way, it was 8:57 my time when I sent the last email, however, my hotmail shows that it was
9:57 pm. Not sure if their server is on Central time or not. Scott, can you help with that question?
Thanks.
Anonymous
From:timezone3@hotmail.com
To:attorney@attorney12345.com; sellis@us.rgl.com
CC:timezone310@hotmail.com
Subject: Norton Anti Virus
Date: Fri, 30 Nov 2007 21:57:16 -0600
Bill and Scott,
I am on the computer now and have a question for you. Can you please call me?
Anonymous

Steganography "Covered Writing"

Steganography tools provide a method that allows a user to hide a file in plain sight. For example, there are a number of stego software tools that allow the user to hide one image inside another. Some of these do it by simply appending the "hidden" file at the tail end of a JPEG file and then add a pointer to the beginning of the file. The most common way that steganography is discovered on a machine is through the detection of the steganography software on the machine. Then comes the arduous task of locating 11 of the files that may possibly contain hidden data. Other, more manual stego techniques may be as simple as hiding text behind other text. In Microsoft Word, text boxes can be placed right over the top of other text, formatted in such a way as to render the text undetectable to a casual observer. Forensic tools will allow the analyst to locate this text, but on opening the file the text won't be readily visible. Another method is to hide images behind other images using the layers feature of some photo enhancement tools, such as Photoshop.

StegAlyzerAS is a tool created by Backbone Security to detect steganography on a system. It works by both searching for known stego artifacts as well as by searching for the program files associated with over 650 steganography toolsets. Steganography hash sets are also available within the NIST database of hash sets. Hash sets are databases of MD5 hashes of known unique files associated with a particular application.

6. FIRST PRINCIPLES

In science, *first principles* refer to going back to the most basic nature of a thing. For example, in physics, an experiment is *ab initio* (from first principles) if it only subsumes a parameterization of known irrefutable laws of physics. The experiment of calculation does not make assumptions through modeling or assumptive logic.

First principles, or *ab initio*, may or may not be something that a court will understand, depending on the court and the types of cases it tries. Ultimately the very best evidence is that which can be easily duplicated. In observation of a compromised system in its live state, even if the observation photographed or videoed may be admitted as evidence but the events viewed cannot be duplicated, the veracity of the events will easily be questioned by the opposition.

During an investigation of a defendant's PC, an examiner found that a piece of software on the computer behaved erratically. This behavior had occurred after the computer had been booted from a restored image of the PC. The behavior was photographed and introduced in court as evidence. The behavior was mentioned during a cross-examination and had not, originally, been intended as use for evidence; it was simply something that the examiner recalled seeing during his investigation, that the list of files a piece of software would display would change. The prosecution was outraged because this statement harmed his case to a great deal. The instability and erratic behavior of the software was one of the underpinnings of the defense. The examiner, in response to the prosecutor's accusations of ineptitude, replied that he had a series of photographs that demonstrated the behavior. The prosecutor requested the photos, but the examiner didn't have them in court. He brought them the next day, at which time, when the jury was not in the room, the prosecutor requested the photos, reviewed them, and promptly let the matter drop.

It would have been a far more powerful thing to have produced the photographs at the time of the statement; but it may have also led the prosecution to an *ab initio* effort—one that may have shown that the defense expert's findings were irreproducible. In an expert testimony, the more powerful and remarkable a piece of evidence, the more likely it is to be challenged by the opposition. It is an intricate game because such a challenge may ultimately destroy the opposition's case, since a corroborative result would only serve to increase the veracity and reliability of the expert's testimony. Whether you are defense, prosecution, or plaintiff, the strongest evidence is that which is irrefutable and relies on first principles. Aristotle defined it as those circumstances where "for the same (characteristic) simultaneously to belong and not belong to the same (object) in the same (way) is impossible." In less obfuscating, 21st-century terms, the following interpretation is applicable: One thing can't be two different things at the same time in the same circumstance; there is only one truth, and it is self-evidentiary and not open to interpretation. For example, when a computer hard drive is imaged, the opposition may also image the same hard drive. If proper procedures are followed, there is no possible way that different MD5 hashes could result. Black cannot be white.

The lesson learned? Never build your foundation on irreproducible evidence. To do so is tantamount to building the case on "circumstantial" evidence.

7. HACKING A WINDOWS XP PASSWORD

There are many, many methods to decrypt or "hack" a Windows password. This section lists some of them. One of the more interesting methods of cracking passwords through the use of forensic methods is hacking the Active Directory. It is not covered here, but suffice it to say that there is an awesome amount of information stored in the Active Directory file of a domain server. With the correct tools and settings in place, Bitlocker locked PCs can be accessed and passwords can be viewed in plaintext with just a few simple, readily available scripts.

Net User Password Hack

If you have access to a machine, this is an easy thing, and the instructions to do it can easily be found on YouTube. Type **net users** at the Windows command line. Pick a user. Type **net user***username*****. (You have to type the asterisk or it won't work.) You will then, regardless of your privileges, be allowed to change any password, including the local machine administrator password.

Lanman Hashes and Rainbow Tables*

- The following procedure can be used to "reverse-engineer" the password from where it is stored in Windows. Lan Manager (or Lanman, or LM) has been used by Windows, in versions prior to Windows Vista, to store passwords that are shorter than 15 characters. The vast majority of passwords are stored in this format. LM hashes are computed via a short series of actions. The following items contribute to the weakness of the hash.
- Password is converted to all uppercase.
- Passwords longer than seven characters are divided into two halves. By visual inspection of the hash, this allows us to determine whether the second half is padding. We can do this by viewing all the LM hashes on a system and observing whether the second halves of any of the hashes are the same. This will speed up the process of decrypting the hash.
- There is no salt. In cryptography, *salt* is random bits that are thrown in to prevent large lookup tables of values from being developed.

Windows will store passwords using the Lanman hash. Windows Vista has changed this. For all versions of Windows except Vista, about 70 GB of what are called *rainbow tables* can be downloaded from the Internet. Using a tool such as the many that are found on Backtrack will capture the actual hashes that are stored for the password on the physical disk. Analysis of the hashes will show whether or not the hashes are in use as passwords. Rainbow tables, which can be downloaded from the Web in a single 70 GB table, are simply lookup tables of every possible iteration of the hashes. By entering the hash value, the password can be easily and quickly reverse-engineered and access to files can be gained. A favorite method of hackers is to install command-line software on remote machines that will allow access to the Lanman hashes and will send them via FTP to the hacker. Once the hacker has admin rights, he owns the machine.

Password Reset Disk

Emergency Boot CD (EBCD) is a Linux-based tool that allows you to boot a computer that has an unknown password. Using this command-line tool, you can reset the administrator password very easily. It will not tell you the plaintext of the password, but it will clear it so that the machine can be accessed through something like VMware with a blank password.

Memory Analysis and the Trojan Defense

One method of retrieving passwords and encryption keys is through memory analysis—physical RAM. RAM can be acquired using a variety of relatively nonintrusive methods. HBGary.com offers a free tool that will capture RAM with very minimal impact. In addition to extracting encryption keys, RAM analysis can be used to either defeat or corroborate the Trojan defense. The Responder tool from HBGary (single-user license) provides in-depth analysis and reporting on the many malware activities that can be detected in a RAM environment. The Trojan defense is commonly used by innocent and guilty parties to explain unlawful actions that have occurred on their computers. The following items represent a brief overview of the types of things that can be accomplished through RAM analysis:

- A hidden driver is a 100% indicator of a bad guy. Hidden drivers can be located through analysis of the physical memory.
- Using tools such as FileMon, TCPView, and RegMon, you can usually readily identify malware infections. There is a small number of advanced malwares that are capable of doing things such as rolling up completely (poof, it's gone!) when they detect the presence of investigative tools or that are capable of escaping a virtualized host. All the same, when conducting a malware forensic analysis, be sure to isolate the system from the network.
- RAM analysis using a tool such as HBGary's Responder can allow reverse-engineering of the processes that are running and can uncover potential malware behavioral capabilities. As this science progresses, a much greater ability to easily and quickly detect malware can be expected.

User Artifact Analysis

There is nothing worse than facing off against an opposing expert who has not done his artifact analysis on a case. Due to an increasing workload in this field, experts are often taking shortcuts that, in the long run, really make more work for everyone. In life and on computers, the actions people take leave behind artifacts. The following is a short list of artifacts that are readily viewed using any method of analysis:

- Recent files
- OLK files
- Shortcuts
- Temporary Internet Files (TIF)

- My Documents
- Desktop
- Recycle Bin
- Email
- EXIF data

Users create all these artifacts, either knowingly or unknowingly, and aspects of them can be reviewed and understood to indicate that certain actions on the computer took place—for example, a folder in My Documents called "fast trains" that contains pictures of Europe's TGV and surrounding countryside, TIF sites that show the user booking travel to Europe, installed software for a Casio Exilim digital camera, EXIF data that shows the photos were taken with a Casio Exilim, and email confirmations and discussions about the planned trip all work together to show that the user of that account on that PC did very likely take a trip to Europe and did take the photos. Not that there is anything wrong with taking pictures of trains, but if the subject of the investigation is a suspected terrorist and he has ties with a group that was discovered to be planning an attack on a train, this evidence would be very valuable.

It is the sum of the parts that matters the most. A single image of a train found in the user's TIF would be virtually meaningless. Multiple pictures of trains in his TIF could also be meaningless; maybe he likes trains or maybe someone sent him a link that he clicked to take him to a Web site about trains. *It's likely he won't even remember having visited the site.* It is the forensic examiner's first priority to ensure that all the user artifacts are considered when making a determination about any behavior.

Recovering Lost and Deleted Files

Unless some sort of drastic "wiping action" has taken place, as in the use of a third-party utility to delete data or if the disk is part of a RAIDed set, I have almost always found that deleted data is *immediately* available in EnCase (forensic software I use) within 20 to 25 minutes after a hard disk image is mounted. This is especially true when the drive has not been used at all since the time the data was deleted.

Software Installation

Nearly every software installation will offer to drop one on your desktop, in your Start menu, and on your quick launch tool bar at the time of program installation. Whenever a user double-clicks on a file, a link file is created in the Recent folder located at the root of Documents and Settings. This is a hidden file.

Recent Files

In Windows XP (and similar locations exist in other versions), link files are stored in the Recent folder under Documents and Settings. Whenever a user double-clicks on a file, a link file is created. Clicking the Start button in Windows and navigating to the My Recent Documents link will show a list of the last 15 documents that a user has clicked on. What most users don't realize is that the C:\Documents and Settings\$user name$ \Recent folder will potentially reveal *hundreds* of documents that have been viewed by the user. This list is indisputably a list of documents that the user has viewed. Interestingly, in Windows 2000, if the Preserve History feature of the Windows Media Player is turned off, no link files will be created. The only way to make any legitimate determination about the use of a file is to view the Last Accessed time, which has been shown in several cases to be inconsistent and unreliable in certain circumstances. Be very careful when using this time stamp as part of your defense or prosecution. It is a loaded weapon, ready to go off.

Start Menu

The Start menu is built on shortcuts. Every item in the Start file has a corresponding . LNK file. Examining Last Accessed or Date Created time stamps may shed light on when software was installed and last used.

Email

Extracting email is an invaluable tool for researching and finding out thoughts and motives of a suspect in any investigation. Email can be extracted from traditional client-based applications such as Outlook Express, Lotus Notes, Outlook, Eudora, and Netscape Mail as well as from common Webmail apps such as Gmail, Hotmail, Yahoo Mail, and Excite. Reviewing log files from server-based applications such as Outlook Webmail can show a user, for example, accessing and using his Webmail after employment termination. It is important that companies realize that they should terminate access to such accounts the day a user's employment is terminated.

Internet History

Forensic analysis of a user's Internet history can reveal much useful information. It can also show the exact code that may have downloaded on a client machine and resulted in an infection of the system with a virus. Forensic examiners should actively familiarize themselves with the most recent, known exploits.

Typed URLs is a registry key. It will store the last 10 addresses that a user has typed into a Web browser address field. I once had a fed try to say that everything that appeared in the drop-down window was a "typed" URL. This is not the case. The only definitive source of showing the actual typed URLs is the registry key. Just one look at the screen shown in Figure 9.4 should clearly demonstrate that the user never would have "typed" all these entries. Yet that is exactly what a Department of Homeland Security Agent sat on the witness stand and swore, under oath, was true. In Figure 9.4, simply typing in **fil** spawns a list of URLs that were never typed but rather are the result of either the user having opened a file or a program having opened one. The highlighted file entered the history shown as a result of installing the software, not as a result of the user "typing" the filename. Many items in the history wind their way into it through regular software use, with files being accessed as an indirect result of user activity.

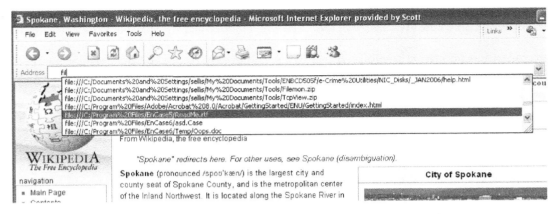

FIGURE 9.4   Spawning a list of URLs that were never typed (the Google one is deleted).

8. NETWORK ANALYSIS

Many investigations require a very hands-off approach in which the only forensics that can be collected is network traffic. Every machine is assigned an IP address and a MAC address. It is like an IP address on layer 3, but the MAC address sits on Layer 2. It is quite like a phone number in that it is unique. Software that is used to examine network traffic is categorized as a *sniffer*. Tools such as Wireshark and Colasoft are two examples of sniffers. They can be used to view, analyze, and capture all the IP traffic that comes across a port.

Switches are not promiscuous, however. To view the traffic coming across a switch you can either put a hub in line with the traffic (between the target and the switch) and plug the sniffer into the hub with it, or ports can be spanned. Spanning, or mirroring, allows one port on a switch to copy and distribute network traffic in a way such that the sniffer can see everything. The argument could be made in court that the wrong port was accidentally spanned, but this argument quickly falls apart because all network packets contain both the machine and IP address of a machine. ARP poisoning is the practice of spoofing another user's IP address, however. This would be the smartest defense, but if a hub is used on a switched port, with the hub wired directly to the port, a greater degree of forensic certainty can be achieved. The only two computers that should be connected to the hub are the examiner and target machines.

Protocols

In the world of IP, the various languages of network traffic that are used to perform various tasks and operations are called *protocols*. Each protocol has its own special way of organizing and forming its packets. Unauthorized protocols viewed on a port are a good example of a type of action that might be expected from a rogue machine or employee. Network sniffing for email (SMTP and POP) traffic and capturing it can, depending on the sniffer used, allow the examiner to view live email traffic coming off the target machine.

Viewing the Web (HTTP) protocol allows the examiner to capture images and text from Web sites that the target is navigating, in real time.

Analysis

Once the capture of traffic has been completed, analysis must take place. Colasoft offers a packet analyzer that can carve out and filter out the various types of traffic. A good deal of traffic can be eliminated as just "noise" on the line. Filters can be created that will capture the specific protocols, such as VoIP. Examination of the protocols for protocol obfuscation can (if it is not found) eliminate the possibility that a user has a malware infection, and it can identify a user that is using open ports on the firewall to transmit illicit traffic. They sneak legitimate traffic over open ports, masking their nefarious activities over legitimate ports, knowing that the ports are open. This can be done with whitespace inside of an existing protocol, with HTTP, VoIP, and many others. The thing to look for, which will usually be clearly shown, is something like:

VOIP > SMTP

This basically means that VOIP is talking to a mail server. This is not normal.[3]

Another thing to look for is protocols coming off a box that isn't purposed for that task. It's all context: who should be doing what with whom. Why is the workstation suddenly popping a DNS server? A real-world example is when a van comes screaming into your neighborhood. Two guys jump out and break down the door of your house and grab your wife and kids and drag them out of the house. Then they come and get you. Seems a little fishy, right? But it is a perfectly normal thing to have happen if the two guys are firemen, the van was a fire truck, and your house is on fire.

9. CYBER FORENSICS APPLIED

This section details the various ways in which cyber forensics is applied professionally. By no means does this cover the extent to which cyber forensics is becoming one of the hottest computer careers. It focuses on the consulting side of things, with less attention to corporate or law enforcement applications. Generally speaking, the average forensic consultant handles a broader variety of cases than corporate or law enforcement disciplines, with a broader applicability.

10. TRACKING, INVENTORY, LOCATION OF FILES, PAPERWORK, BACKUPS, AND SO ON

These items are all useful areas of knowledge in providing consultative advisement to corporate, legal, and law-enforcement clients. During the process of discovery and warrant creation, knowledge of how users store and access data at a very deep level is critical to success.

3. M. J. Staggs, FireEye, Network Analysis talk at CEIC 2008.

Testimonial

Even if the work does not involve the court system directly—for example, a technician that provides forensic backups of computers and is certified—you may someday be called to provide discovery in a litigation matter. Subsequently, you may be required to testify.

Experience Needed

In cyber forensics, the key to a successful technologist is experience. Nothing can substitute for experience, but a good system of learned knowledge that represents at least the last 10 years is welcome.

Job Description, Technologist

> Practitioners must possess extreme abilities in adapting to new situations. The environment is always changing.

Job description:
Senior Forensic Examiner and eDiscovery Specialist Prepared by Scott R. Ellis, 11/01/2007.

- Forensics investigative work which includes imaging hard drives, extracting data and files for ediscovery production, development of custom scripts as required to extract or locate data. On occasion this includes performing detailed analyses of user activity, images, and language that may be of an undesirable, distasteful, and potentially criminal format. For this reason, a manager must be notified immediately upon the discovery of any such materials.
- Creation of detailed reports that lay out findings in a meaningful and understandable format. All reports will be reviewed and OK'd by manager before delivery to clients.
- Use of software tools such as FTK, EnCase, VMware, Recovery for Exchange, IDEA, LAW, and Relativity.
- Processing ediscovery and some paper discovery.
- Be responsive to opportunities for publication such as papers, articles, blog, or book chapter requests. All publications should be reviewed by manager and marketing before being submitted to requestor.
- Use technology such as servers, email, time reporting, and scheduling systems to perform job duties and archive work in client folders.
- Managing lab assets (installation of software, Windows updates, antivirus, maintaining backup strategy, hardware installation, tracking hardware and software inventory).
- Some marketing work
- Work week will be 40 hours per week, with occasional weekends as needed to meet customer deadlines.
- Deposition or testimony as needed.
- Occasional evenings and out of town to accommodate client schedules for forensic investigative work.
- Occasional evenings and out of town to attend seminars, CPE or technology classes as suggested by self or by manager, and marketing events.

• Other technology related duties as may be assigned by manager in the support of the company mission as it relates to technology or forensic technology matters.

Job Description Management

A manager in cyber forensics is usually a working manager. He is responsible for guiding and developing staff as well as communicating requirements to the executive level. His work duties will typically encompass everything mentioned in the previous description.

Commercial Uses

Archival, ghosting images, dd, recover lost partitions, etc. are all applications of cyber forensics at a commercial level. Data recovery embraces a great many of the practices typically attributed to cyber forensics. Archival and retrieval of information for any number of purposes, not just litigation, is required as is a forensic level of system knowledge.

Solid Background

To become a professional practitioner of cyber forensics, there are three requirements to a successful career. Certainly there are people, such as many who attain certification through law-enforcement agencies, that have skipped or bypassed completely the professional experience or scientific training necessary to be a true cyber forensic scientist. That is not to degrade the law-enforcement forensic examiner. His mission is traditionally quite different from that of a civilian, and these pros are frighteningly adept and proficient at accomplishing their objective, which is to locate evidence of criminal conduct and prosecute in court. Their lack of education in the traditional sense should never lead one to a desultory conclusion. No amount of parchment will ever broaden a mind; the forensic examiner must have a broad mind that eschews constraints and boxed-in thinking.

The background needed for a successful career in cyber forensics is much like that of any other except that, as a testifying expert, publication will give greater credence to a testimony than even the most advanced pedigree. The exception would be the cyber forensic scientist who holds a Ph. D. and happened to write her doctoral thesis on just the thing that is being called into question on the case. Interestingly, at this time, this author has yet to meet anyone with a Ph. D. (or any university degree for that matter), in cyber forensics. We can then narrow down the requirements to these three items. Coincidentally, these are also the items required to qualify as an expert witness in most courts:

• Education
• Programming and Experience
• Publications

The weight of each of these items can vary. To what degree depends on who is asking, but suffice it to say that a deficiency in any area may be overcome by strengths in the other two. The following sections provide a more in-depth view of each requirement.

Education/Certification

A strong foundation at the university level in mathematics and science provides the best mental training that can be obtained in cyber forensics. Of course, anyone with an extremely strong understanding of computers can surpass and exceed any expectations in this area. Of special consideration are the following topics. The best forensic examiner has a strong foundation in these areas and can qualify not just as a forensic expert with limited ability to testify as to the functions and specific mechanical abilities of software, but as a cyber expert who can testify to the many aspects of both hardware and software.

Understand how database technologies, including MS SQL, Oracle, Access, My SQL, and others, interact with applications and how thin and fat clients interact and transfer data. Where do they store temporary files? What happens during a maintenance procedure? How are indexes built, and is the database software disk aware?

Programming and Experience

Background in cyber programming is an essential piece. The following software languages must be understood by any well-rounded forensic examiner:

- Java
- JavaScript
- ASP/.NET
- HTML
- XML
- Visual Basic
- SQL

Develop a familiarity with the purpose and operation of technologies that have not become mainstream but have a devoted cult following. At one time such things as virtualization, Linux, and even Windows lived on the bleeding edge, but from being very much on the "fringe" have steadily become more mainstream.

- If it runs on a computer and has an installed base of greater than 10,000 users, it is worth reviewing.
- Internet technologies should be well understood. JavaScript, Java, HTML, ASP, ASPRX, cold fusion, databases, etc. are all Internet technologies that may end up at the heart of a forensic examiner's investigation.
- Experience. Critical to either establishing oneself in a career as a corporate cyber forensic examiner or as a consultant, experience working in the field provides the confidence and knowledge-base needed to successfully complete a forensic examination. From cradle to grave, from the initial interviews with the client to forensic collection, examination, reporting, and testifying, experience will guide every step. No suitable substitute exists. Most forensic examiners come into the career later in life after serving as a network or software consultant. Some arrive in this field after years in law enforcement where almost anyone who can turn on a computer winds up taking some cyber forensic training.

Communications

- Cyber forensics is entirely about the ability to look at a cyber system and subsequently explain, in plain English, the analysis. A typical report may consist of the following sections:
  - Summary
  - Methodology
  - Narrative
  - Healthcare information data on system
  - User access to credit-card numbers
  - Date range of possible breach and order handlers
  - Distinct list of operators
  - Russell and Crist Handlers
  - All other users logged in during Crist/Russel Logins
- Login failures activity coinciding with account activity
- All Users:
  - User access levels possible ingress/egress
  - Audit trail
  - Login failures
  - Conclusion
  - Contacts/examiners

Each section either represents actual tables, images, and calculated findings, or it represents judgments, impressions, and interpretations of those findings. Finally, the report should contain references to contacts involved in the investigation. A good report conveys the big picture, and translates findings into substantial knowledge without leaving any trailing questions asked and unanswered. Sometimes findings are arrived at through a complex procedure such as a series of SQL queries. Conclusions that depend on such findings should be as detailed as necessary so that opposing experts can reconstruct the findings without difficulty.

Almost any large company requires some measure of forensic certified staff. Furthermore, the forensic collection and ediscovery field continues to grow. Virtually every branch of law enforcement—FBI, CIA, Homeland Security, and state and local agencies—all use cyber forensics to some degree. Accounting firms and law firms of almost any size greater than 20 need certified forensic and ediscovery specialists that can both support their forensic practice areas as well as grow business.

Publications

Publishing articles in well-known trade journals goes a long way toward establishing credibility. The following things are nearly always true:

- A long list of publications not only creates in a jury the perception that the expert possess special knowledge that warrants publication; it also shows the expert's ability to communicate. Articles published on the Internet typically do not count unless they are for well-known publications that have a printed publication as well as an online magazine.

- Publishing in and of itself creates a certain amount of risk. Anything that an expert writes or says or posts online may come back to haunt him in court. Be sure to remember to check, double check, and triple check anything that could be of questionable interpretation.
- When you write, you get smarter. Writing forces an author to conduct research and refreshes the memory on long unused skills.

Getting published in the first place is perhaps the most difficult task. Make contact with publishers and editors at trade shows. Ask around, and seek to make contact and establish relationships with published authors and bloggers. Most important, always seek to gain knowledge and deeper understanding of the work.

11. TESTIFYING AS AN EXPERT

Testifying in court is difficult work. As with any type of performance, the expert testifying must know her material, inside and out. She must be calm and collected and have confidence in her assertions. Often, degrees of uncertainty may exist within a testimony. It is the expert's duty to convey those "gray" areas with clarity and alacrity. She must be able to confidently speak of things in terms of degrees of certainty and clear probabilities, using language that is accessible and readily understood by the jury.

In terms of degrees of certainty, often we find ourselves discussing the "degree of difficulty" of performing an operation. This is usually when judges ask whether or not an operation has occurred through direct user interaction or through an automated, programmatic, or normal maintenance procedure. For example, it is well within the normal operation of complex database software to reindex or compact its tables and reorganize the way the data is arranged on the surface of the disk. It is not, however, within the normal operation of the database program to completely obliterate itself and all its program, help, and system files 13 times over a period of three weeks, all in the time leading up to requests for discovery from the opposition. Such information, when forensically available, will then be followed by the question of "Can we know *who* did it?" And that question, if the files exist on a server where security is relaxed, can be nearly impossible to answer.

Degrees of Certainty

Most cyber forensic practitioners ply their trade in civil court. A typical case may involve monetary damages or loss. From a cyber forensics point of view, evidence that you have extracted from a computer may be used by the attorneys to establish liability, that the plaintiff was damaged by the actions of the defendant. Your work may be the lynchpin of the entire case. You cannot be wrong. The burden to prove the amount of damages is less stringent once you've established that damage was inflicted, and since a single email may be the foundation for that proof, its provenance should prevail under even the most expert scrutiny. Whether or not the damage was inflicted may become a point of contention that the defense uses to pry and crack open your testimony.

The following sections may prove useful in your answers. The burden of proof will fall on the defense to show that the alleged damages are not accurate. There are three general categories of "truth" that can be used to clarify for a judge, jury, or attorney the weight of evidence. See the section on "Rules of Evidence" for more on things such as relevance and materiality.

Generally True

Generally speaking, something is generally true if under normal and general use the same thing always occurs. For example, if a user deletes a file, generally speaking it will go into the recycle bin. This is not true if:

- The user holds down a Shift key when deleting
- The recycle bin option "Do not move files to the recycle bin. Remove files immediately when deleted," is selected
- An item is deleted from a server share or from another computer that is accessing a local user share

Reasonable Degree of Certainty

If it smells like a fish and looks like a fish, generally speaking, it is a fish. However, without dissection and DNA analysis, there is the possibility that it is a fake, especially if someone is jumping up and down and screaming that it is a fake. Short of expensive testing, one may consider other factors. Where was the fish found? Who was in possession of the fish when it was found? We begin to rely on more than just looking at the fish to see if it is a fish.

Cyber forensic evidence is much the same (see checklist: "An Agenda For Action For Retrieval And Identification Of Evidence"). For example, in an employment dispute, an employee may be accused of sending sensitive and proprietary documents to her personal Webmail account. The employer introduces forensic evidence that the files were sent from her work email account during her period of employment on days when she was in the office.

AN AGENDA FOR ACTION FOR RETRIEVAL AND IDENTIFICATION OF EVIDENCE

The computer forensics specialist should ensure that the following provisional list of actions for retrieval and identification of evidence are adhered to (Check All Tasks Completed):

_____1. Protect the subject computer system during the forensic examination from any possible alteration, damage, data corruption, or virus introduction.

_____2. Discover all files on the subject system. This includes existing normal files, deleted yet remaining files, hidden files, password-protected files, and encrypted files.

_____3. Recover all (or as much as possible) of discovered deleted files.

_____4. Reveal (to the greatest extent possible) the contents of hidden

---

files as well as temporary or swap files used by both the application programs and the operating system.

_____5. Access (if possible and legally appropriate) the contents of protected or encrypted files.

_____6. Analyze all possibly relevant data found in special (and typically inaccessible) areas of a disk. This includes but is not limited to what is called unallocated space on a disk (currently unused, but possibly the repository of previous data that is relevant evidence), as well as slack space in a file (the remnant area at the end of a file in the last assigned disk cluster, that is unused by current file data, but

once again, may be a possible site for previously created and relevant evidence).

_____7. Print out an overall analysis of the subject computer system, as well as a listing of all possibly relevant files and discovered file data.

_____8. Provide an opinion of the system layout; the file structures discovered; any discovered data and authorship information; any attempts to hide, delete, protect, and encrypt information; and anything else that has been discovered and appears to be relevant to the overall computer system examination.

_____9. Provide expert consultation and/or testimony, as required.

Pretty straightforward, right? Not really. Let's go back in time to two months before the employee was fired. Let's go back to the day after she got a very bad performance review and left for the day because she was so upset. Everyone knew what was going on, and they knew that her time is limited. Two weeks later she filed an EEOC complaint. The IT manager in this organization, a seemingly mild-mannered, helpful savant, was getting ready to start his own company as a silent partner in competition with his employer. He wanted information. His partners want information in exchange for a 20% stake. As an IT manager, he had administrative rights and could access the troubled employee's email account and began to send files to her Webmail account. As an IT administrator, he had system and network access that would easily allow him to crack her Webmail account and determine the password. All he had to do was spoof her login page and store it on a site where he could pick it up from somewhere else. If he was particularly interested in keeping his own home and work systems free of the files, he could wardrive her house, hack her home wireless (lucky him, it is unsecured), and then use terminal services to access her home cyber, log into her Webmail account (while she is home), and view the files to ensure that they appear as "read." This scenario may seem farfetched but it is not; this is not hard to do.

For anyone with the IT manager's level of knowledge, lack of ethics, and opportunity, this is likely the *only* way that he would go about stealing information. There is no other way that leaves him so completely out of the possible running of suspects.

There is no magic wand in cyber forensics. The data is either there or it isn't, despite what Hollywood says about the subject. If an IT director makes the brash decision to reinstall the OS on a system that has been compromised and later realizes he might want to use a forensic investigator to find out what files were viewed, stolen, or modified, he can't just dial up his local forensics tech and have him pop in over tea, wave his magic wand, and recover all the data that was overwritten. Here is the raw, unadulterated truth: If you have 30 GB of unallocated clusters and you copy the DVD *Finding Nemo* onto the drive until the disk is full, nobody (and I really mean this), *nobody* will be able to extract a complete file from the unallocated clusters. Sure, they might find a couple of keyword hits in file slack and maybe, just maybe, if the stars align and Jupiter is in retrograde and Venus is rising, maybe they can pull a tiny little complete file out of the slack or out of the MFT. Small files, less than 128 bytes, are stored directly in the MFT and won't ever make it out to allocated space. This can be observed by viewing the $MFT file.

When making the determination "reasonable degree of forensic certainty," *all* things must be considered. Every possible scenario that could occur must flash before the forensic practitioner's eyes until only the most reasonable answer exists, an answer that is supported by all the evidence, not just part of it. This is called *interpretation*, and it is a weigh of whether or not a preponderance of evidence actually exists. The forensic expert's job is not to decide whether a preponderance of evidence exists. His job is to fairly, and truthfully, present the facts and his interpretation of the individual facts. Questions an attorney might ask a cyber forensics practitioner on the stand:

- Did the user delete the file?
- Could someone else have done it?
- Could an outside process have downloaded the file to the computer?
- Do you know for certain how this happened?
- Did you see Mr. Smith delete the files?
- How do you know he did?
- Isn't it true, Mr. Expert, that you are being paid to be here today?

These are not "Yes or no" questions. Here might be the answers:

- I'm reasonably certain he did.
- Due to the security of this machine, it's very unlikely that someone else did it.
- There is evidence to strongly indicate that the photos were loaded to the computer from a digital camera, not the Internet.
- I am certain, without doubt, that the camera in Exhibit 7a is the same camera that was used to take these photos and that these photos were loaded to the computer while username CSMITH was logged in.
- I have viewed forensic evidence that strongly suggests that someone with Mr. Smith's level of access and permissions to this system did, in fact, delete these files on 12/12/2009.
- I'm not sure I didn't just answer that.
- I am an employee of The Company. I am receiving my regular compensation and today is a normal workday for me.

Be careful, though. Reticence to answer in a yes-or no fashion may be interpreted by the jury as uncertainty. If certainty exists, say so. But it is always better to be honest and admit uncertainty than to attempt to inflate one's own ego by expressing certainty where none exists. Never worry about the outcome of the case. You can't care about the outcome of the trial. Guilt or innocence cannot be a factor in your opinion. You must focus on simply answering the questions in front of you that demand to be answered.

Certainty without Doubt

Some things on a computer can happen only in one fashion. For example, if a deleted item is found in the recycle bin, there are steps that must be taken to ensure that "it is what it is":

- Was the user logged in at the time of deletion?
- Are there link files that support the use or viewing of the file?
- Was the user with access to the user account at work that day?
- What are the permissions on the folder?
- Is the deleted file in question a system file or a user-created file located in the user folders?
- Is the systems administrator beyond reproach or outside the family of suspects?

If all of these conditions are met, you may have arrived at certainty without doubt. Short of reliable witnesses paired with physical evidence, it is possible that there will always be other explanations, that uncertainty to some degree can exist. It is the burden of the defense and the plaintiff to understand and resolve these issues and determine if, for example, hacker activity is a plausible defense. I have added the stipulation of reliable witnesses because, in the hands of a morally corrupt forensic expert with access to the drive and a hex editor, a computer can be undetectably altered. Files can be copied onto a hard drive in a sterile manner that, to most trained forensic examiners, could appear to be original. Even advanced users are capable of framing the evidence in such a way as to render the appearance of best evidence, but a forensic examination may lift the veil of uncertainty and show that data has been altered, or that something *isn't quite right*. For example, there are certain conditions that can be examined that can show with certainty that the time stamps on a file have been somehow manipulated or are simply incorrect, and it is likely that the average person seeking to plant evidence will not know these tricks (see Table 9.4). The dates on files that were overwritten may show that "old" files overwrote newer files. This is impossible.

As shown here, the file kitty.jpg overwrites files that appear to have been created on the system after it. Such an event may occur when items are copied from a CDROM or unzipped from a zip file.

TABLE 9.4   Example of a Forensic View of Files Showing Some Alteration or Masking of Dates

Filename	Date Created	File Properties	Original Path
Kitty.jpg	5/12/2007	File, Archive	
summaryReport.doc	7/12/2007	File, Deleted, Overwritten	Kitty.jpg
Marketing_flyer.pdf	2/12/2008	File, Deleted, Overwritten	Kitty.jpg

12. BEGINNING TO END IN COURT

In most courts in the world, the accuser goes first and then the defense presents its case. This is for the very logical reason that if the defense goes first, nobody would know what they are talking about. The Boulder Bar has a Bar manual located at www.boulder-bar.org[4] that provides a more in-depth review of the trial process than can be presented here. Most states and federal rules are quite similar, but nothing here should be taken as legal advice; review the rules for yourself for the courts where you will be testifying. The knowledge isn't necessary, but the less that you seem to be a fish out of water, the better. This section *does not* replace true legal advice, it is strictly intended for the purpose of education. The manual located at the Boulder Bar Web site was created for a similar reason that is clearly explained on the site. The manual there was specifically developed without any "legalese," which makes it very easy to understand.

Defendants, Plaintiffs, and Prosecutors

When someone, an individual or an organization, decides it has a claim of money or damages against another individual or entity, they file a claim in court. The group filing the claim is the plaintiff, the other parties are the defendants. Experts may find themselves working for strictly defendants, strictly plaintiffs, or a little bit of both. In criminal court, charges are "brought" by an indictment, complaint, information, or a summons and complaint.

Pretrial Motions

Prior to the actual trial, there may be many, many pretrial motions and hearings. When a motion is filed, such as when the defense in a criminal case is trying to prevent certain evidence from being seen or heard by the jury, a hearing is called and the judge decides whether the motion has any merit. In civil court, it may be a hearing to decide whether the defense has been deleting, withholding, or committing other acts of discovery abuse. Cyber forensic practitioners will find that they may be called to testify at any number of hearings prior to the trial, and then they may not be needed at the trial at all, or the defense and plaintiff may reach a settlement and there will be no trial at all.

Trial: Direct and Cross-Examination

Assuming that there is no settlement or plea agreement, a case will go to trial. The judge will first ask the prosecutor or plaintiff whether they want to make an opening statement. Then the defense will be asked. Witnesses will be called, and if it is the first time appearing in the particular trial as an expert, the witness will be qualified, as discussed in a moment. The party putting on the witness will conduct a direct examination and the other side will very likely cross-examine the witness afterward. Frequently the two sides will have reviewed the expert report and will ask many questions relating directly to it.

4. Boulder Bar, www.boulder-bar.org/bar_media/index.html.

"Tricks" may be pulled by either attorney at this point. Certain prosecutors have styles and techniques that are used in an attempt to either rattle the expert's cage or simply intimidate him into a state of nervousness so that he will appear uncertain and unprepared. These prosecutors are not interested in justice. They are interested in winning because their career rotates around their record of wins/losses.

Rebuttal

After a witness has testified and undergone direct examination and cross-examination, the other side may decide to bring in an expert to discuss or refute. The defendant may then respond to the prosecution's witness in *rebuttal*. In criminal court, when the state or the government (sometimes affectionately referred to by defense attorneys as "The G") brings a case against an individual or organization, the attorneys that prosecute the case are called the state's attorney, district attorney, assistant U.S. attorney (AUSA), or simply prosecutor.

Surrebuttal

This is the plaintiff (or prosecutor's!) response to rebuttal. Typically the topics of surrebuttal will be limited to those topics that are broached in rebuttal, but the rules for this are probably best left to attorneys to decipher; this author has occasionally been asked questions that should have been deemed outside the bounds of the rebuttal. This could most likely be attributed to a lack of technical knowledge on the part of the attorneys involved in the case.

Testifying: Rule 702. Testimony by Experts

Rule 702 is a federal rule of civil procedure that governs expert testimony. The judge is considered the "gatekeeper," and she alone makes the decision as to whether or not the following rule is satisfied:

> If scientific, technical, or other specialized knowledge will assist the trier of fact to understand the evidence or to determine a fact in issue, a witness qualified as an expert by knowledge, skill, experience, training, or education, may testify thereto in the form of an opinion or otherwise, if (1) the testimony is based upon sufficient facts or data, (2) the testimony is the product of reliable principles and methods, and (3) the witness has applied the principles and methods reliably to the facts of the case (U.S. Courts, Federal Rules of Evidence, Rule 702).

There are certain rules for qualifying as an expert. In court, when an expert is presented, both attorneys may question the expert on matters of background and expertise. This process is referred to as *qualification* and, if an "expert" does not meet the legal definition of expert, he may not be allowed to testify. This is a short bullet list of items that will be asked in qualifying as an expert witness:

• How long have you worked in the field?
• What certifications do you hold in this field?
• Where did you go to college?

- Did you graduate? What degrees do you have?
- What are your publications?

You may also be asked if you have testified in other proceedings. It is important to always be honest when on the stand. Perjury is a very serious crime and can result in jail time. All forensics experts should familiarize themselves with Federal Rules 701–706 as well as understand the purpose, intent, and results of a successful *Daubert* challenge, wherein an expert's opinion or the expert himself may be challenged and, if certain criteria are met, may have his testimony thrown out. It is accepted and understood that experts may have reasonably different conclusions given the same evidence.

When testifying, stay calm (easier said than done). If you've never done it, approaching the bench and taking the witness stand may seem like a lot of fun. In a case where a lot is on the line and it all depends on the expert's testimony, nerves will shake and cages will be rattled. The best advice is to stay calm. Drink a lot of water. Drinking copious amounts of water will, according to ex-Navy Seal Mike Lukas, dilute the affect of adrenalin in the bloodstream.

Testifying in a stately and austere court of law may seem like it is the domain of professors and other ivory tower enthusiasts. However, it is something that pretty much anyone can do that has a valuable skill to offer, regardless of educational background. Hollywood often paints a picture of the expert witness as a consummate professorial archetype bent on delivering "just the facts." It is true that expert witnesses demand top dollar in the consulting world. Much of this is for the reason that a great deal is at stake once the expert takes the stand. There is also a very high inconvenience factor. When on the stand for days at a time, one can't simply take phone calls, respond to emails, or perform other work for other clients. There is a certain amount of business interruption that the fees must make up for somehow.

Testifying is interesting. Distilling weeks of intense, technical investigation into a few statements that can be understood by everyone in the courtroom is no small task. It is a bit nerve wracking, and one can expect to have high blood pressure and overactive adrenalin glands for the day. Drinking lots of water will ease the nerves better than anything (non-pharmaceutical). It can have other side effects, however, but it is better to be calm and ask the judge for a short recess as needed than to have shaky hands and a trembling voice from nerves. Caffeine is a bad idea.

Correcting Mistakes: Putting Your Head in the Sand

The interplay of examiner and expert in the case of cyber forensics can be difficult. Often the forensic examiner can lapse into speech and explanations that are so commonplace to her that she doesn't realize she is speaking fluent geek-speak. The ability to understand how she sounds to someone who doesn't understand technology must be cultivated. Practice by explaining to any six-year-old what it is you do.

Direct Testimony

Under direct questioning, your attorney will ask questions to which you will know the answer. A good expert will, in fact, have prepared a list of questions and reviewed the answers with the attorney and explained the context and justification for each question thoroughly. If it is a defense job, you will likely go first and testify as to what your investigation has revealed. Avoid using big words and do make some eye contact with the jury if you feel you need to explain something to them, but generally speaking, you should follow the attorney's lead. If she wants you to clarify something for the jury, you should do so, and at that time you should look at the jury. Generally, the rule of thumb is to look at the attorney who asked you the question. If the judge says, "Please explain to the jury ..." then by all means, look at the jury.

Cross-Examination

The purpose of a cross-examination is to get the testifying expert to make a mistake or to discredit him. Sometimes (rarely) it is actually used to further understand and clarify things that were discussed in direct. In most cases, the attorney will do this by asking you questions about your experience or about the testimony the expert gave under direct. But there is another tactic that attorneys use. They ask a question that is completely unrelated to the topic you talked about. They know that the vast majority of time you spend is on the issues in your direct. For example, you may give a testimony about Last Accessed time stamps. Your entire testimony may be about Last Accessed time stamps. It may be the only issue in the case you are aware of. Then, on cross, the attorney asks a question about the behavior of the mail icon that appears on each line next to the subject line in an email. "Great," the expert thinks. "They recognize my expertise and are asking questions."

Stop. They are about to ask you an arcane question about a behavior in a piece of software in the hopes that you are overconfident and will answer from the hip and get the answer wrong. Because if you get this wrong, then everything else you said must be wrong, too. *Whenever* you are asked a question that does not relate to your previous testimony, pause. Pause for a long time. Give your attorney time to object. He might not know that he should object, but the fact is that you might get the answer wrong and even if there is no doubt in your mind that you know the answer, you should respond that you had not prepared to answer that question and would like to know more details. For example, what is the version of the software? What is the operating system? What service pack? If it is Office, what Office service pack? You need to make it clear that you need more information before you answer the question because, frankly, if the opposition goes down this road, they will try to turn *whatever* you say into the wrong answer.

As a forensic examiner, you may find yourself thinking that the reason they are asking these questions in such a friendly manner is because they forgot to ask their own expert and are trying to take advantage of your time because possibly this came up in a later conversation. This could very well be the case. Maybe the counselor is not trying to trip up the expert. Maybe the Brooklyn Bridge *can* be purchased for a dollar, too.

What is the best response to a question like this? If you give it a 10 count and your attorney hasn't objected, and the asking attorney has not abandoned the question, you may have to answer. There are many schools of thought on this. It is best to understand that a number of responses can facilitate an answer to difficult questions. One such response might be, "That is not really a forensics question" (if it's not), or "I'm not sure how that question relates back to the testimony I just gave." Or, if it is a software question, you can say, "Different software behaves differently, and I don't think I can answer that question without more details. I don't typically memorize the behavior of every piece of software, and I'm afraid that if I answer from memory I may not be certain." At the end of the day, the expert should only speak to what he knows *with certainty*. There is very little room for error. Attorneys can back-pedal a certain amount to "fix" a mistake, but a serious mistake can follow you for a very long time and can hamper future testimony. For example, if you make statements about time stamps in one trial, and then in the next trial you make statements that interpret them differently, there is a good chance that the opposition will use this against you.

Fortunately, when cyber forensic experts testify in a defense trial, the testimony can last a number of hours. Great care is usually taken by the judge to ensure that understanding of all the evidence is achieved. This can create a very long transcript that is difficult to read, understand, and recall with accuracy. For this reason, rarely will bits and pieces of testimony be used against a testifying expert in a future trial. This is not, of course, to say that it can't or won't happen.

It is important, in terms of both setting expectations and understanding legal strategy, for an expert witness to possess passable knowledge of the trial process. Strong familiarity with the trial process can benefit both the expert and the attorneys as well as the judge and the court reporter.

13. SUMMARY

Computers have appeared in the course of litigation for over 36 years. In 1977, there were 291 U.S. federal cases and 246 state cases in which the word *computer* appeared and which were sufficiently important to be noted in the Lexis database. In 2012, according to industry analysts, those figures in the U.S. have risen dramatically, to 3,250,514 U.S. federal cases and 2,750,177 state cases in which the word *cyber* appeared. In the UK, there were only 20 in 1977, with a rise to 220,372 in 2012. However, as early as 1968, the computer's existence was considered sufficiently important for special provisions to be made in the English Civil Evidence Act.

The following description is designed to summarize the issues rather than attempt to give a complete guide. As far as one can tell, noncontentious cases tend not to be reported, and the arrival of computers in commercial disputes and in criminal cases did not create immediate difficulties. Judges sought to allow cyber-based evidence on the basis that it was no different from forms of evidence with which they were already familiar: documents, business books, weighing machines, calculating machines, films, and audio tapes. This is not to say that such cases were without difficulty; however, no completely new principles were required. Quite soon, though, it became apparent that many new situations were arising and that analogies with more traditional evidential material were beginning to break down. Some of these were tackled in legislation, as with the English 1968 Act and the U.S. Federal Rules of Evidence in 1976. But many were addressed in a series of court cases. Not all of the key cases deal directly with computers. But they do have a bearing on them as they relate to matters that are characteristic of cyber-originated evidence. For example, cyber-originated evidence or information that is not immediately readable by a human being is usually gathered by a mechanical counting or weighing instrument. The calculation could also be performed by a mechanical or electronic device.

The focus of most of this legislation and judicial activity was determining the admissibility of the evidence. The common law and legislative rules are those that have arisen as a result of judicial decisions and specific law. They extend beyond mere guidance. They are rules that a court must follow; the thought behind these rules may have been to impose standards and uniformity in helping a court test authenticity, reliability, and completeness. Nevertheless, they have acquired a status of their own and in some cases prevent a court from making ad hoc common sense decisions about the quality of evidence. The usual effect is that once a judge has declared evidence inadmissible (that is, failing to conform to the rules), it is never put to a jury; for a variety of reasons that will become apparent shortly. It is not wholly possible for someone interested in the practical aspects of computer forensics (that is, the issues of demonstrating authenticity, reliability, completeness, or lack thereof) to separate out the legal tests.

Finally, let's move on to the real interactive part of this Chapter: review questions/exercises, hands-on projects, case projects and optional team case project. The answers and/or solutions by chapter can be found in the Online Instructor's Solutions Manual.

CHAPTER REVIEW QUESTIONS/EXERCISES

True/False

1. True or False? Cyber forensics is the acquisition, preservation, and analysis of electronically stored information (ESI) in such a way that ensures its admissibility for use as either evidence, exhibits, or demonstratives in a court of law.
2. True or False? EnCase is a commonly used forensic software program that does not allow a cyber forensic technologist to conduct an investigation of a forensic hard disk copy.
3. True or False? On a server purposed with storing surveillance video, there are three physical hard drives.
4. True or False? Cyber forensics is one of the many cyber-related fields in which the practitioner will be found in the courtroom on a given number of days of the year.
5. True or False? A temporary restraining order (TRO) will often be issued in intellectual property or employment contract disputes.

Multiple Choice

1. Typically the forensic work done in a _____ will involve collecting information about one of the parties to be used to show that trust has been violated.
    A. Security incident
    B. Security breach
    C. Computer virus
    D. Divorce case
    E. Security policy

2. When one company begins selling a part that is _____ by another company, a lawsuit will likely be filed in federal court.
   A. Assigned
   B. Breached
   C. Detected
   D. Patented
   E. Measured
3. When a forensics practitioner needs to capture the data on a hard disk, he/she does so in a way that is:
   A. Forensically acquired
   B. Forensically mirrored
   C. Forensically sound
   D. Forensically imaged
   E. Forensically booted
4. Before conducting any sort of a capture, all steps should be documented and reviewed with a _____ before proceeding
   A. Observer
   B. Investigator
   C. Counsel
   D. Forensic Expert
   E. Judge
5. FAT12, FAT16, and FAT32 are all types of file systems?
   A. FAT12
   B. FAT16
   C. FAT32
   D. FAT64
   E. All of the above

EXERCISE

Problem

Why Cyber Forensics?

Hands-On Projects

Project

How long does data recovery take?

Case Projects

Problem

Are there instances where data cannot be recovered?

Optional Team Case Project

Problem

What can an organization do to protect their data and minimize their chances of losing data?

Cyber Forensics and Incident Response

Cem Gurkok
Verizon Terremark

1. INTRODUCTION TO CYBER FORENSICS

Cyber forensics and incident response go hand in hand. Cyber forensics reduces the occurrence of security incidents by analyzing the incident to understand, mitigate, and provide feedback to the actors involved. To perform incident response and related activities, organizations should establish an incident plan, a computer security incident response team (CSIRT), or a computer emergency response team (CERT) to execute the plan and associated protocols.

Responding to Incidents

In an organization, there is a daily occurrence of events within the IT infrastructure, but not all of these events qualify as incidents. It is important for the incident response team to be able to distinguish the difference between events and incidents. Generally, incidents are events that violate an organization's security policies, end-user agreements, or terms of use. SANS (sans.org) defines an incident as an adverse event in an information system or network, or the threat of an occurrence of such an event. Denial-of-service attacks, unauthorized probing, unauthorized entry, destruction or theft of data, and changes to firmware or operating systems can be considered incidents.

Generally, incident response handling comprises incident reporting, incident analysis, and incident response. Incident reporting takes place when a report or indications of an event are sent to the incident response team. The team then performs an incident analysis by examining the report, available information, and evidence or artifacts related to the event to qualify the event as an incident, correlate the data, and assess the extent of damage, source, and plan potential solutions. Once the analysis is over, then the team responds to mitigate the incident by containing and eradicating the incident. This is followed by the creation of a detailed report about the incident.

Applying Forensic Analysis Skills

Forensic analysis is usually applied to determine who, what, when, where, how, and why an incident took place. The analysis may include investigating crimes and inappropriate behavior, reconstructing computer security incidents, troubleshooting operational problems, supporting due diligence for audit record maintenance, and recovering from accidental system damage. The incident response team should be trained and prepared to be able to collect and analyze the related evidence to answer these questions. Data collection is a very important aspect of incident response since evidence needs to be collected in a forensically sound manner to protect its integrity and confidentiality. The incident responder needs to have the necessary skills and experience to be able to meet the collection requirements.

Forensic analysis is the process whereby the collected data is reviewed and scrutinized for the lowest level of evidence (deleted data in slack space) it can offer. The analysis may involve extracting email attachments, building timelines based on file times, reviewing browser history and in-memory artifacts, decrypting encrypted data, and malware reverse engineering. Once the analysis is complete, the incident responder will produce a report describing all the steps taken starting from the initial incident report till the end of the analysis. One of the most important skills a forensic analyst can have is note taking and logging, which becomes very important during the reporting phase and, if it ever comes to it, in court. These considerations related to forensics should be addressed in organizational policies. The forensic policy should clearly define the responsibilities and roles of the actors involved. The policies should also address the types of activities that should be undertaken under certain circumstances and the handling of sensitive information.

Distinguishing between Unpermitted Corporate and Criminal Activity

We previously defined incidents as events that are not permitted by a certain organization's policies. The incident response team should also be aware of several federal laws that can help them to identify criminal activity to ensure that the team does not commit a crime while responding to the incident. Some of these federal laws are:

- The Foreign Intelligence Surveillance Act of 1978
- The Privacy Protection Act of 1980
- The Computer Fraud and Abuse Act of 1984
- The Electronic Communications Privacy Act of 1986
- The Health Insurance Portability and Accountability Act of 1996 (HIPAA)
- The Identity Theft and Assumption Deterrence Act of 1998
- The USA Patriot Act of 2001

When an incident response team comes across incidents relevant to these laws, they should consult with their legal team. They should also contact appropriate law enforcement agencies.

2. HANDLING PRELIMINARY INVESTIGATIONS

An organization should be prepared beforehand to properly respond to incidents and mitigate them in the shortest time possible. An incident response plan should be developed by the organization and tested on a regular basis. The plan should be written in an easily understood and implemented fashion. The incident response team and related staff should also be trained on an ongoing basis to keep them up to date with the incident response plan, latest threats, and defense techniques.

Planning for Incident Response

Organizations should be prepared for incidents by identifying corporate risks, preparing hosts and network for containment and eradication of threats, establishing policies and procedures that facilitate the accomplishment of incident response goals, creating an incident response team, and preparing an incident response toolkit to be used by the incident response team.

Communicating with Site Personnel

All departments and staff that have a part in an incident response should be aware of the incident response plan and should be regularly trained as to its content and implementation. The plan should include the mode of communication with the site personnel. The site personnel should clearly log all activity and communication, including the date and time in a central repository that is backed up regularly. This information should be reviewed by all of the incident response team members to assure all players are on the same page. Continuity and the distribution of information within the team is critical in the swift mitigation of an incident. An incident response team leader should be assigned to an incident and should make sure all team members are well informed and acting in a coordinated fashion.

Knowing Your Organization's Policies

An organization's policies will have an impact on how incidents are handled. These policies are usually very comprehensive and effective computer forensics policies that include considerations, such as contacting law enforcement, performing monitoring, and conducting regular reviews of forensic policies, guidelines, and procedures. Banks, insurance companies, law firms, governments, and health care institutions have such policies. Generally, policies should allow the incident response team to monitor systems and networks and perform investigations for reasons described in the policies. Policies may be updated frequently to keep up with the changes to laws and regulations, court rulings, and jurisdictions.

Forensics policies define the roles and responsibilities of the staff involved, including users, incident handlers, and IT staff. The policy indicates when to contact internal teams or reach out to external organizations. It should also discuss how to handle issues arising from jurisdictional conflicts. Policies also discuss the valid use of anti-forensics tools and techniques (sanitation and privacy versus malicious use, such as hiding evidence). How to maintain the confidentiality of data and the retention time of the data is also governed by organizational policies.

Minimizing the Impact on Your Organization

The goals of incident response include minimizing disruption to the computer and network operations, and limiting the exposure and compromise of sensitive data. To be able to meet these goals, incident response preparedness, planning, and proper execution following related policies are crucial. Incident response teams should minimize the downtimes of business critical systems once the evidence has been gathered and the systems have been cleared of the effects of the incident. Incident response teams should also identify an organization's risks and work with appropriate teams to continuously test and eliminate any vulnerability. Red team/blue team-type exercises whereby one team plays the role of malicious people and the other team the role of incident responders can provide good training for the staff and expose previously unknown risks and vulnerabilities. To minimize the impact of incidents, organizations should also establish and enforce security policies and procedures, gain management support for security policies and incident response, keep systems updated and patched, train IT staff and end users, implement a strong credential policy, monitor network traffic and system logs, and implement and routinely test a backup policy.

Identifying the Incident Life Cycle

SANS (sans.org) defines the phases of the incident life cycle (see Figure 10.1).

Preparation

It's a matter of when rather than if an incident will happen. Therefore, it has become a top priority for an organization to be prepared for an incident. To be prepared, an organization must establish security plans and controls, make sure these plans and controls are

FIGURE 10.1   Incident response life cycle.

continuously reviewed and updated to keep up with the evolving threats, and see that they are enforced in case of an incident. Organizations should be prepared to act swiftly to minimize the impact of any incident to maintain business continuity. Incident response teams should continuously train; test, and update the incident response plan to keep their skills honed.

Detection, Collection, and Analysis

The detection of an incident involves the observance and reporting of irregularities or suspicious activities to security or IT department staff members. Once an event has been reported and escalated to the incident response team, the event is evaluated to determine whether it warrants classification as an incident. If the event has been classified as an incident, the incident response team should move in to perform data collection on the affected systems that will later be used for analysis. During collection, it is important to work in accordance with the organization's policies and procedures and preserve a valid chain-of-custody. The person involved in collecting the data should make sure that the integrity of the data is maintained on both the original and working copies of the evidence. Once the relevant information has been captured, the incident response team should analyze the data to determine who, what, when, where, how, and why an incident took place.

Containment, Eradication, and Recovery

Once the involved systems and offending vectors have been analyzed, the incident response team should move in to contain the problem and eradicate it. It is crucial to contain an incident as fast as possible to minimize its impact on the business. This action can be as easy as disconnecting the system from the network or as hard as isolating a whole server farm from the production environment. Containment and eradication should strive to protect service integrity, sensitive data, hardware, and software. The recovery phase depends on the extent of the incidence. For example, it is easier to recover from an intrusion that was detected while it was affecting a single user than from an intrusion in which the lateral movement of the intruder is extensive. Most of the time, recovery involves backing up the unaffected data to use on the new systems. Operating systems and applications are usually installed fresh to avoid any type of contamination.

Post-Incident Activity

The post-incident phase involves documenting, reporting, and reviewing the incident. Documentation actually starts as soon as an event has been classified as an incident. The report should include all of the documentation compiled during the incident, the analysis methods and techniques, and all other findings. The person writing the report should keep in mind that the report might someday be used by law enforcement or in court. Finally, the incident response team should go over the report with the IT department and other involved parties to discuss how to improve the infrastructure to prevent similar incidents.

CAPTURING VOLATILE INFORMATION

Computer systems contain volatile data that is temporarily available either until a process exits or a system is shut down. Therefore, it is important to capture this data before making any physical or logical changes to the system to avoid tampering with evidence. Many incident responders have unwittingly destroyed memory-only resident artifacts by shutting down a system in the name of containment.

Volatile data is available as system memory (including slack and free space), network configuration, network connections and sockets, running processes, open files, login sessions, and operating system time. System memory can be captured by using sampling tools (MoonSols Windows Memory Toolkit, GMG Systems' KnTDD) as a file and analyzed with the Volatility Framework to obtain the volatile data previously mentioned. The volatile data can also be captured individually with tools that are specific for each data type. The Microsoft Windows Sysinternals suite provides an extensive set of tools that can capture volatile data, such as login sessions, registry, process information, service information, shares, and loaded DLLs.

3. CONTROLLING AN INVESTIGATION

To control an investigation, the incident response team should have a forensics investigation plan, a forensics toolkit, and documented methods to secure the affected environment. An investigator should always keep in mind that the evidence collected and the analysis performed might be presented in court or used by law enforcement. Related documentation should be detailed and contain dates and times for each activity performed. To avoid challenges to the authenticity of evidence, investigators should be able to secure the suspect infrastructure, log all activity, and maintain a chain of custody.

Collecting Digital Evidence

It is important to an investigator to preserve data related to an incident as soon as possible to avoid the rapid degradation or loss of data in digital environments. Once the affected systems have been determined, volatile data should be captured immediately, followed by nonvolatile data, such as system users and groups, configuration files, password files and caches, scheduled jobs, system logs, application logs, command history, recently accessed files, executable files, data files, swap files, dump files, security software logs, hibernation files, temporary files, and complete file listings with times.

Chain of Custody and Process Integrity

The incident response team should be committed to collect and preserve evidence using methods that can support future legal or organizational proceedings. A clearly defined chain of custody is necessary to avoid allegations of tampering evidence. To accomplish this task, the team should keep a log of every entity who had physical custody of the evidence, document all of the actions performed on the evidence with the related date and time, make a working copy of the evidence for analysis, verify the integrity of the original and working copy, and store the evidence in secured location when not in use [1]. Also, before touching a physical system, the investigator should take a photograph of it. To ensure the integrity of the process, a detailed log should be kept of all the collection steps, and information about every tool used in the incident response process should be included.

Advantages of Having a Forensic Analysis Team

Forensic analysis is usually associated with crime investigations. Nowadays, due to the increase in computer-related malicious activity and growing digital infrastructure, forensic analysis is involved in incident response, operational troubleshooting, log monitoring, data recovery, data acquisition, audits, and regulatory compliance. Therefore, organizations can no longer rely on law enforcement due to resource and jurisdictional limitations. A violation of organizational policies and procedures might not concern law enforcement, leaving the organization to its own devices. It has become evident to organizations that maintaining capabilities to perform forensic analysis has become a business requirement to satisfy organizational and customer needs. While it may make sense for some organizations to maintain an internal team of forensic analysts, some might find it more beneficial to hire outside parties to carry out this function. Organizations should take cost, response time, and data sensitivity into consideration before making this decision [1]. Keeping an internal forensic analysis team might reduce cost depending on the scale of the incident, provide faster response due to familiarity with the infrastructure, and prevent sensitive data from being viewed by third parties.

Legal Aspects of Acquiring Evidence: Securing and Documenting the Scene

Securing the physical scene and documenting it should be one of the first steps an incident responder should take. This activity involves photographing the system setup, cabling, and general area, collecting and documenting all cables and attached devices, write-protecting all media, using anti-static packaging for transportation, maintaining proper temperature for stored devices, avoiding exposure to excessive electromagnetic fields, and logging all access to the area. The incident response team should keep an inventory of evidence handling supplies (chain of custody forms, notebooks, evidence storage bags, evidence tape), blank media, backup devices, and forensics workstations.

Processing and Logging Evidence

The goal of an investigation is to collect and preserve evidence that can be used for internal proceedings or courts of law. Investigators should be able to prove that the evidence has not been tampered with. To be able to get this evidence, the incident response team members should receive training specifically addressing these issues and should practice these skills on an ongoing basis to stay sharp.

To properly process and log evidence, investigators should keep the evidence within a secured and controlled environment where all access is logged, and should document the collected evidence and its circulation among investigative entities. We cannot stress how important it is to associate each activity with a date and time.

4. CONDUCTING DISK-BASED ANALYSIS

To be able to process evidence in a manner that is admissible in a court of law, a lab and accompanying procedures should be established. This will ensure that the data integrity is not breached and that the data remains confidential—in other words, that the evidence remains forensically sound.

Forensics Lab Operations

To ensure forensic soundness, an investigator's process needs to be reliable, repeatable, and documented. To have a controlled and secure environment for the investigator to follow these steps, a forensic lab becomes a necessity.

The lab should be established in a physically secure building that is monitored 24/7; have a dedicated staff; have regularly upgraded and updated workstations dedicated to forensic analysis with related software installed; and have a disaster recovery plan in place.

Acquiring a Bit-Stream Image

Acquiring a bit-stream image involves producing a bit-by-bit copy of a hard drive on a separate storage device. By creating an exact copy of a hard drive, an investigator preserves all data on a disk, including currently unused and partially overwritten sectors. The imaging process should not alter the original hard drive to preserve the copy's admissibility as evidence. Selecting a proper imaging tool is crucial to produce a forensically sound copy. The National Institute of Standards and Technology (NIST) lists the requirements for a drive imaging tool as follows [1]:

- The tool shall make a bit-stream duplicate or an image of an original disk or a disk partition on fixed or removable media.
- The tool shall not alter the original disk.
- The tool shall be able to access both IDE and SCSI disks.
- The tool shall be able to verify the integrity of a disk image file.
- The tool shall log input/output (I/O) errors.
- The tool's documentation shall be correct.

The imaging of a hard drive can be performed using specialized hardware tools or by using a combination of computers and software.

SPECIALIZED HARDWARE

The Image MASSter Solo series hard drive duplicators generally support SATA, IDE, USB, eSATA, uSATA, SAS hard drives, and flash memory devices. They can hash the disk images, besides providing write-blocking, to ensure the integrity of the copies. The imaging process can be either disk-to-disk or disk-to-file.

The Digital Intelligence Forensic Duplicator units have the same properties as the Image MASSter Solo series. But they provide access to different hard drive formats through their protocol modules.

TABLE 10.1   Creating an Image of a Drive

$ dcfldd if = /dev/sdb hash = md5 hashwindow = 2G md5log = md5.log hashconv = after bs = 512 conv = noerror,sync split = 2G splitformat = aa of = driveimage.dd

SOFTWARE: LINUX

The dd or dcfldd has been fully tested and vetted by NIST as a forensic imaging tool. It is a freeware utility for any Linux-based system and can copy every sector of hard drives. dcfldd is a dd-based software that enhances dd's output by providing status and time-to-completion output as the disk gets imaged and can split the output to smaller chunks. It can also hash the output to ensure data integrity. The following command as seen in Table 10.1 will read block sizes of 512 bytes, produce 2 GB chunks of a disk device defined as /dev/sdb, and calculate the MD5 hashes every 2 GB to ensure integrity. The hash values will be written to a file named md5.og. In the event of a read error, dcfldd will write zeroes in the copy.

WINDOWS   The AccessData FTK (Forensic Toolkit) Imager tool is a commercial disk-imaging tool distributed by AccessData. FTK supports storage of disk images in EnCase's file format, as well as in bit-by-bit (dd) format.

On the other hand, the Guidance EnCase tool is a commercial disk-imaging tool distributed by Guidance Software. Disk images are stored in the proprietary EnCase Evidence File Format, which contains compressed data prefixed with case metadata and contains hashes of the image data.

Enabling a Write Blocker

Write blockers are hardware- or software-based tools that allow the acquisition of hard drive images while preventing any data from being written to the source hard drive. Therefore ensuring the integrity of the data involved. Write blockers can do this by only allowing read commands to pass through by blocking write commands or by letting only specific commands through. While copying data with a hardware write blocker, both the source and destination drives should be connected to the write blocking device, and in case of a software blocker, the blocking software should be activated first before copying [2]. After imaging is performed with a write blocker, calculating the hashes of both the source and destination images is essential to ensure data integrity. Some hardware write blockers that are used in the industry are as follows:

- Tableau Forensic Bridges
- WiebeTech WriteBlocker

Establishing a Baseline

It is important to maintain the integrity of the data being analyzed throughout the investigation. When dealing with disk drives, to maintain integrity, calculating the hashes of the analyzed images becomes crucial. Before copying or performing any analysis, the investigator should take a baseline hash of the original drives involved. The hash could be either just MD5 or a combination of MD5, SHA-1, and SHA-512. The baseline hash can be compared with hashes of any copies that are made thereafter for analysis or backup to ensure that the integrity of the evidence is maintained.

Physically Protecting the Media

After making copies of the original evidence hard drives, they should be stored in a physically secure location, such as a safe in a secured storage facility. These drives could be used as evidence in the event of prosecution. The chain of custody should also be maintained by labeling the evidence and keeping logs of date, time, and persons with whom the evidence has come into contact. During transportation, the hard drives should be placed in anti-static bags and should not be exposed to harsh environmental conditions. If possible, photographs of the evidence should be taken whenever they are processed, starting from the original location until the image acquisition stages.

Disk Structure and Recovery Techniques

Once a forensically sound copy of the evidence has been made, we can proceed to analyze its contents. There are different kinds of storage media: hard disk drives (HDD), solid state drives (SSD), digital video disks (DVD), compact disks (CD), flash memory, and other kinds. An investigator needs to be mindful about how each media stores data differently. For example, while data in the unused space on an HDD is stored as long as new data is not written, the data in the unused space of a SSD is destroyed within minutes of switching it on. This difference in retaining data makes it difficult to obtain a forensically sound image and recovering data (see checklist: An Agenda for Action for Data Recovery).

AN AGENDA FOR ACTION FOR DATA RECOVERY

The cyber forensic specialist should ensure that the following provisional list of actions for data recovery are adhered to (check all tasks completed):

_____1. Make sure you are ready and have procedures in place for disasters like floods, tornadoes, earthquakes, and terrorism when they strike.

_____2. Make sure you are ready and have a plan in place to take periodic image copies and send them off-site.

_____3. Perform change accumulation to reduce the number of logs required as input to the recovery, which saves time at the recovery site. However, performing this step consumes resources at the home site.

_____4. Evaluate your environment to decide how to handle the change accumulation question/problem in action/task 3.

_____5. Make sure you have procedures in place to implement your plan.

_____6. Check your assets to make sure they're ready as part of your plan.

_____7. Make sure you build your recovery Job Control Language (JCL) correctly. JCL is tricky, and you need to get it exactly right. Data integrity and your business rely on this task.

_____8. Make sure you clean your RECON data sets. It can take hours if done manually, and it's an error-prone process. When your system is down, can you afford to make mistakes with this key resource?

_____9. Make sure you test your plan. There's a lot to think about. In the real world, there's much more.

_____10. Make sure your plan works before you are required to use it!

_____11. Make sure you have procedures in place to deal with issues of increased availability, shrinking expertise, and growing complexity, failures of many types, and the costs of data management and downtime.

Disk Geometry Components

With regard to HDD geometry, the surface of each HDD platter is arranged in concentric magnetic tracks on each side. To make accessing data more efficient, each track is divided into addressable sectors or blocks as seen in Figure 10.2. This organization is known as formatting. Sectors typically contain 512 bytes or 2048 bytes of data in addition to the address information. Newer HDDs use 4096 byte sectors. The HDD controller uses the format and address information to locate the specific data processed by the operating system.

Now, with regard to SSD geometry: Compared to HDDs, SSDs store data in 512-kilobyte sectors or blocks, which are in turn divided into 4096-byte long pages. These structures are located in arrays of NAND (Negated AND or NOT AND) transistors.

Inspecting Windows File System Architectures

File systems, including Windows, can be defined in six layers: Physical (absolute sectors), data classification (partitions), allocation units (clusters), storage space management (FAT or MFT), and information classification (folders), and application level storage (files).

FIGURE 10.2 Physical structure of a drive.

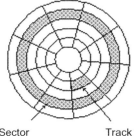

Zone Density Recording   Sector   Track

Knowing these layers will guide the investigator as to what tool is needed to extract information from the file system. Windows file systems have gone through an evolution starting from FAT and continuing to NTFS.

FAT (FILE ALLOCATION TABLE)

FAT has been available widely on Windows systems starting with the MS-DOS operating system. This file system's incarnations include FAT12, FAT16, FAT32, and exFAT. The volume is organized into specific-sized chunks based on the version numbering of the file system. FAT12 has a cluster size of 512 bytes to 8 kilobytes, whereas FAT16 has cluster sizes ranging from 512 bytes to 64 kilobytes. FAT32 file systems can support disk sizes up to 2 terabytes using cluster sizes ranging from 512 bytes to 32 kilobytes. FAT file systems begin with the boot sector and proceed with FAT areas 1 and 2, the root directory, files and other directories. FAT provides a table to the operating system as to which cluster in the volume is used for a file or folder. In a FAT file system, file deletion is accomplished by overwriting the first character of the object's name with 0xE5 or 0×00 and by setting the table entry of the related clusters to zero. FAT file times are stored by using the local system's time information.

NEW TECHNOLOGY FILE SYSTEM (NTFS)

As the name suggests, NTFS was developed to overcome the limitations inherent in the FAT file system. These limitations were the lack of access control lists (ACLs) on file system objects, journaling, and compression, encryption, named streams, rich metadata, and many other features. The journaling features of NTFS make it capable of recovering itself by automatically restoring the consistency of the file system when an error takes place [1]. It also should be noted that NTFS file times are stored in the Universal Coordinated Time (UTC) compared to FAT where the operating system's local time is used. There are mainly two artifacts in NTFS that interests a forensics investigator: MFT (master file table) and ADS (alternate data streams).

MASTER FILE TABLE (MFT)   MFT or $MFT can be considered one of the most important files in the NTFS file system. It keeps records of all files in a volume, the files' location in the directory, the physical location of the files on the drive, and file metadata. The metadata includes file and folder create dates, entry modified dates, access dates, last written dates, physical and logical file size, and ACLs of the files. The file and directory metadata is stored as an MFT entry that is 1024 bytes in size. The first 16 entries in the MFT belong to system files, such as the MFT itself. From a forensics investigator's perspective, entries are very interesting because when a file is deleted an entry gets marked as unallocated while the file content on the drive remains intact. The file name in the MFT entry can be overwritten due to MFT tree structure reorganization, so most of the time file names are not maintained. File data eventually is overwritten as the unallocated drive space gets used.

ALTERNATE DATA STREAMS (ADS)   NTFS supports multiple data streams for files and folders. Files are composed of unnamed streams that contain the actual file data besides additional named streams (mainfile.txt:one-stream). All streams within a file share the file's metadata, including file size. Since the file size does not change with the addition of

ADSs, it becomes difficult to detect their existence. Open source forensics tools, such as The Sleuth Kit (TSK), can be used to parse MFT entries and reveal the existence of ADSs. Specifically, the TSK command fls can be used to list the files and the associated ADSs.

Locating and Restoring Deleted Content

Depending on the method of deletion, time elapsed since the deletion, and drive fragmentation; files can be fully or partially recovered. A deleted or unlinked file is a file whose MFT entry has been marked as unallocated and is no longer present in the user's view. The file can be recovered based on the metadata still present in the MFT entry, given that too much time has not passed since the deletion. The Sleuth Kit (TSK) can be used to parse the MFT to locate and recover these files. The investigator would need to execute the command fls to get a listing of the deleted file's inode and use that inode to extract the file data with the command icat.

Orphaned files' MFT entries on the one hand are no longer fully intact, and therefore the related metadata, such as file name might not be available. On the other hand, the file's data may still be recovered using the same method employed for deleted files.

Unallocated files' MFT entries have been reused and/or unlinked. In this scenario, the only way to recover the file would be to "carve" the data out of the unallocated drive space. Carving involves using tools (foremost, scalpel) that recognize specific file formats, such as headers and footers to find the beginning and end of the file and extract the data.

Overwritten files' MFT entries and content have been reallocated or reused. Complete recovery would not be possible. Fragments of the file can be recovered by searching through the unallocated spaces on the drive with tools, such as grep.

5. INVESTIGATING INFORMATION-HIDING TECHNIQUES

Hidden data can exist due to regular operating system activities or deliberate user activities. This type of data includes alternate data streams, information obscured by malicious software, data encoded in media (steganography), hidden system files, and many others.

Uncovering Hidden Information

Collection of hidden data can be a challenge for an investigator. The investigator needs to be aware of the different data-hiding techniques to employ the proper tools.

Scanning and Evaluating Alternate Data Streams

Open-source forensics tools, such as The Sleuth Kit (TSK), can be used to parse MFT entries and reveal the existence of ADSs. Specifically, the TSK command fls can be used to list the files and the associated ADSs as seen in Table 10.2.

In the example above, we can see that the file ads-file.txt contains two streams named suspicious.exe and another-stream. The numbers seen in the beginning of each listing is the inode. This value identifies each file and folder in the file system. We should note that 63 bytes were skipped starting from the beginning of the drive since that data belongs to

TABLE 10.2   Listing Files from a Raw Disk Image

$fls−o 63-rp evidence-diskimage.dd

r/r 11315-158-1: ads-folder/ads-file.txt

r/r 11315-158-4: ads-folder/ads-file.txt:suspicious.exe

r/r 11315-158-3: ads-folder/host.txt:another-stream

TABLE 10.3   Extracting a File from a Raw Image with its Inode

$ icat −o 63 evidence-diskimage.dd 11315-158-4 > suspicious.exe

the master boot record (MBR). To extract the file data from the file system, the TSK command icat can be used in combination with the inode values, as seen in Table 10.3.

Executing Code from a Stream

Malicious software can attempt to hide its components in ADSs to obscure themselves from investigators. Such components could be executable files. Executable ADSs can be launched with the Windows start command or by other scripting languages, such as VBScript or Perl by referring to the ADS file directly: start ads-file.jpg:suspicious.exe. Executable hidden in ADSs can be automatically launched on system start-up by defining it to do so in the Windows registry key "HKEY_LOCAL_ MACHINE\Software\Microsoft \Windows\CurrentVersion\Run" by creating a string value containing the full path of the ADS file.

Steganography Tools and Concepts

Steganography is the science of hiding secret messages in nonsecret messages or media in a manner that only the person who is aware of the mechanism can successfully find and decode it. Messages can be hidden in images, audio files, videos, or other computer files without altering the actual presentation or functionality. While steganography is about hiding the message and its transmission, cryptography only aims to obscure the message content itself through various algorithms. Steganography can be performed by using the least significant bits in image files, placing comments in the source code, altering the file header, spreading data over a sound file's frequency spectrum, or hiding encrypted data in pseudorandom locations in a file. Several tools perform steganography:

- S-Tools is a freeware steganography tool that hides files in BMP, GIF, and WAV files. The message can be encrypted with algorithms, such as IDEA, DES, 3DES, and MDC before being hidden in the images.
- Spam Mimic is a freeware steganography tool that embeds messages in spam email content. This tool would be useful when real spam messages are numerous and the fake spam message would not wake any suspicion.

- Snow is a freeware steganography tool that encodes message text by appending white space characters to the end of lines. The tool's name stands for and exploits the steganographic nature of whitespace. It also can employ ICE encryption to hide the content of the message in case of the detection of steganography. While most of the time it's visually undetectable, it can be discovered by a careful investigator or a script looking for this tool's artifacts.
- OutGuess is an open-source tool that hides messages in the redundant bits of data sources. OutGuess can use any data format as a medium as long as a handler is provided.

Detecting Steganography

During an incident, an investigator might suspect that steganography has been used by the suspect due to an admission, a discovery of specific tools, or other indicators. Traces of the use of steganography tools can be found in the recently used files (MRU) key, the USERASSIST key, and the MUICache key in the Windows registry; prefetch files, Web browser history, deleted file information in the file system; and in the Windows Search Assistant utility. File artifacts generated by these tools can also be a good indicator of the tools' use.

The presence of files (JPEG, MP3) that present similar properties, but different hash values, might also generate suspicion. The investigator might be able to discover such pairs of carrier and processed files to apply discovery algorithms to recover the hidden messages. Steganalysis tools can also be used to detect the presence of steganography:

- Stegdetect is an open-source steganalysis tool that is capable of detecting steganographic content in images that have been generated by JSteg, JPHide, Invisible Secrets, OutGuess, F5, Camouflage, and appendX.
- StegSpy is a freeware steganalysis tool that can currently identify steganography generated by the Hiderman, JPHideandSeek, Masker, JPegX, and Invisible Secrets tools.
- Stegbreak is used to launch dictionary attacks against JSteg-Shell, JPHide, and OutGuess 0.13b-generated messages.

Scavenging Slack Space

File slack or slack space refers to the bytes between the logical end of a file and the end of the cluster in which the file resides. Slack space is a source of information leak, which can result in password, email, registry, event log, database entries, and word processing document disclosures. File slack has the potential of containing data from the system memory. This can happen if a file can't fill the last sector in a cluster and the Windows operating system uses randomly selected data from the system memory (RAM slack) to fill the gap. RAM slack can contain any information loaded into memory since the system was turned on. The information can include file content resident in memory, usernames and passwords, and cryptographic keys. File slack space can also be used to hide information by malicious users or software, which can become challenging if the investigator is not specifically looking for such behavior. Volume slack is the space that remains on a drive when it's not used by any partition. This space can contain data if it was created as a result of deleting a partition. While the partition metadata no longer exists, its contents still remain on the drive. Partition slack is the area between the ending of a logical partition and the ending of a physical block in which the partition is located. It is created when the number of sectors in a partition is not a multiple of the physical block size. Registry slack is formed when a registry key is deleted and the size value is changed to a positive value. Normally, key sizes are negative values when read as signed integers. The registry key data still remains on the drive. Jolanta Thomassen created a Perl script called "regslack" to parse registry hives and extract deleted keys by exploiting the negative to positive conversion information.

Inspecting Header Signatures and File Mangling

Users or malware with malicious intent can alter or mangle file names or the files themselves to hide files that are used to compromise systems or contain data that has been gathered as a result of their malicious actions. These techniques include but are not limited to renaming files, embedding malicious files in regular files (Pdf, Doc, Flash), binding multiple executable in a single executable, and changing file times to avoid event time-based analysis. For example, a malicious Windows executable "bad.exe" can be renamed "interesting.pdf" and be served by a Web page to an unsuspecting user. Depending on the Web browser, the user would get prompted with a dialog asking whether the user would like to run the program; and most of the time the user will dismiss the dialog by clicking the OK button. To analyze a file disguised in different file extensions, a header-based file-type checker, such as the Linux "file" command or the tool TrID (also available in Windows), can be used. Table 10.4 presents a sample of the malware Trojan.Spyeye hidden in a file with an Acrobat Pdf document extension being detected by the tool file.

Combining Files

Combining files is a very popular method among malware creators. Common file formats, such as Microsoft Office files and Adobe Pdf and Flash files, can be used as containers to hide malicious executables. One example is a technique where a Windows executable is embedded in a PDF file as an object stream and marked with a compression filter. The stream is usually obfuscated with XOR. The Metasploit Framework provides several plug-ins to generate such files for security professionals to conduct social engineering in the form of phishing attacks. The example in Table 10.5 uses Metasploit to generate a Pdf file with an embedded executable file.

TABLE 10.4   Inspecting File Headers

```
$ file hidden.pdf

hidden.pdf: PE32 executable for MS Windows (GUI) Intel 80386 32-bit

Example of a PDF Header:

0000000: 2550 4446 2d31 2e36 0a25 e4e3 cfd2 0a31 %PDF-1.6.%.....1

Example of a Windows Executable Header:

0000000: 4d5a 9000 0300 0000 0400 0000 ffff 0000 MZ.............
```

TABLE 10.5 Creating a Malicious PDF file with the Metasploit Framework

$ ./msfcli exploit/windows/fileformat/adobe_pdf_embedded_exe INFILENAME = /samples/base.pdf payload = windows/meterpreter/bind_tcp E

[*] Please wait while we load the module tree...

. . ..

INFILENAME = > ./base.pdf

payload = > windows/meterpreter/bind_tcp

[*] Reading in './base.pdf'...

[*] Parsing './base.pdf'...

[*] Parsing Successful.

[*] Using 'windows/meterpreter/bind_tcp' as payload...

[*] Creating 'evil.pdf' file...

[+] evil.pdf stored at .../local/evil.pdf

To discover such embedding, an investigator can use Didier Stevens's tool Pdf-parser to view the objects in a Pdf file.

Binding Multiple Executable Files

Binding multiple executable files provides the means to pack all dependencies and resource files a program might need while running into a single file. This is advantageous since it permits a malicious user to leave a smaller footprint on a target system and makes it harder for an investigator to locate the malicious file. Certain tools, such as the WinZip Self-Extractor, nBinder or File Joiner can create one executable file by archiving all related files whose execution will be controlled by a stub executable. When executed, the files will be extracted, and the contained program will be launched automatically. Some of these file binders can produce files that can't be detected by some anti-viruses, and if downloaded and run by an unsuspecting user, it can result in a system compromise.

File Time Analysis

File time analysis is one of the most frequently used techniques by investigators. File times are used to build a storyline that could potentially reveal how and when an event on a system caused a compromise. The file time of a malicious executable could be linked to a user's browser history to find out which sites were visited before the compromise occurred.

The problem with this type of analysis is that sometimes the file times can be tampered with and can't be relied upon as evidence. The tool Timestomp, created by James Foster and Vincent Liu, allows for the deletion or modification of file MACE times (modified, accessed, created, entry modified in MFT times) in the MFT's $STANDARD_INFORMATION attribute. Timestomp can't change the file MACE times in

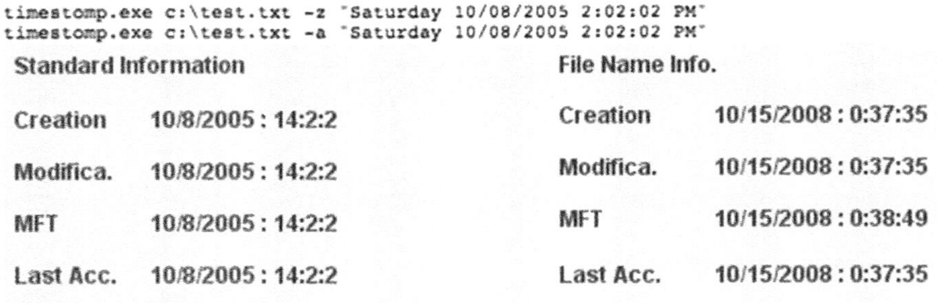

```
timestomp.exe c:\test.txt -z "Saturday 10/08/2005 2:02:02 PM"
timestomp.exe c:\test.txt -a "Saturday 10/08/2005 2:02:02 PM"
```

Standard Information		File Name Info.	
Creation	10/8/2005 : 14:2:2	Creation	10/15/2008 : 0:37:35
Modifica.	10/8/2005 : 14:2:2	Modifica.	10/15/2008 : 0:37:35
MFT	10/8/2005 : 14:2:2	MFT	10/15/2008 : 0:38:49
Last Acc.	10/8/2005 : 14:2:2	Last Acc.	10/15/2008 : 0:37:35

FIGURE 10.3   Changing timestamps as a result of time stomping.

TABLE 10.6   Compilation Time of an Executable Extracted with Pefile

Compilation timedatestamp: 2010-03-23 23:42:40
Target machine: $0 \times 14C$ (Intel 386 or later processors and compatible processors)
Entry point address: $0 \times 000030B1$

the MFT's $FILE_NAME attribute because this attribute is meant to be modified by Windows system internals only. This time-tampering method can be defeated by using Mark McKinnon's MFT Parser tool to view all eight file times to detect discrepancies, as seen in Figure 10.3.

Executable compile times can also be used as a data point during timeline analysis. The open-source Python module pefile can be used to extract this information from the executable header. For example, if malicious software changes MACE times to a future date, but keeps its original compile time, this can be flagged as suspicious by an investigator as seen in Table 10.6.

6. SCRUTINIZING EMAIL

Although many noncommercial users are favoring Web-mail nowadays, most corporate users are still using local email clients, such as Microsoft Outlook or Mozilla Thunderbird. Therefore, we should still look at extracting and analyzing email content from local email stores. Email message analysis might reveal information about the sender and recipient, such as email addresses, IP addresses, data and time, attachments, and content.

Investigating the Mail Client

An email user will generally utilize a local client to compose and send his or her message. Depending on the user's configuration, the sent and received messages will exist in the local email database. Deleted emails can also be stored locally for some time depending on the user's preferences. Most corporate environments utilize Microsoft Outlook. Outlook will store the mail in a PST (portable storage table) or OST (offline storage table) format. Multiple PST files can exist in various locations on the user's file system and can provide valuable information to an investigator about the user's email specific activity.

Interpreting Email Headers

Generally speaking, email messages are composed of three sections: header, body, and attachments. The header contains source and destination information (email and IP addresses), date and time, email subject, and the route the email takes during its transmission. Information stored in a header can either be viewed through the email client or through an email forensics tool, such as libpff (an open-source library to access email databases), FTK, or EnCase.

The "Received" line in Table 10.7 shows that the email was sent from IP address 1.1.1.1. An investigator should not rely on this information as concrete evidence because it can be easily changed by a malicious sender (email spoofing). The time information in the header might also be incorrect due to different time zones, user system inaccuracies, and tampering.

Recovering Deleted Emails

While most users treat emails as transient, the companies they work for have strict data retention policies that can enforce the storage of email, sometimes indefinitely. User emails

TABLE 10.7 An Email Header

Return-Path: <example_from@acme.edu >

X-SpamCatcher-Score: 1 [X]

Received: from **[1.1.1.1]** (HELO acme.edu)

   by fe3.acme.edu (CommuniGate Pro SMTP 4.1.8)

   with ESMTP-TLS id 61258719 for example_to@mail.acme.edu; Mon, 23 Aug 2004 11:40:10 -0400

Message-ID: <4129F3CA.2020509@acme.edu >

Date: Mon, 23 Aug 2005 11:40:36 -0400

From: Jim Doe <example_from@acme.edu >

User-Agent: Mozilla/5.0 (Windows; U; Windows NT 5.1; en-US; rv:1.0.1) Gecko/20020823 Netscape/7.0

X-Accept-Language: en-us, en

MIME-Version: 1.0

To: John Doe <example_to@mail.acme.edu >

Subject: Sales Development Meeting

Content-Type: text/plain; charset = us-ascii; format = flowed

Content-Transfer-Encoding: 7bit

---

usually are stored in backup archives or electronic-discovery systems to provide means for analysis in case there is an investigation. The email servers also can keep messages in store, although the users remove them from their local systems. Therefore, nowadays it has become somewhat difficult for a corporate user to delete an email permanently. Recovery is usually possible from various backup systems. In cases where there is no backup source and users delete an email from their local system, we need to perform several steps on the user's storage drive, depending on the level of deletion:

- If the user deletes the message, but does not empty the deleted messages folder, the user can move the messages from the deleted folder to the original folder quite easily.
- If the user deletes the email message and removes it from the deleted messages folder, then the investigator needs to apply disk forensics techniques to recover the email. In case of a Microsoft Outlook PST file, when a message is deleted it is marked as deleted by Outlook and the data remains on the disk unless the location on the drive is overwritten by new data. Commercial tools, such as AccessData's FTK or Guidance's EnCase, can be used to recover deleted messages. Another approach would be to use Microsoft's "Scanpst.exe" tool. To apply this technique, the investigator should first back up the PST and then deliberately corrupt the PST file with the command "DEBUG <FILE.pst> -f 107 113 20 −q." If the file is too large and there is insufficient system memory, then the investigator should use a hex editor to make the changes marked in red in the PST file as shown in Figure 10.4.

Once the PST file has been corrupted, then the "Scanpst.exe" tool should be located on the drive. And it should also be executed to repair the file, as seen in Figure 10.5.

```
Offset    0  1  2  3  4  5  6  7  8  9  A  B  C  D  E  F
00000000  21 42 44 4E 4B E7 0A 20 20 20 20 20 20 20 20 20   !BDNKç.
00000010  20 20 20 20 þ0 00 00 00 04 00 00 00 01 00 00 00   [.]..........
00000020  B3 93 07 00 00 00 00 00 F8 7E 27 00 D2 D8 00 00   ³"......ø~'.ÒØ..
00000030  09 35 01 00 09 2A 01 00 00 36 01 00 28 6E 04 00   .5...*...6..(n..
00000040  84 37 01 00 00 36 01 00 00 36 01 00 E0 DA 00 00   „7...6...6..àÚ..
```

FIGURE 10.4 Manipulating a PST file for recovery

FIGURE 10.5 Use of the Scanpst.exe tool

7. VALIDATING EMAIL HEADER INFORMATION

Email header information can be tampered with by users who do not wish to disclose their source information or by malicious users who would like to fake the origin of the message to avoid detection and being blocked by spam filters. Email header information can be altered by spoofing, by using an anonymizer (removes identifying information), and using a mail relay server.

Detecting Spoofed Email

A spoofed email message is a message that appears to be from an entity other than the actual sender entity. This can be accomplished by altering the sender's name, email address, email client type, and/or the source IP address in the email header. Spoofing can be detected by looking at the "Received:" and "Message-ID:" lines of the header. The "Received:" field will have each email server hop the message has taken before it has been received by the email client. An investigator can use the email server IP addresses in the header to get their hostnames from their DNS records and verify them by comparing to the actual outgoing and incoming email servers' information. The "Message-ID:" field uniquely identifies a message and is used to prevent multiple deliveries. The domain information in the "Message-ID:" field should match the domain information of the sender's email address. If this is not the case, the email is most probably spoofed. An investigator should also look out for different "From:" and "Reply-To:" email addresses and unusual email clients displayed in the "X-Mailer:" field.

Verifying Email Routing

Email routing can be verified by tracing the hops an email message has taken. This can be accomplished by verifying the "Received" field information through DNS records and if possible obtaining email transaction logs from the email servers involved. The "Message-ID" information can be searched for in the logs to make sure that the message has actually traveled the route declared in the "Received" field.

8. TRACING INTERNET ACCESS

Knowing the path a perpetrator has taken becomes very valuable when an investigator is building a case to present in court. It adds credibility to the claim and solidifies the storyline by connecting the events. For example, knowing the path an attacker has taken to steal a company's source code can reveal the extent of the compromise (loss of domain credentials, customer information leakage, and intellectual property loss), show intent, and prevent the same attack from happening. Tracing Internet access can also be valuable in the case of employees viewing content that is not compliant with workplace rules.

Inspecting Browser Cache and History Files

An investigator can use various data points to trace a perpetrator's activity by analyzing the browser cache and Web history files in the gathered evidence. Every action of a user on the Internet can generate artifacts. The browser cache contains files that are saved locally as a result of a user's Web browsing activity. The history files contain a list of visited URLs, Web searches, cookies, and bookmarked Web sites. These files can be located in different folders, depending on the operating system (OS), OS version, and browser type.

Exploring Temporary Internet Files

A browser cache stores multimedia content (images, videos), and Web pages (HTML, JavaScript, CSS) to increase the load speed of a page when viewed the next time. For the Internet Explorer Web browser on Windows XP and 2003, the cache files can be located in the folder "Documents and Settings\%username%\Local Settings\Temporary Internet Files"; in Windows Vista/7/2008, they are located in the folder "Users\%username%\AppData\ Local\Microsoft\Windows\Temporary Internet Files":

- On Windows XP/2003 Firefox stores the cached files in the folder "C:\Documents and Settings\%username\Local Settings\ Application Data\Mozilla\Firefox\Profiles", and for Windows Vista/7/2008 in "C:\Users\%username%\AppData\Roaming\Mozilla \Firefox\ Profiles."
- On Windows XP/2003 Google chrome Web browser stores the cached files in the folder "C:\Documents and Settings\%username\Application Data\ Google\Chrome\Default \Cache", and for Windows Vista/7/2008 in "C:\Users\%username%\AppData\Local \Google\Chrome\ Default\Cache".
- The MAC times of these cached files can be used during a timeline analysis to find when certain artifacts, such as malware, get dropped by malicious or compromised Web sites. Malicious executable, Pdf files, or Java files can be located in the cache unless the cache is cleared by the user or malware.

Visited URLs, Search Queries, Recently Opened Files

The Internet Explorer Web browser stores the visited URL, search query, and opened file information in the file "index.dat," accompanied by last modified and last accessed, and expiration times. This file on Windows XP/2003 systems can be located in the folder "Documents and Settings\%username%\Local Settings\Temporary Internet Files \Content.IE5," and in Windows Vista/7/2008 systems, it is located in the folder "Users\ %username%\AppData\ Local\Microsoft\Windows\Temporary Internet Files\Content. IE5," The "index.dat" file contains a LEAK record, which is a record that remains when it's marked as deleted, but can't be deleted due a related temporary Internet file (TIF) still being used.

Mozilla Firefox stores the URL, search, and open files-related history in a SQLite 3 database file Places.sqlite. These files on Windows XP/2003 systems can be located in the folder "C:\Documents and Settings\%username\Local Settings\ Application Data \Mozilla\Firefox\Profiles," and in Windows Vista/7/2008 systems, it is located in the folder "C:\Users\%username%\AppData\Roaming\Mozilla\Firefox\Profiles."

Google Chrome also stores its user activity data in SQLite 3 database files. These files on Windows XP/2003 systems can be located in the folder "C:\Documents and Settings\ %username\Application Data\ Google\Chrome\default," and in Windows Vista/7/2008 systems, it is located in the folder "C:\Users\%username%\AppData\Local\Google \Chrome\ default."

All three browsers' history files, cookies, and cache files can be parsed and interpreted by log2timeline, a tool created by Kristinn Gudjonsson. log2timeline is capable of parsing multiple data sources and producing a timeline with, including but not limited to, file MAC times, registry write times, and Windows event logs. The tool can be pointed to a raw drive image (dd image), and as a result it can produce a "super" timeline in CSV format for all pursuable time-based data sources, as seen Figure 10.6 and Table 10.8.

Researching Cookie Storage

Internet Explorer cookies can be found in the folder "Documents and Settings\%username%\ Cookies" in Windows XP/2003 systems, and in Windows Vista/7/2008 systems, in "Users\%username%\AppData\Roaming\ Microsoft\Windows\Cookies." The cookies are stored in plaintext format.

Mozilla Firefox stores its cookies in a SQLite 3 database Cookies.sqlite located in the folder "C:\Documents and Settings\%username\Local Settings\ Application Data \Mozilla\Firefox\Profiles," and, in Windows Vista/7/2008 systems, it is located in the folder "C:\Users\%username%\AppData\Roaming\Mozilla\Firefox\Profiles".

Google Chrome stores its cookies in a SQLite 3 database file "C:\Documents and Settings\%username\Application Data\ Google\Chrome\default\Cookies" in Windows XP/2003 systems and in the file "C:\Users\%username%\AppData\Local\Google

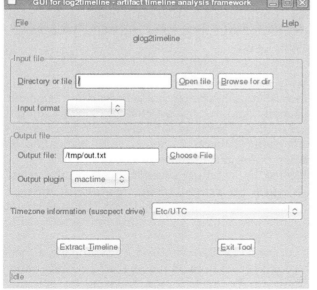

FIGURE 10.6   log2timeline GUI.

TABLE 10.8   Using log2timeline from the Command Line

log2timeline -p -r -f win7 -z EST5EDT /storage/disk-image001.dd -w supertimeline001.csv

\Chrome\default\Cookies" in Windows Vista/7/2008 systems. The cookies files of all three browser types can be parsed and viewed by the tool log2timeline, as previously mentioned.

Reconstructing Cleared Browser History

It is possible to come across cleared browser histories during an investigation. The user could have deliberately deleted the files to hide their Web browsing activity, or a malware could have removed its traces to avoid detection and analysis. Nevertheless, an investigator will look into various locations on the suspect system to locate the deleted browser history files. The possible locations are unallocated clusters, cluster slack, page files, system files, hibernation files, and systems restore points. Using AccessData's FTK Imager on the suspect drive or drive image, an investigator can promptly locate the orphaned files and see if the browser files are present there. The next step would be to use the FTK Imager to look at the unallocated spaces, which should end up being a time-consuming analysis as seen in Figure 10.7. If the drive has not been used too much, an investigator has a high chance of locating the files in the unallocated space.

Auditing Internet Surfing

Knowing what employees are browsing on the Web while they are at work has become necessary to prevent employees from visiting sites that host malicious content (sites with exploits and malware), content that is not compliant with workplace rules, and content that is illegal. Employees can use the Web to upload confidential corporate information, which can cause serious problems for the employer.

Tracking User Activity

User activity can be tracked by using tools that monitor network activity, DNS (Domain Name Server) requests, local user system activity, and proxy logs. Network activity, on the other hand, can be monitored by looking at netflows. Netflow is a network protocol developed by Cisco Systems for monitoring IP traffic. It captures source and destination IP addresses, IP protocol, source and destination ports, and IP types of service.

Local user system activity can be monitored by installing specific agents on the users' systems that can report their activity back to a centralized server. SpectorSoft offers a product called Spector 360 that can be installed on a user system and a central server. The agents on the user systems can track user browser activity by hooking into system APIs and enforce rules set by the employer.

DNS requests can be monitored at the corporate DNS server level or by looking at network traffic. When a user requests a Web page with its domain name, the name gets translated to an IP address via DNS. User activity can be tracked by monitoring for domains

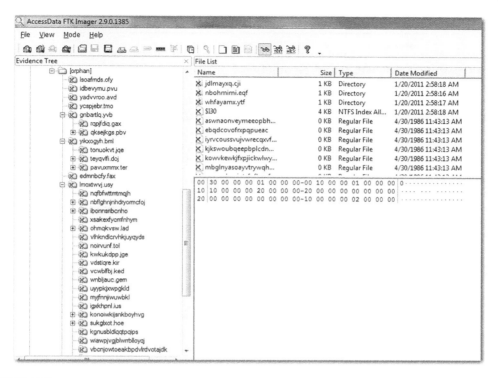

FIGURE 10.7   Use of AccessData FTK Imager.

that are not approved by the employer or domains hosting illegal content in the DNS server's logs.

Most corporate environments utilize a proxy server to funnel Web traffic through. A proxy server acts as the middle-man for requests from users seeking resources from external servers. This position of the proxy server permits tracking user browsing activity and can be used to filter or block certain behavior. Content protected by SSL (Secure Socket Layer protocol) can also be tracked by proxies, by setting the proxy up as an intercept proxy. Squid is one of the most popular open-source proxies available and can carry out the necessary functions to track and block user activity.

Uncovering Unauthorized Usage

Unauthorized Web usage can take multiple forms, such as downloading or viewing noncompliant or illegal content, uploading confidential information, launching attacks on other systems, and more. Once the unauthorized usage has been detected by the previously mentioned means, an investigator can focus on the user's system to corroborate the unauthorized activity. This can be done by analyzing browser history files and related file system activities. Building a "super" timeline with the tool log2timeline can become very useful to find the created cache and cookie files and the browser history entries around the same time the unauthorized activity was detected.

9. SEARCHING MEMORY IN REAL TIME

Analyzing memory in real time can provide very crucial information about the activities of malware or a hacker that would be otherwise unavailable if one were only looking at a system's drives. This information can be network connections and sockets, system configuration settings, collected private information (usernames, passwords, credit-card numbers), memory-only resident executables, and much more. Real-time analysis involves analyzing volatile content and therefore requires swift action by the investigator. The investigator has to quickly act to capture an image of the memory using tools, such as MoonSols Windows Memory Toolkit, GMG Systems' KnTDD, or F-response. F-response is different from the other memory-imaging tools since it provides real-time access to the target systems memory. Real-time access can reduce the time to analyze by permitting the investigator to analyze the memory right away without waiting for the whole memory to be downloaded into a file. You can read more about F-response at www.f-reponse.com.

Comparing the Architecture of Processes

Generally speaking, Windows architecture uses two access modes; user and kernel modes. The user mode includes application processes, such as programs and protected subsystems. The protected subsystems are so named because each of these is a separate process with its own protected virtual address space in memory. The kernel mode is a privileged mode of functioning in which the application has direct access to the virtual memory. This includes the address spaces of all user mode processes and applications and the associated hardware. The kernel mode is also called the protected mode, or Ring 0:

- Windows processes are generally composed of an executable program, consisting of initial code and data, a private virtual address space, system resources that are accessible to all threads in the process, a unique identifier, called a process id, at least one thread of execution, and a security context (an access token).
- A Windows thread is what Windows uses for execution within a process. Without threads, the program used by the process cannot run. Threads consist of contents of the registers representing the state of the processor, two stacks (one for the thread for executing kernel-mode instructions, and one for user-mode), private storage area used by the subsystems, run-time libraries and DLLs (dynamic-link libraries), and a unique identifier named a thread ID.
- DLLs are a set of callable subroutines linked together as a binary file that can be dynamically loaded by applications that use the subroutines. Windows user-mode entities utilize DLLs extensively. Using DLLs is advantageous for an application since applications can share DLLs. Windows ensures that there is only one copy of a DLL in memory. Each DLL has its own import address table (IAT) in its compiled form.

Identifying User and Kernel Memory

Windows refers to Intel's linear memory address space as a virtual address space (VAS) since Windows uses the disk space structure to manage physical memory. In other words 2 GB of VAS is not a one-to-one match to physical memory. 32-bit Windows divides VAS into user space (linear addresses 0x00000000 − 0x7FFFFFFF, 2 GB) and kernel space (linear addresses 0x80000000—0xFFFFFFFF, 2 GB), where user space gets the lower end of the address range and kernel space gets the upper end. To get an idea of how user space is arranged, we can use the !peb command in the Windows debugger. A list of loaded kernel modules can be obtained by running the command 'lm n' in the Windows debugger.

Inspecting Threads

While it is assumed that user and kernel codes are restricted to their own address spaces, a thread can jump from user space to kernel space by the instruction SYSENTER and jump back with the instruction SYSEXIT. Malicious threads can also exist within valid kernel or other user processes. Such hidden or orphan kernel threads can be detected using the Volatility Framework with the plug-in threads, which are shown in Table 10.9.

Discovering Rogue DLLs and Drivers

DLLs can be used for malicious purposes by injecting them through AppInit_DLLs registry value, SetWindowsHookEx() API call, and using remote threads via the CreateRemoteThread() Windows API call. Injected DLLs can be detected using the Volatility Framework's apihooks plug-in. The plug-in provides detailed information regarding the DLLs loaded, such as IAT, process, hooked module, hooked function, from-to instructions, and hooking module, as seen in Table 10.10.

The Volatility Framework plug-in malfind can find hidden or injected DLLs in user memory based on VAD (Virtual Address Descriptor) tags and page. Use of the malfind plug-in to discover injected code is shown in Table 10.11.

The plug-in dlllist in the Volatility Framework can also be used to list all DLLs for a given process in memory and find DLLs injected with the CreateRemoteThread and LoadLibrary technique. This technique does not hide the DLL and, therefore, will not be detected by the plug-in malfind, as seen in Table 10.12.

Employing Advanced Process Analysis Methods

Processes can be analyzed using tools, such as the Windows Management Instrumentation (WMI) and walking dependency trees.

Evaluating Processes with Windows Management Instrumentation (WMI)

WMI is a set of extensions to the Windows Driver Model that provides an operating system interface where components can provide information and notifications. The WMI classes Win32_Process can help collect useful information about processes. The Windows command wmic extends WMI for operation from several command-line interfaces and through batch scripts without having to rely on any other programming language. The command wmic uses class aliases to query related information. It can be executed remotely as well as locally by specifying target node or hostname and credentials. Various commands that can be used to extract various process-related information through wmic are shown in Table 10.13.

TABLE 10.9   Use of the Plug-In Threads

$ python vol.py threads −f /memory_samples/tigger.vmem -F OrphanThread

Volatile Systems Volatility Framework 2.2_alpha

[x86] Gathering all referenced SSDTs from KTHREADs...

Finding appropriate address space for tables...

ETHREAD: 0xff1f92b0 Pid: 4 Tid: 1648

Tags: OrphanThread,SystemThread

Created: 2010-08-15 19:26:13

Exited: 1970-01-01 00:00:00

Owning Process: System

Attached Process: System

State: Waiting:DelayExecution

BasePriority: 0x8

Priority: 0x8

TEB: 0x00000000

StartAddress: 0xf2edd150 UNKNOWN

ServiceTable: 0x80552180

 [0] 0x80501030

 [1] 0x00000000

 [2] 0x00000000

 [3] 0x00000000

Win32Thread: 0x00000000

CrossThreadFlags: PS_CROSS_THREAD_FLAGS_SYSTEM

0xf2edd150 803d782aeff200   CMP BYTE [0xf2ef2a78], 0x0

0xf2edd157 7437   JZ 0xf2edd190

0xf2edd159 56   PUSH ESI

0xf2edd15a bef0d0edf2   MOV ESI, 0xf2edd0f0

0xf2edd15f ff35702aeff2   PUSH DWORD [0xf2ef2a70]

0xf2edd165 ff   DB 0xff

0xf2edd166 15   DB 0x15

0xf2edd167 0c   DB 0xc

TABLE 10.10 Use of the Apihooks Plug-in to Detect Hooking

$ python vol.py -f coreflood.vmem -p 2015 apihooks

Volatile Systems Volatility Framework 2.1_alpha

****

Hook mode: Usermode

Hook type: Import Address Table (IAT)

Process: 2015 (IEXPLORE.EXE)

Victim module: iexplore.exe (0x400000 - 0x419000)

Function: kernel32.dll!GetProcAddress at 0x7ff82360

Hook address: 0x7ff82360

Hooking module: <unknown >

Disassembly(0):

0x7ff82360 e8fbf5ffff   CALL 0x7ff81960

0x7ff82365 84c0   TEST AL, AL

0x7ff82367 740b   JZ 0x7ff82374

0x7ff82369 8b150054fa7f   MOV EDX, [0x7ffa5400]

0x7ff8236f 8b4250   MOV EAX, [EDX + 0x50]

0x7ff82372 ffe0   JMP EAX

0x7ff82374 8b4c2408   MOV ECX, [ESP + 0x8]

WMI output can be used to get a clean baseline of a system to periodically run comparisons. The comparisons can show any new process that has appeared on the system and can help to update the baseline if the new process is a known one.

Walking Dependency Trees

Viewing the dependencies of a process can provide valuable information about the functionality of a process. A process's dependencies may be composed of various Windows modules, such as executables, DLLs, OCX (object linking and embedding control extension) files, and SYS files (mostly real-mode device drivers). Walking a dependency tree means to explore a process's dependencies in a hierarchical view, such as a tree. The free tool Dependency Walker provides an interface that presents such a view, which is shown in Figure 10.8.

Figure 10.8 lists all of the functions that are exported by a given Windows module and the functions that are actually being called by other modules. Another view displays the minimum set of required files, along with detailed information about each file, including a full path to the file, base address, version numbers, machine type, and debug information. Dependency Walker can be used in conjunction with the tool Process Explorer (a free

TABLE 10.11   Use of the Malfind Plug-In to Discover Injected Code

---

$ python vol.py -f zeus.vmem malfind -p 1645

Volatile Systems Volatility Framework 2.1_alpha

Process: explorer.exe Pid: 1645 Address: 0x1600000

Vad Tag: VadS Protection: PAGE_EXECUTE_READWRITE

Flags: CommitCharge: 1, MemCommit: 1, PrivateMemory: 1, Protection: 6

0x01600000 b8 35 00 00 00 e9 cd d7 30 7b b8 91 00 00 00 e9   .5.....0{.....

0x01600010 4 f df 30 7b 8b ff 55 8b ec e9 ef 17 c1 75 8b ff   O.0{..U.....u..

0x01600020 55 8b ec e9 95 76 bc 75 8b ff 55 8b ec e9 be 53   U....v.u..U....S

0x01600030 bd 75 8b ff 55 8b ec e9 d6 18 c1 75 8b ff 55 8b   .u..U.....u..U.

0x1600000 b835000000   MOV EAX, 0x35

0x1600005 e9cdd7307b   JMP 0x7c90d7d7

0x160000a b891000000   MOV EAX, 0x91

0x160000 f e94fdf307b   JMP 0x7c90df63

0x1600014 8bff   MOV EDI, EDI

0x1600016 55   PUSH EBP

Microsoft tool) to detect malicious DLLs. This can be achieved by comparing the DLL list in Process Explorer to the imports displayed by the Dependency Walker.

Auditing Processes and Services

Auditing changes in process and service properties, as well as their counts on a system, can provide valuable information to an investigator about potentially malicious activity. Rootkits, viruses, trojans, and other malicious software can be detected by the auditing process and service creation or deletion across a period of time. This technique is frequently used in malware behavioral analysis in sandboxes. We can audit Windows processes and services by using tools that utilize system APIs or system memory for live analysis. To view information through the system APIs, we can use the tool Process Hacker. The Process Hacker provides a live view of processes and services that are currently being executed or are present on the system. It provides an interface to view and search process information in detail, such as process privileges, related users and groups, DLLs loaded, handles opened, and thread information, which is shown in Figure 10.9. Service information can also be viewed in the services tab. Process and service information can be saved periodically and compared across time to detect any suspicious variations.

System memory can also be analyzed with the Volatility Framework for audit purposes. Periodic memory samples can be obtained using tools, such as F-response, MoonSols Windows Memory Toolkit, or GMG Systems' KnTDD. The Volatility Framework plug-in

TABLE 10.12   Use of the Dlllist Plug-In to Detect DLL Iijection

$ python vol.py dlllist -f sample.vmem -p 468

Volatile Systems Volatility Framework 2.2_alpha

****

wuauclt.exe pid: 468

Command line : "C:\WINDOWS\system32\wuauclt.exe"

Service Pack 2

Base   Size Path

- -

0x00400000   0x1e000 C:\WINDOWS\system32\wuauclt.exe

0x7c900000   0xb0000 C:\WINDOWS\system32\ntdll.dll

0x7c800000   0xf4000 C:\WINDOWS\system32\kernel32.dll

0x77c10000   0x58000 C:\WINDOWS\system32\msvcrt.dll

0x76b20000   0x11000 C:\WINDOWS\system32\ATL.DLL

0x77d40000   0x90000 C:\WINDOWS\system32\USER32.dll

0x77f10000   0x46000 C:\WINDOWS\system32\GDI32.dll

0x77dd0000   0x9b000 C:\WINDOWS\system32\ADVAPI32.dll

0x77e70000   0x91000 C:\WINDOWS\system32\RPCRT4.dll

TABLE 10.13   List of WMI Commands to Get Process Information

wmic /node: /user: process where get ExecutablePath,parentprocessid	Find the path to a specific running executable and its parent process (for all, leave off 'where name = ').
wmic /node: /user: process where get name, processid,commandline,creationdate	Find command-line invocation of a specific executable, as well as the creation time for the process (for all, leave off "where name = ").
wmic startup list full	Find all files loaded at start-up and the registry keys associated with autostart.
wmic process list brief | find "cmd.exe"	Search for a specific process name, such as cmd.exe.

pslist can be used to audit processes, while the plug-in svcscan can be used to audit services.

Investigating the Process Table

The process table (PT) is a data structure kept by the operating system to help context switching, scheduling, and other activities. Each entry in the process table, called process

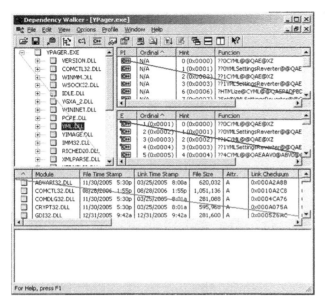

FIGURE 10.8 Using the dependency walker.

context blocks (PCBs), contains information about a process, such as process name and state, priority, and process id. The exact content of a context block depends on the operating system. For example, if the operating system supports paging, then the context block contains a reference to the page table. While to a user a process is identified by the process id (PID), in the operating system the process is represented by entries in the process table. The process control block is a large data structure that contains information about a specific process. In Linux this data structure is called task_struct, whereas in Windows it is called an EPROCESS structure. Each EPROCESS structure contains a LIST_ENTRY structure called ActiveProcessLinks, which contains a link to the previous (Blink) EPROCESS structure and the next (Flink) EPROCESS structure.

A listing of processes represented in the PT can be obtained by using the plug-in pslist in the Volatility Framework. This plug-in generates its output by walking the doubly-linked list. Certain malware or malicious users can hide processes by unlinking them from this linked list by performing direct kernel object manipulation (DKOM). To detect this kind of behavior, the Volatility Framework plug-in psscan can be used since it relies on scanning the memory to detect pools similar to that of an EPROCESS structure instead of walking the linked list.

Discovering Evidence in the Registry

We have already covered one method to inject code into a process. Another method is to add a value in the AppInit_DLLs registry key (HKEY_LOCAL_MACHINE\Software \Microsoft\Windows NT\CurrentVersion\Windows\AppInit_DLLs) that makes a new process to load a DLL of malicious origin.

AppInit_DLLs is a mechanism that allows an arbitrary list of DLLs to be loaded into each user mode process on the system. Although a code-signing requirement was added

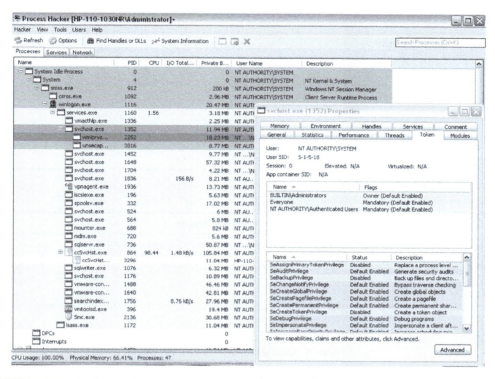

FIGURE 10.9 Using Process Hacker to view process and service information.

in Windows 7 and Windows Server 2008 R2, it is still being utilized by various malicious software to hide and persist on a system.

The Volatility Framework can also be used to analyze the registry that has been loaded to memory. The plug-ins that are available from the Volatility Framework for registry analysis are shown in Table 10.14.

A listing of services can be obtained from the registry in memory from the registry key "HKEY_LOCAL_ MACHINE\SYSTEM\CurrentControlSet\Services." This key contains the database of services and device drivers that get read into the Windows service control manager's (SCM) internal database. SCM is a remote procedure call (RPC) server that interacts with the Windows service processes.

Other registry keys that might be of interest are the keys located in the registry key "HKEY_LOCAL_ MACHINE\ SOFTWARE\ Microsoft\ Windows\CurrentVersion." The keys that are part of the auto start registries are "Run," "RunOnce," "RunOnce\Setup," "RunOnceEx," "RunServices," and "RunServicesOnce." Malware can set values in these keys to persist across system restarts and get loaded during system start-up.

DEPLOYING AND DETECTING A ROOTKIT

Rootkits are composed of several tools (scripts, binaries, configuration files) that permit malicious users to hide their actions on a system so they can control and monitor the

TABLE 10.14   List of Volatility Framework Plug-Ins to extract Registry Information from Memory

hivescan	finds the physical address of CMHIVE structures, which represent a registry hives in memory.
hivelist	takes a physical address of one CMHIVE, returns the virtual address of all hives, and their names
printkey	takes a virtual address of a hive and a key name (e.g., "ControlSet001\Control"), and display the key's timestamp, values, and subkeys.
hashdump	dump the LanMan and NT hashes from the registry.
lsadump	dump the LSA secrets (decrypted) from the registry.
cachedump	dump any cached domain password hashes from the registry.

TABLE 10.15   List of Volatility Framework plug-ins to detect rootkit hooking

Rootkit Technique	The Volatility Framework Plug-In
IAT (import address table) Hooks	Apihooks—detect overwritten IAT entry for a PE file
EAT (export address table) Hooks	apihooks
Inline API Hooks	apihooks
IDT (interrupt descriptor table) Hools	Idt—detects overwritten IDT entries that point to malicious interrupts or processor exceptions
Driver IRP (I/O request packets) Hooks	Driverirp—detects overwritten IRP function table entries (modified to monitor buffer data)
SSDT (system service descriptor table) Hooks	Ssdt—detects hooking of pointers to kernel mode functions in the SSDT that occurs per thread
Hiding with Orphan Threads in Kernel	Threads—detects orphan threads that can unlink or unload its driver

system for an indefinite time. Rootkits can be installed either through an exploit payload or after system access has been achieved. Rootkits are usually used to provide concealment, command and control (C2), and surveillance. A rootkit will usually try to hide system resources, such as processes, Registry information, files, and network ports. API hooking is a popular rootkit technique that intercepts system calls to make the operating system report inaccurate results that conceal the presence of the rootkit. To skip all of the system-level subversion, we can look into the memory directly to detect rootkits. The Volatility Framework provides various plug-ins to detect rootkit concealment techniques, as seen in Table 10.15.

10. SUMMARY

In this chapter we have seen the importance of having a well-documented incident response plan and process, and having an incident response team that is experienced in cyber forensics analysis. Besides having these important components, an organization needs to have strong policies and procedures that back them. Incident response is not only about countering the incident, but also about learning from it and improving on the weaknesses exposed. We should always keep in mind that preparedness is paramount since it is a matter of when rather than if an incident will strike.

With regard to the near future, the amount of data that needs to be gathered and analyzed is increasing rapidly, and as a result we are seeing the emergence of big-data analytic tools that can process disparate data sources to deal with large cases. Tomorrow's incident response teams will need to be skilled in statistical analysis as well as forensics to be able to navigate in this increasingly hostile and expanding cyberspace. As you can see, incident response and cyber forensics needs to be a step ahead of the potential causes of threats, risks, and exploits.

Finally, let's move on to the real interactive part of this chapter: review questions/exercises, hands-on projects, case projects, and optional team case project. The answers and/or solutions by chapter can be found in the Online Instructor's Solutions Manual.

CHAPTER REVIEW QUESTIONS/EXERCISES

True/False

1. True or False? Cyber forensics and incident response go hand in hand.
2. True or False? In an organization there is a daily occurrence of events within the IT infrastructure, but not all of these events qualify as incidents.
3. True or False? Forensic analysis is not usually applied to determine who, what, when, where, how, and why an incident took place.
4. True or False? When an incident response team comes across incidents relevant to these laws, they should consult with their legal team.
5. True or False? An organization should be prepared beforehand to properly respond to incidents and mitigate them in the longest time possible.

Multiple Choice

1. How do incident response and cyber forensics fit together?
   A. They don't
   B. Incident response helps cyber forensics in analyzing evidence
   C. Cyber forensics provides answers to questions that need to be answered for proper incident response
   D. None of the above
   E. All of the above
2. Which option below might be classified as an incident?
   A. Phishing attack
   B. Unauthorized access
   C. Intellectual property theft
   D. Denial-of-service attack
   E. All of the above

3. Which of these options should be considered volatile data and be captured immediately?
   A. Configuration files
   B. Database files
   C. Documents
   D. System Memory
   E. All of the above
4. Which considerations would be involved in monitoring employee email?
   A. Technical factors
   B. Legal factors
   C. Organizational factors
   D. All of the above
   E. None of the above
5. Which tool below can be used to extract the MFT of a Windows system from a drive?
   A. The Sleuthkit
   B. The Volatility Framework
   C. The KntDD
   D. Truecrypt
   E. All of the above

EXERCISE

Problem

How does an organization ship its hard drives?

Hands-On Projects

Project

How does an organization get its data back?

Case Projects

Problem

As an exercise to practice what you have learned in this chapter, you will analyze your own Windows workstation:

1. Create an image of your disk drive and save it to an external drive using AccessData FTK Imager.
2. Create a memory sample from your system using MoonSols Windows Memory Toolkit and save it to an external drive.
3. Create a super timeline of the disk image using log2timeline and list the files created within 24 hours.

4. Using the Volatility Framework, get a list of the following objects from the memory sample: processes, DLLs, modules, services, connections, sockets, API hooks.

Optional Team Case Project

Problem

When should an organization consider using a computer forensic examiner?

References

[1] Guide to Integrating Forensic Techniques into Incident Response, NIST, 2006.
[2] Disk Imaging Tool Specification, NIST, 2001.

CHAPTER

11

Network Forensics

Yong Guan

Iowa State University

1. SCIENTIFIC OVERVIEW

With the phenomenal growth of the Internet, more and more people enjoy and depend on the convenience of its provided services. The Internet has spread rapidly almost all over the world. Up to December 2006, the Internet had been distributed to over 233 countries and world regions and had more than 1.09 billion users.[1] Unfortunately, the wide use of computers and the Internet also opens doors to cyber attackers. There are different kinds of attacks that an end user of a computer or Internet can meet. For instance, there may be various viruses on a hard disk, several backdoors open in an operating system, or a lot of phishing emails in an emailbox. According to the annual *Computer Crime Report* of the Computer Security Institute (CSI) and the U.S. Federal Bureau of Investigation (FBI), released in 2006, cyber attacks cause massive money losses each year.

However, the FBI/CSI survey results also showed that a low percentage of cyber crime cases have been reported to law enforcement (in 1996, only 16%; in 2006, 25%), which means that in reality, the vast majority of cyber criminals are never caught or prosecuted. Readers may ask why this continues to happen. Several factors contribute to this fact:

- In many cases, businesses are often reluctant to report and publicly discuss cyber crimes related to them. The concern of negative publicity becomes the number-one reason because it may attract other cyber attackers, undermine the confidence of customers, suppliers, and investors, and invite the ridicule of competitors.
- Generally, it is much harder to detect cyber crimes than crimes in the physical world. There are various antiforensics techniques that can help cyber criminals evade detection, such as information-hiding techniques (steganography, covert channels),

---

1. Internet World Stats, www.internetworldstats.com.

anonymity proxies, stepping stones, and botnets. Even more challenging, cyber criminals are often insiders or employees of the organizations themselves.

- Attackers may walk across the boundaries of multiple organizations and even countries. To date, the lack of effective solutions has significantly hindered efforts to investigate and stop the rapidly growing cyber criminal activities. It is therefore crucial to develop a forensically sound and efficient solution to track and capture these criminals.

Here we discuss the basic principles and some specific forensic techniques in attributing real cyber criminals.

2. THE PRINCIPLES OF NETWORK FORENSICS

Network forensics can be generally defined as a science of discovering and retrieving evidential information in a networked environment about a crime in such a way as to make it admissible in court. Different from intrusion detection, all the techniques used for the purpose of network forensics should satisfy both legal and technical requirements. For example, it is important to guarantee whether the developed network forensic solutions are practical and fast enough to be used in high-speed networks with heterogeneous network architecture and devices. More important, they need to satisfy general forensics principles such as the rules of evidence and the criteria for admissibility of novel scientific evidence (such as the *Daubert* criteria).[2,3,4] The five rules are that evidence must be:

- *Admissible.* Must be able to be used in court or elsewhere.
- *Authentic.* Evidence relates to incident in relevant way.
- *Complete.* No tunnel vision, exculpatory evidence for alternative suspects.
- *Reliable.* No question about authenticity and veracity.
- *Believable.* Clear, easy to understand, and believable by a jury.

The evidence and the investigative network forensics techniques should satisfy the criteria for admissibility of novel scientific evidence (*Daubert v. Merrell*):

- Whether the theory or technique has been reliably tested
- Whether the theory or technique has been subject to peer review and publication
- What is the known or potential rate of error of the method used?
- Whether the theory or method has been generally accepted by the scientific community

The investigation of a cyber crime often involves cases related to homeland security, corporate espionage, child pornography, traditional crime assisted by computer and

2. G. Palmer, "A road map for digital forensic research," Digital Forensic Research Workshop (DFRWS), Final Report, Aug. 2001.

3. C. M. Whitcomb, "An historical perspective of digital evidence: A forensic scientist's view," IJDE, 2002.

4. S. Mocas, "Building theoretical underpinnings for digital forensics research," Digital Investigation, Vol. 1, pp. 61–68, 2004.

network technology, employee monitoring, or medical records, where privacy plays an important role.

There are at least three distinct communities within digital forensics: law enforcement, military, and business and industry, each of which has its own objectives and priorities. For example, prosecution is the primary objective of the law enforcement agencies and their practitioners and is often done after the fact. Military operations' primary objective is to guarantee the continuity of services, which often have strict real-time requirements. Business and industry's primary objectives vary significantly, many of which want to guarantee the availability of services and put prosecution as a secondary objective.

Usually there are three types of people who use digital evidence from network forensic investigations: police investigators, public investigators, and private investigators. The following are some examples:

- Criminal prosecutors. Incriminating documents related to homicide, financial fraud, drug-related records.
- Insurance companies. Records of bill, cost, services to prove fraud in medical bills and accidents.
- Law enforcement officials. Require assistance in search warrant preparation and in handling seized computer equipment.
- Individuals. To support a possible claim of wrongful termination, sexual harassment, or age discrimination.

The primary activities of network forensics are investigative in nature. The investigative process encompasses the following:

- Identification
- Preservation
- Collection
- Examination
- Analysis
- Presentation
- Decision

In the following discussion, we focus on several important network forensic areas (see checklist: "An Agenda For Action For Network Forensics").

AN AGENDA FOR ACTION FOR NETWORK FORENSICS

The cyber forensics specialist should ensure the following are adhered to (Check All Tasks Completed):

_____1. Provide expert data visualization techniques to the problem of network data pattern analysis.

_____2. Apply standard research and analysis techniques to datasets provided by a company or organization.

_____3. Apply the lessons learned from company-provided datasets to

---

open datasets as the research advances.

_____4. Provide initial datasets, project initiation, and training in network traffic datasets and analysis techniques.

_____5. Provide expert network forensical rule-based algorithms for incorporation by researchers.

_____6. Repeatedly test and verify new visualization techniques and procedures to ensure that new patterns are, in fact, accurate representations of designated activities.

_____7. Develop a test database.

_____8. Develop a design methodology for visualizing test data.

_____9. Develop a query interface to the database.

_____10. Map data structures to a visualization model.

_____11. Build a prototype.

_____12. Refine a prototype.

_____13. Incorporate live Internet data.

_____14. Test live Internet data.

_____15. Deliver a final build.

_____16. Produce new visualization techniques to streamline and enhance analysis of network forensic data.

_____17. Produce a Web browser compatible prototype that demonstrates these techniques to visualize and query vast amounts of data. The resulting interactive visualization interface will advance the usability of the system, solve the volumetric problem with analyzing these datasets, and advance the adaptation of the solution in the INFOSEC market.

_____18. Routinely archive all e-mail as it is received on your server for a certain period of time (say, 30–60 days).

_____19. Clear the archives after an additional specified time.

_____20. Physically segregate the back-up copies of the e-mail system from back-ups of the rest of the computer system.

_____21. Automatically erase e-mail from the computer system, including back-ups, after a short period (15–30 days).

_____22. Apply uniform retention and deletion standards and features outside the server to workstations and laptops.

_____23. Formulate and distribute a statement that the automatic deletion of electronic records will be suspended and steps taken to preserve records in the event of investigation or litigation.

_____24. Maintain an appropriate SOP document. All agencies that seize and/or examine digital evidence must do this.

_____25. Clearly set forth in this SOP document all elements of an agency's policies and procedures concerning digital evidence, which must be issued under the agency's management authority.

_____26. Review the SOPs on an annual basis to ensure their continued suitability and effectiveness.

_____27. Make sure that the procedures that you use are generally accepted in the field or supported by data gathered and recorded in a scientific manner.

_____28. Maintain written copies of appropriate technical procedures.

_____29. Use hardware and software that is appropriate and effective for the seizure or examination procedure.

_____30. Record all activity relating to the seizure, storage, examination, or transfer of digital evidence in writing.

_____31. Make sure that all digital evidence is available for review and testimony.

_____32. Make sure that any action that has the potential to alter, damage, or destroy any aspect of original evidence is performed by qualified persons in a forensically sound manner.

_____33. Be alert. One of the best ways to ensure that your network is secure is to keep abreast of developing threats. Security experts agree that ignorance is the most detrimental security problem. Most hacks occur because someone wasn't paying attention. Web sites such as the CERT home page (http://www.cert.org) are excellent places to get current information.

_____34. Apply all service patches. Many companies will sit on patches rather than put them to use. Others are not diligent enough about searching for and downloading the latest virus definitions. Smart hackers bank on the negligence of others.

_____35. Limit port access. Although just about any application that uses TCP requires a port, you can minimize exposure by limiting the number of ports accessible through a firewall. NNTP (Network News Transport Protocol) is an excellent example: Unless your shop requires newsgroup access, port 119 should be shut down.

_____36. Eliminate unused user IDs and change existing passwords. Poor maintenance is almost as dangerous as ignorance.

_____37. Make sure that system administrators routinely audit and delete any idle user IDs.

_____38. Make sure that in order to limit the likelihood of successful random guessing, that all user and system passwords be system-generated or system-enforced.

_____39. Avoid the use of SNMP across the firewall.

_____40. Check routers to make sure they do not respond to SNMP commands originating outside the network.

_____41. Secure remote access. Try to break into your own network. You can learn a lot by hacking into your own system.

_____42. Test your packet-filtering scheme. If you can gain access to your systems from a workstation outside your network, you can easily test your packet-filtering scheme without any outside exposure. If you do spot a weakness, you'll be one step ahead of the hackers.

_____ **43.** Ask a consultant when in doubt. If you don't have the technical wherewithal in-house or if your staff is too busy working on other projects, don't hesitate to call in a consultant. Many companies offer security assessment and training services.

_____ **44.** Assess your company's networking needs and shut down any ports that aren't necessary for day-to-day operations, such as port 53 for DNS access and port 119 for NNTP (Network News Transfer Protocol) services.

_____ **45.** Be sure to eliminate unused user IDs and to avoid provisioning SNMP services through the firewall.

3. ATTACK TRACEBACK AND ATTRIBUTION

When we face the cyber attacks, we can detect them and take countermeasures. For instance, an intrusion detection system (IDS) can help detect attacks; we can update operating systems to close potential backdoors; we can install antivirus software to defend against many known viruses. Although in many cases we can detect attacks and mitigate their damage, it is hard to find the real attackers/criminals. However, if we don't trace back to the attackers, they can always conceal themselves and launch new attacks. If we have the ability to find and punish the attackers, we believe this will help significantly reduce the attacks we face every day.

Why is traceback difficult in computer networks? One reason is that today's Internet is stateless. There is too much data in the Internet to record it all. For example, a typical router only forwards the passed packets and does not care where they are from; a typical mail transfer agent (MTA) simply relays emails to the next agent and never minds who is the sender. Another reason is that today's Internet is almost an unauthorized environment. Alice can make a VoIP call to Bob and pretend to be Carol; an attacker can send millions of emails using your email address and your mailbox will be bombed by millions of replies. Two kinds of attacks are widely used by attackers and also interesting to researchers all over the world. One is IP spoofing; the other is the stepping-stone attack. Each IP packet header contains the source IP address. Using IP spoofing, an attacker can change the source IP address in the header to that of a different machine and thus avoid traceback.

In a stepping-stone attack, the attack flow may travel through a chain of stepping stones (intermediate hosts) before it reaches the victim. Therefore, it is difficult for the victim to know where the attack came from except that she can see the attack traffic from the last hop of the stepping-stone chain. Figure 11.1 shows an example of IP stepping-stone attack.

Next we introduce the existing schemes to trace back IP spoofing attacks, then we discuss current work on stepping-stone attack attribution.

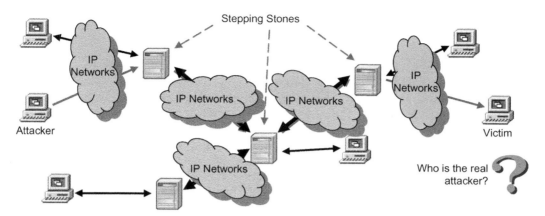

FIGURE 11.1 Stepping-stone attack attribution.

IP Traceback

Here we review major existing IP traceback schemes that have been designed to trace back to the origin of IP packets through the Internet. We roughly categorize them into four primary classes:

- Active probing[5,6]
- ICMP traceback[7,8,9]
- Packet marking[10,11,12,13,14]

5. H. Burch and B. Cheswick, "Tracing anonymous packets to their approximate source," in *Proceedings of USENIX LISA* 2000, Dec. 2000, pp. 319–327.

6. R. Stone, "Centertrack: An IP overlay network for tracking DoS floods," in *Proceedings of the 9th USENIX Security Symposium*, Aug. 2000, pp. 199–212.

7. S. M. Bellovin, "ICMP traceback messages," Internet draft, 2000.

8. A. Mankin, D. Massey, C.-L. Wu, S. F. Wu, and L. Zhang, "On design and evaluation of 'Intention-Driven' ICMP traceback," in *Proceedings of 10th IEEE International Conference on Computer Communications and Networks*, Oct. 2001.

9. S. F. Wu, L. Zhang, D. Massey, and A. Mankin, "Intention-driven ICMP trace-back," Internet draft, 2001.

10. A. Belenky and N. Ansari, "IP traceback with deterministic packet marking," *IEEE Communications Letters*, Vol. 7, No. 4, pp. 162–164, April 2003.

11. D. Dean, M. Franklin, and A. Stubblefield, "An algebraic approach to IP traceback," *Information and System Security*, Vol. 5, No. 2, pp. 119–137, 2002.

12. K. Park and H. Lee, "On the effectiveness of probabilistic packet marking for IP traceback under denial of service attack," in *Proceedings of IEEE INFOCOM* 2001, Apr. 2001, pp. 338–347.

13. S. Savage, D. Wetherall, A. Karlin, and T. Anderson, "Network support for IP traceback," IEEE/ACM *Transactions on Networking*, Vol. 9, No. 3, pp. 226–237, June 2001.

14. D. Song and A. Perrig, "Advanced and authenticated marking schemes for IP traceback," in *Proceedings of IEEE INFOCOM* 2001, Apr. 2001.

- Log-based traceback[15,16,17,18]

Active Probing

Stone[19] proposed a traceback scheme called *CenterTrack*, which selectively reroutes the packets in question directly from edge routers to some special tracking routers. The tracking routers determine the ingress edge router by observing from which tunnel the packet arrives. This approach requires the cooperation of network administrators, and the management overhead is considerably large.

Burch and Cheswick[20] outlined a technique for tracing spoofed packets back to their actual source without relying on the cooperation of intervening ISPs. The victim actively changes the traffic in particular links and observes the influence on attack packets, and thus can determine where the attack comes from. This technique cannot work well on distributed attacks and requires that the attacks remain active during the time period of traceback.

ICMP Traceback (iTrace)

Bellovin[21] proposed a scheme named *iTrace* to trace back using ICMP messages for authenticated IP marking. In this scheme, each router samples (with low probability) the forwarding packets, copies the contents into a special ICMP traceback message, adds its own IP address as well as the IP of the previous and next-hop routers, and forwards the packet to either the source or destination address. By combining the information obtained from several of these ICMP messages from different routers, the victim can then reconstruct the path back to the origin of the attacker.

A drawback of this scheme is that it is much more likely that the victim will get ICMP messages from routers nearby than from routers farther away. This implies that most of the network resources spent on generating and utilizing iTrace messages will be wasted.

15. J. Li, M. Sung, J. Xu, and L. Li, "Large-scale IP traceback in high-speed Internet: Practical techniques and theoretical foundation," in *Proceedings of 2004 IEEE Symposium on Security and Privacy*, May 2004.

16. S. Matsuda, T. Baba, A. Hayakawa, and T. Nakamura, "Design and implementation of unauthorized access tracing system," in *Proceedings of the 2002 Symposium on Applications and the Internet (SAINT 2002)*, Jan. 2002.

17. K. Shanmugasundaram, H. Brönnimann, and N. Memon, "Payload attribution via hierarchical Bloom filters," in *Proceedings of the 11th ACM Conference on Computer and Communications Security*, Oct. 2004.

18. A. C. Snoeren, C. Partridge, L. A. Sanchez, C. E. Jones, F. Tchakountio, B. Schwartz, S. T. Kent, and W. T. Strayer, "Single-packet IP traceback," *IEEE/ACM Transactions on Networking*, Vol. 10, No. 6, pp. 721–734, Dec. 2002.

19. R. Stone, "Centertrack: An IP overlay network for tracking DoS floods," in *Proceedings of the 9th USENIX Security Symposium*, Aug. 2000, pp. 199–212.

20. H. Burch and B. Cheswick, "Tracing anonymous packets to their approximate source," in *Proceedings of USENIX LISA 2000*, Dec. 2000, pp. 319–327.

21. S. M. Bellovin, "ICMP traceback messages," Internet draft, 2000.

An enhancement of iTrace, called *Intention-Driven iTrace*, has been proposed.[22,23] By introducing an extra "intention-bit," it is possible for the victim to increase the probability of receiving iTrace messages from remote routers.

Packet Marking

Savage et al.[24] proposed a *Probabilistic Packet Marking* (PPM) scheme. Since then several other PPM-based schemes have been developed.[25,26,27] The baseline idea of PPM is that routers probabilistically write partial path information into the packets during forwarding. If the attacks are made up of a sufficiently large number of packets, eventually the victim may get enough information by combining a modest number of marked packets to reconstruct the entire attack path. This allows victims to locate the approximate source of attack traffic without requiring outside assistance.

The *Deterministic Packet Marking* (DPM) scheme proposed by Belenky and Ansari[28] involves marking each individual packet when it enters the network. The packet is marked by the interface closest to the source of the packet on the edge ingress router. The mark remains unchanged as long as the packet traverses the network. However, there is no way to get the whole paths of the attacks.

Dean et al.[29] proposed an *Algebraic Packet Marking* (APM) scheme that reframes the traceback problem as a polynomial reconstruction problem and uses techniques from algebraic coding theory to provide robust methods of transmission and reconstruction. The advantage of this scheme is that it offers more flexibility in design and more powerful techniques that can be used to filter out attacker-generated noise and separate multiple paths. But it shares similarity with PPM in that it requires a sufficiently large number of attack packets.

22. A. Mankin, D. Massey, C.-L. Wu, S. F. Wu, and L. Zhang, "On design and evaluation of 'Intention-Driven' ICMP traceback," in *Proceedings of* 10*th IEEE International Conference on Computer Communications and Networks,* Oct. 2001.

23. S. F. Wu, L. Zhang, D. Massey, and A. Mankin, "Intention-driven ICMP trace back," Internet draft, 2001.

24. S. Savage, D. Wetherall, A. Karlin, and T. Anderson, "Network support for IP traceback," IEEE/*ACM Transactions on Networking,* Vol. 9, No. 3, pp. 226–237, June 2001.

25. D. Song and A. Perrig, "Advanced and authenticated marking schemes for IP traceback," in *Proceedings of IEEE INFOCOM* 2001, Apr. 2001.

26. K. Park and H. Lee, "On the effectiveness of probabilistic packet marking for IP traceback under denial of service attack," in *Proceedings of IEEE INFOCOM* 2001, Apr. 2001, pp. 338–347.

27. D. Dean, M. Franklin, and A. Stubblefield, "An algebraic approach to IP traceback," *Information and System Security,* Vol. 5, No. 2, pp. 119–137, 2002.

28. A. Belenky and N. Ansari, "IP traceback with deterministic packet marking," *IEEE Communications Letters,* Vol. 7, No. 4, pp. 162–164, April 2003.

29. D. Dean, M. Franklin, and A. Stubblefield, "An algebraic approach to IP traceback," *Information and System Security,* Vol. 5, No. 2, pp. 119–137, 2002.

Log-Based Traceback

The basic idea of log-based traceback is that each router stores the information (digests, signature, or even the packet itself) of network traffic through it. Once an attack is detected, the victim queries the upstream routers by checking whether they have logged the attack packet in question. If the attack packet's information is found in a given router's memory, that router is deemed to be part of the attack path. Obviously, the major challenge in log-based traceback schemes is the storage space requirement at the intermediate routers.

Matsuda et al.[30] proposed a hop-by-hop log-based IP traceback method. Its main features are a logging *packet feature* that is composed of a portion of the packet for identification purposes and an algorithm using a data-link identifier to identify the routing of a packet. However, for each received packet, about 60 bytes of data should be recorded. The resulting large memory space requirement prevents this method from being applied to high-speed networks with heavy traffic.

Although today's high-speed IP networks suggest that classical log-based traceback schemes would be too prohibitive because of the huge memory requirement, logbased traceback became attractive after Bloom filter-based (i.e., hash-based) traceback schemes were proposed. *Bloom filters* were presented by Burton H. Bloom[31] in 1970 and have been widely used in many areas such as database and networking.[32] A Bloom filter is a spaceefficient data structure for representing a set of elements to respond to membership queries. It is a vector of bits that are all initialized to the value 0. Then each element is inserted into the Bloom filter by hashing it using several independent uniform hash functions and setting the corresponding bits in the vector to value 1. Given a query as to whether an element is present in the Bloom filter, we hash this element using the same hash functions and check whether all the corresponding bits are set to 1. If any one of them is 0, then undoubtedly this element is not stored in the filter. Otherwise, we would say that it is present in the filter, although there is a certain probability that the element is determined to be in the filter though it is actually not. Such false cases are called *false positives*.

The space-efficiency of Bloom filters is achieved at the cost of a small, acceptable false-positive rate. Bloom filters were introduced into the IP traceback area by Snoeren et al.[33] They built a system named the *Source Path Isolation Engine* (SPIE), which can trace the origin of a single IP packet delivered by the network in the recent past. They demonstrated that the system is effective, space-efficient, and implementable in current or next-generation routing hardware. Bloom filters are used in each SPIE-equipped router to

30. S. Matsuda, T. Baba, A. Hayakawa, and T. Nakamura, "Design and implementation of unauthorized access tracing system," in *Proceedings of the* 2002 *Symposium on Applications and the Internet* (*SAINT* 2002), Jan. 2002.

31. B. H. Bloom, "Space/time trade-offs in hash coding with allowable errors," *Communications of the ACM*, Vol. 13, No. 7, pp. 422–426, July 1970.

32. A. Broder and M. Mitzenmacher, "Network applications of Bloom filters: A survey," *Proceedings of the* 40th *Annual Allerton Conference on Communication, Control, and Computing*, Oct. 2002, pp. 636–646.

33. A. C. Snoeren, C. Partridge, L. A. Sanchez, C. E. Jones, F. Tchakountio, B. Schwartz, S. T. Kent, and W. T. Strayer, "Single-packet IP traceback," *IEEE/ACM Transactions on Networking*, Vol. 10, No. 6, pp. 721–734, Dec. 2002.

record the digests of all packets received in the recent past. The digest of a packet is exactly several hash values of its nonmutable IP header fields and the prefix of the payload. Strayer et al.[34] extended this traceback architecture to IP-v6. However, the inherent false positives of Bloom filters caused by unavoidable collisions restrain the effectiveness of these systems. To reduce the impact of unavoidable collisions in Bloom filters, Zhang and Guan[35] propose a topologyaware single-packet IP traceback system, namely TOPO. The router's local topology information, that is, its immediate predecessor information, is utilized. The performance analysis shows that TOPO can reduce the number and scope of unnecessary queries and significantly decrease false attributions. When Bloom filters are used, it is difficult to decide their optimal control parameters *a priori*. They designed a *k*-adaptive mechanism that can dynamically adjust the parameters of Bloom filters to reduce the false-positive rate.

Shanmugasundaram et al.[36] proposed a *payload attribution system* (PAS) based on a *hierarchical Bloom filter* (HBF). HBF is a Bloom filter in which an element is inserted several times using different parts of the same element. Compared with SPIE, which is a packet-digesting scheme, PAS only uses the payload excerpt of a packet. It is useful when the packet header is unavailable.

Li et al.[37] proposed a Bloom filter-based IP trace-back scheme that requires an order of magnitude smaller processing and storage cost than SPIE, thereby being able to scale to much higher link speed. The baseline idea of their approach is to sample and log a small percentage of packets, and 1 bit packet marking is used in their sampling scheme. Therefore, their traceback scheme combines packet marking and packet logging together. Their simulation results showed that the traceback scheme can achieve high accuracy and scale well to a large number of attackers. However, as the authors also pointed out, because of the low sampling rate, their scheme is no longer capable of tracing one attacker with only one packet.

Stepping-Stone Attack Attribution

Ever since the problem of detecting stepping stones was first proposed by Staniford-Chen and Heberlein,[38] several approaches have been proposed to detect encrypted stepping-stone attacks.

34. W. T. Strayer, C. E. Jones, F. Tchakountio, and R. R. Hain, "SPIE-IPv6: Single IPv6 packet traceback," in *Proceedings of the 29th IEEE Local Computer Networks Conference (LCN 2004)*, Nov. 2004.

35. L. Zhang and Y. Guan, "TOPO: A topology-aware single packet attack traceback scheme," in *Proceedings of the 2nd IEEE Communications Society/CreateNet International Conference on Security and Privacy in Communication Networks (SecureComm 2006)*, Aug. 2006.

36. S. Savage, D. Wetherall, A. Karlin, and T. Anderson, "Network support for IP traceback," *IEEE/ACM Transactions on Networking*, Vol. 9, No. 3, pp. 226–237, June 2001.

37. J. Li, M. Sung, J. Xu, and L. Li, "Large-scale IP traceback in high-speed Internet: Practical techniques and theoretical foundation," in *Proceedings of 2004 IEEE Symposium on Security and Privacy*, May 2004.

38. S. Staniford-Chen and L. T. Heberlein, "Holding intruders accountable on the Internet," in *Proceedings of the 1995 IEEE Symposium on Security and Privacy*, May 1995.

The ON/OFF based approach proposed by Zhang and Paxson[39] is the first timing-based method that can trace stepping stones, even if the traffic were to be encrypted. In their approach, they calculated the correlation of different flows by using each flow's OFF periods. A flow is considered to be in an OFF period when there is no data traffic on it for more than a time period threshold. Their approach comes from the observation that two flows are in the same connection chain if their OFF periods coincide.

Yoda and Etoh[40] presented a deviation-based approach for detecting stepping-stone connections. The deviation is defined as the difference between the average propagation delay and the minimum propagation delay of two connections. This scheme comes from the observation that the deviation for two unrelated connections is large enough to be distinguished from the deviation of connections in the same connection chain.

Wang et al.[41] proposed a correlation scheme using interpacket delay (IPD) characteristics to detect stepping stones. They defined their correlation metric over the IPDs in a sliding window of packets of the connections to be correlated. They showed that the IPD characteristics may be preserved across many stepping stones.

Wang and Reeves[42] presented an active watermark scheme that is designed to be robust against certain delay perturbations. The watermark is introduced into a connection by slightly adjusting the interpacket delays of selected packets in the flow. If the delay perturbation is not quite large, the watermark information will remain along the connection chain. This is the only active steppingstone attribution approach.

Strayer et al.[43] presented a State-Space algorithm that is derived from their work on wireless topology discovery. When a new packet is received, each node is given a weight that decreases as the elapsed time from the last packet from that node increases. Then the connections on the same connection chain will have higher weights than other connections.

However, none of these previous approaches can effectively detect stepping stones when delay and chaff perturbations exist simultaneously. Although no experimental data is available, Donoho et al.[44] indicated that there are theoretical limits on the ability of

39. Y. Zhang and V. Paxson, "Detecting stepping stones," in *Proceedings of the 9th USENIX Security Symposium*, Aug. 2000, pp. 171–184.

40. K. Yoda and H. Etoh, "Finding a connection chain for tracing intruders," in *Proceedings of the 6th European Symposium on Research in Computer Security (ESORICS 2000)*, Oct. 2000.

41. X. Wang, D. S. Reeves, and S. F. Wu, "Inter-packet delay based correlation for tracing encrypted connections through stepping stones," in *Proceedings of the 7th European Symposium on Research in Computer Security (ESORICS 2002)*, Oct. 2002.

42. X. Wang and D. S. Reeves, "Robust correlation of encrypted attack traffic through stepping stones by manipulation of interpacket delays," in *Proceedings of the 10th ACM Conference on Computer and Communications Security (CCS 2003)*, Oct. 2003.

43. W. T. Strayer, C. E. Jones, I. Castineyra, J. B. Levin, and R. R. Hain, "An integrated architecture for attack attribution," BBN Technologies, Tech. Rep. BBN REPORT-8384, Dec. 2003.

44. D. L. Donoho, A. G. Flesia, U. Shankar, V. Paxson, J. Coit, and S. Staniford, "Multiscale stepping-stone detection: Detecting pairs of jittered interactive streams by exploiting maximum tolerable delay," in *Proceedings of the 5th International Symposium on Recent Advances in Intrusion Detection (RAID 2002)*, Oct. 2002.

attackers to disguise their traffic using evasions for sufficiently long connections. They assumed that the intruder has a maximum delay tolerance, and they used wavelets and similar multiscale methods to separate the short-term behavior of the flows (delay or chaff) from the long-term behavior of the flows (the remaining correlation). However, this method requires the intrusion connections to remain for long periods, and the authors never experimented to show the effectiveness against chaff perturbation. These evasions consist of local jittering of packet arrival times and the addition of superfluous packets.

Blum et al.[45] proposed and analyzed algorithms for stepping-stone detection using ideas from computational learning theory and the analysis of random walks. They achieved provable (polynomial) upper bounds on the number of packets needed to confidently detect and identify stepping-stone flows with proven guarantees on the false positives and provided lower bounds on the amount of chaff that an attacker would have to send to evade detection. However, their upper bounds on the number of packets required is large, while the lower bounds on the amount of chaff needed for attackers to evade detection is very small. They did not discuss how to detect stepping stones without enough packets or with large amounts of chaff and did not show experimental results.

Zhang et al.[46] proposed and analyzed algorithms that represent that attackers cannot always evade detection only by adding limited delay and independent chaff perturbations. They provided the upper bounds on the number of packets needed to confidently detect stepping-stone connections from nonstepping stone connections with any given probability of false attribution.

Although there have been many stepping-stone attack attribution schemes, there is a lack of comprehensive experimental evaluation of these schemes. Therefore, there are no objective, comparable evaluation results on the effectiveness and limitations of these schemes. Xin et al.[47] designed and built a scalable testbed environment that can evaluate all existing stepping-stone attack attribution schemes reproducibly, provide a stable platform for further research in this area, and be easily reconfigured, expanded, and operated with a user-friendly interface. This testbed environment has been established in a dedicated stepping-stone attack attribution research laboratory. An evaluation of proposed stepping-stone techniques is currently under way.

A group from Iowa State University proposed the first effective detection scheme to detect attack flows with both delay and chaff perturbations. A scheme named "datatick" is proposed that can handle significant packet merging/splitting and can attribute multiple application layer protocols (e.g., X-Windows over SSH, Windows Remote Desktop, VNC, and SSH). A scalable testbed environment is also established that can evaluate all existing

45. A. Blum, D. Song, and S. Venkataraman, "Detection of interactive stepping stones: Algorithms and confidence bounds," in *Proceedings of the 7th International Symposium on Recent Advances in Intrusion Detection* (RAID 2004), Sept. 2004.

46. L. Zhang, A. G. Persaud, A. Johnson, and Y. Guan, "Detection of Stepping Stone Attack under Delay and Chaff Perturbations," in *25th IEEE International Performance Computing and Communications Conference* (*IPCCC* 2006), Apr. 2006.

47. J. Xin, L. Zhang, B. Aswegan, J. Dickerson, J. Dickerson, T. Daniels, and Y. Guan, "A testbed for evaluation and analysis of stepping stone attack attribution techniques," in *Proceedings of TridentCom* 2006, Mar. 2006.

stepping-stone attack attribution schemes reproducibly. A group of researchers from North Carolina State University and George Mason University utilizes timing-based watermarking to trace back stepping-stone attacks. They have proposed schemes to handle repacketization of the attack flow and a "centroid-based" watermarking scheme to detect attack flows with chaff. A group from Johns Hopkins University demonstrates the feasibility of a "post-mortem" technique for traceback through indirect attacks. A group from Telcordia Technologies proposed a scheme that reroutes the attack traffic from uncooperative networks to cooperative networks such that the attacks can be attributed. The BBN Technologies' group integrates single-packet traceback and stepping-stone correlation. A distributed traceback system called FlyTrap is developed for uncooperative and hostile networks. A group from Sparta integrates multiple complementary traceback approaches and tests them in a TOR anonymous system.

A research project entitled Tracing VoIP Calls through the Internet, led by Xinyuan Wang from George Mason University, aims to investigate how VoIP calls can be effectively traced. Wang et al. proposed to use the watermarking technology in stepping-stone attack attribution into VoIP attribution and showed that VoIP calls can still be attributed.[48]

Strayer et al. has been supported by the U.S. Army Research Office to research how to attribute attackers using botnets. Their approach for detecting botnets is to examine flow characteristics such as bandwidth, duration, and packet timing, looking for evidence of botnet command and control activity.[49]

4. CRITICAL NEEDS ANALYSIS

Although large-scale cyber terrorism seldom happens, some cyber attacks have already shown their power in damaging homeland security. For instance, on October 21, 2002, all 13 Domain Name Server (DNS) root name servers sustained a DoS attack.[50] Some root name servers were unreachable from many parts of the global Internet due to congestion from the attack traffic. Even now, we do not know the real attacker and what his intention was.

Besides the Internet itself, many sensitive institutions, such as the U.S. power grid, nuclear power plants, and airports, may also be attacked by terrorists if they are connected to the Internet, although these sites have been carefully protected physically. If the terrorists want to launch large-scale attacks targeting these sensitive institutions through the Internet, they will probably have to try several times to be successful. If we only sit here and do not fight back, they will finally find our vulnerabilities and reach their evil purpose. However, if we can attribute them to the source of attacks, we can detect and arrest them before they succeed.

48. X. Wang, S. Chen, and S. Jajodia "Tracking anonymous peer-to-peer VoIP calls on the Internet," In *Proceedings of the 12th ACM Conference on Computer Communications Security (CCS 2005)*, November 2005.

49. W. T. Strayer, R. Walsh, C. Livadas, and D. Lapsley, "Detecting botnets with tight command and control," *Proceedings of the 31st IEEE Conference on Local Computer Networks (LCN)*, November 15–16, 2006.

50. P. Vixie, G. Sneeringer, and M. Schleifer, "Events of Oct. 21, 2002", November 24, 2002, www.isc.org/ops/f-root/october21.txt.

Although there have been a lot of traceback and attribution schemes on IP spoofing and stepping-stone attacks, we still have a lot of open issues in this area. The biggest issue is the deployment of these schemes. Many schemes (such as packet marking and log-based traceback) need the change of Internet protocol on each intermediate router. Many schemes need many network monitors placed all over the world. These are very difficult to implement in the current Internet without support from government, manufacturers, and academics. It is necessary to consider traceback demands when designing and deploying next-generation networks.

5. RESEARCH DIRECTIONS

There are still some open problems in attack traceback and attribution.

VoIP Attribution

Like the Internet, the Voice over Internet Protocol (VoIP) also provides unauthorized services. Therefore, some security issues existing in the Internet may also appear in VoIP systems. For instance, a phone user may receive a call with a qualified caller ID from her credit-card company, so she answers the critical questions about Social Security number, data of birth, and so on. However, this call actually comes from an attacker who fakes the caller ID using a computer. Compared with a Public Switched Telephone Network (PSTN) phone or mobile phone, IP phones lack monitoring. Therefore, it is desirable to provide schemes that can attribute or trace back to the VoIP callers.

Tracking Botnets

A botnet is a network of compromised computers, or bots, commandeered by an adversarial botmaster. Botnets usually spread through viruses and communicate through the IRC channel. With an army of bots, bot controllers can launch many attacks, such as spam, phishing, key logging, and denial of service. Today more and more scientists are interested in how to detect, mitigate, and trace back botnet attacks.

Traceback in Anonymous Systems

Another issue is that there exist a lot of anonymous systems available all over the world, such as Tor.[51] Tor is a toolset for anonymizing Web browsing and publishing, instant messaging, IRC, SSH, and other applications that use TCP. It provides anonymity and privacy for legal users, and at the same time, it is a good platform via which to launch stepping-stone attacks. Communications over Tor are relayed through several distributed servers called *onion routers*. So far there are more than 800 onion routers all over the world.

51. Tor system, http://tor.eff.org.

Since Tor may be seen as a special stepping-stone attack platform, it is interesting to consider how to trace back attacks over Tor.

Online Fraudster Detection and Attribution

One example is the auction frauds on eBay-like auction systems. In the past few years, Internet auctions have become a thriving and very important online business. Compared with traditional auctions, Internet auctions virtually allow everyone to sell and buy anything at anytime from anywhere, at low transaction fees. However, the increasing number of cases of fraud in Internet auctions has harmed this billion-dollar worldwide market. Due to the inherent limitation of information asymmetry in Internet auction systems, it is very hard, if not impossible, to discover all potential (committed and soon to be committed) frauds. Auction frauds are reported as ascending in recent years and have become serious problems. The Internet Crime Complaint Center (IC3) and Internet FraudWatch have both reported Internet auction frauds as the most prevalent type of Internet fraud.[52,53] Internet FraudWatch reported that auction fraud represented 34% (the highest percentage) of total Internet frauds in 2006, resulting in an average loss of $1,331. Internet auction houses had tried to prevent frauds by using certain types of reputation systems, but it has been shown that fraudulent users are able to manipulate these reputation systems. It is important that we develop the capability to detect and attribute auction fraudsters.

Tracing Phishers

Another serious problem is the fraud and identity theft that result from phishing, pharming, and email spoofing of all types. Online users are lured to a faked web site and tricked to disclose sensitive credentials such as passwords, Social Security numbers, and credit-card numbers. The phishers collect these credentials in order to illegitimately gain access to the user's account and cause financial loss or other damages to the user. In the past, phishing attacks often involve various actors as a part of a secret criminal network and take approaches similar to those of money laundering and drug trafficking. Tracing phishers is a challenging forensic problem and the solutions thereof would greatly help law enforcement practitioners and financial fraud auditors in their investigation and deterrence efforts.

Tracing Illegal Content Distributor in P2P Systems

Peer-to-peer (P2P) file sharing has gained popularity and achieved a great success in the past 15 years. Though the well-known and popular P2P file sharing applications such as BitTorrent (BT), eDonkey, and Foxy may vary from region to region, the trend of using

52. Internet Crime Complaint Center, Internet crime report, 2006 ic3 annual report, 2006.

53. Internet National Fraud Information Center, 2006 top 10 Internet scam trends from NCL's fraud center, 2006.

P2P networks can be seen almost everywhere. In North America, a recent report stated that around 41%–44% of all bandwidth was used up by P2P file transfer traffic. With the increasing amount of sensitive documents and files accidentally shared through P2P systems, it is important to develop forensic solutions for locating initial illegal content uploaders in P2P systems. However, one technique would not be applicable to all P2P systems due to their architectural and algorithmic differences among different P2P systems. There are many legal and technical challenges for tracing illegal content distributors in P2P systems.

6. SUMMARY

Organizations should have a capability to perform computer and network forensics. Forensics is needed for various tasks within an organization, including investigating crimes and inappropriate behavior, reconstructing computer security incidents, troubleshooting operational problems, supporting due diligence for audit record maintenance, and recovering from accidental system damage. Without such a capability, an organization will have difficulty determining what events have occurred within its systems and networks, such as exposures of protected, sensitive data. Also, handling evidence in a forensically sound manner puts decision makers in a position where they can confidently take the necessary actions.

One of the most challenging aspects of network forensics is that the available data is typically not comprehensive. In many cases, if not most, some network traffic data has not been recorded and consequently has been lost. Generally, analysts should think of the analysis process as a methodical approach that develops conclusions based on the data that is available and assumptions regarding the missing data (which should be based on technical knowledge and expertise). Although analysts should strive to locate and examine all available data regarding an event, this is not practical in some cases, particularly when there are many redundant data sources. The analyst should eventually locate, validate, and analyze enough data to be able to reconstruct the event, understand its significance, and determine its impact. In many cases, additional data is available from sources other than network traffic related sources (data files or host OSs).

Organizations typically have many different sources of network traffic data. Because the information collected by these sources varies, the sources may have different value to the analyst, both in general and for specific cases. The following items describe the typical value of the most common data sources in network forensics.

IDS Software

IDS data is often the starting point for examining suspicious activity. Not only do IDSs typically attempt to identify malicious network traffic at all TCP/IP layers, but also they log many data fields (and sometimes raw packets) that can be useful in validating events and correlating them with other data sources. Nevertheless, as noted previously, IDS software does produce false positives, so IDS alerts should be validated. The extent to which this can be done depends on the amount of data recorded related to the alert and the information available to the analyst about the signature characteristics or anomaly detection method that triggered the alert.

Security Event Management Software

Ideally, SEM can be extremely useful for forensics because it can automatically correlate events among several data sources, then extract the relevant information and present it to the user. However, because SEM software functions by bringing in data from many other sources, the value of SEM depends on which data sources are fed into it, how reliable each data source is, and how well the software can normalize the data and correlate events.

NFAT Software

NFAT software is designed specifically to aid in network traffic analysis, so it is valuable if it has monitored an event of interest. NFAT software usually offers features that support analysis, such as traffic reconstruction and visualization; Firewalls, Routers, Proxy Servers, and Remote Access Servers. By itself, data from these sources is usually of little value. Analyzing the data over time can indicate overall trends, such as an increase in blocked connection attempts. However, because these sources typically record little information about each event, the data provides little insight into the nature of the events. Also, many events might be logged each day, so the sheer volume of data can be overwhelming. The primary value of the data is to correlate events recorded by other sources. For example, if a host is compromised and a network IDS sensor detected the attack, querying the firewall logs for events involving the apparent attacking IP address might confirm where the attack entered the network and might indicate other hosts that the attacker attempted to compromise. In addition, address mapping (NAT) performed by these devices is important for network forensics because the apparent IP address of an attacker or a victim might actually have been used by hundreds or thousands of hosts. Fortunately, analysts usually can review the logs to determine which internal address was in use.

DHCP Servers

DHCP servers typically can be configured to log each IP address assignment and the associated MAC address, along with a timestamp. This information can be helpful to analysts in identifying which host performed an activity using a particular IP address. However, analysts should be mindful of the possibility that attackers on an organization's internal networks falsified their MAC addresses or IP addresses, a practice known as spoofing.

Packet Sniffers

Of all the network traffic data sources, packet sniffers can collect the most information on network activity. However, sniffers might capture huge volumes of benign data as well.millions or billions of packets.and typically provide no indication as to which packets might contain malicious activity. In most cases, packet sniffers are best used to provide more data on events that other devices or software has identified as possibly malicious. Some organizations record most or all packets for some period of time so that when an incident occurs, the raw network data is available for examination and analysis. Packet sniffer data is best reviewed with a protocol analyzer, which interprets the data for the analyst based on knowledge of protocol standards and common implementations.

Network Monitoring

Network monitoring software is helpful in identifying significant deviations from normal traffic flows, such as those caused by DDoS attacks, during which, hundreds or thousands of systems launch simultaneous attacks against particular hosts or networks. Network monitoring software can document the impact of these attacks on network bandwidth and availability, as well as providing information about the apparent targets. Traffic flow data can also be helpful in investigating suspicious activity identified by other sources. For example, it might indicate whether a particular communications pattern has occurred in the preceding days or weeks.

ISP Records

Information from an ISP is primarily of value in tracing an attack back to its source. This is particularly true when the attack uses spoofed IP addresses.

Send Network Traffic to the IP Address

Organizations should not send network traffic to an apparent attacking IP address to validate its identity. Any response that is generated cannot conclusively confirm the identity of the attacking host. Moreover, if the IP address is for the attacker.s system, the attacker might see the traffic and react by destroying evidence or attacking the host sending the traffic. If the IP address is spoofed, sending unsolicited network traffic to the system could be interpreted as unauthorized use or an attack. Under no circumstances should individuals attempt to gain access to others. systems without permission.

Because network forensics can be performed for many purposes with dozens of data source types, analysts may use several different tools on a regular basis, each well-suited to certain situations. Analysts should be aware of the possible approaches to examining and analyzing network traffic data and should select the best tools for each case, rather than applying the same tool to every situation. Analysts should also be mindful of the shortcomings of tools; for example, a particular protocol analyzer might not be able to translate a certain protocol or handle unexpected protocol data (illegal data field value). It can be helpful to have an alternate tool available that might not have the same deficiency.

Network forensic analysis tools (NFAT) typically provide the same functionality as packet sniffers, protocol analyzers, and SEM software in a single product. Whereas SEM software concentrates on correlating events among existing data sources (which typically include multiple network traffic.related sources), NFAT software focuses primarily on collecting, examining, and analyzing network traffic. NFAT software also offers additional features that further facilitate network forensics, such as the following:

- Reconstructing events by replaying network traffic within the tool, ranging from an individual session (instant messaging [IM] between two users) to all sessions during a particular time period. The speed of the replaying can typically be adjusted as needed.
- Visualizing the traffic flows and the relationships among hosts. Some tools can even tie IP addresses, domain names, or other data to physical locations and produce a geographic map of the activity.
- Building profiles of typical activity and identifying significant deviations.
- Searching application content for keywords (confidential., proprietary).

Finally, let's move on to the real interactive part of this Chapter: review questions/exercises, hands-on projects, case projects and optional team case project. The answers and/or solutions by chapter can be found in the Online Instructor's Solutions Manual.

CHAPTER REVIEW QUESTIONS/EXERCISES

True/False

1. True or False? In many cases, businesses are often eager to report and publicly discuss cyber crimes related to them.
2. True or False? Network forensics can be generally defined as a science of discovering and retrieving evidential information in a networked environment about a crime in such a way as to make it nonadmissible in court.
3. True or False? When we face the cyber attacks, we can detect them and take countermeasures.
4. True or False? The *Deterministic Packet Marking* (DPM) scheme proposed by Belenky and Ansari[28] involves marking each general packet when it enters the network.
5. True or False? The basic idea of log-based traceback is that each router stores the information (digests, signature, or even the packet itself) of network traffic through it.

Multiple Choice

1. Like the Internet, the _____ also provides unauthorized services.
   A. Voice over Internet Protocol (VoIP)
   B. Botnets
   C. Data retention
   D. Evolution
   E. Security
2. What is a network of compromised computers, or bots, commandeered by an adversarial botmaster.
   A. Botnet
   B. Traceback

C. Data retention
D. Process
E. Security

3. _____file sharing has gained popularity and achieved a great success in the past 15 years.:
   A. Evolution
   B. Data retention
   C. Peer-to-peer (P2P)
   D. Process
   E. Security

4. In many cases, businesses are often reluctant to report and publicly discuss _____ related to them:
   A. Security
   B. Data retention
   C. Standardization
   D. Cyber crimes
   E. Evolution

5. Generally, it is much harder to detect cyber crimes than crimes in the:
   A. Physical world
   B. Data retention
   C. Standardization
   D. Data destruction
   E. All of the above

EXERCISE

Problem

How does network forensics help an organization pinpoint the source of intermittent performance issues and conduct investigations to identify the source of data leaks, HR violations, or security breaches?

Hands-On Projects

Project

24×7 access to all network data and network forensics mining tools, allows an organization to do what?

Case Projects

Problem

How would network forensics go about addressing a pesky intermittent network issue, benchmark application performance for SLAs, or investigate a data breach?

Optional Team Case Project

Problem

When network forensics solutions are in place, what types of forensic investigations can an organization conduct?

Index

Note: Page numbers followed by "f", "t" and "b" refers to figures, tables and boxes, respectively.

Printed and bound by CPI Group (UK) Ltd, Croydon, CR0 4YY

08/06/2025

01896868-0015